W9-AFE-053

WITHDRAWN

Musical Life in Guyana

CARIBBEAN
STUDIES
SERIES

Anton L. Allahar and Shona N. Jackson
Series Editors

Musical Life in Guyana

History and Politics of Controlling Creativity

Vibert C. Cambridge

University Press of Mississippi / Jackson

www.upress.state.ms.us

The University Press of Mississippi is a member
of the Association of American University Presses.

Copyright © 2015 by University Press of Mississippi
All rights reserved
Manufactured in the United States of America

First printing 2015

∞

Library of Congress Cataloging-in-Publication Data

Cambridge, Vibert C.
Musical life in Guyana : history and politics of controlling creativity /
Vibert C. Cambridge.
pages cm. — (Caribbean studies series)
Includes bibliographical references and index.
ISBN 978-1-62846-011-7 (cloth : alk. paper) — ISBN 978-1-62674-644-2
(ebook) 1. Music—Social aspects—Guyana—History. 2. Music—Social
aspects—Guyana—History. 3. Guyana—Politics and government I. Title.
ML3917.G93C36 2015
780.9881—dc23   2014042400

British Library Cataloging-in-Publication Data available

To my wife, Dr. O. Patricia Cambridge

Contents

Preface and Acknowledgments

Musical Life in Guyana: History and Politics of Controlling Creativity is the result of a research journey that was started during a visit to Guyana in August 2000. There I attended a surprise party in the capital city, Georgetown. The event was organized by the Woodside Choir to celebrate the eightieth birthday of Guyanese musician William Rutherford Alexander "Billy" Pilgrim, GRAM, CCH (April 27, 1920–April 17, 2006).[1] He had been director of music in the Department of Culture (ca. 1973–92). At the party, Pilgrim reflected on his musical journey and provided interesting insights on the social and cultural life and the political contexts associated with music making in Guyana during most of the twentieth century, particularly his engagement with choral music in Guyana as conductor of the Woodside Choir.

Founded in 1952, the Woodside Choir represented the apex of choral music in Guyana and was an important ensemble in an influential urban-based music community when Pilgrim became its conductor in 1972. He assumed the appointment after the untimely accidental death of Aubrey Joseph (August 19, 1947–August 4, 1973), literally a few hours before the choir's performance in a major competition. In addition to being at the apex of choral music in Guyana, the Woodside Choir represented middle-class respectability and wielded substantial influence in urban cultural life.

By the end of Pilgrim's reflections, he had offered glimpses of the complex relationships that had existed in the urban music-making process in Guyana during most of the twentieth century and had hinted at the influence of governance practices. I was fascinated. A latent interest in the place of music in Guyanese society was awakened, and I wanted to know more. Fortunately, a period of sabbatical leave, engagement in a project to upgrade mass communication and journalism education at the University of Guyana's Center for Communication Studies, and an invitation to participate in the revitalization of the Institute of Creative Arts in Guyana's Ministry of Culture, Youth, and Sport provided opportunities to return to Guyana for extended periods between 2006 and 2013.

The research journey has been fascinating. It took me around the world and allowed me to meet and to interview many inspiring persons, from sugar workers in rural Guyana to Guyanese music icons in the diaspora. The journey also revealed how difficult it is to locate crucial data on this aspect of

Guyana's social and cultural history. The research process that undergirds this book has been encouraged and supported by various individuals and agencies in the United States of America, the United Kingdom, Germany, and Guyana. To them I offer my sincerest thanks.

The microfilm collection at Ohio University's Vernon R. Alden Library provided access to a collection of major Guyanese newspapers (the *Daily Argosy*, *Chronicle*, *Guyana Graphic*, and the *Evening Post*) covering the period 1900 to 1980. Alden Library is also the home of the Jari Recordings, a collection of some of the folk music recorded by Peter Kempadoo and Marc Matthews across Guyana during the 1970s.

The US Library of Congress and the Smithsonian Institution made available recordings of Guyanese music. From the British Library in London, I was able to access copies of music Clem Nichols composed for the British Guiana Militia Band's performances at the British Empire Exhibition in 1924. An academic quarter spent at the University of Leipzig in 2006 allowed access to the anthropological literature on Guyana in the university's library. I also had the opportunity to visit the Opera House, from which I received printed programs, reviews, and photographs from the 1966 inaugural performance of Alan Bush's *The Sugar Reapers*, an opera celebrating Guyana's post–World War II struggle for political independence.

Through Guyana's Ministry of Culture, Youth, and Sport, I had access to Guyana's National Archives and to the incomplete records of the National History and Arts Council and the Department of Culture, the precursors of the Ministry of Culture, Youth, and Sport. Research in Guyana's National Archives revealed the fragile nature of its collection. Some of the newspapers in the collection are so brittle that they are no longer available for use. The Guyana National Library was very supportive, providing access to rare documents and photographs. At the University of Guyana's Caribbean Research Library, I was able to explore the A. J. Seymour Papers, a unique collection of one of twentieth-century Guyana's influential cultural animators. His collection of programs from the funerals of prominent citizens was a rich source of information of the music associated with that aspect of life in urban Guyana during the 1970s and the early 1980s.

The Cheddi Jagan Research Center in Georgetown provided access to valuable documents related to the People's Progressive Party (PPP) and cultural life in Guyana between 1950 and the end of the twentieth century. Publications of the People's National Congress (PNC) and those of the PNC-led government, along with interviews with former party officials and autobiographical publications by former Guyanese diplomats and other senior government officials, were pivotal in mapping the crucial twenty-eight-year period from independence in 1966 to the PPP's election to office in 1992. Through Dr. Ovid

Fraser and Neil Fraser, I was able to have access to the collected works of Valerie Rodway, one of Guyana's most prolific composers of patriotic music during the mid-twentieth century. I give special thanks to the late Deryck Bernard for recommending Lloyd Kandasammy and Dwayne Benjamin to serve as my research associates during the research in Guyana in 2006.

Barry Higman critiqued Caribbean historiography for its privileging of official documents in archives. He was concerned about the self-serving bias associated with those documents. He recommend a more inclusive approach—one that sought to give voice to those sectors of society that have traditionally been marginalized or muted in the historical narratives of the Caribbean. I accepted those recommendations and conducted in-depth interviews and focused conversations using the snowball method.

Altogether, more than 200 in-depth interviews and focused conversations were conducted to complement the documents research in Guyana, the United States, and Europe. The interviewees included Guyanese politicians, Guyanese musicians living at home and abroad, music educators and researchers, current and former members of the radio and television community, and journalists. Among the politicians interviewed were the late President Janet Jagan, Brindley Benn, Patricia Benn, Ashton Chase, David Granger, Hamilton Green, Elvin McDavid, Halim Majeed, Dr. Rupert Roopnaraine, and most of Guyana's ministers responsible for culture between 1986 and 2011 (Deryck Bernard, Dr. Dale Bisnauth, Gail Teixeira, and Dr. Frank Anthony).

Interviews with Guyanese musicians at home and abroad sought to examine the diversity of musical genres—folk, classical, popular, religious, and military—in multi-ethnic Guyana. The interviews with Andron Alphonso, Lionel Britton, Joan Cambridge, David Campbell, Marjorie Cambridge-Carr, Dr. Desry Fox, Serena Hewitt, Dr. Roy Ibbott, Peter Kempadoo, Eusi Kwayana, Wordsworth McAndrew, Leslie Mohammed, Rambir Nabi, Arjune Nattai, Pandit Chandreca Persaud, Pandit Reepu Daman Persaud, Dr. Vindyha Persaud, Pandit Gopinauth Prashad, Rakesh Rampertaub, Burchmore Simon, Pritha Singh, Chandradai Suki, Julio Thijs, Mangal Raghunandan, Eze Rockcliffe, Rohan Sagar, and Rudolph "Putagee" Vivierios provided a valuable survey of the folk genres derived from Guyana's Amerindian, African, European, and Indian heritage.

Exploration of Guyana's calypso and shanto traditions benefitted from interviews with Bonny Alves, Joseph Burgan-Trotman (the Mighty Enchanter), Neville Calistro (the Mighty Chief), Monica Chopperfield (Lady Guymine), Malcom Corrica (Lord Canary), Roger Hinds (Young Bill Rogers), Godfrey Phillips (the Mighty Rebel), and Hector Stoute, a former executive in the Guyana Calypsonians Association. Bertram DeVarell, who in 1946 founded Tripoli Steelband, Guyana's first steel band, along with Dr. Dawn

Forde-Arno, Winston Beckles, Rudy Bishop, Aubrey Bryan (inventor of the Aubra pan), Charwin Burnham, Ken Croal, Ronald Gaskin, Roy Geddes, Dr. Edward Green, Derrick Jeffrey, Andrew Tyndall, and Ras Camo Williams, were among those interviewed about the steel band experience in Guyana.

Interviews with Dr. Patricia Cambridge, Valerie Codette, Lynette Cunha, David Dewar, Marilyn Dewar, Joyce Aaron-Elcock, Janet Hunte, Pat Insanally, Dr. Joycelynne Loncke, Mildred Lowe, Charles Knights, Jean Mendonca, Edith Pieters, William "Billy" Pilgrim, Magda Pollard, Hugh Sam, and Clairmonte Taitt provided substantial depth and texture to Guyana's association with classical music during the twentieth century.

Ernest Alstrom, Charmaine Blackman, Nesbit Chhangur, Stanley Cooke, Aubrey Cummings, Bridget Hart-Doman, Derry Etkins, John "Bagpipes" Fredericks, Cy Grant, Eddy Grant, Stanley Greaves, Rannie Hart, Frank Holder, Nigel Hoyow, Ted. E. Jones, Ivor Lynch, Dave Martins, Rector Schultz, Ray Seales, Mike Semple, Winston "Sir" Smith, Keith Waithe, Jimmy Weeks, and Val Wilmer provided illustrations of the experiences of Guyanese musicians in Guyana and around the world since the 1930s. "Bappie" Roopnaraine's interview provided valuable observations on the contributions of Guyanese musicians to diffusing Taan and chutney music around the world. In Guyana's context, religious music refers to the music associated with Christian, Hindu, Moslem, and other religious and spiritual traditions. The interview with Brother Paschal Jordan, an innovator in the "Caribbeanization" of the Roman Catholic liturgy, provided perspective on the Guyanese experience with this aspect of Christian religious music in Guyana. The interview with Pandit Reepu Daman Persaud provided perspectives on Hindu religious music in Guyana.

The interviews with Lt. Col. Keith Booker, formerly of the Guyana National Service and later Permanent Secretary, Ministry of Culture, Youth, and Sport; Cecil Bovell, Assistant Commissioner of Police and bandmaster of the Guyana Police Force Band; Major Elton Briggs, retired Guyana Police Force and the Guyana Defence Force; Major Robert Burns, director of music, Guyana Defence Force; John "Bagpipes" Fredericks; Charles Knights, LRSM; Winston "Sir Wins" Smith; and Jimmy Weeks provided valued perspectives on military music.

Music is more than the arrangement of sound. As Billy Pilgrim hinted, the political context is an influential factor. To this end, I interviewed a number of people who had intimate knowledge of the efforts by successive governments of Guyana to use music to achieve their goals across the twentieth century. Among them was Bert Allsopp, a pioneering fisheries officer who, with Norman Cameron, developed a calypso during the 1950s to promote a government initiative to increase the consumption of unscaled fish among Guyanese. Michael Currica, Hilton Hemerding, and Billy Pilgrim provided a window on these practices in the early post-independence years when Guyana hosted major international political and cultural events and welcomed multiple heads of state and other distinguished international personalities.

During the twentieth century a range of technologies, including radio broadcasting, played a pivotal role in the distribution and consumption of music in Guyana. Interviews and correspondence with former and current radio broadcasters such as Noel Adams, Ave Brewster, Pat Cameron, Ron Cameron, Bertie Chancellor, Ayube Hamid, Terrence Holder, Vic Insanally, Carlton James, Peter Kempadoo, Rafiq Khan, Russell Lancaster, Margaret Lawrence, Wordsworth McAndrew, Rashid Osman, Ishri Singh, Joslyn Small, Sir Ronald Sanders, Ron Savory, Jean Singh, and James Sydney provided valuable insights into the music programming policies and practices of radio broadcasters in Guyana since the end of World War II. Entrepreneurs such as Bonny Alves, Neil Chan, Vic Insanally, Vivian Lee, Gem Madhoo-Nasciemento, and Burchmore Simon opened windows onto the world of private investments in Guyanese musical life. The snowball technique used in populating the interviewing/focused conversations process brought me in contact with many musical innovators. The interviews with Deo Persaud and the members of Buxton Fusion provided details on the motivation behind the fusion of African and Indian percussion traditions for which the ensemble had become known.

The Internet and social media, especially the Facebook groups Guyanese Music Lovers Group, New Amsterdam and Guyanese Musical Life, and Queen's College and Guyanese Musical Life Since 1844, supported valuable conversations with Guyanese professional musicians working in a range of international contexts. Members of the groups include music educators, studio musicians, cruise ship and nightclub entertainers, and Guyanese with opinions about music in Guyana.

In addition to the institutions mentioned previously, the following organizations and their staffs provided great assistance, including access to archival records : the Broadcast to Schools Audio Library, NCERD; Castellani House; Channel 6 Television, Corentyne; Critchlow Labour College; Guyana Cultural Association of New York; the Guyana Learning Channel, Ministry of Education; Little Rock Television, New Amsterdam; National Communication Network; and the National Cultural Center.

To the editorial team at the University Press of Mississippi, thank you for your support at each step in the completion of this book. Thanks to Stanley Greaves for his support, especially his granting permission to use *Old Time String Band* to illustrate the cover.

Special thanks is extended to Dr. Dora Wilson, former Dean of Ohio University's College of Fine Arts, and the anonymous reviewers who read the manuscript for this book and shared their opinions. Thanks are also extended to Eslyn Valerie Stephenson-Aiyeola, Marilyn Dewar, Magda Pollard, Leslie Horwood, Denise Boodie, and others who made rare photographs accessible. My spouse, Dr. Patricia Cambridge, the winner of the Philip Pilgrim Memorial Harp in 1974, was my constant guide and sounding board during this long process.[2]

In the years between the start of the research journey and the publication of this book, my findings were shared through a number of channels. Among them were the fifty-article series "Celebrating Our Creative Personalities" in *Sunday Stabroek* (Guyana) between 2003 and 2006; *Black Praxis—Writings on Guyanese Music 2003–2004*; and several conference papers and public lectures. The lectures included Music and Working People in Guyana During the 20th Century at Critchlow Labour College in 2007; Guyana's inaugural Republic Lecture, Sustaining Guyanese Culture in the Era of Globalization: Music and the Techno-Optimist, in 2011; Music and Social Change in 20th Century Guyana at Moray House in 2012; and Dis Time Na Lang Time: Indian Music and the Guyanese 20th Century Soundscape in 2013 at the conference to commemorate the 175th anniversary of the arrival of Indians to Guyana.

The findings, conclusions, and recommendations offered in this book are preliminary and seen as building blocks upon which to create future works on this aspect of the history of Guyana's social and cultural life. This book is presented in eleven chapters covering 1900 to 2011. The use of the decade format emerged naturally, as each decade was dominated by some significant development in Guyana's economic or political life, which in turn influenced patterns of governance and musical life.

Finally, a note on the usage of "Guiana," Guianese," "Guyana," and "Guyanese" in this book. The spellings "Guiana" and "Guianese" refer to the colony British Guiana and its citizens before political independence on May 26, 1966. The spellings "Guyana" and "Guyanese" refer to the state and its citizens after political independence.

Abbreviations

A&R	Artist and Repertoire
ARCM	Associate of the Royal College of Music
ARCO	Associate of the Royal College of Organists
ASCRIA	African Society for Cultural Relations with Independent Africa
BBC	British Broadcasting Corporation
BC	British Council
BG	British Guiana
BGBS	British Guiana Broadcasting Service
BGEIA	British Guiana East Indian Association
BGEICC	British Guiana East Indian Cricket Club
BGEII	British Guiana East Indian Institute
BGLU	British Guiana Labour Union
BGMTA	British Guiana Music Teachers' Association
BGUCC	British Guiana Union of Cultural Clubs
BPI	Bureau of Public Information
CARICOM	Caribbean Community
Carifesta	Caribbean Festival of the Creative Arts
CARIFTA	Caribbean Free Trade Area
CASBO	Chronicle Atlantic Steel and Brass Orchestra
CCH	Cacique Crown of Honor
CSA	Civil Service Association
DEMBA	Demerara Bauxite Company
DPRK	Democratic People's Republic of Korea
DSO	Distinguished Service Order
DYO	Demerara Youth Rally
Festac	Festival of African Culture
GAWU	Guyana Agricultural Workers Union
GBC	Guyana Broadcasting Corporation
GBS	Guyana Broadcasting Service
GCC	Georgetown Cricket Club
GEMS	General Electrical & Musicians Service
GFC	Georgetown Football Club
GMO	Government Medical Officer

GNS	Guyana National Service
GNTC	Guyana National Trading Corporation
GRAM	Graduate of the Royal Academy of Music
GRECO	Guyana Radio & Electronics Company
GUARD	Guyana Action for Reform and Democracy
GUYSTAC	Guyana State Corporation
IMF	International Monetary Fund
KCMG	Knight Commander of St. Michael and St. George
Kt.	Knight
LCP	League of Coloured People
LRAM	Licentiate of the Royal Academy of Music
LRSM	Licentiate of the Royal School of Music
MBE	Member of the British Empire
MLC	Member of the Legislative Council
MPCA	Manpower Citizens Association
MTCC	Mobile Theatre and Culture Corps
NAMS	New Amsterdam Music Society
NHAC	National History and Arts Council
NLF	National Labour Front
NNDA	New Negro Development Association
NPC	Negro Progress Convention
OBE	Order of the British Empire
PAC	Political Action Committee
PCD	Patriotic Coalition for Democracy
PNC	People's National Congress
PPP	People's Progressive Party
PYO	Progressive Youth Organization
QC	Queen's College
RCA	Radio Corporation of America
RCM	Royal College of Music
UDP	United Democratic Party
UF	United Force
UK	United Kingdom
UNDP	United Nations Development Program
UNESCO	United Nations Educational and Scientific Organization
UNIA	United Negro Improvement Association
USIS	United States Information Service
USO	United Service Organization
WPEO	Women's Political and Economic Organization
WPO	Women's Progressive Organization
YMCA	Young Men's Christian Association
YWCA	Young Women's Christian Association

Musical Life in Guyana

1

Prelude

As Alan Merriam counseled more than fifty years ago, "music cannot be defined as a phenomenon of sound alone ... what we hear as music is "the end result of a dynamic process"—the outcome of many human interactions in the political, economic, social, and technological spheres. The political interactions, especially the practices of national governance—the ways societies make and implement decisions—can exert significant influence on what is recognized and approved as music, how it is distributed, and how it is consumed. For this book the term national governance is used to refer to the personalities, institutions, and bureaucracies engaged in the process of making decisions about the economic, social, and cultural directions of a society and the processes associated with the allocation of the society's resources to implement those decisions. This definition also recognizes that in the case of societies such as Guyana, national governance is invariably guided by an overarching ideology or set of aspirations to which a ruling class and their allies subscribe. This ruling class and their allies draw upon a range of persuasive and coercive practices to achieve their goals. Also associated with the dynamics of national governance are the initiatives and actions taken by personalities and institutions who are excluded or are marginalized from the processes of formal decision making and implementation processes but seek to get their voices heard, their perspectives noted, and their constituencies provided for. National governance is always biased toward the interests of the ruling class.

This book, *Musical Life in Guyana: History and Politics of Controlling Creativity*, is—like Gordon Rohlehr's *Calypso and Society In Pre-Independence Trinidad*, Hollis "Chalkdust" Liverpool's *Rituals of Power and Rebellion*, and Jocelyne Guilbault's *Governing Sound: The Cultural Politics of Trinidad's Carnival Musics*—a contribution to the study of the interactions between the national governance practices and musical communities in the Caribbean. Specifically, this book explores these interactions in Guyana during the three political eras that the society experienced as it moved from being a British colony to an independent nation state. The first era to be considered is the period of matured colonial governance, guided by the dictates of "new imperialism," which extended from 1900 to 1953. The second era is the period of internal self-government—the preparation for independence, which extends from 1953, the year of the first general elections under universal adult suffrage, to 1966, the year the colony gained its political independence. The third phase, 1966 to 2000, is defined as the early post-colonial era.

The term *musical communities* is used here to refer to discrete musical traditions, practices, instruments, and repertoire found in Guyana's urban, rural, and hinterland regions and reflecting the nation's multi-ethnic heritage. To contextualize the three phases of twentieth-century governance practices in Guyana, it is useful to provide an abbreviated introduction to salient aspects of political, economic, social, and cultural life in pre-twentieth-century Guyana. Among the themes to be sketched in the upcoming survey are the peopling of Guyana; governance of the society, especially the influential roles of the governor, the urban-based ruling elite, and the plantocracy; residential patterns and cultural life; and patterns of resistance to the colonial order.

The word *Guiana* means "land of many waters" and refers to the many majestic rivers that drain this region of South America, which Columbus saw during his third voyage to the Americas in 1498 and famously described as "the earthly paradise."[1] At 83,000 square miles, this multi-ethnic and multi-religious nation-state is approximately the size of the United Kingdom. Guyana's neighbors are Venezuela to the west, Suriname to the east and Brazil to the south. To the north is the Atlantic Ocean, populated by the Caribbean islands, with which there is much historical and cultural commonality.

Denis Williams, the Guyanese-born artist, novelist, and influential scholar of early Guyana, concluded that the first inhabitants of Guyana were the Warraus, one of the nine Amerindian ethnic groups present in contemporary Guyana.[2] In the years following 1498, Europeans established several colonies on the northeast coast of South America. The Dutch established three of them—Essequibo, Berbice, and Demerara, named after three of the major rivers—in 1616, 1624, and 1741, respectively. After changing hands many times among European colonial powers during the eighteenth and nineteenth centuries, these three colonies were united in 1831 to become British Guiana.[3] In 1966 British Guiana gained its independence from the United Kingdom and became Guyana. In 1970, Guyana adopted a republican constitution and became the Co-operative Republic of Guyana.

Since the seventeenth century the coast of Guyana has been the primary location for the people who populate the Guyanese nation. Terms such as "the wild coast" and "mud land" have been used to describe the low-lying alluvial "coastal plain that covers an area of 1,750 square miles.[4] This coastal region became the site for the establishment of plantation agriculture and the villages and towns in which the majority of Guyanese still reside. From the seventeenth through the twentieth centuries, Guyana, once identified as the location of El Dorado, has consistently been positioned as a place with the potential to make a fortune from its abundant natural resources.[5] Across this period it has attracted international capital—primarily European and North American investments—in coffee, cotton, tobacco, sugar, and rice on the coast, and the extraction of gold, diamonds, bauxite, balata, and timber from the interior. For almost three hundred years, forced labor (first slavery, and later indentured labor) provided the muscle in the quest to realize profits from these investments. Amerindians were the first to be enslaved in Guyana, and this condition lasted until 1793.[6] The first enslaved Africans, primarily Akan from the Gold Coast, arrived in Essequibo around 1621. These enslaved Africans played a pivotal role in transforming the "wild coast," making it suitable for coffee, cotton, and sugar plantations. According to Walter Rodney, "slaves moved 100 million tons of heavy, water-logged clay with shovel in hand, while enduring conditions of perpetual mud and water" to humanize coastal Guyana.[7]

In time other ethnic groups from West and Central Africa were also enslaved in Guyana, among them "Abuna, Akan, Aku (Yoruba), Egba, Effa, Fula (Fulani), Ibo, Ijesa, Kongo, Kru, Ondo (Doko), Oyeh, and Yagba."[8] The physical enslavement of Africans continued until August 1838, when they were emancipated. By the time of Emancipation, sugar was the colony's raison d'etre. According to Eric Williams, this emphasis on sugar was a strategic mistake and has been the cause of Guyana's subsequent social, economic, and political problems.[9] At Emancipation in 1838, the interests of the colonists—the "plantocracy," primarily European plantation owners—determined the orientation and processes of national governance. These colonists expressed fears about the survival of the sugar industry and the economic and social future of the colony, as they had no confidence in the capacity of the "emancipated class" to manage themselves. A system of indentured labor was developed and funded by the colony to cater to this loss of controlled labor and to exert control on the newly emancipated Africans.

The importation of indentured laborers started with the arrival of forty-eight Portuguese from Madeira in 1835; but caste-dominated India, especially the northern Bhojpuri-speaking region of Bihar and Uttar Pradesh, became the primary source of indentured labor from 1838 until 1917. Indentured laborers also came from the Fujian and Guangdong regions of southern China. Other indentured laborers came from West and Central Africa (especially the Kru/Kroo, Yoruba, and Kongo ethnicities); "liberated Africans"—Africans liberated from the illegal slave trade and lodged on the mid-Atlantic island of St. Helena by the British Royal Navy—also came to British Guiana as indentured laborers.[10] Other indentures came from Barbados, other islands in the

Caribbean, and the United States. A small number of indentured laborers also came from Malta and Germany.[11] Carl A. Braithwaite has reported that in 1881, there were 18,318 West Indian immigrants in British Guiana.[12] Many of these immigrants, including significant numbers from St. Lucia, came to work in the gold and diamond mining industries in the hinterland.

The peopling of Guyana, especially since the seventeenth century, set in motion a number of interrelated processes that have led to the creation of a tense, multi-ethnic, and multi-religious society in which there is an inexorable, although at times imperceptible, dialectic of cultural contact and exchange resulting in the ongoing development of a Guyanese creole identity.

In a multi-ethnic society such as Guyana, and for the purpose of this book, the concepts *musical encounters, musical interaction*, and *musical exchange* are of special importance. These concepts are useful when exploring the transfer and adoption of musical attributes across and among cultural communities— a dynamic that has enduring presence in Guyana's musical life.[13]

Starting in the seventeenth century, Amerindian settlements, especially those close to the coast, were interacting with Europeans through trade. There is evidence that the Moravian missionaries were actively proselytizing the Caribs in Berbice during this early period. Early Moravian missionary practice used music, not the music of the communities they were evangelizing but the hymns of Martin Luther, the sixteenth-century German monk who launched the Protestant Reformation. So, in the seventeenth century, Caribs could have been exposed to and interacting with "Ein' feste Burg ist unser Gott" ("A Mighty Fortress Is Our God") and other hymns of Luther. As we will examine later, musical encounters, interactions, and exchange with Amerindian hinterland musical communities increased during the mid- to late nineteenth century with the establishment and expansion of the extractive industries—gold, diamonds, balata, timber, and bauxite—and this dynamic registered on the Guyanese musical landscape.

There is also evidence to suggest that there were musical encounters, interactions, and exchanges among some of the ethnic and racial groups even before their arrival in the Guiana colonies. Just as the West African Pidgin-English language was acquired and expanded by enslaved Africans in slave-holding warehouses while awaiting shipment to plantations in the Americas, so did musical exchange take place on the ships bringing the enslaved Africans to Berbice, Essequibo, and Demerara.[14] It was common practice to encourage music and dancing on the slave ships. This had nothing to do with aesthetics and leisure; it was primarily to ensure that a relatively healthy cargo was available for sale at the end of the journey. The 30- to 180-day journey across the Middle Passage in chains and in a "tight pack" could lead to muscular atrophy, so forced exercise to music on African instruments was a response. Music and dancing on the slave ships thus was about the maximization of profits.[15]

This practice contributed to the birthing of a synthesized African musical aesthetic and the diffusion of African musical instruments, rhythms, and dance patterns to the New World.[16] Between 1621 and the end of African indentureship in the mid-nineteenth century, many African ethnicities had been brought to British Guiana.[17] The musical interaction and exchange among these African ethnicities and other people of African descent from the West Indies and other parts of the Americas contributed to the core characteristics of African musical expressiveness evident in British Guiana at the end of the nineteenth century. That expressiveness included the use of a range of aerophone, chordophone, membranophone, and idiophone musical instruments; polyrhythmic drumming patterns represented in several drumming "hands"; syncopation; polyphony; vocal styles characterized by call and response and lyrics that emphasize praise and blame; and integration with dance and religion.

Similar exchanges took place in the depots for indentured Indians in places such as Calcutta (Kolkata). According to Kenneth Parmasad, the embarkation point in Calcutta was not only an important site for musical interaction among various Indian ethnicities and castes that were recruited for indentureship contracts; it was also a source of the musicians who traveled to the Caribbean, bringing with them musical traditions from many regions of India, especially those of the Bhojpuri-speaking regions of North India.[18] By the end of the nineteenth century, out of this contact and interaction emerged the musical instruments and multi-dimensional and multi-genre music oriented to religion, time of year, work, and celebration that characterized Indian music in British Guiana.[19]

The ships that brought "liberated Africans," indentured Africans, and indentured Indians to British Guiana between 1838 and the end of the nineteenth century also provided a space for musical encounters, interaction, and exchange. W. H. Angel, the English captain of the clipper ship *Sheila* that brought indentured Indian workers from Calcutta to the West Indies, provided firsthand evidence of the musical interaction that took place during the journey. Writing about the disembarking of the indentured laborers in Trinidad, he noted: "On leaving, my crew awoke the echoes by giving them no end of cheers, and several rousing shanties. The coolies, at the start of the voyage could not make out what that kind of singing meant, it being so strange to their ears; but towards the end, it was amusing to hear their attempts to join in.[20] That experience is indicative of what may have been experienced on ships bringing East Indians to British Guiana. Despite the failure of the indentured workers on the *Sheila* to master the melodies, Ramnarine argues that they were "clearly engaging in the process of musical interaction in learning the crew's sea shanties."

Another body of evidence suggests there may have been encounters between Africans and East Indians before their arrival on sugar plantations in the West Indies. In *Alas, Alas Kongo: A Social History of Indentured African Immigration into Jamaica, 1841–1865*, Guyanese historian Monica Schuler suggests musical interactions could have taken place between Africans liberated from the illegal slave trade and Indian indentured workers who traveled on the same ships out of the mid-Atlantic island of St. Helena for plantations in the West Indies.[21] St. Helena was also an important refueling station for ships transporting indentured Indians to the West Indies. Planters with interests in British Guiana had agents in St. Helena who actively encouraged liberated Africans to come to the colony as indentured workers. The sonic encounters and musical interactions of these African and Indian *jhaji bhais*[22] may have laid the seed for the African and Indian musical fusions that emerged from time to time during the twentieth century, especially in those communities where people of African and Indian ancestry live close together.

This dynamic of musical interaction and exchange was also evident among Portuguese and Chinese immigrants. The Portuguese immigrants were primarily from Madeira, and music styles from that island became the dominant music style among Portuguese in the colony and influenced the tone and rhythm of Roman Catholic liturgy in British Guiana.[23] Portuguese musical aesthetics extended beyond Roman Catholic liturgical music, influencing public music through pioneering ensembles such as the brass band Primeiro de Dezembre and the string band Estudiantina Restauração de Demerara, which were formed in 1876 and 1892, respectively.[24] The Chinese immigrants to British Guiana were primarily Hakka from the Fujian and Guangdong provinces in Southern China, regions with old music traditions. The Hakka style, described as "laid-back in tone," has a history dating back to the seventh century. Chinese immigrants also brought with them public music traditions associated with festivals, which incorporated drumming and elaborate costumes, as in the popular Dragon Dance.[25]

At the end of the nineteenth century, among the consequences of the peopling of British Guiana was the emergence of Creolese—a lingua franca and a social and cultural hierarchy based on race and color. At the apex of the hierarchy were Europeans; the lower rungs were determined by the concept of "comparative lightness."[26] This concept, developed during slavery, conferred social status and prestige to persons whose skin color was closest to whiteness. The schoolyard ditty sums it up: "If you black stand back / If you brown stick around / If you white, you all right!" Ultimately, the hierarchy based on lightness of skin color was applied to all racial groups. In British

Guiana at the end of the nineteenth century, a dark-skinned Madrassi Indian had lower status than a fair-skinned Indian from Northern India. Justification for European domination and the social hierarchy is found in the ideology of racial superiority, specifically white supremacy. This ideology held that Europeans had achieved the highest level of human civilization and, as a result, were ordained to direct national governance and accrue maximum economic and social benefits from the resources of the polity. At the end of the nineteenth century there were increasing covert and overt challenges to this ideology by the subordinated people in the colony. In their increasing demands for political participation, economic justice, and respect for cultural expressions, the subordinated classes would also draw upon their cultural assets, including music and other expressive arts, to establish moments of solidarity and resist white supremacy and colonial domination in urban, rural, and hinterland contexts.

On July 21, 1831, when the colonies of Essequibo, Demerara, and Berbice were united to form British Guiana, the administration of the colony retained significant elements of a system of governance developed during more than two hundred years of Dutch colonial rule. Under this system, white supremacy and economic interests of the colonists—the plantation owners—was the transcendental orientation of national governance.[27] Although there was a governor, the balance of power resided in the Combined Court, which controlled the allocation of the colony's financial resources. In 1893, James Rodway concluded that British Guiana could be "considered a crown colony" with a significant limitation. At the time, the colony was administered by a governor with an "advising executive council consisting of three officials and the same number of colonists, all appointed by the Queen."

The legislative body of the colony was the Court of Policy and comprised the governor and eight elected officials. These officials were elected by a small electorate—"two thousand votes qualified by income or property." In the case of a tie, the governor had the casting vote. According to Rodway, real power was exerted by the six-member College of Financial Representatives. This mechanism was "adjoined with the Court of Policy" to create the Combined Court. The Combined Court body had the special purpose of voting on taxes and expenditures. The colonists had the majority in this body and exerted substantial influence—their interests were paramount.[28]

This arrangement would create tensions and conflicts between the representatives of the colonists—who demanded protection of their economic interests (sugar)—and Britain's new imperial interests, which had become ascendant by the end of the nineteenth century. Several terms have been used to describe British imperial interests at the end of the nineteenth century, among them "new imperialism" and "constructive imperialism." The goals of this policy were to give British industry competitive advantage in the global economy by controlling access to the raw materials of its colonies and ensuring dominance in the markets of the British Empire over which the sun never set. New imperialism was a reaction to increasing competition to British industry by German and American industries and represented a retreat from the ideas of free trade. It was emblematic of the responses to the economic crisis that had characterized the global economy since the 1870s.

At the end of the nineteenth century, the British colonial governor was the lynchpin in the execution of "new imperialism." Sir Henry Barkly (1849–1853),[29] one of British Guiana's early governors, has been recognized as establishing the "hard core professional" managerial style required by a colonial governor.[30] At the end of the nineteenth century, the governor of British Guiana was always male, mostly English-born, product of the upper classes, including the aristocracy, and educated at such exclusive public schools as Eton and Harrow and elite universities like Oxford, Cambridge, London, Edinburgh, and Trinity College. This background gave them unassailable status in the colony's social hierarchy. The governor both represented the dignified and efficient aspect of the Crown in the colony and, through the execution of authority, established the position as the society's single most influential political leader with the ability to dispense patronage in the interest of getting personal and imperial policy executed.[31] The résumés of governors show that many of them had experience with British mercantile companies in India and Southeast Asia and that many were pioneers in adopting deficit financing as a method to spur economic development in the "tropical plantations"—the priority areas in the "new imperialism" visions articulated by Joseph Chamberlain in 1896.[32]

As the commander-in-chief, the governor commanded the colony's coercive power—the police, the militia, and the prisons—and on many occasions during the nineteenth century demonstrated that they were not reluctant to use those assets.[33] The governors' formal attire—various military uniforms, court dress, braided Windsor uniforms, bicorn hats, plumed pith helmets, and other accouterments—reflected this power and authority. Martial music (ruffles and flourishes) was played as governors arrived at formal events, took salutes, and conducted inspections. Martial music punctuated the colonial soundscape with regularity.

In the multiple tasks of executing the policies of new imperialism, the governor was at the apex of a bureaucracy engaged in delivering education, running hospitals, collecting revenue, operating transportation systems, regulating mining, conducting agricultural research, maintaining public order, protecting property, administering justice, running prisons, promoting loyalty to the Crown, and transferring British tastes, decorum, and social and cultural values. By 1891 this bureaucracy was led by sojourning British civil servants.

This group along with their families numbered less than four thousand, just under 1 percent of the population, which in the 1891 census totaled 278,328. The governor and his spouse, senior colonial civil servants and their families, along with members of the establishment clergy, the urban-based representatives of the sugar industry, and the leaders of the colony's commercial sector represented the colony's political and social elite—the ruling class. This community tended to live in enclaves in Georgetown and New Amsterdam. As we will encounter below, it was from these urban enclaves that the colony's social and political elite exerted substantial influence on the colony's musical life.

Earl Grey, one of the early conceptualizers of "new imperialism," wrote in 1852 that Georgetown, in Demerara, and New Amsterdam, in Berbice, were the only two towns "worthy of mention" in British Guiana.[34] Georgetown, which was elevated to a city in 1831, was described as the "Garden City" and "the Venice of the West Indies."[35] New Amsterdam was considered "more like a Dutch town."[36] The social life and the hospitality offered by the residents of these municipalities were legendary. Richard Schomburgk, an Austrian explorer who visited British Guiana during the 1840s, described Georgetown as a place where pleasure was an important social goal, from the elite ruling class to the "poorest negro."[37]

Among the leisure preferences of the urban ruling class were dinner parties and attending balls at venues such as the Assembly Rooms in Georgetown and the Reading Rooms in New Amsterdam.[38] The spouses of governors and other leading colonial officials played important roles in organizing this aspect of colonial leisure time. Other pursuits included reading and listening to "good music."[39] In the context of the nineteenth century, the term refers to what is commonly called classical music. Other genres of music popular among the colonial ruling class included sacred music, military music, songs from the British music hall, art songs, and folk songs from various regions of the United Kingdom. The expansion of the printing industry during the mid-nineteenth century made sheet music readily available in the UK and across the empire.[40] During the late nineteenth century, both Georgetown and New Amsterdam also became destinations for international classical musicians touring the West Indies.[41] As will be explored later, in time the consumption of "good music" by the middle and lower classes was an important social marker, and the ability to perform those genres of music supported upward mobility. This orientation continued into the twentieth century.

The racial and social hierarchies associated with white supremacy meant that, at the turn of the twentieth century, Georgetown and New Amsterdam contained neighborhoods that were almost completely segregated. In Georgetown, sections of wards such as Kingston, Cummingsburg, and Queenstown were inhabited primarily by the white ruling class. Also present in those exclusive wards would be a number of "range yards" that housed the domestic servants—the cooks, washers, butlers, grooms, maids, nannies, and others who serviced the ruling class and their children. Other wards such as Albouystown, Charlestown, and Lacytown were populated primarily by the poor. These communities were characterized by substandard housing, overcrowding, abysmal sanitary facilities, and high levels of crime and unemployment. Those employed worked primarily as laborers—stevedores, cart men, jobbers, and hawkers. These were the urban ghettos with the range of social tensions associated with that reality. These conditions were particularly hard on children.[42] Despite these harsh conditions, music was created in the urban ghettos and there was musical exchange with the urban elite and the urban middle class. In between the elite wards and the urban ghettos were the wards dominated by a growing middle class—the growing number of persons of color employed as junior clerks in civil service, teachers, policemen, and in the commercial sectors. Similar stratification was evident in New Amsterdam.[43]

By the end of the nineteenth century, Georgetown and New Amsterdam were the sites where influential developments in Guyana's intellectual, economic, political and cultural life took place. As we will encounter, for most of the twentieth century there would be an undercurrent of musical rivalry between Georgetown and New Amsterdam in all genres of music. But there was more to British Guiana than the urban centers. There were the coastal villages and hinterland settlements.

The decision to emancipate enslaved Africans in 1838 was not popular among the plantocracy. Variations on the concerns expressed by the planter class at that time still resonated at the end of the nineteenth century. In 1838 the powerful planter class expressed fears about the survival of the sugar industry and the economic and social future of the colony, as they had no confidence in the capacity of the "emancipated class" to manage themselves. The nature of these fears was articulated in memoirs such as *Demerara after Fifteen Years of Freedom*, written under the pseudonym "A Landowner." In this contradictory memoir, the writer claimed that Africans at emancipation were essentially savages, pagans, conceited, cunning, suspicious, lazy, ungrateful, disloyal, and "not yet sufficiently advanced to assume" the responsibilities of freedom.[44] That portrait ignored the Africans' pivotal role in the establishment of the colony's drainage and irrigation infrastructure and their contributions to all aspects of the colony's cultural life during almost three hundred years of contact and interaction with the European planter class.[45] Substantial African contributions to agriculture, medicine, engineering, commerce, religion,[46] language, cuisine, and expressive culture were also ignored.

Across the period of enslavement and up to the end of the nineteenth century, there were ongoing efforts to suppress aspects of African musical and expressive culture through prohibition, derision, deliberate marginalization, and other forms of control. Drumming was banned during enslavement as the drum was seen as a communication channel used in the fomenting and execution of revolts. In 1855 the Obeah Suppression Ordinance was passed outlawing an aspect of African religiosity on the grounds that it also fomented resistance. But efforts to suppress African musicality and other forms of expressive culture in the colony were never successful. Important elements of African musicality remained alive in many hybrid forms, including Kwe Kwe, Masquerade, shanto/calypso, moonlight night/ring play, wakes, and Cumfa. Similarly, efforts to keep people of African ancestry from being active participants in political dynamics of the society, including its governance, also were not successful. For the newly freed Africans, the existential realities nurtured proto-nationalistic responses. How to make this place a better and more humane home where families could be raised with dignity and aspirations? How to create better opportunities for the next generation? How to engage and modify the current institutions and practices of governance in the colony? The Village Movement provided the infrastructure.

Among the consequences of emancipation was the development of the free village movement in rural Guyana. It started in November 1839, when former enslaved Africans from five contiguous sugar estates on the east coast of Demerara pooled their resources and bought Plantation Northbrook for 30,000 guilders (approximately US$132,000 in 2011).[47] After its purchase, the plantation was renamed Victoria after Queen Victoria, the reigning British monarch.[48] This type of village has been described as a communal village.[49] Another type of African village emerging during the early post-emancipation era was the propriety village where individuals purchased "front lots from sugar estates."[50] In time, these two models were applied across the approximately two-hundred-square-mile coastal plain, which extended from the northwestern border with Venezuela to the eastern border with Suriname. Going with the development of the African villages was the introduction of a rudimentary system of representative democracy and transparent governance, contrary to the fears expressed at emancipation.

By the end of the nineteenth century, these coastal villages were the crucibles that tempered a generation of leaders who joined their urban counterparts in challenging European political, social, and cultural domination. The villages were not only locales for alternative practices in the exercise of power, they were also places where the cultural traditions of multiple African ethnicities were integrated, nurtured, and propagated. Kwe Kwe, the pre-marriage ritual, is an example of this dynamic. The lyrics of "Nation" and "All ahwee is waan family," two songs from the ritual's repertoire, recognize the dynamic of ethnic diversity and synthesis in the African experience. This predominantly percussive ritual starts with the arrival of the groom-to-be and his party at the gate of the bride-to-be. At this point, the "tuta" associated with the bride's family raises the song "Nation": "Nation, ah whey yuh nation? Nation, ah whey dem dey? / Nation, me ah call ahwee nation, Nation, ah whey dem deh? / Nation, come tell me yuh nation, Nation, a whey dem deh?"[51]

This song seeks to find out what "nation"/ethnic group the potential groom is from. After this sequence is completed and it is recognized that the potential groom is "acceptable," the "tuta" for the groom's side requests, "Open de door an leh de man come in" because "All awee is one family!" As the nineteenth century came to an end, these villages with their distinctly African creole musical communities (drumming hands and religious/dance/music complexes) became important variables in the colony's political practices.

Another consequence of emancipation was the importation of indentured labor—primarily from the northern Bhojpuri-speaking region of Uttar Pradesh and Bihar. Efforts to keep this population in the colony after the end of their contracts resulted in the expansion of the village system on the coastal plain. This development was initiated in 1896 when the colonial administration purchased Plantation Helena, a former sugar plantation on the Mahaica River, and provided the land free of charge to East Indian laborers whose period of indentureship had ended. This was a strategy to reduce the costs associated with returning immigrants to India and recruiting and transporting new workers to the colony, where they would have to be "seasoned" before they became productive. Central to the profitability of the sugar industry was a constant supply of reliable labor. Free land clinched the deal.

By the end of the nineteenth century, a system of plantation villages had also emerged. These villages were directly associated with active sugar estates such as Port Mourant, Blairmont, Albion, and Enmore and contributed to the relative isolation of East Indians from the wider rural communities.[52] Like the villages developed by the formerly enslaved Africans, the relatively isolated East Indian plantation villages also became places where the ancestral cultural traditions were examined, practiced, nurtured, and propagated, primarily under a primarily Brahmin Pandit caste. These East Indian villages were the loci of distinctive multi-genre musical communities. The development of the African and Indian rural villages on the coastal plain are examples of the segregated residential patterns that characterized British Guiana at the end of the nineteenth century. These villages would substantially influence the governance of society and musical development throughout the twentieth century. The boundaries between coastal villages were porous, as were the boundaries between urban enclaves and range yards, middle-class wards and urban ghettos, and coastal plain and hinterland.

Prior to European colonization, there were established Amerindian settlements in all regions of the territory. Arawaks, Caribs, and Warraus were coastal people, living along the rivers and creeks. The Ackawaio, Arekuna, and Patamona settled in the river valleys. The Macushi and Wapishana were savannah settlers with the Wai Wai settling in the most southernmost region of the hinterland. Like the coastal communities, these hinterland communities were also the homes of discrete musical communities with a range of aerophone, chordophone, membranophone, and idiophone instruments and musical traditions associated with the cycle of life, work, and leisure.[53] Among the discrete musical traditions evident in the colony's hinterland at the end of the nineteenth century was the Banshikilli music of the Spanish Arawaks who arrived in the Moruca region of Essequibo in 1817, fleeing the consequences of the Bolivarian revolution in Venezuela. Other Amerindian musical traditions include Mari Mari. As mentioned earlier, since the seventeenth century, many of these settlements, especially those close to the coast, were interacting with Europeans. Contact between African maroons and Amerindian bounty-hunters during slavery were also sources of encounter and exchange.[54] However, contact with hinterland musical communities accelerated during the late nineteenth century with the establishment and expansion of the extractive industries—gold, diamonds, balata, timber, and bauxite. This expansion also led to the development of new hinterland settlements, such as Bartica, at the junction of the Mazaruni, Potaro, and Essequibo rivers, and the bauxite-mining town McKenzie, named after the Scottish geologist George Bain McKenzie.

The increased encounters with the colony's hinterland had reciprocal consequences for the making and consumption of music in Guyana across the twentieth century. For the coastlanders, the inland terrain—dense tropical rainforests, wide rivers, mountains, waterfalls, and dangerous rapids—inspired musical compositions in a variety of genres ranging from sea shanties, work songs, and folk songs to patriotic songs, art songs, and operatic works. Examples of this creative output are to be found in the sea shanty "Essequibo River" and the folk song "Itanamie," whose refrain "Captain, Captain / Put me ashore / I don't want to go anymore / Itanamie gwine wuk me belly!" speaks to the terror experienced by pork-knockers (small-scale alluvial gold miners) as they encountered "the awesome rawness" of the Itanamie rapids en route to the gold and diamond fields. The majestic Kaieteur Falls (the world's tallest single-drop waterfall) on the gold-bearing Potaro River "discovered" by Charles Barrington Brown in 1870 and majestic Mount Rorima have inspired many compositions, among them Reverend Hawley Bryant's "Song of Guiana's Children" and Phillip Pilgrim's *The Legend of Kaieteur*. The interactions between coastlanders and the aboriginal residents of the hinterland also resulted in the diffusion of some coastal genres, styles, and instruments to the nation's aboriginal hinterland residents, and this in turn had influence on the musical communities of the hinterland. This body of work emerging from contact between the coast and the hinterland would play an important role in the governance of the society, especially in the important task of nurturing a transcendental Guyanese identity in multi-ethnic Guyana.

British Guiana at the end of the nineteenth century was a tense, dynamic space determined by the ideology of white supremacy, the ambitions of "new/ constructive imperialism," and the increasingly vociferous demands for freedom and active participation in the governing of the society by the subordinated classes. It is this mix that would determine a range of governance strategies would be adopted across the twentieth century. Initially, there would be tactical acceptance of the status quo, especially by the urban middle class who depended on government employment and colonial patronage. Always present were voices of resistance with demands for the construction of new institutions and new patterns of governance. Music would have a visible place in all these strategies and associated initiatives.

At the end of the nineteenth century, several concurrent music-making communities and processes could be identified in British Guiana. Among them was an multi-talented, multi-ethnic urban community capable of composing and performing the music needed to serve the "pomp and ceremony" needs of the colony—the monarch's birthday, Empire Day, the opening of the legislature, the start of the judicial seasons, the various parades and route marches, and the music for the ruling class to relax and socialize.

Writing in 1931, on the occasion of the centenary of the British Guiana colony, E. M. T. Moore, W. McDavid, and P. M. de Weever provided valuable perspectives on the state of musical life in the colony at the end of the nineteenth century.[55] All of the writers commented on the presence of musical societies, such as the Athenaeum and the Musical Society; trained teachers; competent performers, including organists and pianists; aspiring composers; and the impact of church doctrine and sacred music on African musicality. Moore noted that the Athenaeum, a choral society, was founded in 1870 and was trained using sol-fa techniques. The Musical Society was founded and led by a Mr. Colbeck in 1883. As a composer, Colbeck had won a prize from the important British colonial publication *Cassell's Magazine*. In 1887, for the Golden Jubilee of Queen Victoria, he conducted the Musical Society's production of Sir A. Sullivan's *Jubilee Ode*.[56] Other noted composers at the end of the nineteenth century included Mr. Smellie, Carrie Moore, S. E. Blades, A. de Weever, and P. M. de Weever. Smellie was the organist at St. Andrew's Kirk and composer of the delightful "Anthem 'For the Lord Jehovah.'" Miss Carrie Moore composed the music to a Jubilee song to Queen Victoria in 1887.[57]

Moore also stated: "It may not be known by everybody that at the Emancipation Jubilee in 1888 Messrs. Blades, A. de Weever, and his brother P. de Weever, composed all the music performed in the Philharmonic Hall on that occasion."[58]

The British Guiana Militia Band, established in 1865, was the principal ensemble providing the musical aesthetics of the colony. This and other bands and orchestras provided the musical accompaniments for the dinners, drawing-room concerts, balls, and other entertainments for the urban, sojourning colonial elite. The established churches provided the sacred music. Other musical communities based on the musical traditions of Amerindians, Africans, East Indians, Portuguese, and Chinese were to be found in urban, rural, and hinterland regions of the colony, also serving the recreational and spiritual needs of those communities. In the course of the twentieth century all of these musical communities would be directly associated with the governance of the society.

Musical Life in Guyana: History and Politics of Controlling Creativity seeks to explore the nature of this interaction and its consequence on music making, distribution, and consumption in multi-ethnic Guyana. The book is divided into three sections. The first focuses on the period 1900–1953, the period of matured colonialism. The second section focuses on the period 1953–1966, the period of internal self-government and preparation for independence. The final section covers the period 1966–2000, with a coda to 2011, and addresses the early post-colonial era.

2

New Imperialism and Domestic Agitations

Between 1900 and 1920 five governors ruled British Guiana.[1] The responses of these proconsuls and their ruling-class allies to the colony's complex set of interrelated challenges influenced Guyana's economic, political, social, and cultural life, including musical life, for the majority of the twentieth century. The constellation of challenges had international and domestic dimensions. On the international level, the border problem with Venezuela appeared to have been resolved in 1899. However, the governors had to respond to the demands of Britain's policy of new imperialism. As mentioned in the previous chapter, the overarching goal of the new imperialism paradigm was to jettison the ideals of free trade and create for the benefit of the United Kingdom a self-sufficient economic system based on the assets of the British Empire. At the start of the twentieth century, overpopulation, along with unacceptable levels of unemployment and underemployment, were among the major issues and concerns in British society. These problems had serious implications for the stability of the British polity and its status as a world power.

The spokesmen for new imperialism—Joseph Chamberlain, Winston Churchill, and Earl Grey—saw "undeveloped tropical estates" such as British Guiana as the source of strategic raw materials needed for British industries. Under this system the raw materials from the tropical estates would enter the United Kingdom at preferential rates, give British industry a competitive edge, and consequently contribute to the reduction of the unacceptably high levels of unemployment and underemployment that had characterized British society since the mid-nineteenth century. In turn, colonies such as British Guiana would be a guaranteed market for British manufactured goods produced from the raw materials harvested from the colonies. This model for economic self-sufficiency was also seen as a strategy for protecting British industry in an international marketplace dominated by ongoing economic crises. Britain's global economic dominance at the start of the twentieth century was being challenged by the assertiveness of Germany and the post–Civil War United States. Ultimately, this competition led to World War I (1914–18).[2]

Another international challenge came from the realm of ideas. The economic philosophy and practice of capitalism, which undergirded British and European imperial expansion from the middle of the nineteenth century, was also under criticism. Socialism was being offered as an alternative way to organize global economic, social, and political life. For Marx and Engels, capitalism was an exploitative system that resulted in the dehumanization of human beings and the construction and maintenance of undemocratic forms of governance. The founders of this resurgent ideology predicted that it would take a revolution to topple the capitalist system and replace it with socialist practices that would lead ultimately to the egalitarianism of communism. Before the end of the second decade of the twentieth century, the Russian Revolution had occurred and the Soviet Union was established as an alternative model for national governance. Governors across the British Empire were required to protect their colonies from the Bolsheviks and their subversive ideas. New imperialism also envisioned the dominion territories of Australia, Canada, and South Africa and some of the colonies as destinations for British migrants. With its landmass of 83,000 square miles and a population of 278,328 in 1900, British Guiana was occasionally considered as a potential destination.

On the domestic front, the governors of British Guiana had to respond to an equally complex constellation of challenges. New imperialism demanded the opening up of the hinterland as a strategy for diversifying the economy and reducing dependency on sugar. By 1895 the colony had collected almost $120,000 in revenue from gold.[3] Despite these early indications of the efficacy of the hinterland thrust, the sugar interests who controlled the Combined Court resisted funding the shift in economic focus, imposed draconian taxes, or offered lukewarm support. Instead, they sought provisions that would benefit the sugar industry, specifically increasing recruitment of indentured labor from India and sanctioning the use of Indian child labor by granting exemptions from the Elementary Education Ordinance, which required compulsory education up to the age of 14.[4] Also at the economic level, the governor and his executive team had to respond to the colony's chronic economic problems, which manifested themselves through increasing bankruptcies, middle-class existential anguish, high levels of unemployment, and increasing demands by the working class for better working conditions and improvement in wages.

Eusi Kwayana is of the opinion that the folk song "Makantali" could be referring to a company (Mack & Tally) whose "money done"—had fallen into hard times and gone into bankruptcy, a shameful condition in the ethos of that era considered an indication of moral weakness.[5] Roy Heath captured the nature of middle-class anguish—the great fear of "coming down" in the world—in his autobiography *Shadows Round the Moon*:

Experience of middle-class family life taught me that coming down in the world was a kind of death. There was nothing sadder than the remnants of affluence in homes marred by such tragedies. If the piano had to be sold and the single shirt laundered with care, photographs of the well-clad family remained displayed on walls as mementoes of better times, and the scent of vanilla still came from the kitchen where offal was prepared once a week instead of the veal and mutton of a once-daily fare.[6]

According to Kimani Nehusi, in the rural areas wages for cane cutters declined more than 50 percent between 1895 and 1901. In the urban areas, the wages of dock workers declined by "at least 25 percent" during the same period.[7] The list of other pressing domestic challenges was substantial. It included demands for electoral reform by the subordinated classes; access to adequate education; and response to the consequences of increased rural-to-urban migration by African Guianese, which was the result of the systematic destabilization of the African-founded coastal villages by the sugar industry. There were also demands for improvements in the public health and social infrastructure to address the problems of poor housing, poor sanitation, malnutrition, overcrowded urban ghettos, and high levels of mortality and morbidity caused by malaria, yellow fever, and cholera. Crime was also increasing in the urban areas. The need for adequate and reliable transportation along the coast and into the hinterland was also an important factor in the various plans proposed by the governors of British Guiana for the economic, political, and social development of British Guiana during the two decades of the twentieth century.

These international and domestic realities informed the priorities and governance styles of the governors of British Guiana during the first two decades of the twentieth century. Central to the development and execution of new imperialism was the use of multiple strategies and techniques to manufacture public opinion and consent in the "mother country" and loyalty across the Empire. Those techniques, based on audience segmentation, used multiple communication channels, among them grand exhibitions; "Buy British" campaigns; posters; films; the music curricula of the primary, secondary, and tertiary education system; public music events; Christian hymnals; the music hall; and Royal patronage of cultural events such as concerts.[8] Jeffry Richards's *Imperialism and Music: Britain 1876–1953* provides valuable details on the musical dimensions of this comprehensive strategy to win hearts and minds.[9]

In British Guiana, during the first two decades of the twentieth century, a number of events and socio-cultural developments in the colony would demonstrate the range of functions music played in society, including its expanding role in the politics of manufacturing public opinion and consent and carving a space for dialogue and resistance by both the ruling elite and the subordinated classes. These events and developments included the increasing importance of leisure-time activities as a surrogate site for political work; Peter M. de Weever's 1902 composition "Me Cawfee in de Marnin'"; the Ruimveldt Riots of 1905; World War I (1914–18); demands for music credentials led by women of the urban elite; the accelerated diffusion of pianos and gramophones across all sectors of the society, especially among the middle classes in urban and rural areas; and the persistence of the colony's multi-ethnic folk music traditions, despite concerted efforts to suppress them. The churn of these issues that arose in the 1920s continued to resonate in Guyanese society during the late twentieth century.

As mentioned earlier, there were increasing numbers of British colonial administrators along with their families living in Georgetown. This ruling community had cultural and leisure demands and expectations. Their primary leisure time activities followed those of the previous century—dinner parties, balls, and concerts of classical music presented by international musicians who visited the colony. According to Brian Moore in the late nineteenth and early twentieth centuries, "local concerts and theatrical performances were . . . very few. Instead, there was a tendency to import artists."[10] Despite its relatively remote location, several world-famous artists and musical groups visited British Guiana during the first two decades of the twentieth century, establishing the colony as a destination in the West Indian concert touring circuit. The repertoires of these visiting musicians reflected the taste of the ruling class and reinforced the musical tastes of the Victorian culture of respectability. As the early decades unfolded, concerts began to feature colonial officials and their spouses, organists from the established churches, members of the British Guiana Militia Band, and members of the middle and working classes who had become skilled in the European musical traditions. The leisure time pursuits and musical orientation of the new, multi-ethnic middle class also reflected this orientation.

In the urban areas there was also public music presented by the British Guiana Militia Band, which was established in 1858,[11] and from established Portuguese bands such as the brass band Primeiro de Dezembro, and the string band Estudiantina Restauração de Demerara, which were formed in 1876 and 1892 respectively.[12] Their repertoires were predominantly European. The British Guiana Militia Band dominated the public sphere through their regular Monday morning route marches, Empire Day concerts, military parades, and weekly band concerts on the Seawall, the Promenade Gardens, and the Botanical Gardens in Georgetown. In New Amsterdam, there were also route marches and band concerts at the bandstand on the Esplanade by the No. 7 Company Military Band. These military bands provided more than music; they were important vehicles in winning hearts and minds and projecting Empire.

The British Guiana Militia Band was brought into existence as a result of the 1856 anti-Portuguese riots, which were fomented by John Sayers Orr—the "Angel Gabriel."[13] The militia was unpopular, and it has been suggested that the band was "formed with a view of popularizing it."[14] According to "Octave":

> The original bandsmen consisted chiefly of retired soldiers from the West India Regiment, local musicians and others drawn from a few of the West Indian Islands. The band at this time was purely a brass band and one of the leading figures was a pure blooded African Sergeant named Thomas who had two large tribal scars on both sides of his face. He played the euphonium and his ability as an instrumentalist was highly appreciated.[15]

Between 1860 and 1920, the band had six bandmasters. Captain A. R. Carroll was bandmaster from March 29, 1893, until his death on February 13, 1920.[16] Capt. A. Fawcett succeeded him in 1921. In addition to "popularizing" the militia, the band promoted classical music and, through its apprenticeship program, became the major music-training establishment for working-class British Guianese, particularly those of African and Portuguese ancestry. By 1920 the band was respected for its high quality of music by locals and international visitors. For example, in 1915, at the end of a performance, an international visitor, an "English lady . . . was so pleased with the playing" that she made a gift of $25.00 to the bandmaster "for the purpose of purchasing new music."[17] During the first two decades of the twentieth century, the British Guiana Militia Band and many of its individual members were in demand as performers at concerts and other forms of light entertainment programs in Georgetown and New Amsterdam.

The Portuguese bands Primeiro de Dezembro and Estudiantina Restauração de Demerara also performed publicly. Primeiro de Dezembro performed in venues such as the Promenade Gardens and participated in various Roman Catholic festivals, including accompanying religious processions associated with the Madeiran version of Roman Catholicism. The band was also popular at fairs and garden parties. According to Menezes and Moore, the band established a reputation for musical excellence.[18] Estudiantina Restauração de Demerara's repertoire was primarily popular music, as opposed to the classical music preferred by Primeiro de Dezembro. A number of new bands also emerged during this period, among them the Ladies' Orchestra,[19] the Demerara Symphony Orchestra,[20] and the B.G. Musicians' Band.[21] These new bands joined the established bands in performing at public venues including events such as Moonlight Concerts in the Promenade Gardens. Many of their performances were for fundraising purposes.

Music-based leisure time activities continued to be important venues in the governance of British Guiana during the twentieth century. Ideas were floated, decisions were taken, alliances were formed, and patronage granted at the balls, dinner parties, and concerts organized by the urban ruling elite. These events were as important as the male-dominated elite social clubs such as the Georgetown Club.[22] The urban middle class also nurtured a range of music-based leisure activities such as drawing-room concerts, which served as locations for articulating their interests. Among the working classes, "The Practice" or "dance practice" was a popular form of entertainment. A contemporary newspaper, aligned to the ruling class, revealed the prevailing anti-"Practice" bias when it offered the following description of "The Practice":

> A discordant nocturnal noise emanating from a tenement room in the city keeps the neighbourhood awake while it provides amusement for a certain class of people who congregate to pass away their time. The noise is a combination of sounds produced by a flute, a steel triangle, and a concertina and all the instruments would seem to have lived their lives already. The dancers comprise domestic servants fresh from the kitchen, butlers, housemaids, porters, etc., and these nightly performances are known as "the practice." Admission to the hall is obtained by the purchase of a ticket for sixpence, which gives the holder the right to dance for one night.[23]

"Practices" were constantly under surveillance and the newspapers were replete with reports of assaults and disorderly behavior associated with these events.[24] Invariably, the "Centipedes" were blamed for this type of behavior. The term was used to describe the multi-ethnic gangs of young men and women who resided in the ghetto areas of urban British Guiana, especially Georgetown, and tended to hang out in public places exhibiting a life style described by the ruling class as disreputable ("rep!"). There is no agreement on the origins of the name. Juanita De Barros offers two suggestions as to the origin: ruling class–generated or self-generated. The rhetoric of the ruling class and the pro–ruling class newspapers saw the gangs as similar to centipedes—"a quick-moving, many-legged, poisonous insect that lived in debris, indistinguishable from one another."[25] She also posited that the name could have been self-generated and linked to "the masquerade tradition in the Caribbean [in which] insects and other non-human characters commonly represent humans and their foibles . . . and during carnivals and festive events when men and women transform themselves into insects, animals, and other non-human forms."[26]

Despite their "disrespectability," during the 1900s the "Centipedes" were expanding the colony's musical repertoire. Masquerade/Centipede music was a musical hybrid, the product of musical exchange that had taken place between the colony's African, Scottish, and Irish heritages and featuring fifes, flutes, pennywhistles, side drums, and the bhoom drum. Throughout the twentieth century, this music, along with an associated cast of characters—the Mad Bull, the Long Lady, the Stilt Man, and the flouncers—defined Christmas festivities in urban Guyana. A turn-of-the-century description stated:

> When the great festal day does not fall on a Sunday, the slumberer is awakened by some music and much noise on the street . . . for drumbeaters are nothing if not energetic, and the musicians are nothing if not merry. There is a law here for the suppression of the drum, but on such a joyous day as this, the custom and inclination rule and our policeman are forgiving. The street band is accompanied by a motley procession of people whose especial business, it seems, is to arouse the whole city. . . . Sometimes in concert, oft times in confusion, drum, flute, coronet and clarionet, shac-shac and steel, tom-tom and tambourine, proclaim the happy morn, while high above all, in dismal diapason, *vox humana* dins into our ear such proclamations as this: "Chris'mas ma'nin come again / An' I ent get no cawfee wata."[27]

Clearly, working-class musical expressions were considered subversive and not embraced by the ruling class and its coercive institutions. The music and associated practices of the working class were seen as carrying the seeds of crime and disloyalty and various laws were introduced to suppress them.

By the start of the twentieth century, piano and violin were the dominant domestic musical instruments in the homes of the ruling elite and the expanding middle class. Other popular stringed instruments including the mandolin, the quarto, banjo, and guitar were among the predominant instruments in the string bands that were popular in creolized urban and rural Guyana. Bugles, clarinets, flutes, trumpet, saxophone, and tuba were found primarily in urban ensembles such as the British Guiana Militia Band and the Portuguese bands Primeiro de Dezembro. The organ had become the dominant instrument in urban Christian establishment churches. These churches played important roles in national governance. Religious institutions—churches, temples, and mosques were also influential venues for music education and performance. We will return to this sector later in this chapter.

During the first two decades of the twentieth century, music had multiple functions in British Guianese society. For all social groups music was a vehicle for recreation, entertainment, and the transmission of cultural heritage. Competent performers were accorded status and prestige. The ruling class was aware of the efficacy of music as an instrument for manufacturing consent and influencing public opinion in the United Kingdom and applied this capacity to the governance of the colony. The subordinated classes in the colony's urban, rural, and hinterland locations were also aware of music's efficacy for facilitating upward mobility as well as a channel for domestic agitations—focusing attention on societal ills, articulating ambitions, motivating solidarity, and mobilizing for action.

In 1901, at the age of 28, Peter Moses de Weever (1863–1937) composed "Me Cawfee in de Marnin.'"[28] P. M. de Weever was the son of an immigrant who came to British Guiana from St. Martin/St. Maarten sometime during the 1850s and established a successful wheelwright's business.[29] By color and occupation in the public sector, Peter Mortimer de Weever was a member of the new middle class. He had personal experience with middle-class anxieties about "coming down" that his grandson Roy Heath wrote about in *Shadows Round the Moon*. The lyrics for "Me Cawfee in de Marnin'" were in Creolese and the music was reminiscent of a revival hymn, a style that was becoming increasingly popular through the Pentecostal denominations and syncretic religious groups such as the Jordanites, which had been established in 1882.[30] "Me Cawfee in de Marnin'" has been described as one of the earliest examples of "creole expression" in Guyanese music, for which the composer was known.[31] The composers of the existing repertoire of Creolese songs prior to 1901 were unknown. Their compositions were categorized either as "plantation lullabies" or topical folk songs.[32] Examples of the latter would be "August marnin come again" (ca. 1839) and "Victoria marrid de German man" (ca. 1840). "August marnin come again" was a song celebrating the anniversary of the physical emancipation of enslaved Africans in British Guiana; "Victoria marrid de German man" was a commentary on Queen Victoria's marriage to Prince Albert of Saxe-Coburg & Gotha in 1840.

The verses of "Me Cawfee in de Marnin'" are meant for solo or unison singing and the chorus is in four parts. The song spoke to the colony's agricultural history, and through the exploration of cuisine addressed the conditions of poor people in the colony at the start of the twentieth century.[33] The first verse introduces the beverage choices the colony's workers had at the start of the day ("choclat," tea, "suga wata," and lemonade) and emphasize the "commentator's" preference for a "bowl o' bilin' cawfee" (a bowl of boiling coffee).

The first verse is followed by the chorus, which celebrates coffee, is repeated after the remaining three verses. The second verse describes the commentator's work ethic, especially the commitment to punctuality, which requires rising "wid de sunrise . . . dry or wet." The verse also identifies the commentator's relationship with religion, which could be compromised by the commitment to work, thus undermining the prevailing notion that

Africans were lazy and sought any excuse to not work. In the third verse, de Weever refers to saltfish and fat as foods that were possible when the working person had it "grand." Other foods available when things were "grand" included yellow plantain, green pepper, rice, and "cawfee wit a gil bread in de marnin.'"

Making it "grand" was rare, given the decline in the wages of urban laborers and rural cane cutters.[34] In the fourth and final verse, the commentator is revealed as an old person who has lived through the difficult post-slavery days, characterized by economic depressions, abusive labor practices, and a political system in which he had no voice.

The commentator created by de Weever does not come across as fatalistic. The "bowl of cawfee, in de Marnin'" can be read as a metaphor suggesting that the oppressive conditions that dominated the lives of the colony's poor were stimulants for the urgently needed social and political change. This work by de Weever is emblematic of the emerging solidarity between the middle and working classes in their resistance to planter-class domination that characterized the colony at the start of the twentieth century. "Me Cawfee in de Marnin'" became popular across the West Indies. In 1992, Jamaica's Ernie Smith recorded a version of the song on a CD celebrating examples of early Jamaican folk music. "Me Cawfee in de Marnin'," the first composition in Creolese for which the composer is known, established a tradition in Guyana that was followed by other Guyanese such as Chuck Gerard, Hilton Hemerding, Roland Phillips, and Terry Gajraj among others in the latter decades of the twentieth century.

The solidarity sentiment evident in "Me Cawfee in de Marnin'" exploded in Ruimveldt on November 28, 1905, during the governorship of Sir Frederick Mitchell Hodgson KCMG, who was no stranger to British Guiana, anti-colonial resistance, or the West Indies. This son of the clergy had served as postmaster general in British Guiana between 1882 and 1888. Between 1888 and 1898 he was the Colonial Secretary of the Gold Coast, in essence the second in command of the colony. In 1892 he established the Gold Coast Rifle Volunteers and as a major commanded this force. In 1898 he became governor and commander in chief of Gold Coast. As a senior colonial officer, Hodgson played a pivotal role in the suppression of the Asante/Ashanti people, the looting of their treasures, and the exiling of the Asantehene—King Prempeh. His insensitive efforts to humiliate the Asante/Ashanti people by demanding the Golden Stool for him to rule on triggered the siege of Kumasi led by Queen Yaa Asantewaa. Her capture in September 1901 culminated the process of annexing the Ashanti Kingdom by Britain and incorporating it into the Gold Coast colony.

When Hodgson arrived in British Guiana, he was a conquering hero and committed to the use of force to ensure the paramountcy of the British monarchy over the dominion and colonies.[35] As Governor of British Guiana, Hodgson demonstrated that he was powerful and had no qualms defending British capital, as was demonstrated with the suppression of the demands by workers for improved wages and working conditions.[36] Recall Kimani Nehusi's observation that the wages for cane cutters and weeders had declined by more than 50 percent between 1885 and 1901. This decision to reverse wage increases is considered to have been one of the factors that ignited the Ruimveldt riots. Guyanese historians have used several terms to refer to the domestic explosion of 1905. Walter Rodney used the term "Ruimveldt Riots"; Kimani Nehusi has referred to the moment as the "Ruimveldt Protest"; Nigel Westmaas has called it the "1905 Rebellion." But all agree that the incident had profound consequences for the society—consequences that have resonated throughout the twentieth century. The triggering factor was the wages paid to the stevedores, which had remained stagnant for nearly three decades. In protest, the primarily black Georgetown stevedores went on strike on November 28, and when it ended on December 3 it had involved a wide swath of the working class—stevedores, domestics, bakers, and other categories of workers in Georgetown and rural sugar workers on estates on the East Bank of Demerara, the West Bank of Demerara, and the West Coast of Demerara. On December 1, sugar workers from estates on the East Bank of Demerara went on strike and, accompanied by "drums and pipes," began a march to Georgetown to show solidarity with the stevedores and also make their case.[37] The marchers were intercepted by a detachment of police and the artillery at Plantation Ruimveldt. Following the instructions of Col. De Rinzy, the police and the artillery fired on the marchers, wounding three. This action triggered several days of rioting in Georgetown. Governor Hodgson was stranded in the Parliament Buildings in Georgetown for a period of time. There were also acts of violence against estate managers on East Bank and West Demerara estates. These actions resulted in more shootings and the dispatch of the British Navy to the colony from Barbados. At the end of the riots, "seven persons were dead and seventeen critically wounded."[38]

Walter Rodney has noted that riots and disturbances were regular occurrences in the history of the British West Indies and that many of these incidents did not affect more than a small sector of those societies. He noted, however, that there were some, such as the Ruimveldt riots, that "were more wide-ranging and the scale of violence larger; as a result of the level of consciousness and organization of the participants . . . it had profound impacts on the colonial authorities."[39] As mentioned earlier, Nigel Westmaas has termed the Ruimveldt riots "the 1905 Rebellion" and associated it with other landmark events in Russia; Bengal, India; and South West Africa, where working people sought improvement of their living and working conditions.[40] Ultimately, the strike action by the stevedores failed but the strike's verve resonated across urban, rural, and hinterland British Guiana, building working-class solidarity and ushering in the birth of trade unionism under the leadership of Hubert Nathaniel Critchlow. Although the evidence is sparse, the Ruimveldt riots demonstrated that the music of the working class, which may have been based on "drums and pipes/fifes," had played an important role in the mobilization and motivation of the striking workers; and as we will see below, this role continued with the growth of organized labor throughout most of the twentieth century.[41]

Walter Rodney also contended that one of the reasons why the workers failed to win any benefits after the 1905 riots was the absence of effective organizations. Starting in 1906, middle-class professionals of African ancestry such as Berbice-born Dr. J. M. Rohlehr, who was a spokesman for the strikers in 1905, urged the formation of a trade union.[42] Critchlow took up this task and continued to use music as a tool for mobilization. As Hazel Woolford, the Guyanese labor historian, noted, "Critchlow was the first secular African Guianese leader to have brass band concerts at the public meetings and as part of its open air concerts geared to mobilizing and strengthening the nascent trade union movement. The 'Faithist' or Jordanites, up until then, were the ones who utilized brass bands as part of their meetings."[43] The domestic economic crisis continued to fester.

Governor Hodgson was replaced by Sir Walter Egerton in July 1912; by 1914 Egerton had articulated a development plan for the colony that attracted the attention of the *New York Times* of May 17, 1914. Under the headline SCHEME TO DEVELOP BRITISH GUIANA, the article revealed a plan that aimed to pull the colony out of its state of economic inactivity by "building a railway from the coast to the Brazilian frontier, a distance of some 340 miles, which would open up the vast wealth known to be awaiting enterprise in the interior." According to the article, several problems needed to be resolved before the plan could be implemented. These included the "rag of a Constitution" which placed too much power in the hands of the Combined Court for financial matters and the absence of representative democracy.[44] On July 28, 1914, just less than three months after the relatively optimistic article in the *New York Times*, World War I began.

The outbreak of World War I in 1914 brought dramatic increases in the cost of living and reaffirmed the need for trade unions. Ironically, WWI also provided some economic relief for the colony's unemployed. British Guianese soldiers proudly marched off to war to local folk-flavored marches such as "Georgetown Boys Forever" and "What you gunn do to Kaiser?" The participation by non-white British Guianese in WWI triggered many changes in British Guianese society. It helped temporarily undermine some of the stereotypes that had emerged about people of African ancestry among the white ruling class in British Guiana and across the West Indies. Black Guianese and their counterparts across the West Indies were anxious to demonstrate their loyalty to Great Britain and were prepared to give their lives in the service of the Empire. The British War Office "was initially hostile and reluctant to accept Black West Indians. The idea of people of color fighting and killing Europeans was anathema."[45] However, the massive loss of lives by British soldiers in the European theatre demanded a change in British War Office policy. A notice signed by Col. G. C. De Rinzy, Commandant, Local Forces dated June 22, 1915, invited "Recruits from British Guiana to Join His Majesty's Army for the Duration of the War." The notice announced:

> Smart, healthy, young men of good character between the ages of 19 and 38 years anxious to serve with the British Guiana Contingent of recruits being raised for the purpose of proceeding to England to join His Majesty's Army for the duration of the great war, can apply in Georgetown and New Amsterdam personally at the Militia Barracks between the hours of 7 to 9 a.m., 12 noon to 2 p.m., and 4 to 6 p.m. on weekdays until further notice.[46]

The upper age limited was extended to 45 years for "Ex-soldiers." All "candidates had to be [no] "less than 5ft. 3in in height and [have] 33.5 ins chest measurement, [and were] required to undergo a strict medical examination, including eye-sight test."[47] Recruits were offered a shilling a day pay and promised another shilling per day when they became "efficient." In addition, family allowances were offered for wives and children. Given the state of unemployment among the working class in British Guiana at the start of WWI, there were many recruits. However, the medical examinations in British Guiana and across the West Indies revealed that the health of the working-class volunteers was poor, leading to high levels of rejection.[48] Glenford Howe's *Race, War and Nationalism* and Cedric Joseph's *The British West Indies Regiment 1914–1918* chronicle the racism, poor housing, underpay, and physical abuse that West Indian recruits experienced when they got to England and during their military service in Palestine, Jordan, Egypt, Mesopotamia, East Africa, India, France, Italy, and Belgium.[49]

It has been concluded that among the consequences of the participation of black West Indians in WWI was the "exacerbation of [the] underlying tensions and contradictions implicit in West Indian society, stimulating the growth of working-class consciousness and facilitating the growth of black consciousness and nationalism."[50] As we will see in the sphere of labor relations, those conclusions held true for British Guiana. In addition to heightening political consciousness, participation in WWI also exposed British Guianese soldiers to new musical trends and songs that were popular in Europe. The African American Lt. James Reese Europe and the members of the 369th US Infantry "Hell Fighters" Band from Harlem, New York, was popularizing jazz in France and all across Europe, while soldiers from the British Empire were marching to songs such as "It's a Long Way to Tipperary." That song would come to British Guiana and serve as a mobilizing song for the nascent labor movement.

The end of World War I in 1918 did not bring about any immediate change to the ideology of white supremacy in the colony. However, there were significant changes in the political and social equations. On the international front, the successful Russian Revolution strengthened concerns about the possibility of radical change in the colony. As a result, the Seditious Publications Bill was passed in 1919 to ban the importation of Marcus Garvey's *Negro World*. The first trade union was established in 1919.

When the Indian Indentureship program ended in 1917, the hierarchy that placed Europeans at the apex remained unchanged. The colony's administration continued to be dominated by sojourning British-born officials.[51] There were also increased efforts at using cultural power in the governance of the society and this is evidenced in the increasing role of the governor and the ruling class in the promotion of music education—the credentialing of music competence. The leader in this cause was Sir Wilfred Collet, who served as the colony's governor from April 15, 1917, to April 4, 1923. Under his governorship British music examinations would become available in the colony. In addition to the institutionalizing of British credentials, the post–World War I era also brought with it acceleration in the diffusion of music making and distribution technologies. As will be addressed later, folk music persisted in rural and hinterland regions in the post–WWI era.

The importance of music as a social marker and the growing popularity of concerts and other forms of public musical performances led to demands for elevating standards through formal music education. These demands came primarily from women associated with the elite and the new middle class. By 1915 *Catechism of Music*, "compiled by a Local Teacher," had joined Hemy's *Royal Modern Tutor for the Pianoforte* as the primary texts used by the increasing number of piano teachers in Georgetown and New Amsterdam. In a society where there were aspirations for upward mobility, music students, especially women, sought credentials that would demonstrate that they understood and could perform European classical music. This led to demands for credentials from recognized British institutions. In 1916 a list was published in the *Daily Argosy* of students from the Ursuline Convent, Georgetown, who were successful at the elementary and junior examinations of the London College of Music.[52] A year later the same newspaper reported on an important development in music education in British Guiana:

Following a long series of correspondence with the Royal Academy of Music and the Royal College of Music, Miss. Ivy K. D. Davis, LRAM, ARCM, etc., has been successful in persuading the Board in London to consent to the holding of theory examinations in Georgetown under the aegis of the Board and the examinations will take place next year, probably in March coincident with the holding of the examination in England. Sir Chas. Major, Kt., and Mr. T. A. Pope, both of whom are interested in music, have consented to act as Honorary Local representatives of the Associated Board, and to preside over examinations.[53]

This meant that British Guianese students no longer needed to travel to England for the examination. By 1918 music students in British Guiana also had the opportunity to sit the theory examination of the Trinity College of Music.[54] Eventually, local-born graduates from the London College of Music, Trinity College, the Royal Academy of Music, and the Royal College of Music—such as Lynette Dolphin, Billy Pilgrim, Ruby McGregor, Joyce Aaron, Cicelene Baird, Francis Percival Loncke, Rosemary Ramdehol, and Joyce Ferdinand—would exert significant influence on the development of music in Guyana. By the end of the 1920s a music teacher held high status and had an important role in the formal and informal governance of the colony. The elite schools (Queen's College and Bishop's High Schools) had music teachers and solid music programs. T. A. Pope was the Headmaster at Queen's College. In time, this orientation would occasionally expand to include the entire educational system. Music was recognized as a vehicle that could develop and inculcate values and perspectives that nurtured loyalty to the ideology of the state. This was made even easier with common texts and hymnals. The establishment churches, those that received subventions from the state (Anglicans, Catholics, and Scottish Presbyterians) were also important institutions in the musical community associated with the urban-based ruling class. Central to this aspect of the musical community were church organs and choirs.

Between 1900 and 1920, the organ became a popular instrument in major Christian churches in urban British Guiana. Regular organ concerts were presented at St. George's Cathedral, Christ Church, St. Andrew's Kirk, and St. Philip's in Georgetown and at the All Saint's (English) Church in New Amsterdam. The popularity of the organ as a concert instrument can be traced back to December 11, 1822, when the first Sacred Concert in British Guiana was held at St. Andrew's Kirk. The installation of the "kist of pipe" in St. Andrew's was ahead of many a Kirk in Scotland and was as "good as any organ as might be found then in the West Indies."[55]

In time, the organ spread to urban and rural churches. For example, by 1914 the Edinburgh's New Congregational Church in Berbice dedicated a "beautiful American organ."[56] During the first two decades of the twentieth century, an organ concert circuit connected churches in Georgetown, New Amsterdam, and the contiguous African villages. In addition to showcasing the organ and virtuosos such as G. W. Nusum, these concerts provided space for other instrumentalists and singers. For example, the gala concert organized by the All Saints' (English) Church in New Amsterdam to present the "opening of [its] new organ" on Tuesday, 9 September 1913, featured performers from Georgetown including G. W. Nusum, Miss Downer (contralto), Kirton Tucker (bass), and H. E. Anderson (violinist). The pianist and accompanist was C. H. Bagot.[57]

The organ concerts established the churches as important venues for musical interaction and exchange in urban, rural, and hinterland environments. In 1919 the Lutheran Church started to evangelize among East Indians in the colony, especially in Berbice. The outcome of interaction and exchange within the Christian churches would become most evident in the growth of choral music, a topic we will address in upcoming chapters. The period under review also witnessed acceleration in the diffusion of music making and delivery technologies. These technologies introduced new musical tastes, established new musical connections, and in the process reinforced aspects of the society's racial architecture.

During the first two decades of the twentieth century, the London Electric Cinema, Olympic Picture Theater, Royal Picture Palace, and Gaiety Picture Palace were established in Georgetown. Pianists such as Oscar Dummett, Arthur Seaton, and Banks Greene accompanied the silent movies that were shown at these cinemas.[58] In New Amsterdam, Anna Mclean, the aunt of the celebrated author Edgar Mittelholzer, was sought after as an accompanist for the silent movies that were shown in the town's two cinemas. Edgar Mittelholzer's *A Swarthy Boy* provides a snippet of the musical accompaniment she provided for the 1914 serial *The Exploits of Elaine* when it was shown at New Amsterdam's Olympic Cinema. For a sequence in which the heroine is in "great peril," Mrs. McLean weaves together extracts from musical favorites of the time: "*The Destiny Waltz* merging into *The Blue Danube* merging into *The Merry Widow* merging into *The Druid's Prayer* merging into *Beautiful Dreamer*."[59]

In addition to showing silent movies with piano accompaniment and live musical performers between pictures, these cinemas, along with the Assembly Rooms, the Town Hall, and Christ Church School Hall, were also the venues for concerts by local and visiting artists. The local performers included the spouses of colonial officials, members of the new multi-ethnic middle class, and members of the British Guiana Militia Band. In New Amsterdam, Messrs. Mittelholzer and Fryer were popular violinists.[60] Dancers from Ivy Davis's Melisma Academy of Music, Classical Ballet, and Dramatic Arts were also popular performers.[61] Among the international acts who performed in local cinemas between 1900 and 1920 were the Royal Marionettes; the W. S. Harkin Players; the Morton Opera Company; the Spanish pianist Senorita Maria Mercedes Padrosa; Alma Simpson, America's Metropolitan Soprano Recitalist; the "Italian songstress" Madame Olivari; the acrobat Prince Otto Taka; and the Chinese conjurer Professor Hen-Akie. These concerts tended to be fundraisers for organizations that were part of the informal network of institutions engaged in the governance of society. These concerts also gave colonial officials and local politicians visibility as patrons.[62]

In addition to the cinemas, other new music technologies were also diffused in British Guiana, especially in the urban centers, during the first two decades of the twentieth century. Among these were barrel organs, Pianolas by the Autopiano Company, sound post cards, the gramophone, and kits for crystal radio sets. Credit terms and installment payment plans ensured that Victrola and Columbia gramophones became important furnishings in upper- and middle-class homes. These technologies, especially the gramophone, facilitated the introduction of additional musical styles and the development of new musical tastes. From Europe came waltzes; from the United States came "coon music" such as "The Laughing Nigger Boy"; and from Trinidad came "Manuelita," "Sarah," "Oil Fields," "Mango Vert," "Pauline," "Mary Jane," "505 Stop," and other waltzes and paseos performed by Lovey's Trinidad String Band.[63] Reflecting the impact of World War I, marches were also popular gramophone recordings.

Hack's Cycle Depot, "the premier gramophone music house," ran advertisements announcing a supply of "stirring band marches" from Columbia Records. These included Souza's "Double Eagle," "Thunder," "El Albanico," "El Capitan," "Manisot," "Under the Double Eagle," "With Russian Banners," "Invincible Eagle," "Yankee Doodle," "Over There," and the "American Republic."[64] Another advertisement a few months later announced the availability of "War Songs from 'Yankee Doodle' down to 'Over There' [and] all the stirring, tuneful songs our men have sung through many a hard-fought campaign." The advertisement reminded the reader: "For music that is patriotic, played with a snap and a sparkle that reflect the very spirit of the theme, the proper combination is Columbia [records and the Columbia] Grafonolas."[65] These developments in music performance and the diffusion of new music technologies such as Victrolas, Grafonolas, and phonographs between 1900 and 1920 led to the diversification in forms of music-based entertainment during this period. Among the popular new forms were steamer and train excursions, subscription dances, jazz dances, café chantants, and vaudeville shows.[66]

Despite efforts by the ruling class to ban, mute, and denigrate the musics of the subordinated classes during the nineteenth century, the first two decades demonstrated that those efforts were not effective. In the years following the

1905 riots, rural-to-urban migration accelerated. This movement also brought the musical traditions of rural Africans and East Indians into the urban space. By 1911, 65 percent of the colony's European (excluding Portuguese) population resided in Georgetown, while 57 percent of the Portuguese population did. Almost 5 percent of East Indians in the colony were now living in Georgetown and nearly 25 percent of all Africans were now living there. Twenty-four percent of the Chinese in the colony lived in Georgetown and were concentrated in the Charlestown ward, where in 1913 the Chinese community experienced severe loss of property and life when a fireworks factory exploded, destroying a large area and taking more than twenty lives.[67] In addition, almost 50 percent of the mixed-race population was to be found in Georgetown. This exacerbated the already poor housing and public health situation in areas such as La Penitence, Charlestown, Albouystown, and sections of Kitty, Alberttown, Cummingsburg, Lodge, and Kingston. However, despite these structural deficiencies, the residential arrangements increased interracial contact and, as a result, encouraged musical interaction and exchange. From the rural African villages came the music/dance complex associated with births; marriage; birthdays; "moon-light night"; wakes; and the religious works associated with Cumfa and other African-based syncretic religions. Of these, the pre-marriage Kwe Kwe ritual was very influential. Kwe Kwe has given Guyana some of its most memorable folk songs.[68]

At the start of the twentieth century, religious and folk music dominated the soundscape of the predominantly East Indian rural villages. According to Peter Manuel, the religious music was influenced by "*bhakti*-centered Hinduism, which encouraged inter-caste fraternization and group singing" in temples and other venues.[69] This orientation privileged Rama and Krishna and festivals such as Diwali and Phagwah. Another manifestation of religious music was the various "works" such as nine-day bhagvats and various pujas that took place in yards and was referred to as "ground singing." Maha Kali was an influential deity for the darker-skinned Madrassis, and regular drum-based ecstatic pujas were organized for this deity. The dominant religious genre was the bhajan. The folk music in predominantly East Indian villages was based on Bhojpuri folk music traditions. Peter Manuel identified the following dominant categories: "work songs, . . . songs associated with life cycle events, . . . songs associated with seasons and seasonal festivities, . . . and songs associated with Ramlila theatre."[70] Other secular traditions include biraha, maujing, and tassa drumming. Matticore/Dig Dutty, like the African Kwe Kwe, was a pre-marriage ritual associated with Hindus. In 1900 the ritual also served to prepare the young couple for marriage life. In a private, all-female ceremony, the bride-to-be was "educated" by the older women on sexual matters. This education was said to be vivid and explicit and made memorable by lively lyrics and hot rhythms on the two-sided drum known as the dholak. That lyrical and rhythmic style was called Chatni. Like Kwe Kwe, the music from this aspect of the rural Indian soundscape would have an impact on music in Guyana during the twentieth century, especially after independence in 1966. In addition to the dholak, harmonium, the tadjah drum, dhantal, sarenghi, and majeera were some of the popular instruments used in music making by East Indians at the start of the twentieth century. Not all East Indians were Hindu. At the start of the twentieth century, between 10 and 15 percent of the Indian population were Muslims. Of special importance for this chapter was the festival of Muharram or Hosay. The festival was public and featured replicas of Tazias—the tombs of Hassan and Hussein. It was this constellation of musical traditions that rural East Indians brought with them to the urban center.

As a result of migration, residents of these urban communities and contiguous rural villages encountered a soundscape that included sacred genres, which included hymns and cantatas from the churches; marching melodies of the Salvation Army and the brass bands of the Jordanites; the "Sankeys" of "way-side" churches; bhajans from Hindu temples; and the call to prayer and from mosques. There were also the pulsating Cumfa drums on Punt Trench Dam and village back dams. There were songs from Kwe Kwe and Matticore; the songs of wakes, the drums of tadjah, the drums and flutes of masquerade band music, and the "bruk up" sessions of old-time fiddle and clarinet bands that performed at "practices," "dignity balls," and birthday parties in lodge halls and in private homes.[71] These sounds also wafted into the proximate middle- and upper-class communities, creating discomfort and demands to curb them. However, these encounters would flavor the society's musical repertoire for the remainder of the twentieth century.

As unemployment continued to increase, urban and rural working people sought opportunities in the hinterland, where further musical encounters, interactions, and exchange took place. The new terrain, the waterfalls, the rapids, and the type of work inspired songs composed to accompany work in the gold and diamond fields and the timber grants. The workers came primarily from the African villages of the east coast of Demerara (Belladrum, Buxton, Clonbrook, and Golden Grove) and west coast Berbice (Hopetown) and brought with them the West and Central African–inflected compositional and performance style based on call and response and inspired by the repertoires of Kwe Kwe and Cumfa.[72] The songs were composed to coordinate work and for recreation. Some of the songs also referred to the mythologies of the indigenous peoples. The term *shanty* has been used to describe this genre of folk composition. These creations did not remain in the hinterland. They came to urban and rural areas with returning workers and in time became part of the nation's repertoire of folk music. In addition, increased penetration of the hinterland led to the establishment and expansion of a number of hinterland settlements such as Bartica, Mahadia, and Kurupung, which, as we will note in the next chapter became destinations for touring calypsonians and other popular musicians during the 1930s.

Prior to the accelerated penetration of the hinterland during the 1900 to 1920 period, Christian missionaries had been there seeking to convert the indigenous peoples. As mentioned previously, there is evidence of this starting with the Moravians as early as the seventeenth century in the Berbice area. This evangelizing did have some impact on the music of the indigenous. Some music-based traditions, such as the feasting and drinking sprees associated with successful hunts or special religious services of the Ackawaio and Arekuna, were defined as savage and restricted by the missionaries. The efforts to suppress these practices were not successful. The work of the missionaries also influenced the instruments used by indigenous peoples.[73] However, when coastal workers penetrated the hinterland to work in the gold and diamond fields and the timber grants, they encountered the rich, diverse, and complex musical environment of the indigenous peoples. In addition to diversity of musical instruments—bone flutes, reed whistles, trumpets, panpipes, drums, viol, Aeolian harp, sambora, maracas, and rattles—there was also a range of vocal practices, which included chants that were associated with distinct religious and spiritual practices.[74] In addition, there were significant examples of musical exchange. For example, in the gold-mining Upper Mazaruni region, the Hallelujah religion practiced by the Ackawaio and Arekuna revealed the interaction and exchange with the Christian hymnals.[75] In the northwest region of the colony, the Spanish Arawaks, who migrated to British Guiana in the 1800s fleeing from persecution in Venezuela, were using violins, banjos, guitars, flutes, maracas, and sambora in their music. The music, known as Banshikilli, was directly influenced by the Joropo rhythms of Venezuela. Banshikilli music was the dominant music of the region and performed by Warraus and Arawaks, the other indigenous people in the northwest region.[76] In timber extracting areas, workers from the coast would have been exposed to the music and related cultural practices of the Caribs. The "coastlanders" who went into the savannahs of the Rupununi would have encountered the musical expressions of the Wai Wai, Macushi, and Patamona. These encounters would be reciprocal.

Accelerated penetration of the hinterland between 1900 and 1920 also fostered increased interaction with indigenous peoples. Some of them worked in the gold, diamond, and timber industries; others supplied fish, meat, and other foodstuff to coastal workers. They also shared their mythologies and exposed the coastlanders to festivals and the music of these festivals: Mari

Mari, Parachari, and Mash-ir-e-meh-i, a celebration after a successful community effort. These hinterland experiences came back to the coastal plain. The flora, fauna, and mythologies of the hinterland became materials for Guianese patriotic and art music that would emerge from the new middle class in the 1930s and continue for the reminder of the twentieth century.

The colony's urban soundtrack during the period was created by many musical instruments, featured multiple styles, and involved several musical communities. However, despite this diversity, the governance practices of the colony state ensured that the musical aesthetics of the state reflected the ideology of the ruling class and its allies. The first two decades of the twentieth century also set in motion a number of political, social, and cultural developments, including the creation of ethnic institutions. Reflecting on this period, Garner noted, "Groups began to organize along class, ethnic, and ultimately, national lines to contest domination by the British colonial administration."[77]

3

The Rise of Ethnic and Class Consciousness:
1921–1930

Five governors administered British Guiana between 1921 and 1930, and among their central tasks were addressing constitutional issues, operationalizing development strategies, and responding to increased agitation by ethnic and working-class movements. The administration of Sir William Collet (1917–23) is illustrative of the indelible impact governors had on the colony's musical life. Collet, who joined the Colonial Service in 1881 at the age of twenty-five, had studied music at Trinity College, London. He had an interesting family background—his "great-great-great uncle, Joseph Collet, had been an official in the East India Company and President of Madras (January 8, 1717–January 18, 1720); his father, Collet Dobson Collet, was a noted radical reformer . . . and [the future governor of British Guiana] Wilfred Collet and his sister Clara had close contacts with Karl Marx and his family."[1] Prior to the governorship in British Guiana, he held Colonial Service appointments in Fiji, Cyprus, and British Honduras.[2] Between 1920 and 1923, he had to respond to the ongoing crisis with the Combined Court in executing the economic development plan articulated by Sir William Egerton, who Collet replaced as governor in 1917. Collet also had to respond to demands for reopening immigration of indentured labor from India and to the improved organization among the colony's ethnic communities and the working class, who continued to clamor for political and economic justice. Important elements in Governor Collet's responses to the constellation of challenges were promoting sports, especially cricket, and encouraging music. In early twentieth-century social theory, sports, especially cricket, taught teamwork and playing by the rules, and music had liberating potential. During his tour as governor, he was patron for a number of musical organizations, wrote the music for "Reginae Collegium," Queen's College's school song, and in retirement established the Collet Medal at Trinity College. Collet and his successors administered the colony during a blooming of European musical culture among the middle and working classes in urban British Guiana. The proliferation of organizations supported this effort.

As mentioned in the previous chapter, Walter Rodney contended that one of the reasons workers failed to win any benefits after the 1905 riots was the absence of effective organizations. The period 1921 to 1931 brought with it a proliferation of organizations. Most represented racial and ethnic interests; some had their genesis in earlier periods. The Chinese Association was founded in 1920. In 1921 E. F. Fredericks, a lawyer from Buxton, founded the Negro Progress Convention (NPC). By 1922 the British Guiana East Indian Association was active. In 1924 the Portuguese Club was founded, and in 1929 the St. Andrew's Association was revived to promote the interests of Scots in the colony. All of these organizations were headquartered in Georgetown, led by members of the new middle class, and, in addition to providing for the social and cultural needs of their members, had strong political agendas. They were all committed to expanding the franchise, becoming involved in the political process, and seeking active involvement in national governance.

According to Harold Lutchman, by the 1920s middle-class politicians were comprised of "the more educated Negroes, Portuguese, East Indians, Chinese and Coloured[s]," the beneficiaries of an educational system whose construction had started during the nineteenth century by Christian denominations and included Queen's College, which was established in 1844. By the 1920s many of the middle-class Guianese leaders had also studied abroad and were qualified in many academic and professional fields. Lutchman also proposed that many middle-class leaders shared similar cultural values with the ruling class, and added that some middle-class leaders "did not reject the dominant British values but embraced them with a fervor which even the Europeans could not surpass."[3] Despite this congruence with British values, these middle-class politicians were proto-nationalists. Their engagement in politics was not merely for status, although that was a factor, but also was about using this access to decision making and resource distribution for the benefit of their constituencies and, more narrowly, their ethnic groups. Their tactics were informed by a mix of international strategies, especially those being applied by blacks in the United States, specifically the strategies of accommodation articulated by Booker T. Washington and the Tuskegee Institute; the politics of confrontation as articulated by W. E. B. Du Bois; and the politics of nationalism and separation as expressed by Marcus Garvey.[4] Accommodation was based on the notion that economic development should be pursued ahead of political and racial equality—it meant the tactical accommodation of the dominant paradigm of racial superiority. Du Bois's politics of confrontation saw the black educated class—the Talented Tenth—as having the responsibility for mobilizing and leading the subjugated out of the conditions of oppression. For Marcus Garvey, the solution lay in self-government and an independent and unified Africa.

The Negro Progress Convention was clearly guided the philosophy and practices of Booker T. Washington and sought to promote educational and economic development for people of African ancestry through self-help and the types of assertiveness that characterized the creation of the African village movement in 1839. Elements of the ruling class described the organization as socialist, Soviet, or anti-capitalist. Sections of the print media accused the NPC of sowing seeds of dissention. Throughout this decade, the *Daily Argosy* published articles, columns, and cartoons that were derisive of Guianese of African ancestry. It must be noted that the NPC was not the only organization that sought to organize people of African ancestry in the colony; others included Marcus Garvey's United Negro Improvement Association (UNIA) and the New Negro Development Association.

The British Guiana East Indian Association (BGEIA) is considered the successor of the British Guiana East Indian Institute (BGEII), which was created in Berbice in 1892 by Thomas Flood, Verasammy Mudaliar, James Wharton, and William Hawley Wharton, who has been identified as the leader. BGEII lasted for under a year. According to Clem Seecharan, among the reasons for the short life of the BGEII was "the atmosphere of indifference to intellectual and political pursuits prevalent among Indo-Guyanese in the 1890s." Another reason was the loss of leadership. W. H. Wharton left British Guiana in 1893 to study medicine at Edinburgh University, where he was probably "the first Indian in the Caribbean to study at a British university."[5] Headquartered in Georgetown, the BGEIA sought to improve the living and working conditions of East Indians in British Guiana and lobbied the government for the renewal of Indian immigration under better terms. J. A. Luckhoo, a barrister and an influential member of the Indian community, even proposed the establishment of an Indian colony in British Guiana:

> ... [A]lthough we form 40 percent of the population, we feel and we have always felt that we are scattered sons of India, and that India should stretch her hands across to us and try and help us and lift us up. The only way of doing this is to increase our numbers in the colony ... we hope that in the future British Guiana will become a great Indian Colony. We appeal to the Head of the Indian Office, and to leaders of Indian authority and opinion to give us their help. We feel that you have our destiny in your hands, and we ask you to remember that these people who emigrate to British Guiana will have the same rights, and that if they will come in sufficient numbers, we shall be able to build up an Indian Colony which will be a credit to India and the Empire.[6]

Seecharan concluded that although the proposal did not materialize, it "was a barometer of the rising Indian self-confidence in British Guiana." Starting in the late nineteenth century, there was increased interest in the intellectual and cultural heritage of Aryan India by British and European scholars. Friedrich Max Muller, the German-born Oxford scholar, who has been described as "a formidable authority in Sanskrit with an extraordinary empathy with the soul of ancient and modern India," asserted "that Indian and European peoples were descended from a common, ancient Aryan 'race.' Their ancestors were the South-Eastern and North-Western Aryans, respectively." Muller also argued "that all Indo-European languages had a common origin; and that the ancient Aryans in India and their language, Sanskrit, was related to European peoples and their original languages, ancient Greek and Latin."[7] This interest by British and European scholars and assertions by researchers such as Muller, along with the work of Indians, contributed to what Clem Seecharan has termed a "virtual Hindu renaissance." This renaissance stimulated "an all-India pride in its Hindu antecedents. This answered the void, the shame, fed by centuries of alien rule—Muslim, then British."[8] Among the other consequences was the development of organizations for reforming Hinduism and promoting Indian political autonomy. In 1875 Swami Dayananda found the *Arya Sumaj* with the aim of "cleansing contemporary Hinduism of its layers of superstition and other excrescences." For him, the goal was to return to the *Vedas*, the original texts of the Aryans, and the eradication of the caste system, Brahmin privilege, idolatry, and polytheism.[9] On the political front, the Indian National Congress was formed in 1895 with what could be described as having accommodationist goals—"an active role in governing their own country, albeit as part of the Empire."[10] At its founding the Indian National Congress was not against British rule. This position changed dramatically in 1907, when the party split into two wings. One wing, the Garam Dal, led by Bal Gangadhar Tilak, demanded complete independence.[11]

These intellectual and political developments were also felt in British Guiana. As in India, these developments nurtured self-confidence and optimism among those East Indians in British Guiana, like Joseph Ruhoman, who were "literate and inquisitive."[12] It has been pointed out that, at the turn of the twentieth century, East Indians like Ruhoman were dissatisfied with the "intellectual and social void within the Indian community; and contrasted this with what [was] considered the superior mental, moral, religious, and social accomplishments of the Black and Coloured peoples ... [and the] growing tendency of the latter to provide higher education for their children—secondary, as well as professional, education in Britain."[13] As Seecharan has stated, Ruhoman was impatient and was anxious to erase the shame of being a "coolie" in British Guiana and replace it with racial pride and dignity. In the early 1900s, Ruhoman's quest was not the top priority for a significant proportion of the East Indians in British Guiana, whose "energies were directed to the acquisition of land" needed for their participation in the nascent rice and cattle industries. The pursuit of western-style education in that context was seen as a distraction.[14]

The idea that East Indians and Europeans were related through common Aryan ancestors did not provide much leverage in the politics of British Guiana during the 1920s. It may have caused some East Indians to believe that they were superior to blacks but did not do much to change the power equation or the way they were perceived by the white ruling class, who still regarded them as "the menial, ignorant coolie … [serving] the purpose for which they [were] imported to the colony very admirably." This reality "gnawed at the dignity of educated Indians," especially the leadership of the BGEIA.[15] To respond to this reality, the Georgetown-based BGEIA established a cricket club, hosted fairs, and promoted drama and music that were European in orientation.

In the 1920s there were 8,247 persons of Portuguese origin or descent in British Guiana and this represented fewer than 3 percent of the population, which stood at 309,676. The creation of the Portuguese Club in 1924 was not the first effort to create their own social institutions and develop strategies to become involved in the political and cultural life in rural and urban British Guiana. In 1875 the Portuguese Benevolent Society was established. However, only male Catholic Portuguese of "good conduct" could become members. The primary purpose of the society was "first and foremost, to encourage Members to care for and share their wealth with the more needy of their fellow-countrymen and women; to give relief to the sick, the elderly, the imprisoned, the unemployed, those unable to work, widows and orphans and to provide funeral and burial expenses."[16] By the 1920s the urban Portuguese community, like the African and East Indian urban communities, was stratified with discrete upper, middle, and lower categories. Despite wealth and other assets, the Portuguese did not have access to the social institutions of the ruling Anglo-Saxons. As a result, in May 1924 the Portuguese Club was opened in Non Pariel Park, Georgetown.

Whiteness was internally differentiated in British Guiana. Scots and Scot-Irish did not enjoy the same status as the English. For most of the nineteenth century and up to the 1920s, Scots in British Guiana dominated the overseer ranks of the sugar industry and the middle and some upper echelons of the civil service, primarily in the coercive sectors—police, prisons, and militia. The growing restiveness of the subordinate classes during the third decade of the twentieth century challenged their dominance in those positions. One response was the reactivation of the St. Andrew's Association, which served to celebrate their ethnicity and to reaffirm their important role in the building of the "Mighty British Nation." Scottish pride kept the bagpipe, the fife, and the airs of the Highlands alive in British Guiana during the third decade of the twentieth century.

On January 1, 1919, Hubert Nathaniel Critchlow, one of the situational leaders of the 1905 Ruimveldt revolt, formed the British Guiana Labour Union (BGLU) and launched the nation's trade union movement. Unlike the ethnic organizations, the trade union movement transcended race and sought to establish solidarity among the working class and the new middle class with its tenuous economic realities. Like the ethnic organizations, the early trade union movement also had social, cultural, and political agendas that influenced the development of music in the colony.

In addition to challenging the stifling political system and jockeying for political advantages in the changing political landscape, these new organizations also contributed to developments in music in the colony. These contributions included the creation of new spaces for the presentation of concerts and other forms of musical entertainment—thus reducing dependency on the elite controlled venues such as the Assembly Rooms and City Hall in Georgetown. The Negro Progress Convention established the NPC Hall, which became a popular venue for concerts. The British Guiana Labour Union's hall also became a popular concert and dance hall. These organizations also held annual conferences, which invariably had a substantial musical component. Through these and other forms of promotion, the new organizations helped expand the colony's musical repertoire. For example, the NPC, through its connection with Booker T. Washington's Tuskegee Institute in the United States, played a pivotal role in popularizing Negro spirituals and African American art music in the colony during the 1920s. The NPC had an extensive rural network that was connected with churches, and this facilitated the circulation of black American vocal music.

The BGLU also used music as a tool for education and building solidarity. During this decade, the labor movement continued to organize, demonstrate solidarity across races and class lines, and agitate for better wages and working conditions. On July 12, 1922, the BGLU was recognized under the Trade Unions Ordinance of June 1922, making it the first trade union in British Guiana. Music played an important role in the early life of the BGLU. Ashton Chase has noted that one of the union's first investments was the purchase of a piano. In September 1921 the union organized a concert and dance in Georgetown. The concert, organized by W. Hosannah, featured classical music, inspirational labor songs, and instrumentals.[17] "The Beleaguered" (poem by Henry F. Chorley and music by Arthur and Sullivan) was performed by the union's chorus. It was a call to action: "Fling wide the gates! Come out! Dauntless and true."[18]

"The Beleaguered" was composed as a four-part work (for two tenors and two baritones), and this rendition by a larger chorus must have been inspiring. During its early years, the BGLU developed a songbook that was used in the education of the juvenile members of the union.[19] The use of songs such as "The Beleaguered" was emblematic of the use of music by the international labor movement to mobilize working people. During the early years of the twentieth century, the music of organized labor in the United States served to recruit and mobilize workers, galvanize support, direct attention to dangerous working conditions, celebrate heroes and heroines, and create a "common bond."[20]

The ethnic organizations also contributed to the preservation and promotion of distinctive cultural expressions, including music. For example, by the 1920s, Portuguese culinary and musical expressions had become part of the British Guianese cultural assets. Carne de porco do aljo (garlic pork), bolo de mel (honey cake) and malasadas (pancakes), and bacalhau (dried salted cod) were firmly part of the colony's cuisine.[21] By the 1920s the influence of Portuguese music was evident in secular and sacred contexts, including the Roman Catholic church. The Portuguese in British Guiana were primarily from Madeira, and the Catholicism practiced there has been described as "folksy." There, various religious feast days (of which there were many) were celebrated with "joyful abandon and with much pomp and splendour ... accompanied by the clergy, government officials, the military and bands of music."[22] This tradition was brought to British Guiana and was most evident in the celebration of Christmas, with the Midnight Mass and roving bands of musicians that took to the streets on Christmas Day. As Van Sertima reminded us: "The merrymakers go by, and anon other merry makers, equally high-spirited, come forward, all stir the sound signifying a season of frolic and festivity and rejoicing. Guitars and other stringed instruments also are heard in pleasant contrast. These come not in battalions nor in noisy company. The players, mostly Portuguese, discourse music that is soft and sweet ..."[23]

These practices helped consolidate the bonds of Portuguese in urban and rural British Guiana. Music was an integral part of Portuguese life in urban British Guiana, especially Georgetown. In the late nineteenth century and during the first decades of the twentieth century, performances on the Seawalls or in the Promenade Gardens by bands such as the Primeiro de Dezembro, the Estudiantina Restauração de Demerara, and the Tuna Uniao Recretiva Portugueza were more than concerts; they were venues for courting. It has been stressed that "[w]hether it was the classical music of the Primeiro de Dezembro Band or the popular music of the Estudiantina String Band; whether the music was played at the Town Hall, Philharmonic Hall, Assembly Rooms, Promenade or Botanic Gardens, the Portuguese bands were very much part of the musical scene in the colony and contributed in no small way to the social entertainment of a wide cross section of the population."[24]

During the 1920s three important musical developments emerged from the Portuguese community. The first was the creation of the British Guiana

Table 3.1 Music Teachers in Urban British Guiana			
Gender	**Georgetown**	**New Amsterdam**	**Total**
Males	3	6	9
Females	12	4	16
Total	15	10	25

Source: Compiled from a sample of the Daily Argosy, 1920–1931.

Musicians Band, led by Jules da Cambra, a former member of the British Guiana Militia Band; the second was the formation of the Goveia Orchestra; and the third the emergence of the baritone Frank Brazao, affectionately known as "the jewel in [British Guiana's] musical crown."[25] The Goveia Orchestra popularized jazz in British Guiana, and Brazao would eventually play an important role in developing the art of radio programming in the colony.

This expansion in music performance in urban British Guiana, along with the increased availability of sheet music, demanded competence in the European musical vocabulary and technique. The growing number of music teachers and the bands associated with the colony's uniformed services—the British Guiana Militia Band, the No. 7 Company Military Band (New Amsterdam), and the British Guiana Police Force Drum and Fife Band—supported this demand.

As shown above, by the third decade of the twentieth century, working-class and middle-class British Guianese were demonstrating achievement in the musical sphere. The results from the London School of Music, the Associated Board of the Royal Academy of Music and the Royal College of Music, Victoria College of Music, and Trinity College revealed the presence of a number of music teachers in Georgetown and New Amsterdam. Table 3.1 above shows the distribution of these teachers.

As the table above shows, females dominated the music-teaching field in both Georgetown and New Amsterdam during the 1920s. A close examination of the names of these teachers indicates that they were either the spouses of expatriate administrators or middle-class spinsters. In addition to these teachers, music education was also provided at the Bishop's High School for Girls in Georgetown and the Ursuline Convent in New Amsterdam.

Among the students who were successful in the 1924 Trinity College of Music examinations was Philip Pilgrim, who passed at the "First Steps" level. This was the beginning of a short but illustrious musical career. He was a student of Winifred McDavid. In 1927, Edna Elcock, a student of Miss Morris's Musical Academy, won the Sir Wilfred Collet's Gold Medal from the Trinity

College. On May 10, 1927, Sir Wilfred Collet wrote to Miss Morris from his home at 13, South Hill Park Gardens, Hampstead, N.W. 3, London:

Dear Miss Morris,

I send you a line of congratulation on the fact that a pupil of yours has won my Trinity College Medal for 1927. In view of the number of candidates and of Dr. Borland's great experience as an examiner, you may well be proud of your pupil's achievement.

(Sgd.) Wilfred Collet[26]

As we will note later, Philip Pilgrim and Edna Elcock (later Jordan) exerted significant influence on the direction of music in Guyana during the twentieth century.[27]

In addition to the creation of organizations to represent ethnic and working-class interests, this decade also witnessed the growth of a number of musical societies, clubs, and groups dedicated to classical music in urban British Guiana. Both the British Guiana Musical Society and the Berbice Musical Society were founded in 1920. The colony's governor, Sir Wilfred Collet, accepted the position as chief patron of the British Guiana Musical Society, which held its inaugural concert on January 27, 1920.[28] The president and musical director of the Berbice Musical Society was C. H. Bagot. The Intermediate Musical and Recreation Club, the Music Lovers Club, the Brotherhood Movement, and New Emerald Orchestra were established between 1926 and 1928.

These urban music organizations produced operas and other large musical works, concerts, and lectures and promoted "promising young musicians" at venues such as the Town Halls in Georgetown and New Amsterdam and school halls. In 1921 the British Guiana Musical Society presented the opera *Merrie England*, and in 1926 the Intermediate Musical and Recreation Club presented *Hansel and Gretel*.[29] In 1928 the Music Lovers Club organized a Grand Concert featuring "promising young musicians such as Mr. A. Johnson, Miss Serena Callender, Miss W. McDavid, Miss P. Johnson, and Miss E. Johnson to support the West Indies Hurricane Relief Fund."[30]

The practice of presenting young musicians in concert was well established in Georgetown and New Amsterdam by the start of the 1920s. It was expected that music teachers would arrange concerts featuring their students who were successful at the examinations conducted by the London School of Music, the Associated Board of the Royal Academy of Music and the Royal College of Music, Victoria College of Music, and Trinity College. This practice, variously titled an "Annual Musical Recital and Distribution of Certificates and Prizes,"

"A Musical Entertainment," or a "Vocal and Instrumental Recital," invariably attracted the patronage of the governor, the bishop, or some other dignitary or representative of the ruling class.[31] This practice has continued into the first decade of the twenty-first century. In addition to concerts featuring local performers organized by musical societies and music teachers, churches were also active organizers of concerts. These were popular fundraising strategies. Sometimes the fundraising concerts were presented as Shilling Concerts and Concert Parties.[32]

Urban churches and lodges regularly presented concerts of Christian sacred music. During the Easter season it was not uncommon for the choirs of the main denominations to present John Stainer's *Crucifixion*, *The Daughter of Jairus*, John Henry Maunder's *Olivet to Cavalry*, and other cantatas. During the Christmas season, church-related service organizations such as the Brotherhood Movement regularly presented concerts that featured choirs of up to one hundred voices singing carols.[33] Peter Moses de Weever pioneered these large choirs.[34] In addition to concerts, during the early decades of the twentieth century churches of the main denominations also expanded their musical repertoire and began to incorporate revivalist hymns, especially the hymns of Ira D. Sankey. Between 1877 and 1891, Sankey and Dwight L. Moody pioneered an evangelical movement that preached a gospel of social reform, which encouraged the "[rousing] singing of the Gospel." The style was so popular that on Sunday, May 6, 1923, Reverend W. Hawley Bryant preached at a "Special Evangelical Service at Smith's Memorial Church, Brickdam." The newspaper announcement for the service advised, "Sankey's Hymns will be used."[35] Smith Memorial Church was the principal church of the Congregationalists in British Guiana and was named after Reverend John Smith—the Demerara Martyr.[36]

In addition to concerts of sacred music, churches continued to present concerts of classical music, and the organ remained the dominant concert instrument in these venues. By the end of the decade many of the major churches were either acquiring new organs or carrying out major repairs to existing instruments. In 1930 the Roman Catholic Cathedral in Georgetown bought a new organ from Messrs. J. W. Walker and Sons, Ltd., of Southfield Road, London for £5,000 or $24,400.00 in British Guianese currency.[37]

The administration of the colony required martial music. Music was required for high ceremonial events, route marches, reveilles, and formal entertainments by the governor. Martial music was a significant element of the urban soundscape. During the 1920s the colony had four ensembles to deliver martial music: the British Guiana Militia Band; the New Amsterdam-based No. 7 Company Military Band, New Amsterdam, Berbice; the Drum and Fife Band of the British Guiana Police Force; and the Onderneeming Boys School Band.

By the start of the 1920s, the British Guiana Militia Band had established a stellar reputation for its musicality; members of the band were among the regular performers in the concert scene, especially as the woodwind and brass sections of local symphony orchestras. When Capt. A. R. Carroll died on February 13, 1920, the leadership of the band fell to Sgt. E. A. Griffith, a colored man from Barbados, who held the post as bandmaster until Capt. Fawcett was recruited in 1922. The Militia Band presented weekly public concerts at the Seawall and the Promenade and Botanic Gardens. The repertoire for these public concerts included popular European martial music and other favorites from the European classical playbook. The band also provided music for public events such as Empire Day and Armistice Day parades, the opening of the Combined Court, and weekly route marches in Georgetown. The British Guiana Militia Band expressed the musical preferences of the colony's ruling elite.

By 1923 talk about the British Empire Exhibition in Wembley, England, was evident in British Guiana. The exhibition, which was opened by King George V on April 23, 1924, was an important element in the new imperialism policy and was organized to "stimulate trade, strengthen bonds that bind mother Country to her Sister States and Daughters, to bring into closer contact the one with each other, to enable all who owe allegiance to the British flag to meet on common ground and learn to know each other."[38]

British Guiana was one of fifty-eight colonial territories that participated in the exhibition. Music had a central place there. In 1923 the idea was floated to send a "West Indian Band" to Wembley. However, that idea did not find favor in British Guiana, because at that time, the British Guiana Militia Band was "unquestionably the best in the West Indies" and was recognized as being able to "hold its own against many of the regimental Bands in England."[39] The British Guiana Militia Band was an important part of the British Guiana contingent to the exhibition and had a successful tour. The band "played daily at one of the bandstands around the Exhibition" and gained recognition as one of the top bands in the British Empire. The march "Dear Demerara," composed by Lance Corporal Clement E. N. Nichols on January 18, 1924, became popular at the exhibition and attracted much critical acclaim. Other compositions by Nichols during the tour included "The Mighty Kaieteur" and "Beautiful England." According to the score published by J. A. Barbour James of 84 Goldsmith Avenue, London, W.3, the march "Dear Demerara" was "written in honour of the British Guiana Militia Band taking part in the British Empire Exhibition."

The synopsis for "Mighty Kaieteur" states:

The march depicts a true representation of the "Mighty Kaieteur." Distant as he dwells within the interior of the "Magnificent Province" of British Guiana, he forewarns both man and beasts, of his wild, hungry and raging waters, miles before arriving at his wonderful descent.

Birds are his only friends; they tease him from morn 'till night, soaring above or beside his descending waters, filling the air with peculiar rhythmical tunes, thus represented by the Piccolos and E. flat Clarionets. The skies are also put on scenes most picturesque by mystic hands, and heavy clouds are ready to empty their folds of water o'er him, again this is told by the beautiful Bass Solo, while in the trio, his swift, wild, rushing and hungry waters run continuously singing a song, which, only nymphs could word his theme.[40]

The synopsis for the march "Beautiful England" states:

In this March, the Composer is struck by the beautiful scenes of England. Especially travelling through the Channel: The English breeze, the pretty clouds, hilly landscapes, etc.; but stop! The busy life in London, the aero planes; which amidst pleasure and business lend the beautiful Bass Solo to this march. The busy soldiers on parade, commanded by a loud toned Instructor, all blended in nature's concord; with the blessings of the "Divine." *Britons never shall be slaves.*[41]

The publisher for all of Clem Nichols's compositions during the British Empire Exhibition was J. A. Barbour James, a Guianese who may have been the first black publisher of music in England.[42] Barbour James, who left British Guiana in 1902 at the age of thirty-five, had a social circle in London that included many celebrated persons of African ancestry in the Edwardian United Kingdom. Among them were Samuel Spencer Alfred Cambridge, the British Guiana–born barrister and tutor at the Inns of Court; and the composer Samuel Coleridge Taylor.[43] Among the other members of the British Guiana Militia Band who attended the Wembley Exhibition were two apprentices, Bert Rogers and Vincent De Abreu. On his return to British Guiana, Bert Rogers brought back an E-flat saxophone, which was said to have been the first in British Guiana. Rogers mastered the instrument and through that exerted substantial influence of popular music in British Guiana from the 1930s to his death in the 1980s.[44] Twenty-three years after attending the exhibition, Vincent De Abreu would become the first Guianese to become bandmaster of the British Guiana Police Force Band, the successor band to the British Guiana Militia Band.[45]

When the band returned from England, a decision was taken to have it tour the rural districts. The *Daily Argosy* of July 3, 1927, supported the decision and described the response that band had received at a recent rural performance:

The decision to send the Militia Band to different village centers in the three counties to give the inhabitants a free musical treat is much appreciated. At

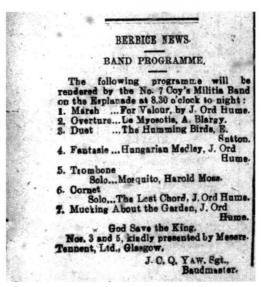

Figure 3.1. Program for concert by No. 7 Company Militia Band, *Daily Argosy*, August 3, 1930.

Mahaicony a few Mondays ago the people in the district turned out in full force to enjoy the fine music for which the band is famous. Performances have been arranged for the West Bank and for Buxton and more are to follow. The Buxtonians are preparing to give the Band a hearty welcome sometime in August, and it is expected that the place of meeting, the Buxton Park will hardly hold the huge [crowd] that is looking forward to the treat. . . . Our people are naturally musical and in these days when everything seems out of joint in this unfortunate colony any such effort to keep their spirits up is appreciated.[46]

A review of the music performed at the band's public concerts revealed an impressive and diverse list of European composers. For example at the band concert held on April 11, 1926, in the Botanical Gardens featured the following: Triumphal March: "Cleopatra" (Mancinelli); Overture: "Private Otheris" (Ansell); First Grand Selection: "Faust" (Gounod); The Celebrated "Largo" (Handel); Grand Pastoral and Hunting Fantasia: "Le Fremersberg" (Koennemann). However, the popular and dance music of the day was sometimes incorporated. "Uncle Stapie," a popular fictitious character apparently of Barbadian origin, in a column written by "Theo," noted that the band needed to refresh that aspect of its repertoire. He complained that the band had played two popular songs ("Sara" and "Horsey keep you tail up") with such frequency "till ill not only de babies know it, but deh very leaves pan de trees does close up an' go sleep soon as dah ban' starts pan dem pieces deah."[47]

The bandmaster for the New Amsterdam–based No. 7 Company Militia Band during this period was Sgt. J. C. Q. Yaw. This band's repertoire was also primarily classical. The program from an evening concert held at the Esplanade on Sunday, August 3, 1930 gives an idea of its repertoire (see Fig. 3.1).

Sponsorship of tunes was also practiced in the concerts presented by the British Guiana Militia Band in Georgetown.[48] This practice influenced the repertoire of the bands.

The British Guiana Police Force created the Drum and Fife band in 1925. A year later four sets of bagpipes were presented by leaders of the Scottish community in British Guiana.[49] In 1927 "Theo" instructed "Uncle Stapie" to:

> better go an' see you friend Broadburn [the Scottish Commissioner of Police] an aks he is whah happen to Blackwood foo-foo—ah begs pard'n ah means de late Mr. Col. Blackwood semi-military police drum an' fife ban. Fo' ah lang time ah ent hear it neida ah can' hear nutt'n bout dem bag-pipe what certain police Highlandrees from de Eas' Coas' was to play. A see Berbice gat deh ban' an even de Guvment technical school at Onterneemin' still gat oe dat goin' stron'. Go an' fine out bout dis ting fo' me ah ent want to say nutt'n yet bout'man dead grass grow at he door.[50]

The bands of the uniformed services, especially, the British Guiana Militia Band and the No. 7 Company Militia Band, produced many musicians who influenced classical and popular music in Guyana, the Caribbean, the United Kingdom, and the United States during the twentieth century. Among the "graduates" of these bands were Rudolph Dunbar, Ranny Hart, George Mootoo, Ron White, John "Bagpipes" Fredericks, Charles Knights, and Harry Whittaker.

The Onderneeming Boys School was a reformatory established in 1879 in response to crisis with the male children of the poor in urban areas. According to one commentator, a colonial magistrate:

> One of the saddest features of the colony is the condition of the children of the poor. There seems to be a spirit of lawlessness amongst them, an impatience of control, a thirst for independence and license which bodes ill for their future and the future of the colony. The boys are idle and dissolute, the girls dirty, and foul-mouthed and dishonest. At an age so early as to be incredible, many of them have become thieves, and later prostitutes.[51]

Juanita de Barros has argued that the school was established with the "implicitly racialist project of encouraging young Afro-Guyanese males to return to the agricultural sector."[52] The reformatory's curriculum included agriculture and music. Each student had to keep a plot of land for which he was entirely responsible and each had to learn a musical instrument. This emphasis on using music in the curriculum at Onderneeming suggests that the institution was implementing contemporary educational theory, which held that music was an effective tool for rehabilitating at-risk youth and juvenile delinquents. This theory had been applied internationally since the turn of the twentieth century. The Home for Colored Waifs in New Orleans and the Roman Catholic–operated Alpha Boys School (for wayward boys) in Kingston, Jamaica, were other institutions that incorporated music in their curriculum. The world-renowned African American trumpeter Louis "Satchmo" Armstrong and the pioneering Jamaican ska trombonist Don Drummond were graduates of the Home for Colored Waifs and Alpha Boys School. The first schoolmaster for the Onderneeming Boys School was P. M. de Weever. According Roy Heath, his grandson, de Weever "learned to play a number of musical instruments in order to teach his charges, and in the process read every musical manual he could lay his hands on."[53] In time the school's band became the band of choice for official functions in Essequibo.

The classical music concert scene in urban British Guiana, especially Georgetown, was very active during the 1920s. The colony remained a destination in the West Indian concert circuit and several nonwhite world-class performers from the United States visited. Among them was the British Guianese–born soprano Alyce Fraser and Anita Patti Brown. Prior to her return to British Guiana in 1926, Alyce Fraser had not visited her land of birth since 1914. Since that time she had established herself as an important soprano and music teacher in Harlem, New York, and was active in the Harlem Renaissance. The *Amsterdam News*, an important Harlem newspaper of the period, noted in a review that her recital included songs in French and Italian and the audience was "large and highly appreciative." The review also described her voice as "well placed and her singing was marked with its diction and purity of tone."[54] Madame Fraser performed in the colony twice during 1927. The wide range of her repertoire can be discerned from the program for her third concert in 1927.

"The Lord Is My Light"	(Frances Aillisten)
"Estrellita" [Spanish]	(Manuel Ponce)
"Inter Noe"	(Ale McFaydne)
"Birthday"	(Huntingdon Woodman)
"Suicidio" [Italian]	(Ponchinelli)
"May Morning"	(Denza)
"Ave Maria"	(Maillard)
"Weigenlied" [German]	(Brahms)

Figure 3.2. Bust of Madame Alyce Fraser in Guyana's National Cultural Center, courtesy of the author.

"Save Me O God"	(Randegger)
"Were You There" [Negro Spiritual]	(H. T. Burleigh)
"It's Me O God" [Negro Spiritual]	(Laurence Brown)
"Joshua Fit the Battle of Jericho" [Negro Spiritual]	(J. Rosamond Johnson)
"So Near to God"	(Fisher)
"Inflamatus" [from *Stabat Mater*]	(Rossini)[55]

Fraser's concerts did much to consolidate and promote Negro spirituals as a concert genre in British Guiana, especially the arrangements of H. T. Burleigh.[56] One of the originators of the African American art song, Burleigh was Antonin Dvorak's personal assistant when the Czech composer arrived in the United States in 1892 to become Head of the National Conservatory and is recognized as the African American musician who influenced him.[57] Madame Fraser would return to British Guiana regularly during the next three decades, and her recitals were highly anticipated. On occasion she would donate proceeds from her concerts to the Negro Progress Convention's Tuskegee Students Fund.[58] The Friends of Alyce Fraser Committee presented a bust to the Guyana National Cultural Center on August 12, 1992.

Anita Patti Brown was one the outstanding black singers of the era and was also described as "a favourite Cantatrice (soprano) of unprecedented fame." She toured the colony in 1930 and presented two concerts. Like Alyce Fraser, she presented concerts featuring both secular and sacred music.[59] On Friday, January 31, 1930, Brown performed at the London Theatre and presented the following program:

"Care Salve"	Handel
"Neet Tree"	Schumann
"Waltz Song"	Gounod
"Le The"	Koechlio
"Song of India"	Koreakoff
"Erl-King"	Schubert
"You Must Have That True Religion"	Boatner
"By and By"	Burleigh
"Calvary"	Bushell
"Sometimes I Feel Like a Motherless Child"	Brown
"Shout Over Heaven"	Manney
"Villanella"	dell'Acqua
"Why Adam Sinned"	Rogers
"Mighty Lak' a Rose"	Nevin
"Laughing Song"	Seguin

The second concert on Sunday, February 2, featured many Negro spirituals arranged by Burleigh. The program included the following:

"The Publicans"	De Water
"I Know the Lord"	Brown
"Allelujah"	Mozart
"Oh Divine Redeemer"	Gounod
"Sinner Please Don't Let This Harvest Pass"	Burleigh
"Going Home"	Divorak [sic]
"You Got to Reap Just What You Sow"	Dawson
"Glory, Glory, Hallelujah"	Boatner
"Go Down Moses"	Burleigh
"Dost Thou Know That Sweet Land"	Thomas
"I Stood on the River Jordan"	Burleigh
"Every Time I Feel the Spirit"	Brown

Like many of the international visitors before and after her, Madame Anita Patti Brown also performed in New Amsterdam at venues such as the London Theatre.

Other musicians coming to British Guiana from the United States during this period were members of the growing British Guianese and West Indian diaspora in New York. Among this new group was the Trinidad-born comedian/calypsonian Sam Manning. His tour in 1929 reflected two things: the growing diversity in urban musical tastes and the influence of three new technologies—phonographs (records), radio, and cinema. Manning was no stranger to British Guiana, as prior to World War I he was a well-known jockey and comedian who had visited regularly. When the war started, he traveled to England and joined the Middlesex Regiment and later served with the British West Indian Regiment in Egypt. On demobilization, he went to the United States, where he started to work as a journalist and eventually returned to the New York stage, where he originated "the [stereotypical] West Indian character." Manning was also one of the first West Indians to sign a recording contract in the United States. In the 1920s he signed contracts with Columbia Gramophone Company and OKeh Records and recorded a number of hits, among them "Lignum Vitae," "Sweet Willie," "Lita," "Camilla," "Barbados Blues," "Emily," "Hold Him Joe," and "Jamaica Blues." Accompanying Manning on the 1929 tour to British Guiana was his lover, Amy Ashwood Garvey, and Syd Perrin. Perrin, who was making his first trip to British Guiana, was an important African American music composer and stage performer who appeared in the musical *Black-Birds*, which toured Europe and had more than 250 performances in London and featured Eubie Blake, Florence Mills, Bill "Bojangles" Robinson, and Adelaide Hall. *Black-Birds* helped launch the Charleston dance craze in England. British Guiana got a chance to see the real thing performed by Syd Perrin. Sam Manning's farewell show in British Guiana was titled "The Temple of Jazz."[60] By 1930 calypso and jazz had established themselves as popular genres in the colony's urban soundscape. Eventually radio broadcasting, phonographic records, cinema, vaudeville shows, fairs, and local touring troupes would diffuse these and other popular genres and the associated dances to the rural and hinterland regions of British Guiana.

The proliferation of music stores in British Guianese urban areas and itinerant music vendors in rural areas allowed access to gramophone records of the music of the Roaring 20s. Because of this technology British Guianese were aware of Manning's music before he arrived. Throughout the 1920s, stores such as Pradasco Cycle Store, R.G. Humphrey, Barrow's Furniture Store, Ferreira and Gomes Ltd., T. Geddes Grant (and its sub-agent S. Davson & Co., in New Amsterdam), and Bookers Garage sold records produced by companies such as Broadcast, Columbia, Edison, Gennett, Goodson, OKeh, and Victor. Through these labels, British Guianese were listening to jazz, American patriotic music, popular songs, West Indian music, Chinese music, and Hindustani music.

For radio, the big leap forward took place on June 27, 1927, when the British Guianese wireless station announced that it was launching experiments in "local broadcasting." The plan was to relay programming from New York simultaneously over the telephone service and from an experimental broadcast transmitter from 8:00 p.m. to 10:00 p.m. daily. A year later, listeners in British Guiana were listening to WGY Schenectady, New York; KDKA, Pittsburgh, PA; 5SWBBCC, Chelmsford, England; PC JJ, Eindhoven, Holland; PCUU, The Hague, Holland; and CJRX, Winnipeg, Manitoba, Canada.[61] The majority of the programming on these stations was music—classical and popular.

In terms of local programming, by 1930 the experimental station (now with the call letters VRY) was broadcasting British Guiana Militia Band concerts from the Sea Wall,[62] church services,[63] dance music concerts from "ballrooms," and recorded music by local musicians. A drawing-room concert—featuring the Music Lover's Orchestra along with Miss R. Cendrecourt, Miss S. Callendar, and Messrs. F. Brazao, S. da Silva, F. Philips, A. de Freitas, Bert Rogers, and Jules de Cambra, popular performers of that time—originating from the home of E. Neblett at 189 Church Street, Georgetown, was aired on June 5, 1930.[64] The ballroom of the Regent Hotel was the venue for a concert of dance music aired Sunday, November 2, 1930. Many of the performers on early music broadcasts were active in Portuguese musical circles.

Radio broadcasting from British Guiana, with its significant music programming, was heard around the West Indies. A Trinidadian writing under the pseudonym "Short Wave Length" expressed dissatisfaction with VRY's music programming in a letter to the *Trinidad Guardian* on July 17, 1930, which was reprinted on page 8 of the *Daily Argosy* on July 30, 1930:

Sir, Listening-in on Sunday night last to the usual broadcasting from Demerara, several of us heard the announcer enquire what his hearers thought of the British Guiana programmes generally.

Apart from some quite excellent music, well rendered by a saxophonist who is distinctly above the common rut of instrumentalists, the general opinion of the party was that the programme was no better, and thank the stars no more worse than usual. At any rate the general consensus of opinion was that Station VRY did not send out anything worthy of the self-styled Garden of the West Indies.

On a recent night I switched off savagely as I refused to have my ears tortured by the sound of school children practicing their scales. . . .

A series of hackneyed melodies broadcast from cracked phonographic records
hardly induces one to keep on the VRY wavelength very long.

These and similar reactions would inform the development of radio programming in British Guiana over the next decade.

By the end of the decade, British Guianese had another source of music, the
"talkie" film. A March 26, 1930, newspaper headline announced: TALKIE FILMS.
INSTALLATION OF MACHINERY—ENGINEER AND ELECTRICIANS ARRIVE.[65] The
installation was completed quickly, and on April 6, 1930, His Excellency, the
Officer Administering the Government, the Hon. C. D. Douglas-Jones, CMG,
was the patron for a special showing of "The Talkie-Singing-Dancing Revue:
Broadway Scandals."[66] Also introduced between 1921 and 1930 were portable
gramophone players and portable radio receivers, developments that also
influenced the consumption of music in Guyana throughout the twentieth
century. This was evident at public events such as fairs, pageants, excursions,
and dances.

Despite stringent economic times brought about by the international
economic depression, urban British Guianese of all social classes continued
to attend fairs and pageants, go on picnics and excursions, and attend balls
and dances. It was expected that there would be music at fairs, pageants, and
excursions, and the advertisements for these events made that point; "Moonlight Excursion on the Demerara on Friday Night . . . Music on Board"[67] and
"Morning Cruise along the Coastline by S.S. Queriman . . . Piano and Jazz
Band on Board"[68] are typical examples.

Several types of balls and dances were popular during this decade. Terms
such as "Grand Dance," "Grand Cabaret Dance," "Fancy Dress," "Carnival
Dance," "Spot-light Dance," and "Swizzle Dance" were used to describe those
organized by the elite and middle strata of urban British Guiana. Among the
popular venues for the upper and middle classes were the Assembly Rooms,
the Government House, the Park Hotel, the Regent Hotel, the Bel Air Hotel,
and the Catholic Guild Hall. The younger members of these classes embraced
new trends in popular music, especially jazz, and organized dances that featured this type of music.

Working-class persons continued to organize "practice sessions," "Basket
socials," "birth night parties," and, as A. J. Seymour has noted, would "throng . . .
the dance halls" such as Dyers Hall, Frolic Hall, Kaieteur Hall, King George
Hotel, National Hotel, Prince's Dance Hall, and various lodge halls. Throughout this decade, the ruling and middle classes continued to express concerns
about the "entertainments" of the working class, especially about what was
transpiring in the dance halls. This extract from Cyril Bishop's June 3, 1921,

letter to the editor of the *Daily Argosy* is supportive of a previous "anti-Dancing Halls" editorial and reflective of prevailing sentiments:

> Sir—I crave your indulgence to endorse heartily everything contained in your editorial of Tuesday under the caption "The Dancing Halls" and to add something to what has been already said. I am to state that the type of dancing halls spoken of are nothing but in short brothels. There the most lawless, immoral aspects of humanity congregate for no other purpose than to pollute the atmosphere with filthy language, increase crime and lower the moral standard of the poor victims who, not in their sphere, but becoming susceptible, fall prey. I trust that the time is not far distant when the Government will introduce some legislation to limit in a very marked degree or even stop the issuance of such licenses.

From the advertisements in newspapers for this period, the following were among the popular bands: the Harry Banks Orchestra, the British Guiana Orpheans, W. Cumberbatch's Orchestra, Ferraz's Full Orchestra, Syd Martin and Harry Crossman, Demerara Ice House Jazz Orchestra, Taite's Jazz Band, Gouveia Full Jazz Band, the Surprise Jazz Band (conducted by Herman Jones), Jimmy Cammy's Orchestra, Lew Spencer's Rhythm Stompers, the Brace Brothers (New Amsterdam), and Bert Rogers and the Sunny Siders Orchestra. Sometimes these bands and orchestras performed as the whole units or as sub-sets. For example, an advertisement may say "Gouveia's (3 piece) Orchestra" or "Gouveia's Full Jazz Band." A close examination of the engagements of these bands during this decade reveals class associations, patronage, ethnic alliances, and economic investments. Gouveia's Jazz Band, formed at the start of the decade and led by a Portuguese, was recognized as the pioneer in the performance of jazz during this decade. Indeed, the band was considered the standard to measure jazz band music. When the Pradasco Cycle Store advertised the arrival of a new shipment of recorded music, the copy noted, "a wide selection of music is available including Jazz Band Music (as played by Gouveia's Jazz Band)."[69] The Harry Banks Orchestra, led by Harry Mayers of the British Guiana Militia Band, was popular among the upper classes. Bert Roger's Sunny Siders, led by Bert Rogers (also of the British Guiana Militia Band), also enjoyed similar patronage. No doubt the patronage was based on their musicianship and the disciplined nature of the band members. Until 1958 members of the British Guiana Militia Band were permitted to form their own ensembles and to perform with other orchestras and bands performing classical and popular music.

Disorderly conduct and being a public nuisance were common charges brought against lower-class urban dwellers, particularly those that lived in the urban ghettos. A unique case of disorderly behavior was reported in 1930 when Princess Stephens, familiarly known as Mama, was charged with "having on November 22, at Cummings Street, Alberttown, sung an offensive song to the annoyance of John Tudor." The defendant pleaded not guilty and said she was only singing the ordinary hymn "Sow your seeds to everybody." When the magistrate asked her if the hymn was one of those popularized by the Salvation Army, she replied, "Yes, Sir."[70]

By far the most significant problem of the 1920s related to economic life. There was high unemployment in the urban areas; all of the primary exports—rice, sugar, and bauxite—were affected by the global depression which caused a dramatic lowering of prices of these commodities on the world markets. Droughts affected rural areas, and sugar estates went out of business. In the early years of the decade, the government of British Guiana, as a way for augmenting declining revenues, introduced an entertainment tax, under which taxes were collected on the tickets sold to patrons of concerts, cinemas, and dances.

On March 31, 1924, the BGLU called a strike to support a demand for improved wages by the predominantly black dockworkers at Sanbach Parker & Co. in Water Street, Georgetown. A day later, the government banned all assemblies in Georgetown after massive disorder in Georgetown. Headlines in the *Daily Argosy* of April 2, 1924, proclaimed STRIKE DISORDER IN GEORGE-TOWN and WAR ON THE COMMUNITY and reported that for four hours the "rabble" overran the city, invading houses and causing businesses to close and railway and electricity services to be suspended. Also on April 2, the predominantly Indian workers on Plantations Houston, Farm, Peter's Hall, and Providence—sugar estates on the East Bank of Demerara, estates owned by the Demerara Company, the owners of Sanbach Parker & Co.—also went on strike for better wages, improved working conditions, and a number of other grievances. On April 3, more than four thousand workers from these estates marched toward Georgetown to meet with Sir Greame Thomson, the governor, and present their grievances. According to a contemporary report, the marchers were "armed with flags, agricultural implements, and sticks, and accompanied by a Tadjah band."[71] In a scenario similar to that in Ruimveldt in 1905, the marchers were stopped by the police and the military at La Penitence, a district very close to Ruimveldt. Fifty-two rounds were fired; thirteen persons were killed, among them eight women; and more than twenty were seriously injured. This would not be the last time female sugar workers gave their lives in the labor struggle.

The editor of the *Daily Argosy* described the incident not as a labor struggle but a confrontation between the forces of law and order and those of ignorance, violence, and destruction. The newspaper was also very harsh with their criticisms of Critchlow, whom they described as "more rogue than fool."[72] In addition, in an editorial titled "Tragedy," the newspaper set about to undermine the evident working-class solidarity and further demonize people of African ancestry by stating: "But if it is inevitable that somebody must suffer in the conflict between order and anarchy it is regrettable that the victims should be decent hard-working East Indian agriculturalists instead of members of the Centipede gangs, the lawless elements of the city who were responsible for Tuesday's disturbances."[73]

An editorial in the same newspaper, published on Sunday, April 6, 1924, under the title "Lessons of the Week," again set about destabilizing interracial working-class solidarity by suggesting "the unfortunate [East Indian] people of the East Bank have been the victims of the machinations of the Labour Union and the Negro Progress Association."[74] Critchlow replied to the newspaper's characterization of the labor protests and described the shooting of workers as another example of "*might* trampling *right*" and reinforced his point by quoting from "When wilt thou save the people," a hymn from *Labour Hymnal*.[75]

It was reported that during the riots a group of protesters entered the home of Mrs. R. B. Craig, at Robb and King Street, but did not attack one of the young ladies who was playing the piano. A member of the mob was heard to say, "Don't let we trouble she, she playing too sweet."[76]

The labor unrests of 1924 left many raw nerves in urban Georgetown. A letter writer using the pseudonym of "European" wrote a letter to the *Daily Argosy* describing the British Guiana Labour Union as "the Union of Strife and Unrest." The letter also described the strikers as displaying "a burst of hooliganism and riotous display by a portion of the Negro population of this city." The writer contended that what was afoot was really "pent-up hatred for the White race of this colony" and criticized the "Government Police Department for giving permission "to the nightly preaching in seditions at different street corners for over a year, be it Critchlowism, Garveyism, or Osborneism, or a mixture of each." The letter also referred to the red and black flags as symbolizing race hate [and Socialism].[77] Among the reactions of the government to the 1924 strike and riots was the rounding up and public humiliation of the Jordanites, a primarily black millenarian sect headquartered in Agricola, a village about four miles outside of Georgetown on the East Bank Demerara. Like the Garveyites, the Jordanites proposed a God that looked like black people. The *Daily Argosy* of Tuesday, April 8, 1924, carried a report about the arrest and subsequent humiliation of the Jordanites:

> On Sunday evening the Police collected a number of the "Jordanites," wearing their "falls," who had gathered at Jonestown, from other parts of the East Bank and Georgetown. They were holding a meeting in connection with their sect

when Capt. P. E. Cressall, with a couple of armed men, visited the spot in a motor lorry in which the people were conveyed to the Brickdam police station, persons on the way down jeering them. They were warned and allowed to depart. Yesterday Jordan, an elderly black man who wears a beard, and the leader of the sect, was taken to the Brickdam for the purpose of identification. He was released; it is understood, with a warning. The male of the sect wear long white gowns and Turbans, while the females wear "falls."

The 1924 negotiations for increased wages failed. However, agitations by organized labor continued in British Guiana and across the West Indies in the years following the 1924 riots. In 1926 West Indian labor leaders such as Hubert Critchlow and A. K. Dinally from British Guiana, Arthur Cipriani from Trinidad and Tobago, and W. J. Lesperan from Surinam met in British Guiana for a labor conference. Among their resolutions was an appeal "for a federation of the West Indies with self-government and dominion status."[78] The idea of a West Indian Federation was prominent in the political discourse in London and in the West Indies. A year later, the first West Indian Conference was held in London and a four-person delegation represented British Guiana. West Indian labor leaders were, in the main, supportive of the federal idea.

Also in 1926, L. S. Avery, the British Secretary of State for the Colonies, appointed a parliamentary commission to "consider and report on the economic position of the colony, the causes which have hitherto been [disregarded] and the measures which could be taken to promote development, and any facts which they consider to have bearing on the above matters." The commission reported in 1927 that a major cause of the "colony's stagnation" was the constitution, which fostered an undemocratic electoral system, and negative race relations.[79] Coupled with the fear of nonwhite majority rule if the franchise was extended, the constitution of British Guiana was amended to that of a Crown Colony in 1928. As James Rose has written, "the Court of Policy and the Combined Court were replaced by a single Legislative Council comprising fourteen elected representatives and fifteen nominated members. This latter category was made up of two ex officio members, namely the Colonial Secretary and the Attorney General, eight nominated officials and five nominated unofficial members sitting with the Governor. Ten members sitting with the Governor constituted a quorum."[80] This constitutional arrangement gave the governor special powers allowing him to "overturn an adverse vote in the Legislative Council."[81] This meant that the governor of British Guiana constitutionally became the colony's maximum leader.

The depressing economic conditions at the end of 1930 had disproportional impact on children. A commission reported that that "out of a total of 10,816 boys and girls who left school during the past three years [1927 and

1930], there are 3,757 or 35 percent who are known to be unemployed." All together, more than eight thousand youth were unemployed in Georgetown. That reality, coupled with drought in the rural areas, energized interest in the extractive industries in the hinterland. As a result, the urban and rural unemployed, especially those from the coastal African villages such as Belladrum, Buxton, Golden Grove, Hopetown, along with international investors moved into the hinterland in search of El Dorado. As mentioned earlier, this development, which accelerated during the next decades, had significant influence on music in Guyana during the twentieth century, especially folk music.

4

Public Spectacles: 1931–1940

During this decade of continued economic hard times and pent-up frustrations, a number of state-funded, -sponsored, or -sanctioned public entertainments were organized to celebrate key events in the colony's history or important developments in British imperial life. The practice of organizing public entertainments to placate its citizenry during economic and other crises was refined by the *pane et circe* ("bread and circus") strategies of Caesar Augustus, the first Roman emperor. For Augustus, "bread and circus" provided opportunities to temporarily deflect a society's attention from current problems, release in a controlled manner pent-up frustrations, and "pump up" loyalty and patriotism.[1] The celebrations to mark the Golden and Diamond Jubilees of Queen Victoria in 1887 and 1896 respectively established the format and content for imperial public entertainments in the British Empire, including British Guiana.

Special events during the decade, organized according to the imperial public entertainment template, included the British Guiana Centenary celebrations (1931); the Centenary of the Abolition of Slavery (1934); Georgetown's Centenary (1937); the Coronation of George VI (1937); and the Centenary of East Indian Immigration to British Guiana (1938). The music associated with elements of these events—religious services, parades, rallies, balls, and dances—identified the musical aesthetics of the ruling class, provided a snapshot of what was popular, demonstrated the scope of the musical proficiency of Guyanese-born musicians, and offered an opportunity to hear and appreciate the thrust of contemporary Guyanese creativity in all musical genres. The execution of these five mega-events also demonstrated radio's capacity to mobilize society and influence its musical taste. During this decade Guyanese became more aware of the musical achievements of its diaspora, and literary arts signaled acceleration in the crystallization of Guyanese nationalist consciousness. The decade ended with the outbreak of World War II, which brought some economic improvement to the colony as a result of the American military bases that were established in the colony. It also increased musical dialogue and exchange.

Figure 4.1. Rev. W. Hawley Bryant, courtesy of Guyana National Library.

In October 1931 British Guiana celebrated the centenary of the union of the colonies of Berbice, Demerara, and Essequibo to create the single colony British Guiana. Despite the stringent economic conditions caused by the global depression, an ambitious program, including the publishing of books,[2] the organizing of exhibitions and fairs, military displays, pageants, and rallies with schoolchildren, feeding programs for the poor, dances, and balls was planned by the ruling class, with Georgetown and New Amsterdam being the centers of attention. Music had a central place in the program of events. The three bands of the uniformed services provided music for the many official functions. In Georgetown, the British Guiana Militia Band performed at the garden party hosted by the governor, Sir Edward Brandis Denham (serving 1930–35), and Lady Denham on the lawns of the Government House in Georgetown; the British Guiana Police Force's Drum and Fife Band performed at the open-air church and the military display. In New Amsterdam, the No. 7 Company Military Band performed similar functions. Private bands provided music for numerous public dances held in Georgetown and New Amsterdam. In Georgetown, Harry Mayers and the Harry Banks Orchestra, described as the colony's leading orchestra, entertained those attending a "Centenary Carnival" at the British Guiana Cricket Club (BGCC) on Monday, October 12. Special efforts were taken to bring in new music for the Centenary Carnival, including "the latest hits from Broadway."[3]

Schoolchildren participated in several events. A rally was held on the grounds of the BGCC on Friday, October 16. In addition to an address by the governor and a tableau titled "British Guiana 1831–1931," there was the

Figure 4.2. Rev. M. A. Cossou. Photograph courtesy of Denise Boodie.

inaugural singing of "Song of Guiana's Children" by a combined schools choir. The British-born Reverend Hawley Bryant of the Smith's Congregational Church (named after John Smith, the Demerara Martyr) composed the music and lyrics.

The music, composed in G major, was upbeat, reminiscent of a march. The lyrics referred to the colony's natural beauty and the wealth that lay in the hinterland and urged the youth to strive for greatness, signaling a shift in colonial sensibility: the tropical estates were developing national identities. In the first verse, Bryant directs attention to the mighty Mt. Roraima and the colony's great, wide, and deep rivers. The verse is followed by a rousing and memorable chorus: "Onward, upward, may we ever go / Day by day in strength and beauty grow, / Till at length we each of us may show, / What Guyana's sons and daughters can be."

Subsequent verses speak to the "shining splendor" of the Kaieteur Falls, and the ongoing quest for El Dorado's diamonds and "bright shining gold," and prayed that Guianese children will through "faith, love, and labor" build "God's golden city which will never grow old."

Rev. Bryant's ministry took him into the hinterland, so he was aware of the majesty of Roraima, the magnificence of Kaieteur, and the wealth of the natural resources. "The Song of Guiana's Children" was taught to succeeding generations of schoolchildren and became one of Guyana's national songs. At the start of the twenty-first century, it remains a powerful bond that unites Guyanese at home or in the diaspora, especially the generations that came of age between 1931 and 1992. The bond that is experienced when sung together at home or in the diaspora is an example of what Benedict Anderson in *Imagined Communities* describes as "unisonality"—a bond that nourishes a nationalism that transcends race and class.[4]

By 1931 the competitive tension between Georgetown and New Amsterdam to be the colony's musical capital was evident. A review of the musical scope of the New Amsterdam celebrations supports this perception. New Amsterdam's weeklong program was opened with "a feast of music at the Congregational Church, Mission Chapel."[5] The Rev. Mortimer Aloysius Cossou (ca. 1880–1957), a Berbice-born theology graduate of Howard University in Washington, D.C., conducted "a specially trained" choir of one hundred voices, which rendered Mozart's *Gloria*, Haydn's *The Heavens Are Telling*, and the premiere of *Drums of Freedom*.

Ruby McGregor, P. M. de Weever's prize-winning student, accompanied the hundred-voice choir. The choir "was [also] assisted by the full No. 7 Company Military Band and a violin orchestra." A contemporary press report of the event noted that "attendance was large" and reported the renderings were "superb and reflected great credit upon all those who took part."[6] Other participants in the "feast of music" were Mrs. J. D. Taitt and Nellie Davis. Their solos were described as "very creditable" renditions.[7] Mrs. Taitt, the wife of the government medical officer at Port Mourant on the Courantyne, later moved to Georgetown, where she exerted substantial influence on the colony's musical life.

Rev. Cossou, who studied theology at Howard and attended the 1919 Pan-African Movement in Paris organized by W. E. B. Du Bois, later wrote the lyrics and composed the music for "My Native Land." The song's lyrics are emotional and evoke a national identity rooted in the earthiness of the Guianese landscape. This song was coastal in its orientation and a counterpoint to the alien pastoral and bucolic visualization of England that tended to dominate Guianese works of imagination at that time. In this song, Cossou suggests that there is beauty in the flood, mud, and pestilential coastal landscape of the colony. Compared to Bryant's "Song of Guiana's Children," the music is more sophisticated, melodically more like an art song, with variations in the accompaniment for each verse. The song was originally composed for voice and piano but is most often performed by children's choirs sung in unison. Like "Song of Guiana's Children," "My Native Land" became an iconic Guyanese patriotic song.[8] The first verse declared, "Oh I care not that others rave over fair lands afar, / Where silvern lakes and placid streams mirror the evening star; / I care not though their wealth be great, their scenery be grand, / For none so fair as can compare with my own native land."[9]

Like Georgetown's, the New Amsterdam celebrations included illuminated buildings; an exhibition of craft, art, and agricultural produce grown by Berbice primary schools; public dances; a band concert at the Esplanade; and a rally for schoolchildren at the New Amsterdam racecourse. The accessible contemporary record is silent on the celebrations in Essequibo; it is conceivable that the Onderneeming Boys School Band provided musical accompaniment for whatever celebrations took place. The records are also silent on celebrations in rural and hinterland locations.

One of the flagship events of the British Guiana Centenary was the Exhibition and Fair, held in Georgetown from Tuesday, October 13 to Saturday, October 18, 1931. The event served to display the colony's agricultural, mineral, and industrial potential and targeted visitors from abroad (tourists and potential investors). The venue for the Exhibition and Fair were the grounds of the elite Georgetown Cricket Club (the world-famous test cricket venue, Bourda) and the contiguous and equally elite Georgetown Football Club was converted into an "Amusement Park." There were many innovations at this event. For example, at the right of the only entrance to the Exhibition and Fair was a twenty-foot-high, six-foot-wide model of the Kaieteur Falls, which was "discovered" by Charles Barrington Brown on April 29, 1870, and was being positioned as the centerpiece of an emerging tourism industry, which targeted an earlier generation of American, Canada, and European "ecotourists." A contemporary report described the model as "a most realistic spectacle."[10]

Among the other innovations in public entertainment were the introduction of a beauty contest and the cooption of musical expressions associated with the working class in state-sponsored programs. The Miss Guiana beauty contest was the first to be held in British Guiana. A prize of $30 and a gold medal was offered to the "most beautiful girl in the colony." There were even hints that the winner might go on to Hollywood and become a film star.[11] Given the reality of Hollywood and the state of social life in British Guiana during this period, it could be safely assumed that Miss Guiana was expected to have Caucasian attributes. The judges for the contest were drawn from the white ruling class and included "Colonel W. E. H. Bradburn, Inspector General of Police and Commandant of the Local [Military] Forces; Capt. F. Burnett, M.C.; and Mesdames L. Clavier, A. G. King, and J. B. Smith."[12] The females on this panel were the spouses of senior colonial administrators. The contest was phased over three nights and there was a variety show preceding each phase of the contest. Among the musicians who performed in the variety shows were the golden-voiced baritone Frank Brazao; the pianist Oscar A. Dummett; and the bandleader and saxophonist Bert Rogers. In addition to these local musicians were performers from the now popular vaudeville circuit. In addition, there were also international musicians.

Among the international musicians was the calypsonian Lord Beginner (Egbert Moore), who "composed a song of about twelve verses on the Centenary" performed at the Exhibition and Fair on two nights. This long-form calypso style was more akin to the Guianese Shanto style that was being popularized in the West Indies and internationally by Augustus Hinds, whose stage name was Bill Rogers. This visit by Lord Beginner has been identified as the start of sustained visits by Trinidadian calypsonians to British Guiana during the twentieth century. In 1950 Lord Beginner achieved international fame with his calypso "Victory Test Match," which celebrated the West Indian victory over England at the Oval—"Cricket, Lovely Cricket!" was the popular chorus.

The inclusion of performers from the vaudeville circuit and a calypsonian can be interpreted as a nod to working-class tastes and another shift in the orientation of the governance of the colony. Contemporary press reports indicate that the results of the beauty competition were not popular. Genevieve De Abreu was declared the winner, with Joan Sharples second and Barbara Osborne third. The columnist "Uncle Stapie" also commented on the situation by asking the populace to accept the "umpires'" decision as final.[13]

Clearly there was more to the outcry and Uncle Stapie's admonition about the judges' decision being final. There were concerns about generalized racial exclusion. Were there concerns expressed that mixed-race Joan Sharples should have been first instead of Portuguese Genevieve De Abreu? Clearly there is some justification for that question, as another beauty contest was organized in 1932 "with new and exciting conditions." This time around, the contest had "seven classes according to races in the colony."[14] This development was just one example that race continued to be a sensitive issue in the colony in the early 1930s; the introduction of the beauty contests can be perceived as another vehicle for reinforcing the proposition that Caucasian standards defined what was beautiful and attractive. Could it be that the fears that justified the introduction of the status of Crown Colony were also being manifested in the realm of beauty? It could be concluded that De Abreu's victory in the first beauty contest was an important sign of the incorporation of the mainland Portuguese into the social category of white. Beauty contests remained a part of Guiana's social scene until the 1980s, when they were "banned" by the socialist government of Linden Forbes Sampson Burnham on the grounds that they were akin to cattle auctions and were disrespectful to women.

Public lectures and talks were also part of the celebrations. P. M. de Weever presented a public talk on the history of music in British Guiana between 1831 and 1931. The presentation celebrated the progress made in musical proficiency in the colony over the century but expressed sadness about the decline of African-based folk music and the associated dances: "The African dances have ceased to be the modes of entertainment in the colony, due to the influence of the churches, which pronounce these dances as devilish and have frequently denied religious rites to members of their several denominations, who had been found guilty of the heinous sin of dancing the tango according to African custom."[15]

Among the other public lectures on music was J. Wood Davis's "A comparison of music past and present" at the Combined Choirs Centenary Concert, held at Providence Congregational Church on Sunday, October 18, 1931.[16] E. M. T. Moore's "Random remarks in Social Music" and W. McDavid's "The Progress of Music in BG" were two essays related to the development of music in the colony over the century published in *British Guiana Women's Centenary Effort*, one of the special publications for the Centenary. All of these lectures spoke to the progress made in musical proficiency, confidence in performing the European classical repertoire, and the role these competencies in music played in social mobility. There were snide and snobbish remarks about the "talentless" who sought kudos as performers.

For those unable to attend the Exhibition and Fair and other events in Georgetown and New Amsterdam, radio broadcasts brought some of it to them. The music of the British Guiana centenary celebrations revealed that at the start of the 1930s, the musical aesthetics of the colony remained primarily European and privileged polyphony and choral music. However, there were clear indications that calypso, jazz (especially swing), and other genres were making their presence felt in urban sections of the colony. Was this an indicator of tactical accommodation by the ruling class? A letter to the editor of the *Daily Argosy* from Essequibo claimed that failure to provide funds for entertaining schoolchildren to the Centenary Celebration Committees of New Amsterdam and Suddie was "unfair discrimination . . . likely to bring His Excellency's Administration into contempt even among ordinary law-abiding citizens."[17] That letter was indicative of a more restive reality that was expressed forcibly in a column in the *Daily Argosy* of October 18, which described the celebrations providing "some amount of relaxation, but at a sore cost to many a pocket" and was nothing more "than a horrible sham" given the disintegration of the "rich colony." This condition was blamed on mismanagement, neglect, and favoritism, and called for a new era in the governance of the society. The column stressed: "What 'B.G' wants is a Napoleon who will lead her on to a new birth, a man who will demand and see that she is no longer treated as a pariah and that the country shall expand as she is capable of doing. The resources of which so much is heard must be exploited and not wasted any more by mismanagement or neglect."[18]

The depression showed no sign of ending in 1934. It appeared to be worsening. As a result, on June 24 the colony was divided into nineteen "Poor Relief

Districts" "for the purposes of administration of relief to the destitute poor."[19] It was in this context that a program of events was organized to commemorate the centenary of the abolition of slavery in British Guiana. The Negro Progress Convention (NPC) played the primary role in organizing the events to commemorate this centenary. There was little financial support from the colony's administration. The commemoration used a template similar to the one used for the British Guiana Centenary. Books were published; the second volume of Norman Cameron's *The Evolution of the Negro* was published to coincide with this anniversary. The first volume, published for the British Guiana Centenary in 1931, had focused on "African Medieval Civilizations." The second volume was divided into two books; "Book I [dealt] with slavery in the Americas; Book II with development from Emancipation to [1934],"[20] with special reference to British Guiana. The publication was praised for its "painstaking research and . . . impartial handling of data."[21] A contemporary editorial noted:

> [T]he writer has admirably succeeded in convincing his readers that there is no stigma in being termed descendants of slaves, for he makes it abundantly plain that "all countries in this world have had slavery among them, and that many of them have had vast numbers of their people enslaved by other nations at some period or other of their history, and that even the high and mighty of this earth may themselves be the descendants of slaves."[22]

Cameron was taking a leadership role in lifting the burden of shame, one of the psychological scars of enslavement and an experience that was consistently used to put people of African ancestry "in their place."[23] The Negro Progress Convention's theme for the commemoration had two dimensions. One dimension was introspective; the other, guided by ideas and practice of Booker T. Washington at the Tuskegee Institute in Alabama, was action oriented. Dr. Theo E. McCurdy articulated the action-oriented future for the NPC as an institution preparing engineers, manufacturers, farmers, and scientists for the "enrichment" of the country "far beyond the realization of any of us."[24]

One of the goals of the Negro Progress Convention was to establish a "local Tuskegee" in Demerara. By 1934 the NPC had sent students to the Tuskegee Institute in preparation for this project; one of the students was Vesta Lowe. The commemoration events were folded into the organization's thirteenth annual assembly, which started on August 1 at the Town Hall, Georgetown and ended on August 13 with a meeting at the Rose Hall Scots School in Corentyne, Berbice. Dr. T. T. Nichols, one of the founder members of the NPC, who became the provisional president when E. F. Fredericks died on April 6, 1934,

Table 4.1

Partial list of music performed during events organized by the NPC and others to commemorate the centenary of the Abolition of Slavery, August 1–13, 1934

Title	Genre	Composer	Performer(s)
O God Our Help	Hymn	Isaac Watt (1719)	Group singing
Canaan, Bright Canaan	Hymn	American Folk	Group singing
Old Black Joe	Song	Stephen Foster (1861)	Ms. R. Sealey, Violin Solo
Go Down Moses	Negro Spiritual	n.a.	Miss Harte and NPC Juveniles
Blest be the ties that Bind	Hymn (Sankey)	John Fawcett (1782)	Group singing
Lift Every Voice	Anthem	J. Weldon Johnson (1900)	Providence and St. Stephen's Choir
Listen to the Lambs	Negro Spiritual	n.a.	Miss Harte and NPC Juveniles
Come Sing to Me	n.a.	n.a.	Miss E. Younge
Mighty Lak' a Rose	Irish dialect Song	Frank L. Stanton (1901)	Miss. E. Stanton
Waltz Suite, Opus no. 2	Classical (piano)	Samuel Coleridge Taylor	Millicent Douglas
Opus no. 3	Classical (piano)	Samuel Coleridge Taylor	Millicent Douglas
Ocean thou Mighty Monster	Aria from *Oberon*	Carl Von Weber (1826)	Serena Callender
Pleading	Song	F. H. Martin-Sperry	Serena Callender
Norwegian Dance	Classical (piano duet)	Grieg	Lynette Dolphin and L. Nicholson
n.a	Classical (violin duet)	n.a.	P. F. Loncke and P. Koulen
John Brown's Body	Marching Song	n.a.	Group singing
Earth, with all thy thousand voices	Hymn	Samuel Coleridge Taylor	Group singing
Praise in Songs the Eternal King	Hymn	n.a	Group singing
Now Thank we all our God	Hymn	Martin Rinkart (ca. 1636)	Group singing
And the Glory of the Lord	Anthem from *Messiah*	Handel (1741)	Trinity Methodist Choir
Queen's College Song	School Song	Clementi and Collet	R. Hoyte, Hodge, and Harte
Peace, Perfect Peace	Hymn	Edward H. Bickersteth Jr. (1875)	Group singing
Lift up your heads	Anthem from *Messiah*	Handel (1741)	All Saints' Choir under Ruby McGregor
Deep River	Negro Spiritual	n.a.	Miss E. Bentick (Town Hall, New Amsterdam, August 3, 1934)
Down by the Bend of the Road	Negro Spiritual	n.a.	Mr. Donald Jones
Hallelujah	Anthem from Messiah	Handel (1741)	All Saints' Church Choir under Ruby McGregor

Source: Compiled from a sample of the *Daily Argosy*, August 1934.

chaired the opening ceremony. From contemporary newspaper accounts it would appear that the convention was dominated by speeches. Yet, a diversity of music—hymns, Negro spirituals, European classical music, and patriotic songs—was woven throughout the fourteen-day program of events. Two orchestras participated. One was identified as the Berbice Orchestra. At the time of this writing, there was no accessible information on that orchestra or the orchestra that performed in Georgetown. Table 4.1 provides a partial list of the music performed during the events organized to commemorate the centenary of the abolition of slavery in British Guiana.

Table 4.1 shows the sources of the music were varied. The tenor of the music was uplifting, rousing, and consciously aligned with Negro struggle in the United States. Like the British Guiana centenary celebrations, choral music was again the dominant performance style.

Running parallel to the program organized by the NPC was a campaign orchestrated by the *Daily Argosy*, the mouthpiece of the colonial establishment. The *Argosy* used its centenary coverage as a moment to minimize African efficacy and agency and pay homage to William Wilberforce, Thomas Buxton, Thomas Clarkson, Granville Sharpe, the Duke of Montague, and the superiority of British morality, which ended the enslavement of more than one million slaves throughout the British Empire on August 1, 1834. An especially superficial editorial titled "One Hundred Years" pointed out that there were some consequences of abolition that "cannot be forgotten." Specifically, it referred to the "ruin to thousands of planters" within the British Empire and that in British Guiana, "the sugar industry was for a period on the brink of collapse and the cotton and tobacco industries as a result of competition from America, soon ceased to exist." According to the editorial, the sugar industry was saved from collapse by the introduction of indentured labor, especially from India. This formulation refreshed the mythology of Indians saving British Guiana and the good Raj from economic ruin caused by indolent and ungrateful blacks. As Robert Moore has noted, the post-abolition encounters, especially between Africans and Indians, established some of the most intractable and unfortunate racial stereotypes in Guyana: the lazy, foppish, profligate, overeducated, and hyper-sexed black; and the conniving, sickly, effeminate, revengeful, clannish, murderous Indian have their unfortunate origins in this moment.[25] The editorial, like the general campaign, fanned the flames that kept those stereotypes hot. Divide and rule (*divide et impera/ divide et regnes*) was a conscious and deliberate tactic of colonial governance.

The same editorial also described the progress made by the descendants of slaves in British Guiana since 1834 as "amazing." This description was quickly modified by a number put-downs such as the important but questionable contributions the Christians, especially the London Missionary Society (Congregationalists), made to this progress:

> Unfortunately the early missionaries in their zeal to model him [the ex-enslaved African] on the intellectual Englishman neglected the cultivation of the more practical side of things. The result has been, and this is the case not only in British Guiana, that by far too large a proportion of these people ape the manners and customs of Englishmen without possessing the means of sustaining the practice of these manners and customs.[26]

The editorial concluded that the descendants of enslaved Africans in British Guiana had not only lost their numerical superiority as a result of indentured labor, but were also losing their status as the intellectual leaders of the nonwhite community. Further, because they had shown no ability in commerce, they were experiencing more economic problems. This stance failed to acknowledge the racism associated with the difficulty African Creoles had in accessing credit and Portuguese commercial infrastructure, which included dedicated shipping and access to a sophisticated trading regime with Portugal.[27] This editorial posited conclusions that reinforced negative stereotypes about Guianese of African ancestry. Many of these stereotypes have become normalized and have influenced self-perceptions and influenced ethnic relations throughout the twentieth century and into the first decade of the twenty-first century. At the level of national governance, the *Daily Argosy*—an influential stakeholder in the governance process—undermined black aspirations with faint praise.

A hint of optimism was evident in British Guiana in 1937 despite the continuing realities of the worldwide depression and the threat of war in Europe. In the years between the celebrations of 1934 and 1937, Governor Denham was succeeded by Sir Geoffrey Alexander Stafford Northcote. Under his administration, the transportation infrastructure was expanded and the use of team sports encouraged. He donated the Northcote Cup for cricket, and a coastal ship, the *Lady Northcote*, was named after his wife. The hint of optimism was the result of increased gold production and plans to expand the industry. The British Guiana Consolidated Goldfields Ltd. announced that it was contemplating "the installation of the modern electrically-operated dredges in the Potaro region," and Bookers Bros. McConnell & Co., the sugar giant, sought exclusive permission to mine a 46,000-acre area in the Puruni district.[28] The idea of a railway system in the hinterland envisioned by Governor Egerton in 1914 was still alive in the popular consciousness. The hopes associated with that infrastructural development was the dominant theme in the popular calypso "Shout All Guiana" that was composed by Ralph Fitz Scott to welcome Sir Wilfred Jackson as the governor of British Guiana, replacing Sir Geoffry Alexander Stafford Northcote in December 1937. The calypso welcomed "most wholeheartedly" the governor and his "attractive consort Lady Jackson" to "this colony of BG." The calypso also prayed that the "supreme grand" will guide the governor's hand to establish and "run the great hinterland railway."[29]

Other optimistic trends included a plan to improve planting methods and for the reorganization of the rice industry.[30] The embryonic tourism industry showed some growth as more international visitors came to visit the Kaieteur Falls and other hinterland vistas.[31] Guianese were also going on international excursions to neighboring Surinam and to Trinidad and bringing back recorded music from Surinam's Comfriari and Trinidad's Carnival.[32]

musicals in cinema

In the cinemas, musicals continued to be the primary fare. For example, on January 1, 1937, *Happiness Ahead*, *King Burlesque*, *Stars over Broadway*, and *In Person* were the "smash hits." The private sector discovered radio as an advertising channel and several companies sponsored music programs. Among them were the *Crown Rum Swizzle Dance Programme*, *Bookers' Drug Store's Sunday Evening Classical Programme*, *Bookers' Drug Store Musical Programme*, and the *De Castro's Wine Programme* featuring recorded music. Other live music programs on radio included *Amateur Hour*, *Regent Swing Kings Dance Orchestra*, *A Hour of Catholic Music*, *Pianoforte Selections by Randolph Profit* (the station pianist for VP3BG), and *Old Favorites with Cecil Rodrigues*.

By 1937 the British Guiana Militia Band had started to feature more Guianese compositions in its regular concerts. Among the works presented regularly were the marches "Choral Greetings" and "Dear Demerara" (composed by Lance Corporal Nichols); "Sons of the Soil" by Bandsman A. Briggs; "Hail Demerara" and "Demerara Drum" by J. L. V. Casimir; and the waltz "Mayflower" by H. Chapman-Edwards. This development also contributed to the emerging optimism.

A number of cultural and infrastructural developments also contributed to the mood. The British Guiana Museum was opened on Friday, February 19, 1937.[33] R. G. Humphrey, who had significant investments in gold mining and urban property, donated $5,000 for the development of the Georgetown Pure Water Supply Scheme,[34] another gesture that generated optimism. The water purification scheme was estimated to cost $120,000 and the aim was to raise the funds through local subscriptions, in the spirit of "assisting ourselves" being encouraged in the face of the economic depression.[35] Against this backdrop of guarded optimism, arrangements were made to celebrate the centenary of the City of Georgetown and the Coronation of King George VI in March and May 1937 respectively.[36]

The organizers of the events to celebrate Georgetown's centenary and King George VI Coronation drew upon the template used for the British Guiana centenary in planning the programs. The final program for the Georgetown centenary included church services; military parades; illuminated buildings,; decorated bicycles; rallies for schoolchildren, featuring mass choirs singing patriotic songs; sporting events, featuring international competitors; theatrical programs; firework displays; public dances; and a competition for a centenary song.[37] M. E. Bayley composed lyrics for the winning song, and she won the £3.3 shillings (three-guinea) prize offered by the Georgetown City Council. Lt. Sydney Henwood, who had become the bandmaster of the British Guiana Militia Band in 1935, composed the music for the winning composition.[38]

The primary public dance was the Centenary Cabaret Night held at the Assembly Rooms on Thursday, March 4. The evening featured a "snappy fast-moving floor show covering the Evolution of Dance Music from 1837 to 1937." The revue presented "the Immortal Favorites of Yesteryears together with the latest Hits from Broadway, Hollywood, and London." Gerald Adamson and his piano accordion provided music for the evening along with Bert Rogers and the Ten Aristocrats. It appeared that Bert Rogers and His Aristocrats had replaced Harry Mayers and His Harry Banks Orchestra as the band preferred by the ruling elite. Also featured at the Centenary Cabaret Ball was the radio pianist Jennie Macaluso.[39] The event was hailed as a "huge success." Again, the music from Cabaret Night was broadcast on VP3MR. In addition, centenary dances targeting the subordinated classes were held at the Surprise Hall and at the Kit Kat Hall, both located on Water Street in Georgetown. These and other dances held at lodge halls and burial societies catered to the working people.

From Saturday, May 8 to Monday, May 17, 1937, virtually every community in British Guiana held activities to celebrate the Coronation of King George VI, which took place in London on Wednesday, May 12. The events in British Guiana were part of Empire-wide celebrations coordinated from London— a demonstration of the command and control associated with management of the Empire. The activities in British Guiana were variations on the templates that were used for the British Guiana and Georgetown centenary celebrations— decorated and illuminated buildings, show-window displays, a Regatta at the Rowing Club, ceremonial parades, torchlight parades, religious services, schoolchildren rallies, horse racing, fairs, fireworks displays, car parades, and fancy dress carnivals, mounted police sports, coronation balls, the governor's banquets, garden parties, Levee (a public gathering), the mass singing of "Come Raise Your Voices," the coronation song that was composed by Rev. Mortimer Aloysius Cossou,[40] and the broadcast of the King's Speech. In accord with current European propaganda techniques, events such as the ceremonial parade demanded a high degree of precision to gain maximum

Coronation celebrations

psychological impact.[41] As a result, there were rehearsals for certain events in Georgetown and New Amsterdam, as in London.

The first event in the celebrations in Georgetown was the Coronation Cabaret Ball organized by Mr. Gerald Adamson, who had organized the successful Georgetown Centennial Cabaret Ball. For this event, the Bert Rogers and Walter Stewart bands provided music. This meant that there was nonstop music. For some music pieces the bands were joined, creating what contemporary observers described as the largest dance band unit ever to perform in British Guiana. Other performers at the Cabaret Ball were Olga Lopes, Thelma Rego, Cicely Smith, John Sadler, Cyril Lord (the "ever-popular baritone"), and Gerald Adamson with his piano accordion. In addition, "several very entertaining acts carefully selected from the local vaudeville stage [ensured] a cabaret show of high quality judged by any standards."[42]

At 6:00 a.m. on Wednesday, May 12, all the church bells were rung to "herald" Coronation Day. At 7:45 a.m. a salute of 21 guns were fired at Fort William Frederick in Georgetown. The time of the firing corresponded with the "sounding of trumpets at Westminster Abbey to indicate the crowning of [King George VI] and synchronized with the firing of a Salute from the Tower of London."[43] At 8:00 a.m. a large crowd at Eve Leary witnessed the ceremonial parade of 351 members of British Guiana Local Forces. The British Guiana Militia Band under Lt. S. W. Henwood and the Police Drum and Fife Band under Sergeant-Drummer Philips were in attendance.[44] Four Guianese were on the King's Coronation Honours List; among them was Sergeant-Major Edward Arden Carter of the British Guiana Militia Band, who was awarded "the Medal of the Civil Division of the Order of the British Empire for meritorious service." Sergeant-Major Carter was born in Barbados on October 16, 1883, and came to British Guiana at the age of eleven. In 1896, at the age of thirteen he joined the British Guiana Militia Band. He was promoted to the rank of lance corporal in 1901 and to corporal in 1910. Carter acted as bandmaster in 1920 after the death of Captain Carroll and was promoted to sergeant major the same year. In 1924 he went to the British Empire Exhibition with the British Guiana Militia Band.[45]

The Georgetown celebrations attracted visitors from all over the colony, including hinterland workers. Ralph Fitz Scott's calypso "Bush women come to town" provides a list of the graphic names of some of the hinterland prostitutes who had come to Georgetown for King George VI's coronation in 1937. "Barima Sluice Box," "Camoudi Coil," and "Land Pirai" were among the persons mentioned.

Planning for the coronation celebrations in New Amsterdam started in January 1937 when the Town Council appointed a forty-eight-person committee

Table 4.2

Partial list of music performed during events to celebrate the Coronation of King George VI in Georgetown, May 8–17, 1937

Title	Genre	Composer	Performer(s)
Festival Prelude from Ein Feste Burg	Hymn	Martin Luther (ca. 1529)	C. H. Harewood, Organist and Choirmaster, the Cathedral Church of St. George
Coronation March	March	German	British Guiana Militia Band
Te Deum Laudamus	Liturgy	n.a.	Congregation
Praise to the Lord the Almighty King of Creation	Hymn	Joachim Neander (1863)	Congregation
Come Raise Your Voices	Coronation Song	Mortimer A. Cossou	Kingston Methodist School Choir

Source: Compiled from the *Daily Argosy*, May 1937.

and voted a sum of not more than $1,000 for the purpose. The committee developed a program similar to Georgetown's. A unique element of the New Amsterdam program was the organizing of a music festival. In less than two decades, the consequences of that initiative would be felt nationally.[46]

The celebrations in New Amsterdam lived up to expectations. Most significant for the New Amsterdam celebrations was the number of choirs that participated, among them the New Amsterdam Anglican School, All Saints Scots School, St. Theresa's Catholic School, New Amsterdam Roman Catholic Boy's School, Berbice High School for Girls, and the Cumberland Methodist School. A number of public concerts were also presented by the No. 7 Co. Militia Band. This made New Amsterdam's celebration the most musical in British Guiana. Rudy McGregor and the choir from the rural primary school, Cumberland Methodist School, played significant roles in this celebration. Compared to Georgetown, New Amsterdam had a wider and more complex musical repertoire for the coronation celebrations. Partial lists of the music performed during the celebrations in Georgetown and New Amsterdam are provided in Tables 4.2 and 4.3.

The music performed during the official Coronation Celebration represented the contemporary musical aesthetics of the state. Without a doubt, the music promoted empire and justified imperial rule. It is also indicative of a theoretical orientation which suggests that choral music is a strategy for developing discipline and fostering cohesion—qualities essential in the management of a colonial polity.

Table 4.3
Partial list of music performed during events to celebrate the Coronation of King George VI in New Amsterdam, May 8–17, 1937

Title	Genre	Composer	Performer(s)
May peace and love be near his throne	Chorus	n.a.	Berbice High School Girls' Choir (New Amsterdam)
Organ Prelude No. 2	Classical	n.a.	n.a.
Here's Health to His Majesty	Chorus	n.a.	Scouts of New Amsterdam
Come raise your voices	Coronation Song	n.a.	Combined Schools' Choir (New Amsterdam)
All People That on Earth Do Dwell	Hymn	n.a.	Combined Church Choir
Praise my soul the King of Heaven	Hymn	n.a.	Congregation
O God our help in Ages Past	Hymn	n.a.	Congregation
The Yale March	n.a.	n.a.	Edith Pieters
Never Let the Old Flag Fall	World War 1 Marching Song	n.a.	Miss Davis, Principal, Berbice High School for Girls and School Choir
God Save the King	National Anthem	n.a.	Communal
A Prayer to their Majesties	Coronation chorus	n.a.	Berbice High School for Girls' Choir (New Amsterdam)
Jubilee Song	Chorus	n.a.	Berbice High School for Girls' Choir (New Amsterdam)
Hurrah for England	n.a.	Franklin Taylor (ca. 1856)	Cumberland Methodist School Choir (with assistance from Rudy McGregor and Donald Jones)
The Men of Harlech	Marching Song (Welsh)	n.a.	Cumberland Methodist School Choir (with assistance from Rudy McGregor and Donald Jones)
The Call of the Empire	n.a.	n.a.	Cumberland Methodist School Choir (with assistance from Rudy McGregor and Donald Jones)
Land of Hope and Glory	n.a.	n.a.	Cumberland Methodist School Choir (with assistance from Rudy McGregor and Donald Jones)
Come raise your voices	Coronation Song	n.a.	Cumberland Methodist School Choir (with assistance from Rudy McGregor and Donald Jones)

Title	Genre	Composer	Performer(s)
Men of England	n.a.	n.a.	Cumberland Methodist School Choir (with assistance from Rudy McGregor and Donald Jones)
Eve of Waterloo	n.a.	n.a.	Cumberland Methodist School Choir (with assistance from Rudy McGregor and Donald Jones)
Recessional	n.a.	n.a.	Cumberland Methodist School Choir (with assistance from Rudy McGregor and Donald Jones)
Henry V before Agincourt	n.a.	n.a.	Cumberland Methodist School Choir (with assistance from Rudy McGregor and Donald Jones)
The Coronation Durbar	n.a.	n.a.	Cumberland Methodist School Choir (with assistance from Rudy McGregor and Donald Jones)
Our Glorious Heritage	n.a.	n.a.	Cumberland Methodist School Choir (with assistance from Rudy McGregor and Donald Jones)
O Salutaria	Liturgy	n.a.	Choir of Church of the Ascension (organist Mrs. De Caries)
Tantum Ergo	Liturgy	n.a.	Choir of Church of the Ascension (organist Mrs. De Caries)

Source: Complied from the *Daily Argosy*, May 1937.

In 1931 the East Indian population was approximately 124,000, just over 40 percent of the total population of British Guiana. At this time there were still East Indians in British Guiana who spoke Hindi, Urdu, or dialects from Uttar Pradesh and Bihar. By the start of the 1930s, more East Indians had joined the legal and medical professions and the colony's civil service. Also by 1938, the rapidly growing East Indian urban middle class had expanded its institutional infrastructure and more attention was now being directed to the social life and arts. In this sphere, urban East Indians revealed accommodationist and assimilationist tendencies. For example, in drama, the European format was used to present plays such as *Savitri* (*Love Conquers Death*), which was first presented in 1937. The traditional folk drama forms from Uttar Pradesh and Bihar, such as the "Leelas," do not appear to have been privileged by the leaders of the urban East Indian population. Was this an indication of "cultural cringe"? Was this a manifestation of shame and the belief that the folk cultural expressions of Uttar Pradesh and Bihar and those expressed by East Indians in rural British Guiana—"coolie culture"—were inferior?

In his 1937 New Year's message to East Indians in British Guiana, Professor Bhaskarand proposed a new slogan from the *Rig Veda*, "Sangachchadhwam savad adhwam samvomannansi janatam," which means "Walk together, speak together, and think together."[47] These ideas—upward mobility and racial solidarity—would guide the program of activities organized to celebrate the centenary of the arrival of the first East Indian indentured laborers on May 5, 1838. The idea of racial solidarity would remain a dominant idea and practice in Guyanese politics throughout the twentieth century and into the first decades of the twenty-first.

The centenary celebrations reflected the aspirations of the urban East Indian, at that time the vanguard of East Indian life in British Guiana. The celebrations became a platform for the leadership to articulate the aspirations of East Indians in British Guiana and a demonstration of institutional completeness—a term referring to the availability of a range of institutions (religious, cultural, economic, and communication) that support and nurture the social fabric of constituent groups in plural societies. Among the institutions that East Indians had by 1938 was a series of radio programs, one of which was *Indian Musical Heroes*, presented by Isaac A. Pollard and broadcast every Tuesday night on VP3MR. Programs featuring Indian music were very popular, and during one period in the 1930s both VP3MR and VP3BG were airing up to four hours of Indian music programming per week. The audiences were not only local; there were active, letter-writing listeners in Trinidad and Surinam. In May 1938 *Indian Musical Heroes* celebrated its first anniversary with a two-hour special. The program, which featured "artists from all over the colony" and was interspersed with "short addresses by prominent Indians," coincided with the centenary anniversary and literally launched the celebrations.[48]

The centenary celebrations extended over a two-week period and also followed the templates used for other centenary celebrations during the decade. There were religious services, an international meeting, and cultural events. On May 5 religious services were held at temples, mosques, and churches reflecting the religious composition of the East Indian community in British Guiana. At the start of the 1930s almost 8,000 East Indians were Christians. The contemporary press reported that a hymn in Hindi was composed especially for the celebrations.[49] The international meeting attracted delegates from India, Trinidad, and Dutch Guiana and was held at the British Guiana East Indian Cricket Club, which had been established in 1927. The meeting was opened by the governor, Sir Wilfred Jackson, who in his address commented on the achievements of East Indians over the past century and focused attention on the future:

Much has been achieved and it is well to commemorate the beginnings from which this achievement has sprung. But fulfillment lies in the future. East Indian colonists have made a great contribution to the progress of the country, but if the hopes, which have been formed of its future development, are to be realized we must believe that better things lie ahead. There are formidable difficulties to overcome, but I feel confident that the same innate qualities which enabled the early settlers to adapt themselves so readily to the conditions and problems of a new environment will enable their descendants to cope with the changing circumstances of the problems with which present developments confront us.[50]

In his address, C. R. Jacobs, a Member of the Legislative Council (MLC) and president of the British Guiana East Indian Association, posited that a key element in the future development of East Indian life in British Guiana was constitutional reform, which would extend the franchise for East Indians. For Jacobs, a second element was the maintenance of a distinct Indian identity. Citing Booker T. Washington, Jacobs noted that he found no "sound logic" for merging into a "Guianese consciousness":

We have brought with us to this Colony our religious customs, traditions and cultural standards. These, combined with our awakened national consciousness and the subtle, silent forces at work among us, does not [sic] permit the surrender of our identity as a distinctive racial group. This desire, however, to remain as a separate and distinctive community would in no [way] interpose difficulties in the way of a hearty co-operation with other racial groups in a common purpose aiming at the development of the Colony and the welfare of the inhabitants.

In the beautiful analogy of Booker T. Washington, "We can be one as the hand though separate as the fingers."[51]

What Jacobs envisaged for the future was an idyllic and bucolic, predominantly rural life that contributed to the building of a "greater India in British Guiana."[52]

Jacobs's speech, flavored with quotations from Rabindranath Tagore, was not only poetic but also carried with it the essence of socialism and hailed the emergence of a political strategy. Like Dr. Theo McCurdy's speech to the Negro Progress Convention, Jacobs's speech envisioned diversification of the economy and exploitation of the colony's natural resources. The speech also reaffirmed perceptions that East Indians did not have an inclusive vision for British Guiana in the future. Jacobs later became one of the leaders of the Manpower Citizens Association, a trade union representing sugar workers that was formed in 1937. Jacobs would also become a founding member of the distinctly socialist People's Progressive Party in 1949. That party, the first mass party in British Guiana, would be swept into power in the first elections held under universal adult suffrage in 1953.

Elements of the thrust of Jacobs's speech were also evident in the many cultural events organized for the centenary celebrations. Among them were the Centenary Fair, dramatic performances, publications, opening of librarues, and feeding the poor. The governor was the patron of the Centenary Fair, which was held in the Promenade Gardens. Among the special attractions at the fair were the Children's Fancy Dress Parade, the Indian Fire dance, exhibitions of fencing and wrestling, and Hoop-la. The British Guiana Militia Band conducted by Lieutenant S. Henwood presented a special concert of music.

On May 6 the Assembly Rooms were the venue for *Footlights of Hindustan* and *The King and the Queen*, two drama productions by the British Guiana Dramatic Society led by Mrs. J. B. Singh. *Footlights of Hindustan* was described as "a centenary variety programme" that featured "Indian instrumental orchestration, gorgeous costumes and settings." *The King and the Queen* was a two-act play written by Rabindranath Tagore and directed by Satyen H. Ghose. The performances were followed by a dance arranged by Harry Mayers (of the British Guiana Militia Band) with music performed by the Harry Banks Orchestra. Centenary celebrations were also held in New Amsterdam and other locations in British Guiana. The show *Footlights of Hindustan* was also presented in New Amsterdam. The New Amsterdam celebrations were again more musically inclusive: there was wide community participation led by Ruby McGregor, a Guianese of African ancestry, and the New Amsterdam–born Mootoo brothers orchestra.

Music had an important place in the Indian centenary celebrations.[53] The urban celebrations, reflecting the emerging sensibilities of the Indian middle class, featured both European and Indian classical music. The presence of European genres in the celebrations was another manifestation of efforts by the emerging local East Indian leadership class, like their African counterparts, to demonstrate that they had acquired European tastes and, by extension, values and norms. The musical programming for the subordinate class of urban East Indians during the celebrations tended to be what was popular among their compatriots at the time—the music of vaudeville. This suggested a few things: (a) the emergence of a common taste culture among the urban working class and (b) the presence of influential East Indian performers of the music popular among the urban subordinated classes, specifically the music of the Mootoo brothers. The Mootoo brothers by this time had established themselves in New Amsterdam, Georgetown, and in Trinidad and Tobago as exponents of the "Bhajee" beat and innovators in the field of calypso music and other styles of music popular on the vaudeville circuit.[54]

The Indian centenary celebrations had the stamp of approval of the establishment and in the main; the program of activities reproduced the established formula for major celebrations. This apparent adherence to the established formula must not be interpreted as acquiescence. As was evident in C. R. Jacobs's various speeches and pronouncements, the celebration was also about advancing strategies for changing the status of East Indians in British Guiana, improving the working conditions of East Indian labor in British Guiana, and rehabilitating the status of India and Indians globally.

One of the themes of the various talks given on the history of music in British Guiana between 1831 and 1931 was about the significant improvement in musical proficiency. The musical programs associated with the centenary celebrations during the 1930s demonstrated this proficiency. The term *musical proficiency* is used here in an inclusive sense; meaning more than the achievement of formal certification from some examining board, it also refers to a level of confidence and pride in musical output and the confidence to share this beyond the community that created it. The term also recognizes the presence of an environment that enables this acquisition of skills and nurtures musical confidence and pride in music. During the 1930s several factors contributed to musical proficiency. Among these were higher levels of accomplishment in formal music education and the development of genres that enjoyed success both domestically and internationally. As we have already indicated, during the 1930s radio expanded in scope and professionalism, and this too contributed to the growth of musical confidence and proficiency in the colony. An additional factor was the colony's ongoing connection with the international music scene and the increasing acclaim that British Guianese musicians, such as Ken "Snakehips" Johnson, were attracting internationally.

Throughout the 1930s, Guianese continued to pursue higher levels of competence "in theoretical and practical music" at home and overseas. An important indicator of musical competence in the 1930s was success at the various examinations set by the Associated Board of the Royal Academy of Music and the Royal College of Music, Victoria College of Music, and Trinity College. During the 1930s several Guianese, including F. P. Loncke and Rosemary Ramdehol, studying in British Guiana went beyond Grade VIII and earned licentiates (diplomas) from the Associated Board of the Royal Academy of Music and the Royal College of Music and Trinity College. Each year, the board offered a single scholarship to the West Indian student who earned the highest scores in the annual examinations. The scholarship winner attended the Royal College of Music. For all of the 1920s and for the first four years of the 1930s, the winner of the single scholarship came from Jamaica, Barbados, or Trinidad. However starting in 1935, three Guianese, Philip Pilgrim, Lynette Dolphin, and William Pilgrim won this highly competitive scholarship. Philip

Pilgrim won the scholarship in 1935, Lynette Dolphin in 1937, and William "Billy" Pilgrim in 1938.

British Guianese also pursued music education through Trinity College. Here, too, they had stellar achievements. In May 1937 Lucille Mabel Nicholson was awarded a Licentiate Diploma from Trinity College"[55] The Collet Medal was the recognition earned for top marks in the highest level of examinations offered by Trinity College. Edna Jordan (nee Elcock) won that medal in 1927. During the 1930s, Rosemary Ramdehol and Nellie Dos Santos were also winners of the Collet Medal.

In early December 1939, four months after the start of World War II, Philip Pilgrim returned to British Guiana having earned the Associate of the Royal College of Music (ARCM) in Performance diploma. Pilgrim had also emerged as one of the top-grade pianists at the college. He first came to national attention in 1924 when his success at the "First Steps" examinations of Trinity College of Music was published. He credited his early teachers for his success:

> At the age of seven I began the piano under Miss W. McDavid, LRSM, who gave me a good grounding in time and rhythm. Miss Gwendoline Moore, LRSM, also tutored me for a few years before she left the Colony for America. My last local teacher was Mrs. F. W. Kerry, LRSM, who, through her experience and example, inspired me to greater effort, resulting in my winning in 1934 the Scholarship of the Associated Board of the Royal Schools of Music.[56]

On his return, Pilgrim immediately became active in the Georgetown concert scene. On December 15, 1939, he gave a concert at the Town Hall, which featured Beethoven's *Moonlight Sonata* and selections from Chopin. Pilgrim had planned to return to the United Kingdom; however, as a result of the ongoing war he remained in Guiana until his untimely death on August 30, 1944, at the age of 27. His magnum opus, *The Legend of Kaieteur*, had its premiere in Georgetown on July 20, 1944. This composition has been described as a "rare example of classical music from the Caribbean."[57] Between 1939 and his death in 1945, Philip Pilgrim was a popular performer on the concert stage.

Classical music continued to be an important component in the musical tastes of urban Guianese during the 1930s. It was, however, possible to detect a tiring with the traditional classical repertoire. There was an emerging interest in compositions with Guianese idioms and flavors. The latter tendency was already evident in the earlier mentioned patriotic songs presented during the various centenary celebrations and the special marches composed by Clem Nichols and other members of the British Guiana Militia Band. The arrival of Lt. Sydney Henwood as bandmaster of the British Guiana Militia Band in 1935 and the return of Philip Pilgrim in 1939 accelerated this. Of equal importance on the musical scene were non-classical compositions—the popular genres.

During the 1930s a number of domestic genres achieved national and international prominence. Chief among these were the "Shanto" and the "Bhagee Beat." These expressions were developed in the urban ghettos and hinterland work camps, and matured in the vaudeville circuit. The term *Shanto*—a conflation of "shanty," the work songs sung in the hinterland, and "calypso"—is attributed to Bill Rogers (1906–1984), who used it to describe a special form of calypso originating in British Guiana. Shantos tended to have multiple verses with between twelve to fourteen lines per verse; choruses were rarely used.[58] During the 1930s the shanto with the "bhagee" beat was very popular in British Guiana and the terms were sometimes used interchangeably. According to Gordon Rohlehr: "The beat of the Bhagee was very infectious, and the major dance bands all played it during intermission, when people would dance to it and sang the ditties. It was also played at the end of dances, resembling in this respect the leggo in Trinidad of the same period, which came after people had danced the lancers, waltz, fox trot, and Charleston."[59]

Many of the shantos and calypsos composed during this period commented on the social and economic conditions that the poor and working-class population were experiencing in urban British Guiana. It was this role as both "searchlight" and "loudspeaker" that made these compositions valuable assets for the labor movement. In this role, the shanto reenergized the praise song/blame song/ridicule song tradition associated with the colony's African heritage and with exponents such as Sweet Sago, who was popular during the 1890s. Writing in 1938, the *Daily Chronicle* columnist Pugagee Pungus described Sweet Sago compositions as having a "corrupting influence." According to Pungus, Sago was an inmate of the leprosy asylum in Mahaica on the east coast of Demerara, who would:

> [P]eriodically ... escape and tramp all the way to the Georgetown, where his arrival would be hailed with delight. He invariably turned up a little before Christmas, or some other festive season, and, followed by huge crowds, he would go from yard to yard, doing his latest "tunes," and of course making frequent collections. His themes and gestures begged description and excursions to the City only terminated when the crowds became so unwieldy, and the turmoil so uproarious, that the police were compelled to intervene all too tardily. "Sweet Sago" would then be hauled before the Magistrate and taken back to his friends at Mahaica.[60]

Sago was considered to have "lowered" the quality of Creole popular song making, according to a biased Pungus; the shantos were of that class and did

not represent a renaissance.[61] Despite Pungus's flummoxing, the shanto continued to grow in popularity, with Bill Rogers as the most versatile and productive
composer and performer. He became the first Guianese to sign a recording
contract and, in November 1934, recorded twenty-eight shantos with RCA's
American Blue Bird label. Sam Manning and Lionel Belasco were two other
West Indian musicians who were recording with Blue Bird at this time.

Among Bill Rogers's 1934 recordings were "The West Indian Weed Woman,"
"Bhagee," and "Ugly or Pretty Woman."[62] "The West Indian Weed Woman" provided an exhaustive list of British Guianese ethno-botanicals and their cura-
tive and restorative attributes: "Sweet Broom, Sweet Sage and Lemon Grass / I
hear dem good for making tea / Well a hear Zeb grass and Wild Daisy / Is good
to cool the body."[63] The song became a hit during the first international calypso
wave of the 1930s and was re-released in the 1950s, the 1970s, and again in the
late 1990s. Harry Belafonte and singers in the Bahamas, Jamaica, Barbados,
and Trinidad have also covered the song. "Bhagee" was not only a recipe for
preparing that variety of callaloo; it could be seen like de Weever's "Me Cawfee in de Marnin'," as a contemporary commentary on the prevailing diet and
conditions of working people during the Depression era. The song concludes
with an anecdote from the household of Lal Beharry and Sookie. Lal Beharry
leaves for work with the understanding that Sookie is going to "cook some rice
and Bhagee." Well, Lal returns home with "his friends and company" prepared
to eat rice and Bhagee and finds that Sookie has "disobeyed his orders" and
prepared dhal pourie, dhal, and curry. According to Bill Rogers, Lal flies in rage
and expresses his disappointment in "deep Hindustani." The rage escalates to
violence when "he up a dhantal and tend to she memory."

In the last verse of "Bhagee," Rogers demonstrates knowledge of East Indian
culinary practices and Hindi that came from growing up in multi-ethnic
Charlestown, a ward in south Georgetown during the 1900s. Also recorded
in 1934 were "Sugar, Cent a Pound," "Kingston Dead Cow," and "Silver Bangle
Dipped in Gold." "Sugar, Cent a Pound" spoke about the sale of sugar salvaged
from a schooner that sank at a local wharf; "Kingston Dead Cow" reflected on
the speed with which the carcass of a cow, which had drowned in the Demerara River near Kingston, was butchered and distributed. Both recordings
commented on the cost of food and the extremes to which poor people went
to get it. "Silver Bangle Dipped in Gold" was commentary on the dress styles
of urban women, especially the pretentious use of imitation gold jewelry.

Bill Rogers was also a touring performer. He toured Dutch Guiana, Trinidad,
Barbados, the United States, and Canada during the 1930s. Gordon Rohlehr
has argued that Rogers's shanto style, "his feel for the dramatic situation, and
his talent for narrative . . . [and his] employment of long lines crammed with
words and syllables and his extended choruses . . . fed into to the musical and

lyrical collective unconscious of the Calypso world to become a definite influence on [Trinidadian calypsonians such as Lord] Melody."[64]

Bill Rogers was not the only composer of shantos and bhagee songs in British Guiana during the early 1930s. Among the others were Joe Coggins, Zeda Martindale, Ralph Fitz Scott, Cyril Lamprey(?), Johnny Murray, Papsi Corrica, Bandula, Red Ants, Lall, and Ezekiel.[65] Shantos were performed in rum shops, at dances, and starting with Rogers's recordings in 1934, were recorded by international recording companies. As suggested earlier, these compositions served as "searchlights" and "loudspeakers" focusing on and commenting on what was transpiring at all levels of society—in high places, on the middle rounds of society, and to quote Rohlehr, with the "bedraggled proto-proletariat existing at the rotting edges of the society." Joe Coggin's "Me an Me Neighbor Don't 'gree" commented on the rags-to-riches-to-rags cycle that so many of the hinterland workers, especially those who worked in the gold and diamond fields—pork-knockers—experienced during the 1930s. Zeda Martindale's "Captain Put Me Ashore" was also about pork-knockers; this shanto refers to a Barbadian contract worker expressing fear as he experiences the awesome rawness of the rapids and waterfalls that had to be surmounted to get to the gold and diamond fields. By the 1950s the song became known as "Itanamie" and earned a prominent place in Guyana's repertoire of folk songs. As mentioned during the examination of the music associated with King George VI's coronation, Ralph Fitz Scott's "Bush Women Come to Town" provides a list of the graphic names of some of the hinterland prostitutes who came to town for King George VI's coronation. The songs of Martindale, Coggins, and Scott are incisive explorations of the intersection of urban and hinterland British Guiana during the 1930s.

In addition to being a pivotal figure in the development and export of bhagee and shanto music, Bill Rogers is also be recognized as one of the first impresarios to take Trinidadian calypsonians on tours of the semi-permanent communities in the hinterland during the late 1930s. His first venture was with Lord Caresser in 1938. Lord Caresser left a record of that tour, including that of his love affair with the Guianese dancer Peggy Daniels in the calypso "Peggy Dearie." That calypso not only tells about his love for Peggy and the "honeymoon" they spent in the Mazaruni gold mining district, it is a veritable lesson on the geography of the hinterland mining communities linked to "happy moments" spent in the Cuyuni, Essequibo, and Demerara, Parry Map (sic), Ol' Macquarie, Matusi Hole, Enachu, Aranapai, Kurupung, Merume Mountain, and Mazaruni and celebrates Peggy's versatility as a dancer of the "Frenchy Toe, the Spanish rumba, the slim sham shimmy and diggy daga do."[66]

Another recording, "No Surrender," documents Lord Caresser's falling out with Bill Rogers, whom he describes as a "bargee composer," an "old time flouncer," and a "sweetie vendor." In his teenage years, Bill Rogers sold sweets at street corners in Georgetown and may have been a dancer in one of the Charlestown masquerade bands.[67]

During this decade, as a result of increasing tours by Guianese musicians to the West Indies, especially Trinidad, and vice versa, there was more reciprocity in the flow of musical ideas between the two British colonies. For example, the Mootoo Brothers Orchestra, led by the Berbice-born, East Indian Charlie Mootoo, became a virtual fixture in Trinidad, and in the process influenced the direction of calypso music in Trinidad during the 1930s and 1940s.[68]

Mootoo [handwritten marginal note]

Here we return to organized labor and its role in facilitating musical proficiency during the 1930s. As has been implied throughout this chapter, the Depression exacted a heavy toll on working-class Guianese during the 1930s, and this catalyzed labor organization. In the years between the centenary of British Guiana in 1937 and 1939, twelve trade unions were registered in British Guiana.[69] In addition to seeking improved wages and working conditions, many of these unions had overt political goals, especially the demand for universal adult suffrage. Some of them espoused support of socialism, and many of the organizers for these unions were described as "communist agitators."[70] Hubert Nathaniel Critchlow, the colony's pioneering trade unionist, visited the Soviet Union in 1932.

Because of low wages and the Depression, the workers had very little if any disposable income. As a result, union dues were very low or nonexistent. This meant that many unions depended on support from international sources. Many of the new unions sought affiliation with the British Labour Party and other international organizations such as Labor and Socialist International and the Canadian Labour Party. However, the primary source of income was music-based events. According to Ashton Chase, son of the vaudeville promoter Sam Chase, throughout the 1930s trade unions depended on "Punch Card Rallies, house-to-house collections, pound sales, Harvest envelopes, Mock Courts, Concerts, Fetes, Children's parties and dances . . . as fund raising sources."[71] Sam Chase, Jack Hylton, and Bill Rogers refined their skills as performers, promoters, and social commentators in this milieu.[72]

Street demonstrations led by brass bands became a major mobilizing strategy of organized labor. These demonstrations tended to take place early in the morning and follow routes that went through working-class districts and ended up in the Parade Ground, where agitations were made. The Parade Ground on Middle Street in Georgetown was a symbolic place for the nascent labor movement, as it was there that the heads of some of the leaders of the 1823 Demerara slave uprising were displayed after they were executed.[73] The premier working-class demonstration was the annual May Day Parade, which

music + labor [handwritten marginal note]

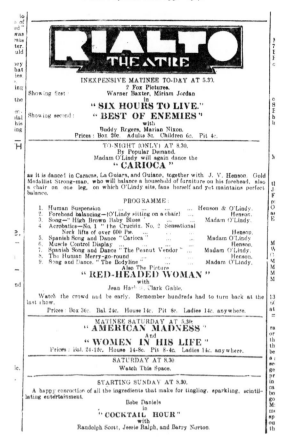

Figure 4.3. Advertisement for show by Madame O'Lindy,
Daily Argosy, July 4, 1935.

was invariably led by a brass band. The popular Barbadian-born, vaudeville comedian Jack Hylton was a regular fixture at the head of the parade.

On the cultural front, vaudeville became an increasingly important aspect of working-class entertainment. Vaudeville shows were held primarily in cinemas. The London, Rialto, and Olympic cinemas in Georgetown and the Gaiety Theatre in New Amsterdam were the primary venues for major vaudeville shows presented by promoters/performers such as Madam O'Lindy and Sam Chase. In the 1930s, vaudeville shows featured multiple acts—strongmen, acrobats, comedians, singers, dancers, and orchestras. For example on July 4, 1935, Madam O'Lindy presented the show *Carioca* at the Rialto Cinema in Georgetown. The promotional materials stated that Madam O'Lindy would again "dance the 'Carioca' as it is danced in Caracas and La Guira."

In addition to producing shows in British Guiana, Madam O'Lindy and her vaudeville troupe toured the West Indies. Another popular dancer for this era was the earlier mentioned Peggy Daniels, who was also famous for performing hip-swinging routines from popular screen musicals such as the "Carioca" (*Flying Down to Rio*, 1933), the "Continental" (*The Gay Divorcee*, 1934), the "Digga Digga Do" (*Stormy Weather*, 1933), and the "Hold Your Man" (*The Lady with the Fan*, 1933). Sam Chase's vaudeville shows would have a similar formula; however, he would add more topical skits and songs. His work in this sphere is seen as playing an important role in educating and mobilizing the urban working class.

Throughout the 1930s radio broadcasting grew in importance and cultural significance. Guianese listeners were now able to receive programming from international broadcasters such as the BBC Empire Broadcasting Service, and from American stations such as W2XAF and W2XAD. These stations provided Guianese listeners with programs that featured choral music, classical music, the light classics, jazz, swing, and other popular dance genres. The music programming on these international stations, especially the American commercial stations, was guided by the principle of lowering program production costs and increasing revenues through commercials. As a result, the program schedules of W2XAF and W2XAD were dominated by music programs. These musical developments in radio broadcasting in the United Kingdom and in the United States influenced radio broadcasting in British Guiana. By 1935 Weiting and Richter, J. P. Santos, and Harlequin Bakery initiated radio advertising using original local compositions.

By the second half of the 1930s, music-based programs sponsored by the commercial sector proliferated on the Guianese airwaves. For example, in 1937 the British Guiana Match Factory, the British Guiana Biscuit Factory, and J. P. Santos were sponsoring programs featuring music provided by Walter Stewart's Swing Orchestra. Also in the same year, the British Guiana Cigarette Company sponsored the revival of *Amateur Hour* on VP3MR. The first show, broadcast from the Town Hall in New Amsterdam, was described as a cabaret show and dance and the purpose was to raise funds for the band of the No. 7 Militia Company. Among the performers were Olga Lopes, Thelma Rego, Frank Stokes, Walter Stewart's Swing Orchestra with Anton Lichtveld, and the British Guiana Harmonica Band.[74] In addition to programs of Anglo-American dance music, there were other music programs. The Indian Musical Association launched *Best Indian Singers on the Air*, the first program of Indian music, on March 3, 1937. The weekly program presented "first-rate Indian singers" and was aired on VP3BG in English and Hindi.[75]

The practice of featuring Guianese musicians on the embryonic radio system provided them with audiences beyond the shores of British Guiana. For

Figure 4.4. Advertisement for show by Ken "Snakehips" Johnson, *Daily Argosy*, August 8, 1935.

example, in 1937 the twenty-one-year-old "jazz-pianist, dance orchestra leader and composer" Ferdinand Eversley and the twenty-three-year-old violinist Anton Lichtveld toured Trinidad, capitalizing on the "fame" they had earned from regular performance on Guianese radio, which was listened to in Trinidad and other parts of the West Indies. Eversley's playing style was described as "a blend of Fats Waller's and Charlie Kunz [of the Casini Club Orchestra]." Anton Lichtveld, who was born in Dutch Guiana, had made British Guiana his home and was considered "the best violinist among those who broadcast from British Guiana."[76] Eversley and Lichtveld joined Phil Madison, Bill Rogers, the Mootoo Brothers, and Madam O'Lindy as Guianese who toured Trinidad and left a legacy that was built upon during the latter half of the twentieth century by King Fighter, Lord Canary, Tony Ricardo, Lady Guymine, and others.

We now return to one of the important musical visitors to British Guiana during the 1930s—Ken "Snakehips" Johnson, who was known in international show-business circles as "British Guiana's Ambassador of Rhythm." Kenrick Reginald Hymans Johnson was born in Georgetown on September 10, 1914, to a black middle-class family. His father was a medical doctor. Kenrick attended Queen's College, the elite boys' grammar school in Georgetown. When Kenrick Johnson left British Guiana in 1929 to study at the prestigious William Borlase School in Marlow, Buckinghamshire, he had already been exposed to a wide range of musical styles and played piano and violin. His uncle was the pianist Oscar Dummett.

Instead of pursuing the study of medicine or law after William Bolase, as were the expectations of his parents, he took up show business and studied dance with the innovative American choreographer Buddy Bradley. As a result of his height, 6' 4", and his fluid and flexible style, Kenrick Johnson earned the nickname "Snakehips." By 1934 Ken was in the United States, appearing in movies and starring in Hollywood cabaret. This 1934 trip to the United States exposed him to swing music as popularized by Cab Calloway and Fletcher Henderson. Prior to returning to England in 1935 and forming the West Indian Orchestra, which has been described as the first regular black band of any size in Britain,[77] he visited British Guiana for a "one night only performance."

For his performance in British Guiana on August 8, 1935, he created a new band—the Aristocrats of Symphonic Jazz. Among the members were Bert Rogers (sax), Ferdie Eversley (piano), and Wallie Browne (trumpet). The program presented is shown in Figure 4.4.[78]

Ken Johnson's West Indian Orchestra became London's leading swing band in the late 1930s and early 1940s. Ken Johnson and his band were the toast of London's cafe society. By 1939 he was described as the "British Negro Jazz star."[79] He died at the age of twenty-six, performing at London's exclusive Café de Paris when it was bombed during a German air raid on March 8, 1941. British Guiana and Georgetown had lost a proud son.

Meanwhile, the Guianese diaspora in New York were also making their musical presence felt. Among them was Edward Stewart, whose accomplishments were reported in a local newspaper under the headline GUIANESE BARITONE MAKES DEBUT IN NEW YORK:

Mr. Edward Stewart, Guianese baritone singer, made his debut in a song recital at St. Peter Clave's Auditorium, Jefferson Avenue, Brooklyn, New York. He was presented by Rev. John T. Ogburn, Priest of St. Cyprian's Church. According to the *Amsterdam News*, the concert was a huge success and Mr. Stewart was highly praised. Mr. Stewart was accompanied by Miss Muriel Braithwaite on piano and he sang Negro Spirituals and songs in five different languages. He closed his performances with the Negro National Anthem—"Lift Every Voice and Sing till Earth and Heaven sings." Mr. Stewart studies at the Brooklyn Conservatory of Music.[80]

Also in New York was Mrs. C. G. Corey, originally from Belfield, East Coast Demerara. She was the composer of the lyrics and music for the song "Shoulder to Shoulder with Uncle Sam" and dedicated it to President Roosevelt in 1934. This song called for increased national effort to overcome the Depression. She received a note of thanks from the president.[81] Other overseas Guianese who were actively engaged in classical music and attracting international critical attention during the 1930s were former British Guiana Militia Band apprentice and clarinetist Rudolph Dunbar, who resided in London, and the New York–based composer Ingram Fox.

On February 16, 1939, four sugar workers were shot to death and "over a dozen were injured" at Lenora Sugar Estate, West Coast Demerara. Like the previous Ruimveldt shootings, women again paid the supreme price. One of the workers killed was Sumintra, a weeder who was identified as a "ring leader."[82] According to the Guyanese labor historian Ashton Chase, the origins of the incident was a strike called by firemen at the Lenora factory to protest their 11½-hour working day.[83] The resolution of the strike included recognition of the Manpower Citizens Association (MPCA) as a union to represent sugar workers.[84]

The Lenora strike was just one of the labor eruptions in British Guiana during the 1930s. Labor agitations were not unique to British Guiana; starting in British Honduras in 1934, riots spread across the British West Indian colonies. According to Breton and Yelvington, "the 1930s were years of popular revolt in the Caribbean," as riots by the working class also took place in Cuba, Haiti, Martinique, and the Dominican Republic.[85] The causes of these riots were myriad and included poor wages, subhuman living conditions, and absolute disrespect by the ruling classes. Mr. Seaford of the British Guiana Sugar Producers Association contemptuously described the "main requirements" of the Guianese worker as "food, shelter, bright and attractive clothing, a little spare money for rum and gambling, and the opportunity for easy love making."[86]

The British government's response to these developments was the establishment of the West Indian Royal Commission, chaired by Lord Moyne. The commission's terms of reference were "to investigate social and economic conditions in Barbados, British Guiana, British Honduras, Jamaica, the Leeward Islands, Trinidad and Tobago, and the Windward Islands, and matters therewith, and to make recommendations."[87] The results of the commission's findings, which had far-reaching consequences for West Indian social and political life, were not released due to the start of World War II.

Coterminous with the activism of the working class were increased anti-colonial fermentations among the middle class, especially in the realm of the literary arts. During this period *Bim* was launched in Barbados, *Beacon* in Trinidad, and *Kyk-Over-All*, edited by the poet A. J. Seymour, in British Guiana. Similar journals emerged in Haiti and Martinique.[88] These journals were characterized as "dealing with Afro-Caribbean themes, documenting 'folk lore,' and religious cosmologies."[89] In retrospect, these journals were proto-nationalist.

5

The American Presence: 1940–1950

We are still dominated by the sun—strangers in a land we call our own. There is no Guianese people. Only an accumulation of persons—end products of a various history. Images
in mud of the distant alien. Here patterns kill us, and the spiritual bullying of foreigners
forever consents to the act. Incoherence, apishness, sentimentality, uncreativeness.... The
truth is, we are a lot of persons and a lot of races, with a super village mentality.[1]
—Denis Williams, 1945

Three governors administered (but did not rule) British Guiana during this
important decade. Sir Wilfred Jackson was replaced by Sir Gordon Lethem in
1941. Governor Lethem's tenure extended to 1947, when he was succeeded by
Sir Charles Woolley. Unlike previous governors, their authority in the colony
was challenged by another force—the presence of the United States. On September 2, 1940, the United States of America and Great Britain signed the
Destroyer-Base Agreement, under which the "United States acquired from
Great Britain the right to lease naval and air base sites in Newfoundland, Ber-
muda, the Bahamas, Jamaica, St. Lucia, Antigua, Trinidad, and British Guiana
for a period of ninety-nine years."[2] Under this agreement the United States
established two military bases in the colony: an air force base at Hyde Park
(subsequently named Atkinson Field after the first base commander) on the
east bank of Demerara, twenty-five miles outside of the capital, Georgetown;
and a seaplane/naval base on the west bank of the Essequibo River.[3] These
bases were crucial to the defense of the Panama Canal and of efforts to clear
the Caribbean of German submarines that were targeting ships bringing in
food to the region and taking out strategic materials such as bauxite and oil.
The bases were also crucial for the execution of Operation Torch—establishing an "Allied bridgehead in North Africa, preparatory to re-opening a second
front against Hitler in Western Europe to complement the German-Russian
eastern front."[4]

The American presence in British Guiana compounded an already complex domestic situation. At the most basic level, the physical conditions under
which the majority of the population lived continued to be unsatisfactory,

even dire. As a result of the submarine-based Battle of the Caribbean, there were ongoing food and fuel shortages. Food intake was deficient in quantity and quality. The cost of living in 1942 was 60 percent higher than it was in 1938 and the average wage was seventy-two cents a day; access to land was limited, in urban and rural areas sanitary conditions were "abominable," and "Malaria was still a scourge."[5] Approximately 44 percent of East Indians and 49 percent of Amerindians were illiterate in 1946.[6] Crime (especially increases in theft of property) created a security crisis. Race, class, and color hierarchies continued to dominate social life and influence individual and collective efficacy and esteem. For Denis Williams, the conditions in the colony were stifling authentic creativity; he characterized Guyanese artistic expression as incoherent, apish, sentimental, and uncreative.[7] Williams's observations were indicative of the nationalist sentiments that had been gathering steam in the political sphere since the previous decade.

In addition, all British Guianese were expected to support the British war effort with treasure and blood, by donating money to purchase warplanes and mobile canteens and supporting the fund-raising efforts of the Red Cross and other voluntary initiatives. Garden fetes at the Government House (the governor's home), gold and silver collections, soccer matches, and even baseball games were some of the fund-raising activities that were initiated during the early years of the war and continued throughout World War II. Patriotic funding-raising was developed to a fine art. Guianese of all ethnicities were recruited to serve in all sectors of the British Armed Services. In a January 3, 1941, announcement, recruiters for the Royal Air Force in British Guiana stated that recruitment to the force was "not restricted to certain races."[8] The statement was necessary as there was the perception, anchored in the experiences of World War I, that persons of color were not acceptable. British Guianese volunteer Cy Grant, a person of African ancestry, would become a flight officer in the Royal Air Force, after being shot down over the Netherlands in 1943, Grant was a prisoner of war for the remainder of the war.[9]

Administrative responses to the colony's social, economic, political, diplomatic, and technological dynamics during the decade would leave an indelible imprint on governance practices in the society for the remainder of the century, and this would influence musical life. Despite this complex of pressures, notwithstanding Denis Williams's observations, musical productivity in British Guiana increased in all musical genres. A number of factors contributed to this. Clearly, one was an environment that encouraged music—stress increases demand for music. This proposition is supported by observations made by Alan John Knight, the bishop of Guiana, at the awards ceremony for British Guianese students who were successful in the 1940 examinations of the Associated Board of the Royal Schools of Music. Reflecting on the powerful and positive role music was playing in the lives of people of England since the start of World War II, he reported, "People who never listened to music were now doing so, during the day and night and some of the best music was being produced for them to satisfy their demands." He also observed that this spontaneous development was a good thing and predicted "the revival in music in England at such a difficult time would be felt in the Colonies."[10]

In British Guiana there were additional reasons for this quantitative and qualitative development. Among them were (a) the arrival of Americans via the establishment of American military bases in the colony; (b) the musical tastes and demands of Guianese working people; (c) innovations in the music of rural East Indians; (d) the return of students who were on scholarships in the United Kingdom and the United States; (e) further growth of music appreciation and performance organizations; (f) technological developments; (g) an influential diaspora on both sides of the Atlantic; and (h) the increasing importance of nationalist politics.

The primarily southern white American servicemen in British Guiana needed recreation and entertainment on and off the bases. According to Leslie Mohamed, who worked in food services at Atkinson Field between 1941 and 1943, the recreation facilities at Atkinson Field included a swimming pool, a bowling alley, and two cinemas—one for officers and an open-air one for the ordinary troops and the local workers. American film stars and other popular entertainers such as John Garfield, the Andrews Sisters, and Al Jolson also entertained American troops at Atkinson Field.[11] The British Guiana Militia Band was one of the local ensembles that provided on-base entertainment. Erica Gomes, the daughter of Captain S. W. Henwood, bandmaster of the British Guiana Militia band, recalls: "The Band would perform for the troops and I particularly remember Harry Mayers (my Dad's Deputy) singing 'God Bless America' (a big hit). There were naturally many marches played and other popular tunes for the entertainment of the troops."[12]

In time the repertoire of the British Guiana Militia Band's regular public concerts was expanded to feature more Broadway show music, Sousa marches, and the national anthem of the United States. Among the other local ensembles that provided on-base entertainment were Gun Fernandes and the Luckies, Al Seales and the Washboards, and Tom Charles and the Syncopaters; their repertoires featured music popular in the United States—the music of Irving and Ira Berlin, Sammy Cahn, Duke Ellington, Hammerstein and Rogers, Johnny Mercer, Glen Miller, and Cole Porter. These Guianese bands became adepts of swing, jive, and jazz and reveled in improvisation. Al Seales and the Washboards emerged as musical innovators, introducing styles such as the Latin-inflected "Bion." In the late 1940s, Al Seales opened GEMS Recording Company, which has been described as "the earliest Recording

Company in region to create a complete production from musical arrangements recorded locally on tape, to the manufacturing and distribution of gramophone records, through MELODISC RECORDS of London, England."[13]

Off-base entertainment was organized by the United Service Organization (USO), a private, nonprofit association established in February 1941 and incorporated in New York. The organization emerged out of a request from President Franklin Roosevelt to six civilian agencies "to provide morale and recreation services to US uniformed personnel."[14] The mission of the organization, as expressed in its constitution and by-laws, was:

> ... to aid in the war and defense program of the United States and its Allies by serving the religious, spiritual, welfare, and educational needs of the men and women in the armed forces and the war and defense industries of the United States and its Allies in the United States and throughout the world, and in general, to contribute to the maintenance of morale in American communities and elsewhere.

Off-base entertainment brought with it challenges associated with American segregationist policies and practices. The first dance organized by the USO in British Guiana was held on Saturday, May 30, 1942, at its "new Club Rooms situated next to the Lighthouse in Kingston." The dance was held under the patronage of Sir Gordon Lethem, the governor of British Guiana, who was conflicted with expectations that the colony's legal system would be modified to accommodate American Jim Crow policies in British Guiana. [15] American ideology held that it would be inappropriate for white soldiers to be judged by magistrates and judges of color.

Gun Fernandes's Luckies Orchestra provided music for the inaugural dance of the USO. Entry was restricted to members of the American armed forces and persons who were issued with USO guest cards. British Guiana's white, urban elite and the colonial political directorate were the patrons and patronesses for this occasion, among them the chief justice, the commissioner of police, and other leaders of the public and private sector.[16] As in Trinidad, which shared with British Guiana similar racial dynamics, "the colony's white inhabitants saw it as part of their duty to offer visiting Americans local knowledge regarding the construction of racial boundaries and the conduct of relations between men and women."[17] The aim of the advisors to the American forces was not to "devalue whiteness" by unbridled public fraternization with "nonwhite women."

As Julia Carson observed, American segregationist practices posed a problem of recruiting and training appropriate junior hostesses throughout the Antilles area. In British Guiana, girls of various racial strains—Chinese, Portuguese, East Indian, and Negro—"cooperated" in club work.[18] One of the "Negro" women who cooperated was Helen Taitt, the daughter of Dr. Jabez and Dorothy Taitt. Her parents were lynchpins in the Georgetown social scene, connecting the subordinated classes with the ruling class. Her father was a Barbadian-born medical doctor who was at that time a government medical officer in Georgetown. Prior to that, he held the same position in Port Mourant on the Corentyne coast of Berbice. He also had an active private practice. Her mother was light-skinned and Guianese-born and was president of the British Guiana Philharmonic Society, of which the colony's governor was the patron. The Taitt family lived in Woodbine House, an impressive property in Murray Street originally owned by Mr. Forshaw, a former mayor of Georgetown. Helen Taitt's family and relatives were well connected. Through those connections she was employed as a typist by the Elmhurst Contracting Company, the company that built the American airbase at Hyde Park, east bank Demerara. In addition to her typing skills, the Bishop's High School graduate was also a trained dancer. She had studied under Mrs. Hoban and had performed in shows such as *The Enchanted Gardens* at the Assembly Rooms.[19]

Because of her job and the social contacts of her family, she attended her first ball at the USO club in Georgetown. In her autobiography *My Life, My Country*, she reported that she danced all night and even performed on stage, singing "Boogie Woogie Bugle Boy of Company B," one of the current hits by the Andrews Sisters. As a result of that performance, she was invited back to perform at the USO Club. On her second outing, she did a Carmen Miranda impersonation, singing "South American Way" and "Ma Ma Yu Care O."[20] Soon after that performance, she left the job at the Hyde Park airbase and joined the fledgling Bureau of Publicity and Information (BPI), a unit of the colonial government responsible for providing pro-British wartime information and organizing events to boost the morale of the citizens. One product from this unit was the musical *You Can't Stop It*. Among her colleagues at BPI were H. R. Harewood, A. J. Seymour, Winfred Gaskin, and C. A. Gomes.

The paucity of white women has always been a reality in British Guiana. So, interracial fraternization was the order of the day for off-base recreation and entertainment. This breached Jim Crow policies. As a result, in 1943 a general order on dating was issued to American forces in British Guiana. According to this order, "officers have been seen in Georgetown with eminently undesirable companions" and that reflected "discreditably on the command and on the US." Here is an extract from the general order, which aimed at ending the practice immediately:

There is a strong color line observed in British Guiana; while it does not in any way affect inter-business relations among local inhabitants, it is very strongly marked in social contacts.

Generally speaking, social life in Georgetown may be divided in the following categories:

(a) British White
(b) Portuguese
(c) Mixed Portuguese
(d) Mixed Colored

Officers' dates should derive from (a) above and to a very limited extent from the upper group (b). Officers are advised that they are not expected to associate with groups in this Colony with which they would not associate at home. British officers and police have certain fixed social contacts. The American officer is categorized similarly and should conform to this social demarcation line.[21]

The order created "a storm of public criticism" and did not stop interracial sexual encounters by officers or their subordinates. Despite these injunctions, the relations developed. As Neptune observed, there may have been several reasons for this. On the part of US officers and servicemen, it may have been satisfying the fantasy of sex with the exotic "other," and in some cases genuine love. For the nonwhite women, he speculated it could have been "the desire for a Yank or by the covetous demand for the Yankee dollar." In her autobiography Helen Taitt supports Neptune's observations:

In the Caribbean, May Anne was "down by the seaside—sifting san wid de Yankee man!' . . . and in Georgetown, the girls were proud to do their seawall walks beside a USA uniform. Soldiers were there to supply us with all sorts of goodies from the P.X. . . . America was the wonderful place where film stars and cowboys and Mickey Mouse came from, and having all those Americans around us was almost as good as being there ourselves![22]

By the time the war ended in 1945, it was reported that there were seventy-nine brothels in Georgetown that catered to American servicemen.[23] The impact of the American presence was not only felt in Georgetown. The demand for prostitutes was also felt in the rural areas. A folk song performed by a retired Indian Guyanese female sugar worker during my field research in Albion, Berbice, in 2007 had the following line, "I don't want no Yankee in me bed." This referred to East Indian women in rural areas who were encouraged to come to Georgetown to work as prostitutes.[24] It was also estimated that during the war years, "one person in ten in the city [Georgetown] had venereal disease."[25] Clearly, access to the "Yankee bladder"—a euphemism for condoms—was limited to Yankees only.

The racial politics associated with the American presence in British Guiana also energized the color/caste dynamics in society. Light-skinned women privileged their European ancestry, hoping to pass for white, land a Yankee, and marry into a happy future. Marriage to women of color by US troops in the West Indies was difficult, as base commanders had to give permission for this. Many of the southern states in the United States did not permit interracial marriages.[26] The "one-drop" rule was also in effect. Many light- and brown-skinned girls found themselves in "temporary marriages," a term used to refer to marriages that took place in the West Indies between white soldiers and West Indian women of color. Those marriages were not considered legal in the segregated states of the United States. So, those marriages were really local and thus temporary. This was the reality enshrined in the chorus of King Radio's 1946 calypso "Brown Skin Girl"—"Brown skin girl stay home and mind baby / I'm goin away, in a sailing boat / And if I don't come back / Stay home and mind baby."[27]

"Brown Skin Girl," along with "Rum and Coca Cola" by Lord Invader and later "Jean and Dinah" by the Mighty Sparrow, is a penetrating appraisal of the racial and sexual dynamics of the presence of the American military in British Guiana and other parts of the West Indies during World War II. This assault on West Indian womanhood and undermining of West Indian masculinity contributed to the further energizing of nationalist impulses and in British Guiana served to encourage membership of the People's Progressive Party, which was founded by Dr. Cheddi Jagan on January 1, 1950.

In addition to its impact on race and social relations, the American presence also influenced the direction of political discourse in British Guiana. According to Carey Fraser, United States foreign policy during the early war years was anti-colonial, supporting self-government and independence for European colonies in the Caribbean. US foreign policy also recommended industrialization and agricultural diversification for these colonies. Although this rhetoric became muted after the successful execution of the Battle of the Caribbean and a shift in attention to Europe, left in place were a development paradigm oriented to industrialization, not mere supply of raw materials, and the idea of a federation-oriented mechanism similar to what Critchlow, Cipriani, Dinally, Lesperan, and other West Indian labor leaders had envisioned when they met in British Guiana in 1926.[28] These development visions informed the work of the US-sponsored and -funded Caribbean Commission. One of its staffers was Dr. Eric Williams, the future prime minister of Trinidad and Tobago and one of the architects of the Caribbean Free Trade Area (CARIFTA), the predecessor of the Caribbean Community (CARICOM). The United States did not formally give up Atkinson Field until 1966, when British Guiana gained its political independence.[29]

As the Americans needed relaxation and entertainment, so did stressed-out Guianese in urban, rural, and hinterland areas. A variety of musical ensembles provided the needed entertainment: swing bands featuring wind and brass instruments and male and female vocalists, calypso bands, and vaudeville musicians. Many villages had their own bands. The predominant instruments in African Guianese villages were guitar, banjo, quarto, mandolin, bass, drums, flutes, coronets, and shak shak. The popular instruments among bands in Indian Guianese bands were dholak, dhantal, harmonium, and finger cymbals. A cadre of musicians who had studied classical music in the United Kingdom started to return to the colony and reinvigorate the colony's classical music repertoire. Improved transportation and the ingenuity of promoters ensured that there was musical interchange among urban, rural, and hinterland musical communities.

Urban swing bands were in demand and performed at a variety of music-based entertainments, dances, picnic, fairs, and excursions. To protect themselves from unscrupulous promoters, bandleaders formed British Guiana Dance Orchestras Union in 1940 and registered it as a trade union on May 31, 1940. The records of the union were not accessible during the writing this book, so it is not possible to say if the union was successful or not. Clearly it was not, as claims of exploitation were still rife in the 1960s and 1970s. However, from the contemporary record it is clear that the bands were large, featuring wind and brass instruments and male and female vocalists. Among the most in-demand bands were the Pan Americans, the Lucky Strike Orchestra, Al Seales and His Washboard Orchestra, Harry Mayers and His Orchestra, Bert Rogers and His Aristocrats, Lew Spencer and His Rhythm Stompers Orchestra, Fred Rose and His Swing Serenaders, Harry Whittaker and His South American Band, Ivan Brace and His Royal Ambassadors, the Mootoo Brothers Orchestra, and Tillack's Indian Orchestra.

In addition to performing for dances, some of these bands were actively engaged in inter-county and inter-colonial swing competitions and the vaudeville circuit. At the inter-county level, the main competitors were Ivan Brace and Pan Americans from New Amsterdam, and Al Seales and the Washboards and Bert Rogers and the Royal Ambassadors from Demerara. Voting at these competitions was by acclamation, so when the competitions were held in Georgetown, the victor was usually a Demerara band; conversely, when the competition was held in New Amsterdam, the Pan Americans were always the winners. It seemed that bands played better on the home turf!

Calypsos became an extremely popular form of musical entertainment during the 1940s. As you may recall, it all started in 1931 with the Mighty Terror's visit for the British Guiana centenary and accelerated when Bill Rogers brought the Lord Caresser to tour British Guiana in 1938. Calypso's popularity continued to increase during the 1940s, and by the early 1950s British Guiana was an important creative venue for calypsonians such as Lord Melody and the Mighty Sparrow. Lord Melody would compose and record some of his classics, such as "The Devil," "Boo Boo Man," and "Happy Holiday," in British Guiana at the studios of Al Seales's GEMS Recording Company. The Mighty Sparrow would make his first recording at GEMS studio. In the 1940s British Guiana, a primarily Protestant Christian society, was the center for calypso during the post-carnival season. Trinidad was a primarily Roman Catholic society that "prohibited" calypso performances during Lent.

Other factors that contributed to the popularity of calypso in British Guiana during the 1940s were the ease of travel between the two countries and the increased availability of phonographs/records. Through recordings Guianese had access to the leading exponents of the art form of that era, among them Attila the Hun, Lord Beginner, the Caresser, the Commander, Lord Executioner, the Mighty Destroyer, the Growler, Lord Iere, the Roaring Lion, King Radio, the Tiger, and Lord Ziegfeld, along with Guianese such as Bill Rogers, Ralph Fitz Scott, Zeda Martindale, and Joe Coggins. The Mootoo Brothers Orchestra was one of the dominant studio bands accompanying Guyanese and Trinidadian calypsonians. The orchestra was also very popular on the Guyanese vaudeville circuit.

By the 1940s vaudeville had matured. In addition to providing popular entertainment, promoters and producers such Sam Chase, Bill Rogers, Prince Taylor, and Reginald Thornhill continued to use the vehicle to comment on social and political conditions. Some of the shows were titled *Fan Me Soldier Boy*, *She Wanted a Yankee*, and *Caribbean Nights*.[30] Vaudeville shows began to feature Trinidadian calypsonians such as Lord Invader. The extempore competitions he would have with Lord Coffee, the Guianese calypsonian, were popular. The Mootoo Brothers Orchestra was in demand. Superlatives have been have been used to describe the contributions of George (1910–1978) and Charlie Mootoo (1915–1955) to calypso music in Guyana and Trinidad. For more than three-decades, the bands these brothers organized accompanied some of the most innovative calypsonians in the world—Lord Beginner, Lord Iere, Lord Ziegfeld, the Commander, the Mighty Caresser, Attila the Hun, Terror, and the Roaring Lion.

These brothers, sons of an East Indian father and a mixed-race mother, had their musical origins in New Amsterdam, Berbice. Their mother introduced them to music and encouraged their pursuit. George's musical skills, especially his dexterity on the clarinet, were sharpened in the New Amsterdam–based No. 7 Militia Company Band. His brother Charlie, who was sight impaired, specialized in the saxophone and was described as a musician who "was sensitive to sounds and played anything that was given to him by George." The Mootoo brothers were trailblazers and the Guianese public enjoyed their musical innovations during the 1940s.[31] The Mootoo Brothers Orchestra accompanied the Tiger when he recorded the wartime calypso "Let Them Fight for a Thousand Years," which promoted the Grow More Food campaign in Trinidad and wittily commented on the exportation of arsenic contaminated sugar from Demerara: "Friends, they nearly kill this Tiger / With that arsenic sugar from Demerara / It appears as if we next door neighbour get bad / Demerara declare war on Trinidad."[32]

Most of the musicians in the Mootoo Brothers Orchestra and in the other popular bands in urban British Guiana were able to read musical scores. This was no doubt a consequence of the state of available music education. Formal, non-formal, and informal music education was provided by a number of organizations including the British Guiana Militia Band, the British Guiana Police Force Drum and Fife Band, the Band of No. 7 Militia Company, and the Salvation Army. The churches with their choirs and youth arms also contributed to this expansion in musical competence. Another contributing factor was the increasing number of private music teachers, who prepared students for the examinations of the Associated Board of the Royal Colleges of Music, London College of Music, Victoria College of Music, and Trinity College. These music educators, along with expansion in radio broadcasting and the spread of record players, also contributed to the broadening in musical tastes.

Another popular musician and bandleader of East Indian ancestry during the 1940s was the versatile Tillack. He was born in Port Mourant, a predominantly Indian plantation village in the Corentyne region of Berbice on April 21, 1904, to parents who had been indentured immigrants from India. He was named Brijbassee at birth, but his nickname was Tillack. In his magisterial book *Sweetening Bitter Sugar*, Clem Seecharan points out that because of the management practices of an early manager, the conditions of the people of the Port Mourant were somewhat better than most estates in British Guiana. The workers were treated more humanely; sanitation was better; workers were provided with land on which to grow rice and rear cattle. As a result it was noted that workers at Port Mourant "were discernibly more independent, confident, and ambitious."[33] But this did not mean life was just. Cheddi Jagan, one of the founders of the People's Progressive Party, and Guyana's president (1992-95), was also born in Port Mourant. He recalled the estate as a place that was segregated physically, socially, and psychologically. He called it a place of two worlds: "the world of the exploiters and the world of the exploited; the world of the whites and the world of the non-whites. One was the world of the managers and the European staff in their splendid mansions; the other the world of the labourers in their logies in the 'nigger yard' and the 'bound-coolie yard.'"[34] It was in this duality that Tillack grew up.

As a youth he was recognized as a musical protégé. He is known to have been a truant, preferring to spend time with the old-time Taan singers in the village. Taan singing is style of singing developed among Indian indentured immigrants in the West Indies and Suriname and is associated with classical Indian forms and sung in Hindi. In the early post-indenture era, a limited range of instruments—dholak, dhantal, manjira, and sitar—usually accompanied this singing style. By the 1930s the harmonium, a European reed organ, became increasingly popular. Initially, Taan singing was dominated by the raga tradition, with Prabhati, Bhairavi, Malkauns, Bihag, Thumri, and Dhrupads being the dominant ragas. However, by the 1930s with the arrival of Hindi film music and the proliferation of sound recordings from India, "film songs" and "record songs" began to influence the Taan singing styles. Taan has been described as a male-dominated, primarily vocal "local-classical music" "performed primarily in the context of weddings, occasional bhagvats, and wakes."[35] Taan signing has been identified as an important development in Indian expressive culture in the West Indies, as it reflected pride in India and progress from the disparaged "coolie culture." British Guiana quickly emerged as an important Taan center.

In rural agricultural areas of British Guiana, especially around the more productive sugar estates such as Port Mourant in the Corentyne, there emerged by the 1940s a class of East Indians who owned land, operated rice mills, reared cattle, and ran small businesses as tailors, tanners, and shopkeepers. From this group came the sponsors of Taan singers, employing them to perform at weddings, wakes, and a variety of religious "works." In many cases, they would take Taan singers into their homes for extended periods of time.

The Taan singer's repertoire was initially based on songs that celebrated the life of Lord Ram, who was emphasized in the religious traditions of the Bhojpuri region of North India—from which a majority of the Hindu and Moslem immigrants living in British Guiana came. Supporting Taan singers was akin to providing help to an ascetic, a holy man. Indeed, some of the influential Taan singers in British Guiana have been Pandits and Mulvis.

Taan singers would organize "ground singing" in public places during these periods as "artists in residence." These weddings, wakes, "works," and ground singing tended to be public events and attracted visitors from far and wide. More importantly, this style of music attributed respectability and was seen as distinct from the more raucous genres of East Indian folk music associated

Figure 5.1. Advertisement for show by Tillack, *Daily Argosy*, July 14, 1944.

with Matticore (a pre-marriage celebration) and in places like rum shops. Taan singers also participated in the performances of *Ramleela* and similar religion-based performances that toured rural East Indian communities in British Guiana during the first four decades of the twentieth century. Rural Indian communities were not cut off from the other entertainment practices that were taking place in the wider society. These communities were aware of the increasing popularity of vaudeville and variety shows. Taan singing became an element in the East Indian variant of the vaudeville and variety show. It was through the latter vehicle that Tillack made his presence felt in Georgetown in the 1940s.

According to the ethnomusicologist Peter Manuel, Tillack became the most revered Taan singer of Guyana during the twentieth century.[36] He also earned many names during his career, including the "Song Bird of Port Mourant." A self-taught multi-instrumentalist, he was versatile on the dholak, tabla, sitar, sarangi, harmonium, accordion, clarinet, saxophone, esraj, violin, banjo, and piano.[37] As a result of these competencies, Tillack was very popular in the Berbice East Indian music circuit. Tillack was also known as a follower of Mahatma Gandhi and for his passionate support of India's independence struggle. According to his son Jawaharlal Tillack, this passion was evident in the lyrics of his many compositions. Jawaharlal tells the story of an Indian dignitary visiting British Guiana in the late 1930s being so impressed by the pro-Indian independence lyrics of his father's songs that he "gave" Tillack the additional name Bal Gangadhar in homage to the Indian freedom fighter Bal Gangadhar Tilak, who is recognized as one of the first and strongest proponents of Swaraj (complete independence) and is considered the father of Hindu nationalism as well.[38] His famous statement "Swaraj is my birth right, and I will have it" is well-remembered in India today.[39] Port Mourant–born Brijbassee carried the name Bal Gangadhar Tillack with pride.

In time, Tillack's popularity extended beyond Berbice. On July 14, 1944, Tillack, "British Guiana's favourite Indian song bird and idol of Port Mourant," gave his first performance in Georgetown at the Cinema Olympic.

Other performers in the ". . . grand . . . Indian Musical Show" were Kamla Bai, Pita Pyrree, Ram Roop, and Master Kisson. The show's format was similar to that used for vaudeville shows of that era. It featured "delightful music, gay songs, and snappy jokes," and the anchor band was Tillack's Indian Orchestra.[40] Directed primarily at the popular Indian masses in urban British Guiana, this show signaled the presence of a significant urban East Indian audience. Prior to that show, many of the variety shows that did include Indian performers presented them as exotica—contortionists, wire walkers, and fire-eaters.

An important member of Tillack's first show in Georgetown was Pita Pyrree. Pita was born in Queenstown, Essequibo, and was orphaned at an early age. Her distinctiveness emerges from the fact that she was a pioneering East Indian female public dancer and singer. According to Rakesh Rampertaub, at the turn of the twentieth century and through most of the early decades of the twentieth century, Indo-Guianese women were prohibited from dancing in the public as it was considered unclean. At that time the practice was for men to perform the roles as female dancers; this was the practice in presentations such as *Ramleela*.

Tillack and Pita Pyrree were indicative of musical exchanges taking place in rural Indo-Guianese communities. Western musical influences were becoming evident in rural Indo-Guianese music. Tillack's dexterity with a wide range of Western musical instruments was one example of this development. New musical genres were incorporated as radios and record players were adopted in rural Guiana. Hindi film scores and recorded music by Indo-Caribbean musicians were also available. These new musical genres and sources would ultimately reduce the popularity of Taan singing and influence other forms of traditional Indian religious, folk, and popular music. These changes were most evident in Berbice.

By the late 1940s Tillack was touring Trinidad and Surinam. In the early 1950s he moved to Georgetown and became the host of the program *Geet Marala* on Radio Demerara, the successor station to VP3BG and VP3MR. Prior to his death in Georgetown in 1964, he had also served as a music tutor in training programs in Indian music organized by the recently created National History and Arts Council.

During the 1930s a number of Guianese went overseas to study music. Among the first was Vesta Lowe, who studied under Dr. William Levi Dawson and Portia Washington Pitman at the Tuskegee Institute in the United States through a Negro Progress Convention scholarship. In 1935 Philip Pilgrim was awarded a scholarship to study at the Royal Academy of Music. Lynette Dolphin and William Pilgrim followed him in 1937 and 1938 respectively. The return of Philip Pilgrim, Vesta Lowe, Lynette Dolphin, and later William Pilgrim to British Guiana had a positive impact on all aspects of music in the society. The effect would be evident in the expansion of musical appreciation, increased music composition, and the development of organizations to advance music education.

Philip Pilgrim returned in 1939 and his impact was evident in a number of ways. Before his sudden death in 1945, he gave a number of illustrated public lectures on music, presented a number of well-received concerts, and composed what has been described as "the most outstanding Caribbean musical composition of the twentieth century." His talks were given to a range of organizations including labor unions, women's clubs, and religious institutions. His concerts were acclaimed for their high quality and he was commended for elevating performance standards in the colony. His concerts were also the sites for innovation. For example, in 1940 and in 1941 he presented a series of recitals for two pianos with John Heuvel. These concerts presented popular classical compositions; for example, the February 11, 1941, concert featured Liszt's "Hungarian Rhapsody," Gershwin's "Rhapsody in Blue," and Grieg's "Peer Gynt Suite."[41] In this series of concerts Philip Pilgrim also demonstrated his virtuosity as a solo pianist. In 1951 the Jamaican music critic Rita Core declared Philip Pilgrim to have been one of the greatest pianists to have ever left the West Indies.[42]

Pilgrim's indelible mark was in the field of composition. On his return to British Guiana, Pilgrim returned to his upper-middle-class social moorings. His father, a fair-skinned Barbadian immigrant, taught mathematics at Queen's College, the elite grammar school for boys, and was the honorary local representative of the Associated Board of the Royal Schools of Music. Philip Pilgrim's social network included the emerging literary and artistic community, which included Arthur J. Seymour, the Bureau Public Information official, poet, and editor of *Kyk Over Al*. As mentioned earlier, this circle was already evincing proto-nationalist tendencies. Specifically, there was increasing interest in Guiana's hinterland mythologies and its flora and fauna; Seymour's epic poem *Legend of Kaieteur* was emblematic of this mood and orientation. The poem not only told the story of how the majestic waterfall got its name; it also helped popularize the theme of sacrifice for peace and nation building. The poem also inspired Pilgrim's composition.

Pilgrim and Seymour collaborated on the epic composition that was first presented on July 29, 1944, at the packed Assembly Rooms.[43] The work, which featured two pianos and allowed for improvisation by one of the pianists, was indicative of new compositional styles already evident in the modernist schools of composition in Europe. This style was a direct result of the musical exchange that had been taking place between jazz and European academic/classical music since the turn of the twentieth century and may have featured in his education at the Royal College of Music. The *Legend of Kaieteur* attracted positive acclaim from the Guianese critics. It was performed in Georgetown and in New Amsterdam. In 2004 the regional publication *Caribbean Beat* identified *Legend of Kaieteur* as the most outstanding Caribbean classical composition of the twentieth century.[44]

Vesta Lowe's return to British Guiana did not attract much fanfare. She had studied at Tuskegee Institute—a "Negro" college in the southern United States—and in those days of high colonialism and pretentiousness, that school, like most American colleges and universities, were not "recognized" by the colony's establishment. Another reason that has been offered was the fact that Lowe was dark-skinned and of rural origins. Despite these obstacles, she was also active in the musical milieu during the early years of the 1940s. One of her earliest acts upon her return to the colony was the creation of the Dawson Music Lovers' Club, named in homage to Professor William Levi Dawson, her mentor at Tuskegee. He had established an international reputation for arranging and conducting African American choral music. Vesta Lowe's early works in British Guiana emphasized her education in African American musical traditions, especially compositions inspired by the slavery experience. The early concerts by the Dawson Music Lovers' Club would invariably feature Negro spirituals including "Kind Jesus is List'ning" (Dawson), "Deep River" (Burleigh), "Listen to the Lambs" (Dett), "My Lord What a Mourning" (Dawson), and "Goin' Home" (Dvorak).[45]

The Dawson Music Lovers' Club did not limit its performances to urban areas of the colony. It also toured the rural areas, and this contributed to Vesta Lowe's efforts to seek out, recover, and promote the folk songs of the colony's African heritage. In addition to promoting music appreciation and conducting research on the colony's folk songs, she was also an effective music teacher. In 1941 Philip Pilgrim paid tribute to her skills as a teacher when he referred to the club's presentation of *Deep River*: "The Choir gave the best performance of 'Deep River' I have ever heard outside the talkies. The members have been trained to a high pitch of excellence by Miss Vesta Lowe, their leader, who has herself belonged to the famous Tuskegee Choir and was among those chosen to sing at the opening of Radio City" [New York].[46]

She also prepared students for the examinations organized by the Associated Board of the Royal Colleges of Music and Trinity College. Lowe, who majored in home economics at Tuskegee, was expected to become a member of the "Little Tuskegee" in British Guiana. This did not materialize, and despite her degree she found it impossible to obtain a permanent appointment in the colony's civil service. Despite those difficulties, she continued to collect and promote folk music. One of the persons she influenced in the process was James Alexander Phoenix—the founder of the Skeldon Music Lovers Choir and, in 1944, the British Guiana Police Force Male Voice Choir.[47] The Police Male Voice Choir's first public appearance was in December 1944, performing Christmas carols for patients at the public hospitals in Georgetown. In time, the British Guiana Police Male Voice Choir would incorporate the colony's folk songs in its repertoire, contributing to Vesta Lowe's goal of developing appreciation of the nation's folk songs, especially those songs associated with Kwe Kwe, work, and social commentary.

When E. O. Pilgrim, the honorary local representative for the Associated Board of the Royal Schools of Music, gave his report on the 1940 examinations, he identified fifty-four music teachers who had prepared students for those examinations. This was an increase of twenty-nine since the period 1920–31. At the same event, Alan John Knight, the bishop of Guiana, announced that, starting in 1941, he was going to award a prize for harmony, as an incentive for more students to study that subject. He also encouraged music teachers and students to draw upon other resources such as listening to "good music" on the radio to supplement what they were teaching and what they were learning. He concluded his remarks with the hope "that as the years progressed they would get more and more local compositions . . . and a large body of local composers."[48]

Lynette Dolphin's return to British Guiana would contribute to the achievement of some of the bishop's aspirations. In 1937 Dolphin was the second Guianese to win a four-year scholarship to study at the Royal Academy of Music in London. However, because of the illness and subsequent death of her mother, she did not take up that scholarship until 1939, arriving in London "September 3, 1939—the day Britain declared war on Hitler's Germany."[49] Lynette spent her early years in rural British Guiana. Her father, E. Lugard Dolphin, was headmaster of the De Willem Primary School on the west coast of Demerara and was known as "a martinet in the treatment of his school and his family."[50] From her accomplishments in the administration of cultural affairs in Guyana, it could be inferred that she developed her sense of order and skills at organization from her father.

Her mother, Clarice, who was born in Essequibo, was a member of the de Weever musical family. Clarice's father was Aloysius de Weever, a solicitor, at one time the organist at Brickdam Cathedral, and probably the first Guianese to build a complete organ and a piano in the colony in which local materials were used. Her uncle was P. M. de Weever, a "well known musician and composer"[51] of "Me Cawfee in de Marnin,'" which by 1940 had become popular across the West Indies to the extent that Jamaica has claimed it as an original example of the Mento style.[52]

Lynette's first music teacher was her mother, a trained primary school teacher and a talented musician. During the 1920s and 1930s Clarice Dolphin played a major role in training schoolchildren on the west coast of Demerara to perform at annual concerts held at De Willem Primary School for visiting inspectors of schools and sugar estate managers who lived in a ten-mile radius of the school.[53] Her musical tastes represented the times she lived in and her upbringing. The songs she taught schoolchildren were similar to the songs sung by schoolchildren in the United Kingdom, Georgetown and New Amsterdam, including "Come to the Field," "Who is Silvia," and "Under the Greenwood Tree." Lynette inherited from her mother a preference for music of the formal English style.

The Dolphin family came to Georgetown when E. Lugard Dolphin was appointed headmaster of the Broad Street Government School, the first non-denominational primary school to be built by the government of British Guiana. Prior to that all, primary schools in the colony were built and managed by churches with subventions from the government—the dual-control model. In Georgetown, Lynette attended Bishop's High School, the elite girls' school, and took music lessons from British Honduras–born Eleanor "Nell" Brown (later Eleanor Kerry). Lynette was an outstanding student and was popular as a soloist or accompanist on the Georgetown concert circuit in the late 1920s and 1930s. She continued to perform publicly until she left for the United Kingdom in 1939.[54] Billy Pilgrim has noted her "studies in London were interrupted when a bomb dropped on the house in which she was living injuring her and necessitating her return [to British Guiana]."[55]

Upon her return to the colony in 1942, she immediately returned to the concert circuit. She also went to work organizing the Schools Annual Musical Festival, a project inspired by her mother's work on the west coast of Demerara. The first festival, held at the Astor Cinema in Georgetown in 1943, featured a choir of one thousand children drawn from twenty-five schools. The British Guiana Militia Band, under the baton of now Major C. Henwood, accompanied the choir. According to a contemporary report, "for the second half of the program [Major Henwood] handed the baton over to Lynette, whose performance as a conductor received high praise from the audience."[56] Among the songs performed at the first Schools Music Festival were "Jerusalem," "Where'er You Walk," "Who is Silvia," "In Derry Dale," "Early One Morning," "Oh No John," "Summer Is a-Coming In," and "Come Follow Me." Sir Gordon Lethem, the governor, congratulated the organizers of the festival and suggested that more local songs be included in the future. In 1944 Hawley Bryant's "Song of Guiana's Children" and the Negro spiritual "Sometimes I feel like a motherless child" were part of the repertoire. Until 1958 the festival remained a fixture on the colony's musical scene. Lynette Dolphin also recognized the important place radio had in promoting music education and expanding musical tastes, so starting in 1944 she organized the series of radio programs titled *Musicians of Tomorrow*. The Bureau of Public Information, precursor to the post-independence Ministry of Information, produced the programs.[57]

Immediately after the end of World War II, Lynette Dolphin returned to the United Kingdom and completed her education. She earned the diplomas of Licentiate of the Royal Academy of Music (LRAM), Associate of the Royal College of Music (ARCM), and Graduate of the Royal School of Music (GRSM). By 1948 she was back in the colony, and became one of the founding members of the British Guiana Music Teachers' Association.

The inaugural meeting of the teachers' association was held on April 7, 1948, at the Georgetown home of Lynette Dolphin. The following were the agreed to aims of the association:

(a) to enlarge and improve the knowledge of music of its members and to stimulate their interest in every branch of musical development;
(b) to promote discussion on matters of interest to music teachers and to make united representation in any matter affecting the teaching of music in this country;
(c) to keep abreast of current musical events and modern methods of teaching;
(d) to undertake any other activity for the betterment of the Association.[58]

The British Council, an arm of British public diplomacy, allowed its offices, with its facilities for film shows and gramophone concerts, to be used as the meeting place for the association until 1960.[59] In May 1948 the teachers' association became a member of the British Guiana Union of Cultural Clubs.[60] As Lloyd Searwar reminisced in 2001, before the advent of the National History and Arts Council (ca. 1958) or the Department of Culture (ca. 1972), "the BG

Union of Cultural Clubs provided the framework of support for the quickening of cultural life" in British Guiana.[61]

In 1949 the British Guiana Music Teachers' Association reported fifty-nine members; forty-two were from "town" and seventeen were "country members." The "immediate need" during the first year "was better acquaintance with the subject matter of the new theoretical syllabus [of the Associated Board of the Royal Schools of Music]."[62] Major Henwood, director of music of the British Guiana Militia Band, was "consulted, and at his suggestion, Mr. Vincent de Abreu, a member of the band, was invited to give three talks on orchestral instruments. The first was on 'Woodwind Instruments,' the second dealt with 'An introduction to the Brass Instruments' and the third focused on 'The Combination of Woodwind and Brass Instruments.'" According to the first annual report, these illustrated talks "gave teachers an opportunity to see all the less familiar instruments and to hear them singly and in combination." De Abreu was accompanied on each occasion "by a small group of Militia bandsmen."[63]

Public education was established as an important task of the British Guiana Music Teachers' Association. Also during the first year, Lynette Dolphin gave a talk on the string quartet. F. H. Martin Sperry, an executive in the private sector (Weiting & Richter), lectured on the symphony. Other members of the association also contributed to the series of lectures on "the life and works" of major European composers. Mrs. Kerry's talk was on Haydn; Edna Jordan's lecture was on Mozart. M. Daniels presented the lecture on Beethoven. Winifred McDavid, E. de Weever, and Valerie Warner (later Valerie Rodway) presented lectures on Schubert, Chopin, and Schumann, respectively. Francis Percival Loncke, who returned to the colony in 1949, also gave a talk on his experiences during his year at Trinity College, where he had earned a licentiate in violin performance. In 1948 Loncke became the first Guianese to be awarded a British Council scholarship to study violin at Trinity College, London. By 1950 the association had seventy members,[64] and in the new decade expanded its influence on the colony's cultural life.

Radio broadcasting in the colony benefited from government investment during the 1940s. Radio became an important element in wartime communication, playing an important role in countering rumor and Axis propaganda while promoting loyalty to the Crown and the Allies. From the British Broadcasting Corporation (BBC) came regular newscasts and an expansive diet of musical programs, establishing a tone that would dominate radio broadcasting in the colony for the next three decades. In addition to serving as an information diffusion tool, radio also served as an important strategic entertainment vehicle. The latter function provided a platform for commercial advertisers and for the creative talents in the Bureau of Public Information (BPI) who

radio + wartime communication

produced musicals, dramatic works, and talks supporting and promoting government initiatives. During the 1940s the BBC also broadcast programs such as *Calling the West Indies* and *Caribbean Voices*, which featured successful Guianese personalities in the United Kingdom.[65]

The Guianese diaspora in London increased after the end of World War II, when some of those who volunteered to serve in the British Armed Forces opted to settle in the United Kingdom. Guianese were part of the great postwar West Indian immigration stream to the United Kingdom. The Guianese diaspora in the United States was also growing, with a majority settling in New York. In both of these locations were a number of musicians whose professionalism and talent was so significant that they had presence and influence in the musical life of their host societies. Among the celebrated during this period were Rudolph Dunbar and Rannie Hart in London and James Ingram Fox in New York.[66]

Rudolph Dunbar (ca. 1902–1985) achieved his peak as an international musician during the 1940s. Having established himself as a world-class clarinetist during the 1930s, by 1940 he had begun to assert himself as a conductor.[67] By the end of the decade he had conducted several of the leading British and European orchestras, including the BBC Symphony, the London Symphony Orchestra, France's Orchestra du Conservatoire, and the Berlin Philharmonic Orchestra. For his compatriots in British Guiana, the success of this former apprentice from the British Guiana Militia Band was especially inspiring.

Dunbar's journey to that place in Europe's classical music scene started in 1916 at the age of fourteen, when he joined the British Guiana Militia Band as an apprentice. After five years he left for New York to study music at the Institute of Musical Arts (now the Julliard School). There, Dunbar studied composition, clarinet, piano, and other musical subjects, and was recognized for being a talented clarinetist. He graduated after five years. While in the United States, Dunbar developed a long-lasting relationship with the African American composer William Grant Still. He also experimented with jazz, and in the mid-1920s was a clarinet soloist in recordings by the Plantation Orchestra.

In 1925 Dunbar traveled to Paris for post-graduate studies in music, specializing in the clarinet, and is credited for making the clarinet a concert instrument. A *Musical Courier* review of one of his concerts at the Salle Chopin (Plepal) stated, "Rudolph Dunbar, Negro clarinetist, gave an unusually beautiful program." The review continued, "It is seldom one sees such rapt attention by a large audience as Mr. Dunbar received. His virtuosity, purity of tone and well-round ability has placed him in the front rank of artists abroad." His repertoire was also extensive; in a contemporary newspaper review of one of his concerts in Paris, French pianist and music critic Maurice Dumesnil observed: "A clarinet recital is in itself a rarity. But an eclectic and tastefully arranged programme, such as Mr. Dunbar played is also uncommon. He went from Mozart to Debussy, through Weber and Chopin, all played with fine qualities, a rich, fluent mechanism, and excellent appreciation for the different styles of the composers. He was recalled many times." In 1931, his reputation as a gifted clarinetist and a world-class musician unassailable, Dunbar moved to London, where he established a school for clarinetists and wrote the influential textbook *Treatise on the Clarinet (Boehm System)*.

Dunbar also composed music and began his career as a conductor in London. He described his composition style as "ultra-modern." An example is *Dance of the 21st Century*, composed in 1938 for the Footlights Dramatic Club, Cambridge University. Dunbar conducted its American premiere during the late 1940s when the National Broadcasting Company (NBC) broadcast it coast-to-coast. This launched his conducting career in the United States. In addition to performing classical music, Dunbar also played jazz. Between 1931 and 1934, he led two orchestras in the United Kingdom: the All British Coloured Band, a.k.a. Rumba Colored Orchestra, and Rudolph Dunbar and His African Polyphony. These bands contributed to what John Cowley has called the underappreciated influence that West Indians musicians had on the evolution of popular music in Britain during the twentieth century.[68]

By the end of the 1940s, Rudolph Dunbar had achieved acclaim as a conductor, composer, and educator. However, by the end of the decade, he had a number of negative experiences with the gatekeepers at the BBC. In an interview with Alex Pascal about six months before his death in 1988, Dunbar spoke about the vindictiveness of a particular producer/director of music at the BBC who derailed his musical career in Europe. Dunbar described that director of music as "despicable and vile" and the BBC "as stubborn as mules and ruthless as rattlesnakes."[69]

Rannie "Hot Lips" Hart (1916–2006) arrived in the United Kingdom in 1948 as part of the massive wave of postwar immigrants from the West Indies. He was born in Hopetown, West Coast Berbice, on July 16, 1916, the youngest of eight siblings—four boys and four girls.[70] Like his older brother Victor, Rannie began his musical career in 1928 as a twelve-year-old apprentice in the British Guiana Militia Band. He spent eleven years in the band, rising through the ranks from second coronet to solo coronet. For his virtuosity on the coronet and his dulcet tone, he acquired the cognomen "Hot Lips." According to Val Wilmer, the British music historian, by the age of eighteen Hart was "British Guiana's hottest trumpeter." She added, "Throughout his life, the way he held his trumpet reflected his strict training as an army bandsman."[71]

Hart's post–militia band career is filled with innovation and travel. He founded the Syncopators Orchestra. When he left for Trinidad and Tobago in the early 1940s to join the Trinidad and Tobago Police Band, Tom Charles took over the Syncopators Orchestra. In 1948 Hart travelled to the United Kingdom and by August was leading a fourteen-piece band at the Queen's Hotel in London's Brixton district. The band had a singular mission: to popularize calypso music in London. In the process Hart gave Lord Kitchener, the Trinidad and Tobago calypso icon, a "break," and the rest is history. Hart and Kitchener became good friends, and he was featured on many of Kitchener's early London recordings.

While Rudolph Dunbar and Rannie Hart were engaging London during the 1940s, James Ingram Fox was facing Jim Crow in the United States and establishing a career as a classical musician. In 1940 the London Symphony Orchestra performed at the Royal Albert Hall the symphony *The Academic*, composed by the British Guiana–born James Ingram Fox (1909–2005) in 1939. When Fox passed away on February 8, 2005, at the age of ninety-six, he was probably Guyana's most prolific composer of classical music. He left an impressive collection of five symphonies, an opera, concerti, piano sonatas, choral works, and sixty songs. His obituary summarized his life as "true ambassador for music all over the world."[72]

Unlike Dunbar and Hart, James Ingram Fox was not a member of the British Guiana Militia Band. He was born into a middle-class family on February 18, 1909, in Georgetown, British Guiana. His father was a dentist, and the family hoped that James would study medicine. Like his relative Ken "Snakehips" Johnson, he too succumbed to the muse of music. In 1932 Fox enrolled at the New York College of Music and studied with Dr. August Fraemcke and Gottfried Kritzler. After earning his B.A. at the New York School of Music, Fox completed an M.A. in Music from Columbia University in 1938. After graduation Fox was unable to find a job as a full-time music teacher; he kept his job as an elevator operator and worked occasionally with Morton Gould, arranging music for Broadway shows. He maintained this relationship with Gould for many years and worked with him on musical compositions for radio.

After *The Academic*, Fox composed four other symphonies: *The Choral* (on the "Ode to Nativity" by Milton), *The Hinterland* (dedicated to the people of Guyana), *The Emancipation*, and *Southland*. Fox's compositions were included in a 1950 concert of symphonic music composed by black composers organized by Dean Dixon. In addition to compositions by Fox, the concert featured music by Samuel Coleridge Taylor (1875–1912) of England, and Ulysses Simpson Kay (1917–1995) and William Grant Still (1895–1978) of the United States. The concert attracted the attention of many influential white musicians such as Aaron Copeland, Samuel Barber, and Serge Koussevitzky, and opened doors for Fox. He obtained his first job as a music director, at Wiley College in Marshall, Texas. His academic music career eventually took him to New York

The New Engineer anxiously wonders if the Brakeman will play his " customary " part.

Figure 5.2. Editorial cartoon, *Daily Argosy*, May 19, 1942.

University, Dartmouth College, Western Michigan University, University of Chicago, and his alma mater Columbia University. While continuing his academic career, he arranged music for Morton Gould and began exploring African rhythms and integrating them into his piano compositions. This creativity is evident in the opera *Dan Fodio*. Dean Dixon considered this opera to be a masterpiece "because of the tessitura (the position of tones in instruments) and the manner in which he used complex rhythms."[73]

Fox never lost his Guyanese roots. He loved and celebrated his African heritage and African musical creativity. In an interview with Talise Moorer of the *New York Amsterdam News* in 1998, Fox reflected: "Black music will add creativity and new dimension to any music you have. . . . I would like to see all students of musicology travel to Africa to absorb these beats."

Throughout the 1940s there were continuing demands for improvements in the British Guianese political environment by trade union leaders, African-Guianese ethnic organizations, and Indo-Guianese religious and ethnic organizations for universal adult suffrage without literacy tests.[74] In 1942 there was anticipation of change with the arrival of Sir Gordon Lethem as governor. He was described as the "new engineer" in a political cartoon published in the *Daily Argosy* on May 19, 1942.

In December 1943 Port Mourant–born Dr. Cheddi Jagan, aged twenty-five, returned from Northwestern University in Chicago, Illinois, to launch his career as a dentist. In the music collection he brought back to British Guiana were recordings by Paul Robeson. His American-born wife Janet (née Rosenberg) also arrived in British Guiana in 1943. Jagan recalled that on his arrival there was no active political party as "the Popular Party of the late 'twenties and 'thirties had become defunct."[75] He described the Legislative Council as a "debating society" and suggested that Critchlow, Edun, and Jacobs, although members of the Legislative Council and representing labor unions, did not form a mass party and did not "involve the people in any significant way in their politics and protests."[76]

Jagan also considered the ethnic organizations to be deficient politically, especially the League of Coloured People (LCP), which had replaced the NPC as the dominant urban organization representing African Guianese interests, and the British Guiana East Indian Association (BGEIA). These perspectives were supported by other members of the society, especially a group that met weekly at the Carnegie Library. In 1946, along with Janet Jagan, Jocelyn Hubbard, and Ashton Chase, Cheddi Jagan formed the Political Action Committee (PAC) and its organ the *PAC Bulletin*. The aims of the PAC were:

> To assist the growth and development of the Labour and Progressive Movements of British Guiana, to the end of establishing a strong, disciplined and enlightened Party, equipped with the theory of Scientific Socialism;

> To provide information, and to present scientific political analyses on current affairs, both local and international; and

> To foster and assist discussion groups, through the circulation of Bulletins, Booklets and other printed matter.[77]

Also formed in 1946 was the Women's Political and Economic Organization (WPEO). Janet Jagan was the founding general secretary; other founding members were Winifred Gaskin and Frances Stafford.

Cheddi and Janet Jagan participated in the 1947 general elections as independent candidates. Janet was a candidate for the Georgetown seat; she lost the election to John Fernandes. However, Cheddi Jagan won his contest against John D'Aguiar. During the election many forces were mobilized against the Jagans. In addition to raising the issues of Cheddi Jagan's race and that he was not a Christian, also invoked was the "red scare"—the anti-communism appeal first used against Hubert Nathaniel Critchlow in the 1920s. As an independent member of the legislature, Jagan's attention focused on the range of political, social, and economic challenges facing British Guiana in the late years of the 1940s. Not only were the Guianese masses not enfranchised, political power still resided in the hands of the white urban elite, with the British governor at the helm. In the 1940s national governance was not participatory; "the voices of the most vulnerable were not heard,"[78] and the decision-making and implementation processes were not transparent, responsive, efficient, or effective.

In 1942 Forbes Burnham was the winner of the single British Guiana scholarship, and proceeded to study at London University, from which he graduated in 1948. On his return to British Guiana, Burnham also became active in the politics of colony. He too was concerned with the conditions of the masses. On January 1, 1950, the Peoples' Progressive Party (PPP) was formed; organized according to Leninist theory, the PPP was a vanguard party with a democratically elected leadership but managed according to "democratic centralism." Command and control was the dominant operational style, which ironically was conceptually similar to the practices that undergirded colonial governance. The only difference was who the intended beneficiaries were. For the PPP, the beneficiaries were to be the British Guianese working class, as opposed to the narrow ruling-class cliques in British Guiana and London. Burnham was the founding chairman of the PPP, Janet Jagan the general secretary, and Cheddi Jagan as leader.[79] This first mass political party to be formed in the colony would influence all aspects of political, economic, and cultural life for the remainder of the century and into the early decades of the twenty-first century.

The 1940s was a decade of "gathering." Several forces and institutions that would inform Guyanese musical life over the next fifty years were already evident. The musical repertoire of the colony was increasingly diverse and was becoming more complex and sophisticated. However, viewing British Guiana from the United Kingdom in 1945, Denis Williams was somewhat disillusioned with the governance practices of the polity and the consequences that had on Guianese creativity and identity. He famously declared:

> We are still dominated by the sun—strangers in a land we call our own. There is no Guianese people. Only an accumulation of persons—end products of a various history. Images in mud of the distant alien. Here patterns kill us, and the spiritual bullying of foreigners forever consents to the act. Incoherence, apishness, sentimentality, uncreativeness. . . . The truth is, we are a lot of persons and a lot of races, with a super village mentality.[80]

Rectifying that reality was the cultural task of the 1950s, and music had a role to play in that effort.

6

The 1950s: The Rise and Fall of Self-Determination

The four governors of British Guiana during the 1950s had to navigate several significant international and domestic realities. As representatives of the Crown they had to implement imperial policies related to decolonization and the "realpolitik" of the Cold War. For Great Britain, India's political independence in 1947 signaled the start of the end of the Empire and the emergence of the Commonwealth—a collectivity theoretically based on equality. So for British Guiana, the question of independence was not if but when. The determination of when had to respond to the dynamics of the Cold War in the hemisphere. Since the end of World War II, the United States was adamant that the Caribbean was not going to be aligned with the Soviet Union and its Communist ideology.

At the start of the decade, the governor was Sir Charles Campbell Woolley. He had been governor since April 1947 and would continue until October 1953. Along with the local ruling elite and their allies in the private sector, the governor was engaged in preparing the colony for political independence, and this included the development of a more inclusive constitution. On January 1, 1950, the first mass party in the colony, the People's Progressive Party, was formed, and among its demands were universal adult suffrage and political independence. Guianese intellectuals, artists, and other creative personalities such as Denis Williams, Elsa Gouveia, Wilson Harris, Martin Carter, Jan Carew, A. J. Seymour, E. R. Burrowes, Lynette Dolphin, Rajkumari Singh, Sydney King, Cicelene Baird, Vivian Lee, and Al Seales subscribed in some form or other to the proposition that political independence had to be constructed upon a foundation of cultural confidence. For these opinion leaders and cultural influentials, cultural confidence required the recognition and celebration of the common histories of struggles that united the colony's people together and nourished and nurtured confident creativity that strove to bring to birth a people—the Guyanese—who transcended individual ethnicities. As a result of the state of organizing capacity in the colony's political and cultural realms, things moved quickly on all fronts—and music was associated with all of them. For example, in July 1952 the first national festival of music was held in the colony.

More than five thousand persons representing musicians from every county in the colony participated in the July 1952 British Guiana Festival of Music. The organization and execution of the festival demonstrated high levels of cooperation and coordination among individuals and institutions in the public sector, the private sector, and civil society. The governor was the festival's patron, and that set the tone for the public sector. The Town Halls in Georgetown and New Amsterdam, along with the auditoriums at Queen's College and Bishop's High School, were available as venues. In addition, the Transport and Harbours Department subsidized transportation for participants from the rural areas who had to travel into Georgetown for the national finals. F. H. Martin-Sperry, a senior executive from Weiting & Richter, a prominent Water Street firm specializing in shipping, ice making, cold storage, and beverage manufacturing, as chairman of the music festival committee spearheaded fund-raising through the recruitment of foundation members from the private sector and civil society. The British Guiana Music Teachers' Association was one of the first foundation members and contributed $100 to the festival fund. The proprietors of the Astor and Plaza cinemas in Georgetown, the Globe Cinema in New Amsterdam, and the Sarswattie Cinema in Richmond, Essequibo, donated those places as venues for the festival. The origins of this multi-partner approach to cultural events in Georgetown can be traced to modus operandi developed by the Union of Cultural Clubs during the 1930s and the 1940s.[1]

The idea of organizing a competitive music festival in Guiana is attributed to Dr. Frederick Stanton, who had visited the colony as the music examiner for the Royal Schools of Music in 1944. The idea was kept alive when the British Guiana Music Teachers' Association was formed in 1948. In 1950, in collaboration with the music officer of the British Council, a music festival committee was formed and the first festival scheduled for 1952. By 1950 the colony had an impressive pool of music teachers and musicians who were aware of the ideas behind competitive amateur musical festivals in the United Kingdom. Those British festivals had their origins in the choral festivals held in British cathedrals and large churches starting in the early 1870s. In Britain the founding goal was to improve the musical competencies of local choirs. Another idea behind the organization of amateur music festivals in the United Kingdom was the theory of "aesthetic force," which held that "good music" had the capability of uplifting the poor. The theory posited that the poor were poor because of their cognitive inferiority, and further proposed that music, "the first of the fine arts . . . has a special 'aesthetic force' that energizes the minds of

Table 6.1

Categories and Test pieces: British Guiana Music Festival 1952.
New Amsterdam Adult Preliminaries, Friday, July 11, 1952

Category	Test Pieces
Soprano Solo	"Unmindful of the Roses" (C. Rosen) and "Still the lark finds repose" (Ella Ivimey)
Mezzo-Soprano	"To the Children"
Baritone Solo	"Sea Fever" (John Mansfield and John Ireland)
Mixed Vocal Duet	"Sweet Phyllis" (F. E. Wetherly)
Vocal Duet (Women's Voices)	"O Happy Fair" (Sir Henry Bishop)
Mixed Vocal Quartet	"Polly Willis" (Dr. T. A. Arne)
Ladies Choir	"The Lord is My Shepherd" (Schubert)
Mixed Voice Choirs	"There us Lady Sweet and Kind" (Peter Warlock) and "Through Bushes and Briars" (Mr. Potpher and Vaughn Williams)
Church Choirs	"Praise the Lord, His Glories Show" (Hal H. Hopson)

Source: *Daily Argosy*, July 9, 1952.

cognitively passive people." It was not much of a leap to transfer this theory to the colonies of the British Empire. Since the late nineteenth century, colonial officials were seeking strategies to address the consequences of being poor in the urban ghettos of British Guiana.[2] In the United Kingdom, it was argued that music's aesthetic force could "civilize the savage."[3] Similar ideas were already being applied in the curriculum for the Onderneeming Boys School. The victors at British music festivals had substantial bragging rights for being the best performers in their categories. In racially hierarchic British Guiana, a victory had race, color, and class implications. It also called into consideration community pride—urban over rural.

For the first festival, there were vocal, instrumental, and verse-speaking competitions. In addition, there was a competition for composition. The festival committee established a curriculum of test pieces, dominated by British compositions; made arrangements for the festival adjudicator; and developed a system of preliminaries in the counties of Berbice, Demerara, and Essequibo. For the first festival there were 974 entries, of which 728 came from Demerara, 186 from Berbice, and 60 from Essequibo.[4] Table 6.1 provides details of test pieces for some of the festival's categories.

Volunteers from the BGMTA, led by Eleanor Kerry and later Elaine Stephenson, established the nimble administrative network needed to execute the colony-wide festival. The festival organizing committee also subscribed to the British system and did not offer monetary prizes for the winners; instead medals, cups, and certificates were to be awarded according to three categories—Honors, First-Class, and Second-Class.[5] The festival's motto was "The object is not to gain a prize, but to pace one another on the road to excellence."

The adjudicator for the inaugural festival was Vernon Evans, MMus, ARCO, who at that time was the music advisor to the Government of Trinidad and Tobago and attached to the Department of Education. Evans earned his academic degrees at the University of Wales and after graduation lectured in music at the Coleg Harlech, Wales. In his professional career he served as an organist at the Cathedral of Llandoff, and in Leeds he was music advisor to the United Kingdom's National Council of Social Services.[6]

The public was enthused. The proliferation of formal and informal music education initiatives such as the British Council's radio programs, public concerts by the British Guiana Militia Band, Sunday afternoon concerts held in urban and rural churches and school halls, and the decade of School Music Festivals had created a society whose musical tastes included the appreciation of the repertoire that was being privileged during the festival of music. As a result of the publicity and promotion program developed by A. J. Seymour, the press showed interest in the event and provided daily details on what was transpiring, including the results from the countrywide preliminaries. For example, the press reported on the start of Berbice preliminaries, which more than five hundred persons attended. In addition to capturing the public's imagination, the festival stoked regional pride and to some extent provided an opportunity to debunk some of the ancient class and color stereotypes. In his opening remarks to the Berbice preliminaries, the mayor of New Amsterdam, J. T. Clark, a Guianese of African ancestry, reminded the adjudicators about "the high musical reputation which Berbice enjoys."[7] He also reflected on the test pieces and hoped that more local compositions would be used in the future.

The nationwide preliminaries began to draw attention to emerging talent. From Georgetown was eleven-year-old Jocelyne Loncke, who was adjudged the best of the fifteen finalists in the Under 14 pianoforte preliminaries and whose test piece was Arne's "Gig on G." Other participants from Georgetown who attracted attention were the pianists Hugh Sam and Ray Luck. The New Amsterdam preliminaries drew attention to performers such as Edith Pieters, Stephen Bobb-Semple, Annie Rambarran, Norma Romahlo, Moses Telford, and Vernon Williams.

Musicians from Georgetown were expected to dominate the festival and win most of the festival's prizes. It was anticipated that the musical ensembles from the British Guiana Philharmonic Society, led by Dorothy Taitt, would dominate the festival. This did not happen! When the final tally was completed, musicians from New Amsterdam topped the list, demonstrating "the high musical reputation" that Mayor Clark had alluded to. Among Berbice's victories were first, second, and third prizes for the Women's Vocal Duets (test piece "O Peaceful Night"); first and second prizes in the Under 14 pianoforte solo competition; third prize in the tenor solo; and first prize in the Children 16 and Under choral completion. Norma Romahlo won the solo pianoforte competition and Moses Telford third (test piece Beethoven's "Rondo" from *Sonata Op. 13*); the New Amsterdam Music Society (NAMS) choir won the competition for Mixed Voices Choir (test piece Vaughn Williams's "Through Rushes and Briars") with a performance that the adjudicator described as "singing such as I have never heard before";[8] Moses Telford and Cicely Hoyte were first and second place winners for the Under 18 Pianoforte solo (test piece Sterndale Bennet's *Rondino*); Telford and Hoyte were also the first prize winners for the piano duet competition; Annie Rambarran won the adult soprano competition. Rambarran and Vernon Williams were winners of the mixed vocal duets; in second place were Edith Pieters and Stephen Bobb-Semple, and in third were Stephanie Campbell and Clarence McKenzie (test piece "Sweet Phyllis"). Edith Pieters won the mezzo-soprano competition (test piece "To the Children"). The Vireo Trio, also from Berbice, won first place in the Women's Vocal Trio with their rendition of William Shields's "O Happy Fair," which was based on words from Shakespeare's *A Midsummer Night's Dream*. The Berbicians Norma Romahlo and Cicely Hoyte also won the pianoforte duets with their rendition of "Allegro and Adagio" from Mozart's *Sonata in B Flat*.

On the final night of the festival, the Berbicians won three of the four cups that were awarded for adult competitions. The NAMS Choir won the best adult choir cup. Annie Rambarran won the cup for best vocal soloist and Norma Romahlo won the cup for best instrumental soloist.[9] In his concluding remarks at the final session of the first British Guiana Festival of Music, Martin-Sperry, president of the festival committee, reported that the festival attracted 974 entries involving 5,250 persons. He also reviewed the organization and outcomes of the festival:

> Competitions included vocal, instrumental, solos, trios, quartettes, choral, verse speaking and composition entries. We used seven different halls, four in Georgetown, two in Berbice, and one in Essequibo. We had in the preliminaries 12 sessions, six in Georgetown, four in Berbice and two in Essequibo and twenty-one sessions for the Adjudicator in Georgetown, i.e., thirty-three in all. The attendance is estimated at rather more than 23,000, including competitors, i.e., about one in nineteen of the whole population in the colony.[10]

The festival was also an organizational achievement. Martin-Sperry provided details on the nature and scope of this achievement in his closing remarks:

Figure 6.1. L to R: Elaine Stephenson, Major Henwood, Mrs. Hough, Lynette Dolphin, V. J. Sanger-Davies, Florizelle Francis. Photograph courtesy of Elaine Stephenson.

You can well imagine the work of organization, classification, preparation of marking sheets, certificates, printing the syllabus, the programmes and tickets, the transportation of pianos and instruments, the accommodation of children, borrowing many articles, hiring halls, lighting, microphones and many arrangements, with the tremendous amount of detail that all this entails, which further, does not include the onerous work of the judges of the preliminary competitions.[11]

Among the key players in executing British Guiana's first music festival were Lynette Dolphin, A. J. Seymour, Celeste Dolphin, and Elaine Stephenson. These persons became the organizational backbone for all the future music festivals and a majority of the major national cultural events to take place in country for most of the next five decades.

The Berbice contingent returned to New Amsterdam as conquering heroes and were celebrated for surpassing "the most optimistic expectations." A public function, chaired by the Hon. W. O. R. Kendall, MLC, was held at the Town Hall in New Amsterdam on July 25 at which gifts were presented to Ruby McGregor, LRSM, Annie Rambarran, and Edith Pieters for "the part they played in training of the choirs under them." Special praise was given to McGregor, who was described as "the chief architect of a glorious festive record." In addition to a gift and check, McGregor was also presented with an illuminated address, which read in part:

Never in the history of the Ancient County, have such feats been accomplished in the realms of song and music, and never was there a more energetic, assiduous, helpful, and successful teacher of music than yourself. Your name will go down to posterity as one who in your day and generation, had done a great service to your community and mankind—a service which generations yet unborn will appreciate and strive to emulate.[12]

The seed sown by Ruby McGregor during the 1930s had borne fruit. At the end of the festival, it was clear that Guianese had demonstrated world-class competence with Western musical styles but did not appear have a body of domestic compositions upon which to evaluate musical proficiencies. The elections of 1953 would identify the range of musical options that were available in the colony to rectify that deficiency.

Recorded music, chants, slogans, folksongs, school yard ditties, and political songs were among the communication devices used by the young People's Progressive Party as they mobilized the nation for the first general elections based on universal adult suffrage in 1953. In addition to universal suffrage, the new constitution shifted power to elected officials; the governor retained power for external affairs—the start of the era of internal self-government, preparation for independence. It was a significant move from the Crown Colony status that had existed since 1928.

Former president Janet Jagan in 2007 recalled the party's use of recorded music played through mobile public address systems to "warm up" the crowds before speeches at public meetings. She recalled the popularity of recordings by Paul Robeson, especially those that celebrated the working-class struggle.[13] Robeson, an African American, was in the 1950s a world-class multi-lingual, basso cantante concert singer. Known for his support of the struggle for civil rights in the United States and his support for the Soviet Union, he was popular among progressive political circles around the world. When the Jagans returned from the United States, recordings by Robeson were part of their record collection. Some members of the PPP developed personal friendships with Robeson as a result of contacts in the international progressive circuit. Brindley and Patricia Benn became close friends with Paul and Eslanda Robeson. Patricia Benn confirmed that their first son Robeson was named after Paul Robeson and their first daughter Eslanda, after Robeson's wife.[14]

Chants of slogans, folk songs, and schoolyard songs were also used effectively during the public meetings. Jai Narine Singh recalled the rhythmic chanting of the slogan "The time has come for change" during the 1953 campaign.[15] Maurice St. Pierre provides an illuminating example of Forbes Burnham using the call-and-response patterns of "Rick-chick-chick/Conga-tay," a song from a schoolyard game, to "elicit positive responses from listeners" at a public meeting held by the PPP at Bourda Pasture/Green. According to St. Pierre, "Burnham established a dialogue with his listeners by utilizing the words of a song used by children at play, during which a child playing the role of first mother hen would seek to protect her chickens form the predatory efforts of a second mother hen," as follows:

First Mother Hen:	Rick chick chick chick
Chickens:	Conga-tay
First Mother Hen:	See fowl mama
Chickens:	Conga-tay[16]

In this situation, Burnham was playing the role of the first mother hen protecting "his listeners from the predatory actions of the second mother hen, Britain, which was known as the mother country."[17] Locally composed political songs were also used in the run-up to the 1953 elections.

The use of locally composed political songs can be traced to the work of Sydney King and Demerara Youth Rally and the Pioneer Youth League, the youth section of the PPP founded in 1952.[18] Lusignan-born King's commitment to utilizing music and drama to raise political consciousness and promote social change was honed in the Demerara Youth Rally (DYR). In that organization he collaborated with the late Cecilene Baird, a fellow East Coaster, to produce the musical *Christus the Messiah*. Eusi Kwayana wrote the libretto and Baird composed the music. The aim of the work was to demonstrate Christ's connection with the masses—a connection that had relevance to the political struggles taking place in British Guiana during the early years of the 1950s.

Kwayana also wrote the lyrics for "The Song of the Demerara Youth Rally," the theme song for the movement.[19] The first of three verses articulated the cause, calling upon young men and women to not be "content with pauper's lots" and urging them to organize to "soon possess our land." The second verse declared "war to kings of greed and selfishness" and "all the prophets of doom" and identified "liberty [and the] pursuit of happiness" as the ultimate destination. The final verse required the youth to "be the allies of the people" in building "a brave new world, not with atom bombs, not with murder, but with toil."

The song was sung to the melody from the *String Quartet in C Major (The Kaiser-Quartet), Op. 76, no. 3* composed by Joseph Haydn in 1797[20] and popularized as the German national anthem and the hymn "Glorious Things of Thee Are Spoken." In addition to local compositions, such as Kwayana's "The Song of the Demerara Youth Rally," DYR also used Paul Robeson's renditions of spirituals such as "Go Down Moses," "Deep River," and "Sometimes I Feel Like a Motherless Child" in its mobilizing work. According to Eusi Kwayana, the struggles that Robeson sang about resonated with the conditions of working people who lived in the villages and estates on the east coast of Demerara.

Robeson's aspirations were in harmony with those of the Guyanese working class at that time. Internationally, throughout the early decades of the twentieth century political songs and anthems had a central place in labor and progressive circles.

By 1953 Kwayana had composed "The Red Flag," the song of the People's Progressive Party. Like "The Song of the Demerara Youth Rally," the dominant themes in this party song focused on mobilization for independence, independence for Guyana, the celebration of human dignity, and resistance to domination. This anthem had four verses. Like "The Song of the Demerara Youth Rally," the first verse articulated the cause, reminding "fighting men" to break the bonds of slavery and create a land of liberty under the PPP: "The mighty land Guyana we / Shall make a land of liberty / We're staying with the P.P.P. / To keep the red flag flying!" The second verse emphasized the intention of building a free society, not one that was "halfway slave and halfway free." The third and fourth verses stressed the importance of being steadfast, with "every woman, every man" working to materialize "our brave progressive plan" and "marching with the PPP to keep the red flag flying!"

Sydney King/Eusi Kwayana remained connected with Guyana's political life for the remainder of the twentieth century. Over the next three decades, Kwayana wrote anthems for other political parties in Guyana. He has made it clear that he is not a composer of music but recognizes the importance of using popular melodies in creating political songs. He has acknowledged his indebtedness to the melodies of the Anglican hymnal and socialist Europe. The melody used for the PPP song is similar to the British Socialist Party's song and the Christmas carol "O Tannenbaum." As Tim Blanning has noted, successful political anthems are invariably built on popular melodies, as this makes for easier memorization and establishes solidarity.[21] Along with the PPP song was the gesture of the raising the index, middle, and ring fingers of the right hand. These three fingers reflected the 3 Ps—the PPP. The 1953 election campaign was hot, with the *Daily Argosy* leading a vigorous anti-communist offensive in which cartoons were used—clearly recognizing the power of images and the significant levels of illiteracy among potential supporters of the PPP.

The PPP won eighteen of the twenty-four contestable seats in the 1953 general elections.[22] H. R. Harewood, the registration officer for the elections, described the elections as "the most orderly election within memory."[23] The *Argosy* reported "polling was heavy and orderly [with] the women out numbering the men by more than 10 to 1 in most cases"; 74 percent of the total electorate voted.[24] On April 30, 1953, six days after the PPP victory, the new governor, Sir Alfred Savage, lifted the ban, which had been imposed since the mid-1930s, prohibiting music bands from accompanying May Day

Figure 6.2. Editorial cartoon, *Daily Argosy*, May 10, 1953.

Parades.[25] The parade for Labour Day 1953 was accompanied by "a steel band and a band of brass music" and was described as being three miles long with "some 30,000 people" participating.[26] On the same day, the new governor also consented to be the patron for the Second British Guiana Festival of Music.[27]

The euphoria associated with the victory of the multiracial mass party did not last for long. Within days there was a leadership crisis within the PPP, which Jagan described in his autobiography *The West on Trial*: "Winning the election was only the first battle. The next was to select ministers and submit names to the Governor. This is where the trouble began. For nearly a whole week the party was plunged into a crisis. The rank and file who were elated by our victory could not understand why. The reason was Burnham's demand to be 'leader or nothing.'"[28] What was taking place was an internal ideological struggle. Contemporary political lore has it that the moderates wanted to get rid of the "Reds." The editorial cartoon presented in the *Daily Argosy* of May 10, 1953, described the struggle between Jagan and Burnham as an example of the PPP's "split personality."

In the absence of a perspective from Forbes Burnham, the Cheddi Jagan interpretation has emerged as gospel. The "moderates" did not get their way.[29] It must be noted that the average age of the new government was twenty-eight, and ministers did show a substantial amount of naïveté in governance and a proclivity to use extreme Marxist/Leninist jargon.[30] Within two months of the PPP's victory, the colony was called upon to celebrate the Coronation of Queen Elizabeth II.

On March 1, 1953, about a month before the general elections, a nineteen-person Coronation Celebrations Advisory and Coordinating Committee was established in the colony under the chairmanship of W. J. Raatgever, C.B.E., president of the Georgetown Chamber of Commerce. Committee members included the mayors of Georgetown and New Amsterdam, Mrs. J. B. Singh, Mrs. D. J. Taitt, and Lynette Dolphin. The committee's secretary was A. J. Seymour, assistant public information officer in the Bureau of Public Information. The presence of Taitt, Dolphin, and Seymour on the committee was a clear indication that music had an important role to play in the coronation celebrations.

The slogan for the Guianese celebrations was "The People Rejoice" and the aim of the celebrations was to demonstrate that British Guiana was joining the British Commonwealth of Nations in rejoicing the coronation of the Queen, "the young mother of a great family of nations embraced within the golden circle of the crown."[31] Like the rest of Empire, efforts were made to incorporate music composed in the United Kingdom and other parts of the Empire in the Guianese celebrations.

British Guiana's celebrations did feature lots of music. Lynette Dolphin, who had demonstrated her effectiveness in organizing and training school choirs, was tasked with preparing a choir featuring the voices of one thousand schoolchildren. The British Council, a public diplomacy arm of the British Government in the colony, played an important role in orienting the colony to London's preferred music for this grand moment. One of the vehicles used was a series of music programs on Radio Demerara. The flagship program for the British Council was *Music for You*, which aired from 9:15 to 10:00 p.m. on Sundays and featured British composers such as Edward Elgar, John Ireland, and Henry Purcell. Radio Demerara, in collaboration with the BBC, presented during May 1953 a "special series of "Coronation Concerts on Sundays from 6:00 to 7:00 p.m." Those concerts dealt "with the festive music associated with the Coronation and [included] music specially composed for the occasion."[32]

Special emphasis was placed on children, with the hope that they would have "lovely memories of the day and the week." In addition to marches, there was a special party for four hundred children at the governor's residence, and special coronation medals, a gift from the Demerara Bauxite Company. The centerpiece of the Guianese children's involvement in the celebrations was the annual music festival for Georgetown schools, which was launched during Coronation Week. As usual, the event took place at the Astor Cinema and featured a thousand-voice choir drawn from twenty schools, conducted by Lynette Dolphin with musical accompaniment provided by the British Guiana Militia Band under the baton of Major S. W. Henwood. Reflecting previous criticisms, the festival's repertoire included international and local compositions. The international compositions included Shaw's "Hymn for the Queen," Thiman's "The Spacious Firmament on High," Alford's "The Smithy," Saville's arrangement of "Here's a Health unto Her Majesty," Holst's "I Vow to Thee My Country," the Valse Lente "Saints and Sinners," and Coates's "Youth of Britain." From Jamaica came Campbell's "A Cloud." Local compositions included the "Coronation March" composed by F. H. Martin-Sperry and the "Song for Queen Elizabeth," whose lyrics were written by A. J. Seymour, who also wrote the lyrics for the two-part song "Buttercup."

For Sir Alfred Savage, who took the governor's office on April 14, 1953, the 1953 Music Festival of Georgetown Primary Schools was his first exposure to non-martial music in British Guiana. At the end of the event, he expressed satisfaction and thanked the pupils for "a very, very happy musical start for Coronation Week." He continued, "It is really a pleasure listening to you and a tremendous pleasure to see over 1,000 children smiling through and look-ing so happy." The governor also extended thanks to Lynette Dolphin for "the wonderful part [she] took in making the festival a success and the choir train-ing which [she had] given." The governor also directed praise to the British Guiana Militia Band. He thanked Major Henwood and the band for their con-tributions to what he described as a day that would remain in his memory. About the British Guiana Militia Band he said, "I heard about you . . . the reputation of this band, while in England and it is worldwide."[33]

The Booker Group of Companies in British Guiana paid between £10,000 and £15,000 to bring the Loyal Tribute exhibition to the colony. The free exhibition was held at a special building erected on the site of the Assembly Rooms, which was destroyed by fire in 1945. This site had been designated as the location for a national cultural center.[34] Beyond the issue of the medals, and the Loyal Tribute exhibition, the other elements of the program reprised the models used in the 1930s for the centenary of the colony (1931), King George's coronation (1937), and the centenary of Georgetown (1939): deco-rated buildings, torchlight parades, fireworks, pageants, balls, and a fair—the Coronation Festival at the Georgetown Football Club's ground. Indicative of changing times, the Coronation Festival featured the Queen of Song and Cor-onation Calypso competitions. The latter was hyped as "War" and as "a fiesta of extemporaneous singing to the infectious beat of the calypso rhythms." The press predicted, "the top-ranking calypso 'warriors' King Cobra and Lord Sweet Dreams . . . [were expected] to out-sing all opposition and level it off to a typical 'Cobra-Dreams' calypso fireworks session."[35]

The public response to the coronation celebrations was overwhelm-ing. More than ten thousand "loyal Guianese" turned out to see the gov-ernor take the salute at ceremonial parade on the Sea Wall. Among the attendees were visitors from Surinam, Venezuela, and Brazil. The

Figure 6.3. Editorial cartoon, *Daily Argosy*, June 7, 1953.

massed bands of the British Guiana Militia and the Police Force were in atten-dance at the parade. Thousands more came into the city to view the decorated and illuminated buildings. As a result, there were traffic jams and train and ferry services were filled to capacity.[36] Adding to the merriment were steel bands that "took to the road playing bright and brisk tunes, and marching with a huge Union Jack floating at the head of their column." The participation by the steel bands was extremely popular. The headline on the front page of the *Daily Argosy* for June 4 read "Carnival Spirit Reigns As Steelbands Roam City." Large crowds "tramped" with the bands throughout the day and into the night. The music presented by the steel bands included "Rule Britannia" and a variety of patriotic airs and "road marches."[37]

Steel band music ceased being ghettoized after the coronation celebrations and became an important political instrument. The *Argosy's* editorial cartoon for June 7 "spoke" to this development. The cartoon showed steel bands lead-ing trampers to the tune of "Rule Britannia" and trampling the Hammer and Sickle. The virulent anti-communist and anti-PPP campaign that character-ized the April general elections was not over!

Schoolchildren were central to coronation celebrations in New Amster-dam. Like Georgetown, a festival of music ushered in Coronation Week in New Amsterdam. There the event was titled the Festival of Coronation Music and featured a massed choir of two thousand students drawn from eight schools. The choir presented eleven songs, among them "The Empire Hymn," "Song of Guiana's Children," "The Coronation Song," Sgt. Clem Nichol's "Elizabeth Regina," Rev. M. A. Cossou's "My Native Land," and F. P. Loncke's "My Guiana." Sgt. Nichols conducted the No. 7 Military Band, which provided the musical accompaniment for the New Amsterdam festival.[38]

On *Sunday-at-Noon*, a Bureau of Public Information radio program aired on June 7, A. J. Seymour reviewed and described the weeklong celebrations as one that "we shall long remember."[39] He reflected on "the modern marvel of radio" that allowed Guianese to hear the ceremony, which was broadcast in real time from Westminster Abbey. Seymour also commented on the fact that during the first three days of the celebrations, more than 62,000 persons took journeys by the Transport and Harbours Department. He considered this another manifestation of the colony's loyalty and was very enthusiastic about the positive contributions the celebrations made to community life. Seymour suggested, "Georgetown is ripe for a permanent Committee to organize yearly galas and festivities which would add zest to the people and colour to community life."[40]

On October 9, 1953, the constitution was suspended and the PPP government was expelled from office for allegedly planning major acts of civil disorder aimed at making the colony a launching pad for Soviet expansionism in the Americas. When the Royal Marines and the Royal Welsh Fusiliers disembarked from the frigates *Bigbury Bay* and *Burghead Bay* on October 9, they immediately took to patrolling the streets with fixed bayonets. They did not find the city filed with hostile people. As Singh recalls: "The people appeared to be in mourning. The streets were practically deserted with hardly anyone venturing outdoors. Even curious children were kept indoors by their parents, and guardians, so that the British military, egged on by the few conservatives in the colony, would not be given an excuse to demonstrate their firepower."[41]

This development was a devastating blow for Guianese nationalists. Soon after the landing of the British troops, the regular band concerts presented by the British Guiana Militia Band at the Sea Wall and the Botanical Gardens, started to feature the regimental marches of the Royal Welsh Fusiliers and the Royal Marines. Also heard around the city were the marches and other martial music of the British troops as they did the route marches and other shows of force. In schoolyards, schoolchildren continued to sing "Rick, Chick, Chick, Chick" and other ditties.

The political climate remained tense throughout the remainder of 1953. The PPP launched a period of passive resistance; under the extended state of emergency many of the PPP leadership were put into detention. Sydney King, Rory Westmaas, Martin Carter, Ajodha Singh and Bally Lachmansingh were arrested on October 24. Others had their movement restricted and organizations like the Pioneer Youth League was declared illegal and banned. The PPP headquarters was closed.[42] In his poem, "This is the Dark Time, My Love," twenty-three-year-old Martin Carter captured for posterity the zeitgeist: "the season of oppression, dark metal, and tears." A time when "the stranger invader" watched you sleep and aimed at your dreams.[43]

Those who were not detained were restricted to specific areas in the colony. Cheddi Jagan was restricted to Georgetown, and was later arrested for breaking the order and sentenced to six months hard labor. He spent his prison term between the Georgetown prison and the penal settlement in the Mazaruni River. His prison experiences are emotionally described in his autobiographical work *The West on Trial: The Fight for Guyana's Freedom.* In that work he speaks about the large crowds that assembled outside of the Georgetown Prison gates to welcome him when he was released on September 12, 1954.[44] That scene was captured in the final movement of Alan Bush's opera *The Sugar Reapers* that was inspired by and dedicated to the anti-colonial struggle of Guyanese working people during the 1950s.[45]

On December 31, 1953, Governor Savage appointed an interim government. British troops, initially the Royal Welsh Fusiliers and later the Argyll and Sutherland Highlanders, used patrols and other forms of psychological operations to defuse the tensions and restiveness associated with the suspension of the constitution and appointment of the interim government. The occupying forces and the interim government recognized that coercion and threats of force were not the only means of bringing calm and stability to the colony. For the troops, starting with the Argyll and Sutherland Highlanders, music and sport became important ingredients in efforts to win the "hearts and minds" of Guianese. Bagpipes and drums again became a part of the soundscape of Georgetown and New Amsterdam as the Argyll and Sutherland Highlanders did route marches and changed the guard. These events drew large crowds.

Bagpipe and drums were not unknown in Georgetown's military services. As indicated earlier, in the 1920s two sets of pipes were donated to the British Guiana Police Force. By World War II, these instruments had fallen out of use and were discarded in an attic room in the police headquarters, Eve Leary. John H. T. Fredericks told the story of his discovery of these discarded instruments, his acquisition of the skills to play the instrument, and the defense of his nickname "Bagpipe." Sometime in 1944 Fredericks discovered the bagpipes and related instruction manuals in the attic of the Police Training School at Eve Leary and taught himself to play. His early attempts at playing attracted the attention and encouragement of Major Henwood of the British Guiana Militia Band. In time, Fredericks became proficient on the instrument and earned his nickname. Until his death in 2008, he was still known affection-ately as John H. T. "Bagpipe" Fredericks.

In 1955 the curfews that had been imposed on Georgetown in 1953 were lifted. However, the colony was still occupied by British troops—now the crack Scottish regiment the Black Watch. As all occupying forces do, they made efforts to win the hearts and minds of the citizenry. This included strategic socializing. Fredericks recalled a story about ranks from the Black Watch who attended the dance at Haley's Hall, a working-class venue, and engaged in friendly banter with Guianese revelers. The soldiers were told that there was a Guianese who could play the bagpipes as good as any Scotsman. The Scotsmen dared them to produce the evidence. A delegation was sent to fetch Fredericks, who was at that time the duty corporal at the Police Train-ing School. British Guiana's pride being at stake during these testing colonial times, arrangements were made for Fredericks to be temporarily relieved. He proceeded to Haley Hall and represented British Guiana. He performed admirably and remembers that the "hat" that was passed around after his per-formance was "very nice." The name "Bagpipes" was reaffirmed.[46]

On the economic and social front, Britain's Colonial Development Cor-poration invested substantial funds for projects, especially on housing and industrial development, during the period of the interim government (1953–57). This was in response to the abysmal conditions in the colony. Accord-ing to Cheddi Jagan, the British Government had earmarked $44 million for development in 1954–55. However, only $26 million "was actually spent."[47] For Jagan and others, British investment was tantamount to a bribe. One of the major sectors for public spending was housing. In 1954 the Interim Govern-ment launched the "most ambitious housing programme in the British West Indies." The "initial target was to build 4,500 working class homes."[48] For the Ruimveldt Housing Scheme, P. A. Cummings, the Minister of Labor, Health, and Housing, anticipated the construction of a bandstand where the Brit-ish Guiana Militia Band would perform regularly, bringing needed culture and respectability to the residents who originally lived in the "nigger yards" of Georgetown's depressed wards. The patronizing theory of aesthetic force maintained salience.

Private-sector investments also increased following the installation of the interim government. By 1956 an area between Plantation Ruimveldt and Plantation Diamond on the east bank of the Demerara River emerged as an industrial corridor.[49] The largest unit in this complex was Bank Breweries, a multi-million-dollar company financed primarily by Guianese capital. Ordi-nary individuals could purchase a single share for a dollar. It was promoted as "people's capitalism." The managing director of the company was Peter Stanislaus D'Aguiar, a Guianese of upper-class Portuguese ancestry, who, like many other upper-class Portuguese of his generation, was educated at Stony-hurst College in the United Kingdom.

Throughout the turbulent 1950s, calypso continued to grow in importance as a communication channel in the society. Banks Breweries recognized the new power of calypso and in 1957, used *The Banks Beer Calypso* as part of the "soundtrack" to launch Banks Beer. In this calypso Peter D'Aguiar and capitalism came in for praise: "Drink a toast in Banks / And let's all say 'Thanks' / To Peter Stanislaus D'Aguiar / Who is the guiding star."[50]

American interests, investment, and expertise were behind aspects of private-sector expansion in the colony during the interim government. Through the United States Information Service (USIS), which was opened offices in Georgetown on November 9, 1955, the United States also became more active in the cultural life of the colony. Using methods similar to the British Council, the USIS used "films, the printed word, and the personal touch" to give Guianese a more authentic view of the American people, their ways of life, past and present, their culture and phychology [sic]."[51] The USIS's library was located in central Georgetown, on Main Street, which still maintained the charm that Kirke had noted in the mid-nineteenth century. The library's collection included an extensive collection of American recorded music. The library also organized exhibitions. In October 1956 an exhibition on "Music in America" was held at the League of Coloured People's Annual Fair. The popularity of that exhibition resulted in increased demand for American music by members of the library.[52] The exhibition at the popular annual fair reinforced the popularity of American music in the colony. By 1956 the music procurement policies of British-owned Radio Demerara had resulted in American music dominating the hit parade. Among the popular tunes in British Guiana in 1956 were Elvis Presley's "Don't Be Cruel," "Blue Suede Shoes," and "Hound Dog"; Little Richard's "Long Tall Sally"; Fats Domino's "Blueberry Hill"; ballads such as "The Great Pretender" by the Platters; and Doris Day's rendition of "Que Será, Será." American popular music dominated the society's airwaves for the next two decades.

In February 1955 the PPP split into two factions: the Jaganite faction, primarily East Indian, and the Burnhamite faction, primarily African. This set in motion an additional dimension to the ethno-political dynamic that has haunted Guyanese national governance ever since. On April 25, 1956, Sir Patrick Muir Renison (who assumed the governorship on October 35, 1955) announced a new constitution. Under the "Renison constitution," there would be "a single-chamber Legislative Council of 12 elected members, counterbalanced by 8 nominated and 4 *ex-officio* members, and an Executive Council of 5 elected members counterbalanced by 4 *ex-officio* and one nominated."[53] General elections were set 1957.

The PPP (Jaganites), the PPP (Burnhamites), the United Democratic Party, the National Labour Front, and the Guiana Nationals were the five parties in the 1957 election. The *Daily Argosy* described the Jaganites as "left-wing progressives" and the Burnhamites as "ambiguous." The National Labour Front, led by Lionel Luckhoo, was described as "right-wing" and John Carter's United Democratic Party was described as "middle of the road Democrats." The only candidate for the "moderate" Guiana Nationals was Frank Allen. It was predicted that 212,000 voters would vote on Monday, August 12.[54]

Calypsonians were active in the 1957 election campaign. The report by the music critic "Clef" on the Mr. Voice and Calypso competition held on the August Bank Holiday weekend at the Guiana Football Club Ground before a large crowd provides an illustration of this engagement. He observed:

> Spontaneous rhymes by Lord Coffee earned him the crown, but it was the opinion of the "crowd" that Lord Canary should have been placed first, instead of second. While all the boys made valiant efforts to boost [*sic*] the party, or in some cases, the leader of that group, Burnham, "The Commander" who was not placed brought an unusual element of music into the picture.
>
> Unnoticed by most of the large crowd "The Commander" used the notes of the pentatonic scale as the basis or structure of his tune, then modulated his key to bring the air of "Song of Guiana's Children" to strengthen his contribution. Unfortunately, however, he was not so rhythmical or engrossing to gain the necessary points for placing.[55]

The Trinidadian calypsonian Lord Melody, a regular visitor to British Guiana, was in the colony during the 1957 election. His 1958 calypso "Apan Jaat" reflected on the nature of the election campaign: its hectic pace ("Night after night crowds get larger") and the promises made ("Some promising money / Some promising milk and honey"). It was also a campaign of appeals to race and ethnicity. According to Lord Melody, the Burnhamites were active: "everywhere you pass is 'Mr. B.'" However, there was an Indian calypsonian name Lal who had Georgetown like Monday Carnival. He not only promoted the Jaganites but demanded ethnic solidarity in voting ("Apan jaat"). This, according to Lal, would ensure the sound trashing of the "Creoles" ("Marsa-ray kay kilwili"). However, in the end, despite complaints by the Burnhamites about who was "entitled to vote . . . the Indian cut dey throat."[56]

calypso + 1957 + elections

In the last line of the calypso, the fictitious calypsonian "Lall" spits with a very contemptuous "Twehhhhh." The calypso also suggested black apathy and demoralization. When all the votes in were tallied, the PPP (Jaganites) won nine seats, the Burnhamites three, and the United Democratic Party and the National Labour Front one each.

Forbes Burnham accepted his defeat stoically. He told a meeting of his supporters in front of his Croal Street chambers two days later, "In a fight such as this a man must be prepared to take as much licks as he could give." A report on the meeting said that at that point one of his supporters "remarked ironically, 'licks like peas'" and Burnham is said to have smiled and said, "Que será, será."[57] The Burnhamite faction "conceded the name PPP to the Jaganites."[58] On October 5 the PPP (Burnhamites) changed its name to the People's National Congress.[59]

Jagan's victory brought with it hope for progress. There was hope that his government would be able to deliver on its 1957 manifesto. An important plank in that manifesto had to do with art, culture, and sports. The manifesto stated: "We will give encouragement and practical assistance in the development of art, drama and music and work for the establishment of the Cultural center in Georgetown as a beginning. Increase of library facilities especially in rural areas and broadening of materials at libraries. The Party will assist in the improvement of Sports in British Guiana."[60] The execution of this task was the responsibility of the chairman of the People's Progressive Party, Brindley Horatio Benn.

Brindley Benn joined the PPP in 1949 and was responsible for forming the Progressive Youth Organization, the youth arm of the PPP.[61] In the 1953 elections he won a seat and served as the deputy prime minister. During the state of emergency in 1953 he was restricted to New Amsterdam. Recorded music was his constant companion during this period. When the PPP split in 1955, he aligned himself with the Jaganite faction and was recognized as "the most prominent African member of that faction."[62] After the PPP's victory in 1957, Brindley Benn was appointed Minister of Community Development and Education.

On June 20, 1958, Brindley Benn appointed a committee (under the chairmanship of A. J. Seymour, now the colony's chief information officer) with the following terms of reference:

> To consider and make recommendations for holding a Guianese History and Culture Week once a year and to formulate a program for the occasion including the estimated cost to Government. The event should be calculated to educate Guianese about their own country and inspire them to work harder for its progress.
>
> The Committee to arrange the program when approved by the Minister.[63]

The other members of the committee were the Barbadian-born E. R. Burrowes, MBE, founder of the Working People Free Arts Class; A. F. Jordan; Vic Forsythe, representing the Theatre Guild; Vesta Lowe, founder of the Dawson

Music Lovers Club and folk music collector; Celeste Dolphin, producer, *Broadcast to Schools*; N. E. Cameron, mathematics master at Queen's College and cultural activist; and Dwarka Nauth, MBE, historian and cultural activist. Notably absent from this list of experienced administrators was Major S. Henwood, who had returned to the United Kingdom. This was due to the fact that under legislation passed in 1956, the British Guiana Militia Band was incorporated into the British Guiana Police Force in 1957. Ninety percent of the Bandsmen accepted the incorporation and were sworn in as policemen; the remainder chose to resign. Among those resigning was Major Henwood. His replacement as bandmaster was Vincent de Abreu, LRAM, ARCM, who was appointed superintendent of police on February 2, 1957.[64] Vincent de Abreu became the first Guianese to hold that post.[65]

In August 1958 the committee submitted a detailed, nationwide program of events for the inaugural National History and Culture Week. The period October 20–24 was selected because the chance of rain was reduced and the sugar industry drama festival would be over, thus allowing for the participation of "the population on the [sugar] estates."[66] "One people, one nation, one destiny" was proposed as the slogan for the week.[67] The slogan was accepted by Brindley Benn and ultimately became the national motto when British Guiana achieved political independence in 1966.

The program proposed for the first National History and Culture Week included art exhibitions, culinary arts festivals, children's pageants, a diary of Guianese history, debates, drama, the publication of a book of Guianese proverbs, folk tales, and riddles; an essay competition for schools, radio broadcasts on Guianese history, public lectures, a display of Guianese books, a special edition of the *British Guiana Bulletin*, and a program of Guianese music. The "rough estimates of costs" was $1,430.[68]

The British Guiana Music Teachers' Association was to be responsible for the program of Guianese music, which included a composition competition and "A Concert of Guianese Music." The concert was held on October 24 in the Georgetown auditorium of the Young Women's Christian Association (YWCA). The patron for the concert was the Honorable Brindley Benn, Minister of Community Development and Education. In a prior time, the governor would have been the patron, demonstrating that the highest office in the land had given his blessing. Things had started to change in the colony; it was now clear that Guianese creativity did not need to be valorized by external agents or agencies—a bold step in decolonization and the development of cultural confidence. The concert's program featured martial music, art songs, choral music, folk music, and featured performances on the steel pan.

The concert started with Cpl. E. Briggs's composition "Overture for Military Band" performed by the British Guiana Police Force Band, and included works by F. P. Loncke ("Four Songs of Guiana" arranged for Piano Forte), Joan Gilkes ("There Runs a Dream"), Vesta Lowe (*arr.* "One Sunday Morning," "Rice Field Joe," "Sancho," and "Ganga Manni"), Martin-Sperry ("Valse des Ombres"), Edward Green ("Ping Pong Solo"), Cecilene Baird ("Ol' Higue"), Hugh Sam ("Fantasia on Three British Guiana Folk Songs"), Horace Taitt ("To the Hibiscus"), Clem Nichols ("Dear Demerara"), and Cecile Nobrega ("Dance and Romance*). The piano was the concert's dominant instrument, used for almost half of the twelve-item concert. Among the featured pianists were Oscar Dummett, Joan Gilkes, Hugh Sam, and Joycelynne Loncke. Edward Green ("Ping Pong Solo") and the Pelcans Steel Band ("Ol' Higue") presented two pieces for steel pans. Vocal performances were presented by the British Guiana Police Force Male Voice Choir, Pauline McKenzie, and John Moses. The four national songs featured in Loncke's arrangement were the now iconic compositions of W. Hawley Bryant ("The Song of Guiana's Children"), Mortimer Cossou ("My Native Land"), Francis Loncke ("My Guiana"), and Cyril Potter ("My Guiana, Eldorado"). Hugh Sam's "Fantasia on Three British Guiana Folk Songs" was the winner of the 1958 National History and Culture Week's composition competition. That composition was inspired by hinterland and rural images: "Itanamie," "Timber Man," and "Satira Gal." The concert ended with Clem Nichols's 1924 march *Dear Demerara*, performed by the British Guiana Police Force Band.

The concert of Guianese music was a welcome development, because concerts in Guiana at that time still tended to privilege European compositions. Norman Cameron could recall only four occasions in twenty years—1931, twice in 1944, and 1951—when there were concerts "devoted to local compositions."[69] The first Guianese History and Culture Week was well received and was recognized as a bold first step in building the cultural confidence needed in the construction of an independent Guyanese nation. The initiative launched in 1958 would continue to influence national cultural policy in Guyana throughout the remainder of the twentieth century. The effort would morph into events like Carifesta in 1972; Guyfesta, launched in 1975; and the many cultural events that surround Mashramani—Guyana's annual republic celebrations. The organizing committee would become the National History and Arts Council, the Department of Culture, and by the end of the twentieth century, the Ministry of Culture, Youth and Sport.

British Guiana's political drama of the 1950s could easily distract attention from private initiatives in the Guianese music scene. These initiatives, especially those by Vivian Lee, Cyril Shaw, Al Seales, and Bing Serrão and the Ramblers in British Guiana, along with those of Rannie Hart, Cy Grant, Freddy Grant, Frank Holder, Mike McKenzie, Iggy Quail, and Robert Adams

in the diaspora, would do much for Guianese music making and the construction of cultural confidence.

Vivian Lee, Cyril Shaw, and Al Seales were entrepreneurs who ran their
businesses in a single block in the Lacytown bordered by Robb Street, Wel-
lington Street, Regent Street, and King Street. Also located in that block was
Freedom House, the headquarters of the Peoples' Progressive Party; Metro-
pole Cinema; Federation Yard, the pan yard of the pioneering steel drum band
Quo Vadis; and "Point." "Point" was at the corner of King and Regent Street
and was the venue where independent musicians were hired by bandleaders
for temporary assignments. During the 1950s that Lacytown block was one of
the most musically creative spaces in the colony, and the consequences of that
creativity reverberated throughout the twentieth century and into the first
decades of the twenty-first century.

Vivian Lee ran the Ace Advertising Agency, which he founded in 1948
after returning from the United States, where he had completed a course in
radio broadcasting at the Cambridge School of Broadcasting in New York.
At that time in the United States, brokerage was a popular program production model. Under this arrangement, the producer bought blocks of times
from a radio station and produced a program in which he sold advertising
at a profit. Lee used that model to guide his radio work in British Guiana.[70]
Ace Advertising Agency specialized in promoting consumer products such as
Ovaltine and alcoholic beverages such as Guinness Stout and XM Rum. Lee
used the radio talent show and variety shows featuring Guianese musicians
as the primary vehicles for promoting his clients and their products. Through
the Ovaltine account he launched *The Ovaltine Amateur Hour*, a live talent
show on ZFY—the dominant local radio station at the start of the 1950s. ZFY
became Radio Demerara in 1951. The show was a Guianese version of the later
American popular television show, *The Gong Show*. For the local production
the *gongmeister* was Harry Mayers and his orchestra was the house band. In
a 2003 interview, Lee reminisced that King Fighter and Lord Canary were
two contestants who, despite being "gonged," went on to garner recognition in
British Guiana and Trinidad as accomplished calypsonians.

Lee launched other trend-setting radio programs such as *Tops in Pops* and
variety shows like the popular *The Gypsy Caravan featuring Miss Snodgrass*. Lee
has described the latter as a "colloquial show with low-brow humor" featuring
a "live band with four or five people—piano, guitar, bass, drums, and singer."[71]
The radio programs produced by Lee were popular and provided an opportunity for showcasing the colony's emerging popular music talent. The shows
featured working-class folks. *Top of the Pops*, sponsored by Auto Supplies, was
a pioneering show that provided a weekly update on what was happening in

the international popular music scene. *Top of the Pops* connected British Guiana with international musical trends. In addition, the program stimulated the emerging record sales sector of the Guianese economy. To respond to this situation, Lee established Ace Records and Ace Records Club—the music recording production and distribution arms of Ace Advertising.

The British Guianese popular musical environment was alive in the 1950s. The colony was an important center in the development of calypso; increased diffusion of record players increased demand for recorded music; and there was increased demand for live shows featuring local and international artists. Since 1938 British Guiana had become a popular destination for Trinidadian calypsonians. In the 1950s Lord Melody and the young Mighty Sparrow were almost permanent fixtures in Georgetown. The popular vaudeville shows stoked the demand for calypsonians; calypso competitions featuring local and Trinidadian competitors were anticipated by wide sectors of the society. It was in British Guiana that the young Mighty Sparrow recorded "Jean and Dinah" on the Ace Records label. As Lee explained, "I used the equipment at the radio station to produce tape recordings and then sent the tapes to Decca, a well-known record company in England. They made the records and sent them to the Ace Record Club"—the sales outlet.[72] The organization that Vivian Lee established in 1950 would play an important role in the society's musical life for the next three decades, producing some of Guyana's iconic pop music hits and long-lasting musical innovations. Cyril Shaw was an impresario who specialized in organizing tours of the colony by popular calypsonians from Trinidad, African American pop singers, and Indian musical stars. The tours organized by Cyril Shaw allowed communities in urban and rural British Guiana to see world-class musical talent.[73]

At the start of the 1950s, Al Seales, leader of the Washboards Orchestra, one of the colony's most popular big bands recognized for its musical innovations such as the introduction of the Latin-inflected "bion" beat, he also recognized the changes taking place in the colony's popular music environment and took steps to diversify his engagement.[74] World War II had ended and the "Yankee dollar" was not around. So by 1950, Al Seales was operating General Electric and Musicians Service (GEMS), a store that specialized in the selling of musical instruments and other aspects of music. According to his son Ray Seales, his father had two ambitions at the start of the 1950s: "One was a well-equipped recording studio, and the second was a record pressing plant."[75] Over a twenty-year period he made some progress with the first ambition through GEMS Records.[76] During the 1950s, GEMS established a house band—the Caribbean All Stars, led by Harry Whittaker—and established a special sound.

This infrastructure placed GEMS in direct competition with Radio Demerara, the local radio station that had new state of the art GATES recording technologies and one of the most modern recording studios in the West Indies. In 1951 the local, privately owned company ZFY was acquired by Overseas Rediffusion Ltd., and rebranded Radio Demerara. The national radio system was the only outlet for Guianese recordings and Radio Demerara officials had the authority not to play a record on air. Agencies such as Ace Records rented Radio Demerara's studios and technicians to record Guianese vocal and instrumental music. Studio rentals, like brokerage, were standard practices in mid-century radio broadcasting in British Guiana.

With his own studio, Al Seales's GEMS Records was a challenge to Radio Demerara's dominance. Ultimately, GEMS needed access to airwaves to make their products known. On many an occasion, the gatekeepers at Radio Demerara denied that access on the grounds that the GEMS product did not meet the expected quality standard. According to his son, Al Seales always believed that officials at the local radio stations frustrated his efforts based on color and class grounds. However, despite tensions with the gatekeepers of the local radio system, GEMS produced some of the first Guianese compositions to make the hit parade and the No. 1 spot. Among those achieving that distinction were Lennox Greaves's "So Long for Now" and Doreen Gravesande's "Ting-A-Ling." In addition, GEMS produced some of the most iconic Guyanese musical expressions. An example is "Happy Holiday" by Billy Moore and the Four Lords. Since 1956 that song has established the spirit of Christmas among Guyanese at home or in diaspora. Because of the unstable political situation in British Guiana during the 1960s, Al Seales's second ambition was never materialized. Like Vivian Lee he sent his recordings to be pressed at Melodisc in London.

One of the reasons why Al Seales decided to diversify his engagement with the Guianese music scene was the changing nature of music-based entertainment in the colony. Big bands were becoming obsolete; they were becoming too expensive to hire. The average party keeper or dance promoter was looking at ways to reduce costs and maximize profits. Another factor was the popularization of the 45-rpm record format. As a result of both of these developments, a niche was opening up for jukebox operators. During the 1950s the equipment of jukebox operators such as "Mr. B's" and "Chance," included a turntable, an amplifier, and a large monaural speaker. The entire unit could operate on AC or DC power, including from a motorcar battery. A jukebox operator could provide hours of musical entertainment at a fraction of the cost of a big band. Urban Guianese still wanted live music, and in the place of the big band emerged small string bands. The pioneer in this development was Bing Serrão and the Ramblers.

In a 2003 newspaper article, Bernard Heydorn posed the rhetorical question, "Did you know that one of the longest standing bands in history is Bing

Serrão and the Ramblers from Guyana?"[77] That year, the three Serrão brothers, Bing, Bernie, and Maurice, celebrated the fiftieth anniversary of the Ramblers with a new CD titled *Three in One Saga*. The title was homage to their popular instrumental "Three in One Saga," which dominated music programming on radio in British Guiana during the late 1950s. In 1953 the Serrão brothers formally started the band with friends Michael Andrews, Romeo Rego, Mark Steeles, and Ambrose De Souza.[78] The early band was made up of many non-traditional and improvised instruments: "an Echo mouth organ, a comb with silver paper from Lighthouse cigarette boxes, maracas of empty tin cans with buck beads (Job's tears), rice and split peas, and un-amplified string instruments—mandolins and string bass—umbilical linkages to the colony's Portuguese musical heritage."[79] The band's popularity spread as a result of playing "all over Guyana—for charities, private parties, hotels (Tower and Park), consulates, Auntie Olga's concerts, Vivian Lee's shows at the cinemas, weddings, birthday parties, business functions, sports clubs [senior staff sports clubs on sugar estates], even at Government House for Governor Savage and Guyanese politicians." As Heydorn also informed his readers, "By 1956, the Ramblers were playing on Radio Demerara on a Lee's Photo studio sponsored 15-minute weekly radio program."[80] This helped take the band's music beyond Georgetown.

When the Ramblers started in 1953, they were a transitional group providing a link between the passing of old-time acoustic string bands and a new generation of electrified string ensembles. They were one of a handful of urban string bands. Stanley Greaves captures this transitional situation in his painting *Old Time String Band*, the cover art for this book. String bands still had a presence in rural British Guiana. Raymond Smith provided a photograph of one such band from Hopetown in his influential book *The Negro Family in British Guiana: Family Structure and Social Status*, illustrating the importance of bands to the community's cultural life. When Bing Serrão and the Ramblers recorded "Three in One Saga" on the Cook Label, the band was amplified. This launched Guyana's amplified string band tradition—a development that would accelerate during the 1960s. Also emerging during this period was the Rhythmaires led by George Simmons.[81]

The British ethnomusicologist John Cowley has commented on the important but under-recognized contributions West Indian musicians made to the evolution of British popular music during the first half of the twentieth century. By the 1950s musicians from British Guiana such as Robert Adams,[82] Freddy Grant, Rannie Hart, Cy Grant,[83] Frank Holder,[84] Mike McKenzie, and Iggy Quail were among the key contributors to this evolution. Freddy Grant and Rannie Hart were noted for their versatility on the woodwind instruments. Freddy Grant played clarinet and flute; Rannie "Sweet Lips" Hart was a trumpet virtuoso. Both men were also bandleaders: Freddy Grant led the Demerarians and Rannie Hart the Caribbean Boys. Mike McKenzie and Iggy Quail were innovative pianists and members of the bands led by Grant and Hart. Grant, Hart, McKenzie, Holder, and Quail influenced the direction of jazz in the UK though their interactions with British-born performers such as Humphrey Lyttleton and Johnny Dankworth. These men along with Cy Grant also contributed to the popularization of calypso music. Freddy Grant and Rannie Hart were featured on most of the seminal calypso recordings made in the United Kingdom during the 1950s. They accompanied the calypso icon Lord Kitchener on a majority of his recordings for the Parlophone label. This group also accompanied Bill Rogers in 1952, when he visited the United Kingdom to record with the Melodisc and Parlophone labels. Bill Rogers's 1952 recordings featured Freddy Grant on clarinet, flute, and maracas; Rannie Hart on trumpet and cigar box; Mike McKenzie on piano; Lawrence Weeks from India on bongos; and Joe Sampson on string bass.[85] Eight 78-rpm records resulted from the sessions. These included remakes of "British Guiana Bargee," "Weed Woman," and "Daddy Gone to Cove and John" that were first recorded in New York in 1934 on Bluebird label. The remaining five recordings were new: "Nice Woman, Ugly Man," "Bald-Plated Emily," "Necromancy," "Sightseeing in the UK," and "The Hungry Man from Clapham." Clearly, Rogers's visit was to capitalize on the "calypso wave" that was then evident in the UK. Of the new recordings one was a "shantoized" version of a popular British music hall song "The Hungry Man from Clapham." While in the United Kingdom, Bill Rogers also did a number of live performances. One of them was on the Humphrey Lyttleton Show at the Royal Festival Hall in London and another at the City Hall in Sheffield. His "British Guiana Bargee" was popular with audiences, and he received enthusiastic reviews from the media.[86]

What the Guianese musical diaspora did in the United Kingdom, Douglas Harper did in Scandinavia. Douglas Harper was born in Georgetown in 1929. His music education started at the age of eight and by the age of fifteen he was recognized for his skills as a jazz pianist. Among his "jamming" partners in British Guiana were Valerie Warner (later Rodway) and Sonny Rodway. In the early 1950 he migrated to the United Kingdom and between 1953 and 1955 he studied at the prestigious Guildhall of Music. He maintained his love for jazz and toured Europe with bands led by Sammy Walker and Herman Wilson. Unlike his many of his compatriots, he settled not in the United Kingdom but in Scandinavia, and worked as a freelance pianist and bandleader during the 1960s. During the 1970s he became a music teacher, teaching jazz piano at the Folkuniversitet in Göteborg. Over the years, he became a prolific composer and continued to incorporate Guyanese folk themes and motifs in compositions, which total more than a hundred. In 2009 he published thirty-four of

Figure 6.4. Douglas Harper. Photograph courtesy of Douglas Harper.

his compositions in *Douglas Harper: A Man and his Music*.[87] In 2012 Harper published his autobiography, *My Life as a Musician* (Sweden: B4Press, 2012).

The 1950s was a pivotal decade in Guyana's political and cultural life. There were qualitative and quantitative developments in the scope of musical life in the colony. The contributions of music critics such as Clef in the "Music Forum" columns in the *Daily Argosy* were essential complements to the developments in the colony's musical life. Clef exemplified the art of the critic. It was not about bashing the performer; his role was to use a valid aesthetic framework to measure performances. His reviews were technical and therefore credible. For example, in his review of a performance by Cecil Huggins, a tenor from Trinidad, he noted that the artist had a "flair for the songs popularized by Mario Lanza, whose style he tries to follow. . . . his expression was often marred by the lack of colouring or shading to give proper effect in some lyrical passages."[88] He offered similar observations on the limits to the technique of O. Britton. He advised her "to be careful with her notes. Such diffusion shows lack of confidence or concentration while an eagerness to lay emphasis on throaty qualities of sound infuses the defect."[89] Clef critically evaluated all of the dominant genres of music in Guiana during the latter part of the decade—classical, folk, religious, spirituals, military, string bands, steel bands, and calypsos. Through his columns he told us about unique musicians such as Moses Josiah, a virtuoso on the musical saw. Clef also left a record of early experimentations with quartet singing and rock and roll in British Guiana.[90]

In addition to aesthetic evaluation, Clef also encouraged musical diversity in the society. For example, he asked why East Indian music was absent during the early History and Culture Week celebrations. A promoter of folk music and music education in schools, he was also a valuable source on developments taking place in the international musical environment. When Charles Knights stated that for music to flourish in a society it needed four elements—composers, performers, audiences, and critics—he was referring to critics with the capacity of Clef.[91] There were other critics, who operated out of the British Council, and their focus was primarily on European classical music. These included Cecily Pilgrim, Sydney Carter, Earl John, and Basil Hinds. Like Clef, they used a formal aesthetic framework to evaluate music. Critics played an important role in music education and the expansion of musical tastes in the colony.

At the end of the decade, political tensions continued. Internationally, there were increasing fears about Soviet expansionism, and the Cold War heated up in the region. The overthrow of President Arbenz Guzman in Guatemala in 1954 and the successful Cuban Revolution in 1959 did not make for a relaxation of political tensions in British Guiana. The fears that the Jagans were hell-bent on making the colony a base for Soviet activities in region were high. When coupled with the prevailing "ethno politics," British Guiana would explode in the 1960s with civil disorder, racial violence, and the PPP would be replaced as the key variable in national governance. The politics of fragmentation and coalitions, which were established during the 1950s, remained a dominant characteristic of politics until the end of the century and into the first decade of the twenty-first century.[92] On February 23, 1966, British Guiana gained its political independence and changed its name to Guyana. The journey to that destination will be explored next. The 1950s was the age of impatience.

7

The 1960s: "Guiana Lament": The Painful Road to Independence

Guyana's flag with its arrowhead now waves over us. The golden arrow points the way to a future which can be one of prosperity for all.

There is no part of the community which will be unaffected by our country's attainment of Independence. Guyana can be a great land, but it can only become great by our own efforts, our own sacrifices, our endurance and our tolerance. There has been, in the past, some emphasis upon the diverse origins of our people.

Today, and for the future, I commend to you our new nation's motto and invite you to join in creating "One People, One Nation, One Destiny."
—**Forbes Burnham,** May 26, 1966[1]

The *Guyana Graphic* souvenir issue to mark Guyana's independence on May 26, 1966, carried several essays focusing on various aspects of Guyanese history, culture, economy, and the new nation's development ambitions. Essays by Robert Moore, Wilson Harris, Basil Hinds, George Lamming, Wordsworth McAndrew, Dwarka Nath, and "Recorder" focused on the contribution the arts played in the struggle for independence. The articles by McAndrew and Recorder emphasized the place of music in Guyanese society. McAndrew emphasized the place of the folk music traditions of rural Guyana and demonstrated how, along with folk stories, they were part of a rich, multiracial and multidimensional oral tradition and important elements in the construction of an authentic national identity. Recorder explored the evolution of the classical and popular music in Guyana, praising the contributions of radio and the British Guiana Music Festival and recognizing the music festivals as an "enriching resource" and an institution that "served to set quality standards in choice and performance."[2] He traced the contributions of composers such as Rev. Hawley Bryant, Rev. Cossou, Francis Percival Loncke, Patricia Loncke, Cecile Nobrega, William A. Pilgrim, R. C. G. Potter, Valerie Rodway, Betty Roe, and Hugh Sam, who gave the new nation a rich collection of patriotic music and songs.

His article also spent several paragraphs saluting the contributions of musicians who specialized in popular music. Among the musicians singled out for praise were Ferdinand Eversley, "the most versatile instrumentalist"; "Gun" Fernandes, "a solid saxist with the Lucky Strike Orchestra"; "the vibraharpist" Denis Evelyn; Rannie Hart, the trumpeter; Jerry Daniel, who served as a "repertoire manager for Cook Records, Trinidad"; Wally Stewart, the leader of the Washboards Orchestra before Al Seales; Harry Mayers, the "waltz king"; and Jack James, the alto saxophonist and leader of the Jazz Kings, who "created traffic jams about the city" when the band was in session. Other musicians in his list included Tom Charles and the Rogers brothers (Bert and Edward).[3] Reflecting on the contemporary musical scene, Recorder noted:

> In the sixties the demand for more bands for parties and dances and improvements in electronics and recording led to the innovation of the jukebox for live orchestras and combos. Just as they were about to rally their cause the electronic guitar came into vogue and signaled the wane of the live brass and wind band.
>
> The guitar vogue came on the wave of pop culture and the rise of the younger generation with their new star system and new sound.[4]

Recorder was somewhat equivocal about the music of the younger generation. "They make noise," he noted. But he quickly admits that "they make beautiful sounds also." He singled out Johnny Braff, Winston "Pepe" Romalho (Combo 7), and Ted E. Jones (Rhythmaires) as singers who had developed their potential. For Recorder, instrumentalists such as Colin Wharton, "Fat Boy" Downer, Wendell Bunyan, Des Glasford, Keith Proctor, and Ralph Blakney were examples of musicians who enjoyed "doing their business without any pretensions of misplaced grandeur."[5]

What Recorder failed to comment on was the dominating popularity of contemporary American popular music, especially soul, R&B, jazz, and rock and roll. He could have also expanded his reflections on the role radio and other technologies such as coin-operated jukeboxes and the transistor radio had in Guyanese society at the dawn of independence. In 1966 James Brown, Ray Charles, Lee Dorsey, Ben E. King, Chubby Checker, Martha and the Vandellas, Doris Troy, Aaron Neville, Lou Rawls, the Supremes, the Temptations, Wilson Pickett, Stevie Wonder, and Percy Sledge had significant airplay through audience-request and "hit parade" programs on the national radio network. This music also had a formidable presence in the coin-operated jukeboxes that were now present in cake shops, bars, and nightclubs in coastal Guyana. The transistor radio meant that the audience could take their music along. Also popular was British rock and roll purveyed by the Animals, the Beatles, Petula Clark, the Kinks, and the Rolling Stones. Eshri Singh, Ayube

Hamid, Sonny Mohamed, through programs such as *Hits from India*, *Indian Songtime*, *Filmi Duniya*, *Indian Memory Album*, and *Indian Melody Time* kept Indian music contemporary.

In addition to connecting Guyanese to industrially determined global musical tastes, the popularity of American, British, and to some extent Indian musicians also animated the concept of the "pop star" in Guyanese society, and this led many individuals and pop bands to aspire to become rich and famous. This music signaled a new dynamic in generational relationships in a new nation state. In the age of the civil rights struggle, youth power, black power, anti-war movements, free love, popular music was an important vector of these ideas. In addition, this international musical diet coupled with other aspects of American popular culture, especially fast food, fashion, and slang contributed to the orientation of the Guyanese baby-boomers that had started to come of age in 1966.

One US innovation that took tenuous root in Georgetown was the coffee shop. Ram John Holder, along with a returned Booker cadet, Stephen DeCastro, was active in the formation and operation of what may have been British Guiana's first bohemian-type coffee shop, the Itabo—an Amerindian word referring to "back passages in rivers." This coffee shop attracted the attention of the youth as a place where locally grown coffee was brewed strong; the conversation was flavored with progressive political ideas and rhythms of Beat poets like Ginsberg and Ferlinghetti. The ambient music was jazz. The music of Ray Charles had special place in this bohemian-inflected environment. The urban youth that came of age in the early 1960s were awed by Charles's versatility on organ, piano, saxophone, and drums. His soulful voice expressed the pain that connected the Guyanese struggle with that of African Americans.[6] Itabo was different; it was Guiana's first engagement with the beatnik culture that was then popular in the United States.

In a secret report to the British Colonial Office, Sir Ralph Grey, the Governor of British Guiana reported on advice he received from a Guianese civil servant, Lloyd Searwar:

> He said that although he did not give much credence to most of the tales about the "Itabo" coffee-bar that has been established below PYO headquarters by Ram John Holder and one Stephen Anthony de Castro and that has attracted some local notoriety as a hang-out of the Guianese version of "beatniks," it was commonly said that this was an institution set up by the Party [the PPP] to serve the PYO. Girls (presumably also "enthusiasts") were procured for duty there to attract young men; other excitements were available for the young men attracted; by these means the recruiting for the PYO (which is already very considerable

through less disreputable means) was stepped up; and food and drinks were provided for the PYO vigilantes.[7]

During this period, Ram John Holder recorded, with the Potaro Pork Knockers, *The Songs of Guiana Jungle*, a long-playing album of folk songs, folk-type songs, and patriotic songs. Some of those recordings such as "Guiana" and "Demerara Boy" have become iconic statements of Guyanese identity. After leaving British Guiana in the late 1960s, Holder settled in the United Kingdom, where he established a successful career as a film and television actor.

All of the articles in the *Guiana Graphic's* independence souvenir issue were written six years into the 1960s, and all reflected the relative peace and optimism that prevailed in the country as it attained political independence on May 26, 1966. The route to independence was fraught with contradictions, tensions, racial conflict, and destructive violence. Racial conflict and violence intensified after the general election of 1961 that was again won by the PPP. In that election the politics of "Apan Jaat"—vote for your own race—which was introduced in the 1930s and amplified in 1957, was pervasive.

The racial polarization of the colony had intensified since the split of the PPP in 1955. Starting in 1958 there were deliberate efforts to use the arts to heighten political consciousness, bring about racial healing, and build national identity, unity, and cohesiveness. In a memorandum related to the events planned for National History and Culture Week in 1959, Cheddi Jagan scribbled on a memorandum: "Role of the Artist—stimulate people to struggle, to transform life. Artist—Art reaches its true height when it performs its function as a force revolutionizing society."[8] Jagan's orientation was also evident in the PPP's manifesto for the 1961 election. That manifesto offered a clear plank for promoting and supporting expressive culture—the arts.[9] In the new dispensation, the charismatic Jagan called on his allies for support in national governance. One ally with a Port Mourant connection was Helen Taitt.

In September 1961, after the PPP won their third election victory, Taitt produced and directed *The Future Is Bright*, a musical comedy "about a country boy going to Georgetown to earn enough money to buy equipment that would bring electricity to his village. He succeeded in the end despite the efforts of a choke-and-rob gang."[10] Compton Pooran, an East Indian tenor, and Yonette D'andrade, a colored (Portuguese and African) music festival "discovery" from Essequibo, were the stars. There was little subtlety in the work. Clearly the "country boy" coming to town was Cheddi Jagan and the "choke-and-rob gang" referred to the PNC. It was not uncommon, since the period of slavery, to refer to black people in groups as menacing thugs. The term *choke-and-rob* describes a predatory tactic used by urban youth to rob individuals. Jagan

deliberate use of culture in unity by PPP

and PPP supporters also used that phrase and others such as "the hooligan elements" to frame black participants in anti-PPP demonstrations throughout the 1960s and beyond. This is not to undermine the fact that there were indeed hooligan elements in anti-PPP demonstrations. But this element was not exclusively black. The same can be said about supporters of the PPP: there were also hooligan elements among these supporters and they were not exclusively East Indians.

The Future is Bright tells a story of hope and optimism. The three-act musical comedy features twelve songs composed by Helen Taitt and Hugh Sam. In Act I there are four songs: "Sticks," "Village Girl," "If You Leave Me," and "Believe in Me." "Sticks" was a counting song based on the number ten and was used to set up an important theme—saving. The song also appeared to be paying homage to the folk game Airy Dory, which was based on Gilli-Danda, the Indian folk game.[11]

"Village Girl" is a calypso-structured homage sung by Guy (Pooran) to the innocence, simplicity, and loyalty of the rural woman, especially his Ana (D'andrade). He declares, "Girls more sweet when they grow in the village."[12] "If You Leave Me" and "Believe in Me" are songs of despair and promise. In "If You Leave Me" Ana expresses concern about the loneliness and fear that will ensue when Guy leaves: "what a life this life will be / when I don't have your love to share."[13] In "Believe in Me," Guy reassures Ana of his undying love: "My heart is with you / Wherever I go."[14]

Act II features three songs. These songs are montages of life in Georgetown and articulate underlying ideological perspectives. The first, "Take Yu Cool Time," presents the hustle and bustle of Georgetown ("the lickin dung") and the other tensions of the times, and makes a call to "calm down" so you "doan kill yourself before yu time."[15] "Girls of Water Street" speaks about the "poor little overworked" and underpaid store workers of Water Street who in order to live must also work as prostitutes "by the light of the moon."[16]

The third song in Act II is "Right Here," which recognizes that emigration was accelerating. It had ceased to be a trickle by the early 1960s and was alarming. Among those leaving at this time were expatriate colonials ending extended sojourns, "local whites" (Anglo Creoles), members of the Chinese and Portuguese private sector, a generation of students off to study at universities in the UK, Canada, and the USA, and the beginnings of the scheme to send domestics to Canada.[17] In a sermon to mark the opening of the new Kingston Methodist Church, Rev. James Davison, chairman of the Methodist Circuit in British Guiana, had called for something to be done "to stop the exodus of persons leaving the country."[18] "Right Here" is a plea to stay and work for the country: "Where would you find the people so kind / Where are the days so sunny / Why set your mind to leave it behind / To go where you know life will never be milk and honey."[19] Helen Taitt was not the only Guianese lyricist commenting about the dramatic increases in Guianese emigration. Francine Rodrigues, who was described as "modest and sedate," wrote the lyrics for "Parting is Hard," which was recorded by Andy Nichols and also explored that theme.[20] The recording, which featured the Crystals Combo, became one of the first Guianese vocal hit songs of the electric-guitar age and launched a parade of local hit songs sung by artistes such as Johnny Braff and produced by Vivian Lee.[21]

Five songs are featured in the third act of *The Future Is Bright*: "Buy a Paper," "Lady Guyana," "The Future Is Bright," "Guy, Ana," and "Soldiers in the Town." "Buy a Paper" provides atmospherics for the third act as it recalls the calls of the itinerant newspaper vendors. Taitt, who wrote the lyrics for this song, would have been exposed to the calls of Oscar, the blind vendor, whose route included Murray Street where her home—the Woodbine House—was located.[22] The lyrics for this song pay homage to Oscar and other itinerant newspaper vendors who roamed the streets of Georgetown proclaiming "Buy a paper . . . Mister, buy a paper from / *Chronicle*! / *Graphic*! / *Argosy*!"[23] "Lady Guiana" sets out to portray Guiana as an alluring young woman with all that is needed to charm eligible bachelors. The metaphor is a not-too-thinly veiled reference to Guiana's need to attract foreign investments and the need for this to be done respectfully. As the song stressed, "don't make your eyes pass the lady."[24]

The lyrics for *The Future Is Bright* contain many references to African musical traditions and practices that had been suppressed or censored in the past. The future was going to be bright for the many hands of African drummers, masquerade bands, steel bands, and calypsonians.[25] *The Future Is Bright* called for all to "sing for a betta morning come."[26] "Guy, Ana" projects the spelling of the name for independent Guiana and is indicative of the process of Guianization then already evident in key sectors of the society.[27] In 1961 independence was seen as close at hand. "Soldiers in Town" is filled with contradictions. It has resignation, accepting the need for the soldiers to maintain peace and in the process providing opportunities for Guianese women where "there is not a local man in sight / who knows how to treat us ladies right."[28]

The production also featured dancers from Ballet Guyana, Helen Taitt's company. The show's musicians were Hugh Sam (piano), Maurice Watson (bass), R. Bunbury (flute), E. Briggs (trumpet), and G. Headley (clarinet). The Pelcan Steel Band was also part of the musical team.[29] *The Future Is Bright* was not Taitt's first venture with large-scale productions; her first was *Stabroek Fantasy*, "centered on a group of Stabroek Market hucksters."[30] That show was presented by Theatre 13, a group of young people, and opened at Queen's College on April 13, 1956. Hugh Sam, who composed the music for the show, remembers Theatre 13 as "a new group formed to include artists from all fields of culture."[31] Vincent De Abreu arranged the music. Patricia Bowen and Sam performed "Stabroek Market," the two-piano overture. Other musicians included the Symphonia Steel Band—a band started at Woodbine House—led by Ron Savory with arrangements by Michael Gilkes and Savory. The Junior Philharmonic Choir provided the female voices. Taitt was the choreographer.[32]

Immediately after *Stabroek Fantasy*, she produced *Song of Guiana*. This show had a cast of forty-two children from Richard Ishmael's Indian Educational Trust College. According to Taitt: "he [Richard Ishmael] came to me the next day [after seeing *Stabroek Fantasy*] and all but demanded a show for his school." This show was again an integration of the arts (song, dance, and recorded speech), a "carefully documented history of the country," and was produced with the "full co-operation of the Director of Archives and the radio station." The profits from the show went to the school's Handicapped Children's Fund.[33]

Her third production was *Amalivaca*, which was based on A. J. Seymour's poem "Amalivaca," which, like "The Legend of Kaieteur," was based on an Amerindian legend. For *Amalivaca*, Taitt was avant-garde. In her autobiography she offers the following details:

> I selected quotes from the poem which were read by Wilbert Holder. Stanley Greaves did excellent décor—the highlight of which was at the opening of the curtain when a huge painting (Stanley's interpretation of the words spoken by Wilbert) split down the middle and the two sides slid silently apart to opposite corners of the stage. Music was by Hugh Sam and I did choreography and lyrics, which were sung by members of the Police Male Voice, Woodside and Bishop's High School choirs. Cicely Robinson did costumes and lighting was by Cecil Barker.[34]

The earlier productions were well received. However, there were different reactions to the 1962 production *The Future Is Bright*. In her autobiography, Taitt writes: "I was thoroughly abused for expressing hope for the future when the party opposing the then government wanted everybody to shout 'gloom and doom.'" The show was not well attended, as she noted: "Many who always came to my shows in the past stayed away! The day of the final dress rehearsal, the police phoned to say that an important member of the cast was in jail—caught stealing a bicycle! He was the head of the choke-and-rob-gang in the show . . . I bailed him out . . . and ON WITH THE SHOW! THE FUTURE IS BRIGHT."[35]

The origins of what Helen Taitt did with *The Future Is Bright*—integrating a political message in an entertainment vehicle—can be traced back to World War II with the 1944 musical *You Can't Stop It*, produced by A. J. Seymour for the Bureau of Public Information. Taitt had worked with Seymour on that project. The practice she resurrected in 1962 has continued in Guyana. The model is apparent in Vivian Lee's 1969 film *If Wishes Were Horses*, which promoted the agricultural co-operatives policy of the PNC and the musicals produced by Billy Pilgrim and others for the special birthday concerts for President Forbes Burnham from the late 1970s to the mid-1980s.

Between 1960 and 1964, the racial conflicts and violence were so intense and seemingly unsolvable that the idea of partitioning the colony into an East Indian section and an African section was offered as a serious alternative. A petition with more than five thousand signatures was sent to the governor supporting that proposal. The petition was denied.[36]

After the 1953 suspension of the constitution British Guiana attracted the attention of the international academic community. I am of the opinion that during this period of the Cold War, policy makers in Washington and Whitehall felt that understanding the social and cultural dimensions of Guyanese life might help explain the hold the PPP had on the society and guide strategies for removing them from power, irrespective of their victories in elections. The research reports of Smith, Jayawardena, Halperin, and Despres contributed to the conclusion that British Guiana was a plural society. According to extant theory, plural societies are characterized as societies in which there were people of many different ethnic origins "who mix but do not combine." Each group holds by its own religion, its own culture and language, its own ideas and ways. As individuals they meet, but only in the marketplace in buying and selling."[37] However, as we will note below, there were indications that combining was taking place in the realm of music and suggestive of a destination beyond the segregation of plural societies theory—the Guyanese nation.

Among the international scholars who were part of this wave was Ved Prakash Vatuk, an Indian-born cultural anthropologist and professor at the University of California, Los Angeles. Vatuk conducted his field research in the Corentyne region of Berbice in 1962. The Corentyne was primarily East Indian and predominantly Hindu. There were other ethnic communities in the Corentyne. For example, Manchester, Rose Hall, and Fyrish were predominantly African. In Rose Hall, there was a "Portuguese Quarter." Also evident in the Corentyne were mixed populations, such as "Douglas" (African and Indian) and "Santantones" (African and Portuguese). The Corentyne was a pivotal element the crucial Berbice bastion of support for Cheddi Jagan and the People's Progressive Party. Berbice represented almost 25 percent of the colony's eligible voters at the start of the 1960s. In 1957 the Corentyne (East Berbice) had a population of 31,947, and represented 15 percent of total voters in British Guiana.[38]

In 1962 the Corentyne was also an important location in creation, production, distribution, and consumption of music in British Guiana. It was a multi-genre musical environment. Hindu devotional music was pervasive. In addition to religious music, there was the folk music of festivals and rites of passage, such as the up-tempo Chatini music of Matticore—the pre-marriage ritual similar to the Kwe Kwe rituals of Guyanese of African ancestry; neoclassical innovations such Taan singing, improvised music performed after work and awaiting transportation from the cane fields; and leisure music forms associated with maujing and rum shop music. Indian music programs on the national radio system and Indian film music were other elements in Corentyne's musicscape. Also popular in homes with record players and on coin-operated jukeboxes was American music, especially country and western. From a musical taste perspective, Corentyne was conservative compared to urban Guyana (dominated by Georgetown). It was, however, a space where there was musical interaction and exchange.

During his field research in 1962, Ved Vatuk collected almost nine hundred songs that could be described as East Indian folk songs. Vatuk used three categories to organize the folk songs he collected: (a) traditional religious and festival songs, (b) "protest" songs, and (c) songs by women who were craving for children. Vatuk published his research findings in two important articles, "Protest Songs of East Indians in British Guiana" and "Craving for a Child in the Folksongs of East Indians in British Guiana." According to his findings, 90 percent of the songs were traditional religious and festival songs, which were similar in form to those sung in India in the "Bhojpuri dialect of Eastern Hindi."[39] About 10 percent of the songs he collected were described as of "recent origin." Of these, about half were protest songs. Vatuk defined *protest songs* as "expressions of the singers' lot in life, against changing times, and against a political and economic atmosphere in which freedom is lacking."[40] He also noted that these protest songs were sung in a language that differed from the Bhojpuri dialect. He described the language as "a creolized Hindi: "... the vocabulary was largely Hindi, but without the grammatical complexities of the standard language as it is written or spoken in India. Words of creole English, taki taki, spoken by working class Indians and Africans alike in British Guiana are interspersed. Some of the songs were almost entirely in taki taki or have creole English verses with a 'creole Hindi' chorus."[41]

The primary instruments used to accompany these songs when Vatuk conducted his research were the dholak, tabla, harmonium, sarangi, and dhantal.[42] Of particular interest are the songs that he described as "songs of recent origin," as these offer insights] into some of the ideas that were dominant in the consciousness of East Indians, in the heartland of PPP support. These songs also help illuminate the dynamics of musical exchange and provide another way of seeing Guyanese society—not as a rigidly plural society but one on the way to Guyanese-ness! The protest songs "discovered" by Vatuk revealed African and Western influences on their structure and lyrics and can be offered as examples of musical exchange. He did, however, "discover" a body of folk songs that reflected the region's strong support for the "native son," Cheddi Jagan. In some of these songs, Jagan is equated with Gandhi and Nehru; in others he is described as the "Father of the Nation." As Vatuk reported, "In one song, the fact that Jagan was jailed for his political activities, as was Gandhi" was a proud badge and was reflected in the lines "He went to jail for us poor people / Jagan is the man for the poor."[43]

Vatuk reported "literally dozens" of songs were created to support Jagan during the 1961 elections. One of those songs described Dr. Jagan as "the savior of the race," compared him to Jawaharlal Nehru, praised him for establishing Palin City and encouraged Guianese to "Vote for Dr. Jagan again."[44] Among the themes of the other songs Vatuk "discovered" were those asking "God to make their leader's wishes come true; others urge people to fly the flag of the People's Progressive Party and to fight for independence." Other songs condemned Peter D'Aguiar for supporting the colonial power and blamed Burnham, "who in political philosophy is very close to Jagan, for putting his aspirations for personal power above the nation's welfare."[45] In the case of Peter D'Aguiar, one song recommended: "Eat what D'Aguiar has to give / Drink the liquor he provides / But vote Jagan."[46] Vatuk's findings did not offer any indication that East Indians in the Corentyne were going to abandon Jagan and the PPP, even if the party and its leadership were on an inexorable march to create a communist state.[47]

The findings of Smith, Jayewardene, Halperin, Despres, and Vatuk energized the realism that guided the foreign policy of the United States in the Western Hemisphere during the early days of the Cold War. Simply stated, the "Reds" had to go. The Soviet Union was not going to be allowed to establish another beachhead in the Americas; Cuba was enough! As a result, the United States and the United Kingdom collaborated to ensure that the PPP would not lead British Guiana into independence. Despite those efforts the PPP won general elections in 1961 and the largest block of votes in the 1964 general elections.

On March 7, 1960, the leaders of British Guiana's three political parties met with the British colonial secretary at Lancaster House, London, for a constitutional conference. The conference was expected to set a date for the colony's independence. The US government was pressing the British to be cautious with their decisions on British Guiana, as they were not convinced that the PPP had changed ideologically since 1953. Further, the PNC and the United Force, although supportive of the idea of independence, were not prepared to support independence for British Guiana under the PPP. The United States took overt and covert steps to achieve the goal of removing the PPP from office.

Substantial work has already been done by Cheddi Jagan (*The West on Trial: My Fight for Guyana's Freedom*, 1997), Hamilton Green (*Pain to Peace*, 1986), Jainarine Singh (*Democracy Betrayed: A Political History 1948–1993*, 1996), Maurice St. Pierre (*Anatomy of Resistance: Anti-Colonialism in Guyana 1823–1966*, 1999), Steven Rabe (*US Intervention in British Guiana: A Cold War Story*, 2005), Colin Palmer (*Cheddi Jagan and the Politics of Power*, 2010), Robert Waters and Gordon Daniels ("Striking for Freedom?," 2010), and others on the consequences of the March 1960 conference and subsequent meetings to decide on a date for British Guiana's independence, the new nation's constitution, and the attendant electoral system. Those writings, drawing on declassified British and American documents, also reveal the overt and covert roles of the United States in determining those decisions. So that story will not be repeated in detail in this book.

Irrespective of their partisan stands or ideological biases, all of those writers agree that the violence that ensued during the period 1962 to 1964 were among the darkest moments in contemporary Guyanese history. In that dark time, the unionized working class was racialized and pitted against itself. Music played a significant role in sustaining the tensions and in calming the society.

The PPP won the general elections of 1961 and articulated a G$250 million economic development plan. In October 1961 Dr. Jagan met with President John Kennedy to discuss US economic aid for the colony. Jagan's ambition was to garner an aid package of US$40 million. This was a significant shift in the governance of the colony. Hitherto, the elected government of British Guiana had little if any role in foreign policy and international relations. Given the needs of the society, aid was considered by Jagan to be "a political necessity." The people of Guiana expected that Jagan would be able to bring back the bacon.[48] Prior to leaving for the United States, Sir Ralph Grey, the New Zealand–born governor of British Guiana, offered Jagan guidance for his encounters with Kennedy and the US media. Jagan had been invited to be a guest on NBC's influential Sunday morning public-affairs program, *Meet the Press*. The meeting with Kennedy is said to "have went well." Jagan is reported to have stressed to Kennedy "that he believed in democracy, an independent judiciary, and an independent civil service."

Jagan is considered to have flunked the *Meet the Press* interview. Stephen Rabe noted that the host of the program, Lawrence E. Spivak, "assumed the role of the red baiting Senator Joseph McCarthy" for his interview with Jagan. His first question was "Are you or are you not pro-Communist?" Jagan's responses to that question and others in the same vein have been described as "imprecise and rambling." Spivak was relentless in his questioning and came across as an inquisitor. The British embassy in Washington called Spivak's treatment of Jagan "character assassination."[49]

Jagan's performance on *Meet the Press* consolidated the perceptions of President Kennedy and Secretary of State Dean Rusk that Jagan was not to be trusted. Jagan left Washington relatively empty-handed. There were "vague promises" of a $5 million aid package.[50] It has been argued that, given that reality, the PPP government attempted to diversify the colony's economic relations by exploring trade and aid deals with the Soviet bloc. For example, there were plans to acquire a glass factory from Hungary, a rice-bran oil factory from the German Democratic Republic, and a loan from Cuba.[51]

The Cuban deal was developed during conversations Jagan had with Ernesto "Che" Guevara in 1960. As Jagan recounted, the deal included:

> [L]oans of equipment and materials—cement, steel, and generators—the equivalent of the external cost of $32 million hydro-electric project at Malali Falls and a loan of $US5 million to establish a government-owned timber and wood pulp project. The loans were offered on very generous terms—a 2 percent rate of interest and repayment in the form of wood pulp and other timber products. The Cuban government wanted long-grain wood-pulp from our timbers to combine with short grain Cuban bagasse (sugar cane waste) for paper making.[52]

This was a dramatic gesture on the part of Cuba, which had its own economic and security challenges. Dr. Jagan did not disclose the quid pro quo in his autobiography *The West on Trial*. None of these projects were approved by the British Foreign Office, which still controlled the colony's foreign policy. According to Jagan, the failure to receive substantial funding from the United Kingdom, the United States, or the World Bank led to a decision to increase taxes so the colony could pay for the development plan that was articulated by the PPP government. That plan included elements visualized in the 1920s and reflected the modernization paradigm—the orthodoxy of the time. An important tactic in the process and in the PPP government's development plan, as expressed in the 1961 manifesto, was industrialization. In 1961, all of the major political parties—the PPP, the PNC, and the United Force—were committed to modernization and industrialization.

In an effort to raise funds for the ambitious development plan, the PPP government enlisted the services of Dr. Nicholas Kaldor, a Cambridge University economist, to make recommendations for a national budget. The budget Dr. Kaldor prepared was presented to the legislative council on January 31, 1962. The budget's primary aim was mobilizing of capital for the development plan. A number of tough tactics were proposed. These included taxes on "capital gains, gifts, net wealth, and turnover on sales."[53] Also proposed was a compulsory saving scheme of between 5 and 10 percent, depending on the level of income. Foreign exchange controls were introduced to stop capital flight, and taxes were levied on luxury and semi-luxuries, such as tobacco, alcoholic drinks, and beverages.[54]

The reaction to the budget was swift, vocal, and public. It was described as "Communistic" and "anti-working class." There was massive public resistance. The Trade Union Council called a general strike on February 13, 1962, that was justified on the ground of the lack of consultation. The situation was exacerbated as some elements in the commercial sector began to profiteer, charging high prices and applying conditions to the sale of foodstuff and other commodities. The commercial sector also introduced a "lock out" and the "Axe the Tax" campaign was launched. What also contributed as an irritant in the system was the power and influence of the three "foreigners"—Nicolas Kaldor, the Cambridge University economist; Jack Kelshall, the Trinidad-born bureaucrat; and Janet Jagan, the US-born wife of Cheddi Jagan.[55]

As agitations against the budget were starting, Prince Philip, the Duke of Edinburgh, paid a state visit to the colony. A float parade in his honor became the site for protest against the budget and the "foreigners." As the floats passed the reviewing stand where the governor and Prince Philip were seated, one of the floats opened up and out came a banner demanding that Trinidadian-born and so-called Communist sympathizer, Jack Kelshall, one of the "foreigners" who was Cheddi Jagan's private secretary, should leave.[56] The soundtrack for that demonstration was Ray Charles's "Hit the Road Jack," which had attained #1 on the *Billboard* Hot 100 list in the United States: "Hit the Road Jack! / And don't you come back, no more, no more, no more, no more / Hit the Road Jack!"

The Duke of Edinburgh departed British Guiana on February 9. One week later, on Friday, February 16, all hell broke loose. The day started with rallies and marches led by Peter D'Aguiar. British troops, garrisoned in the colony since 1953, had to be called out, and calm was not restored in the city until about 8:00 p.m.[57] In his accounting of the toll, Jagan reported:

> In all, 56 premises were destroyed by fire, 21 damaged and 66 both damaged and looted; 29 market stalls were damaged and looted; 5 vehicles and 57 traffic signs were damaged by fire; 3 cars, 1 van and 1 Land Rover belonging to the police were also damaged. Claims rendered to the fire insurance companies totaled about $11 million. But the loss suffered was in fact far greater; most of the property did not carry riot insurance, and few stores were insured against looting. One police officer had been killed, 4 looters lost their lives and 41 other people were injured.[58]

Cheddi Jagan subsequently admitted that the 1962 budget was unfortunate. The budget was withdrawn and the riots weakened his position when he attended the next constitutional conference in London on October 23. It was expected that a decision on the date for independence would be made at the conference; the February disturbances made this a non-starter. Another conference was scheduled for October 1963.

An uneasy calm existed until March 1963, when the colony was again thrust into tensions, conflicts, and violence. During the period of uneasy calm, demonstrations were regular. The legislative assembly was regularly picketed. This was part of the PNC tactic of "passive resistance."[59] The event that initiated the conflict this time was the Industrial Relations Bill, which was brought before the legislature in March 1963. Under this bill, the Ministry of Labor would have the power to certify unions as the agents for specific groups of workers. The evident goal was to replace the MPCA (founded in 1920 and considered a "company union") with GIWU, the PPP-affiliated union as the representatives of the predominantly East Indian sugar workers. A version of the bill was introduced in 1953 and was one of the actions that triggered the suspension of the constitution. Naively, Jagan felt that the PPP electoral victories since 1957 were mandates for his action. He had to be aware that this was taunting not only the British but also the United States, who was by 1961 were overtly and covertly engaged in determining political life in the colony.

This action by the government led to another strike, which was called by the Trade Union Congress (TUC) on April 18. The strike lasted for eighty days. The only sector of society that did not join the strike was the primarily East Indian sugar workers who were members of the Guiana Industrial Workers Union. The TUC again received support from the commercial sector and were also recipients of resources from the International Confederation of Free Trade Unions (ICFTU), Organización Regional Interamericana de Trabajadores (ORIT), and the American Institute for Free Labor Development (AIFLD). As Jagan has argued, the tactic this time was not to burn the city but to impose a sea and air blockade. The hope was that this would lead to the fall of the PPP government.

As a result of the blockade, food, gasoline, and other commodities were in short supply, and despite the increasing availability of local products, including cigarettes (such as Texas 99 and Diamond) manufactured from locally grown tobacco, there was still discontent. The strikers participated in "squattings" around government offices to keep strikebreakers from entering. Some senior civil servants were known to have invited strikers to squat in front of their homes to provide them with an excuse for not going to work. These "squattings"/sit-ins were strategic. It would not be strange for a chief accountant to be prevented from leaving home on the day that he should be in office to sign the pay sheet. The aim was to frustrate the strikebreakers.

Songs from the US labor movement and the civil rights movement were among the most popular sung during the eighty-day strike. "Solidarity forever," "We shall not be moved," and "We shall overcome" were among the popular marshaling cries. The strikers also did variations on these songs. The author recalls being part of a group of strikers squatting in front of the Queenstown, Georgetown home of a senior civil servant. The group was lustily singing, "We shall not be moved," when the wife of the civil servant opened the front window to see what was going on. On seeing the assembled squatters, she released a few choice expletives. This led to a variation on "We shall not be moved": "Lulu is a cuss bird / We shall not be moved!"

Union halls were important social venues during the 1963 strike. In addition to playing games and collecting a weekly supply of food rations, strikers were also engaged in cultural activities. The influential Civil Service Association formed the CSA Folk Singers, led by W. J. Simmons. Other members of the group included Joseph Simmons and Pauline Thomas. Stylistically, the choir's rendition of Guyanese folk songs was in four-part harmony sung a cappella. A recording of a CSA Folk Singers performance during a concert of Guianese music for a US diplomat resident in Georgetown during the early 1960s is available at the Library of Congress in Washington, D.C.

The strike was violent. Hamilton Green and others have argued that the cycle of violence started on March 23, when a school bus taking the children of the senior staff of an East Coast sugar plantation to school in Georgetown was blown up en route. The explosion killed Godfrey Teixeira and injured several others. According to Green, the act was condemned by the wider society. During this moment, the PPP's newspaper, the *Mirror*, published an insensitive editorial asking who wept with Kowshilla's children when their mother was killed during the Enmore massacre in the 1948. The outcry to this editorial was widespread and the *Mirror* had to print a front-page apology.[60] Irrespective of when or where it started, the situation in Guiana went into a vicious downward spiral. Racial violence took place all across the coastal region of the colony. These were some of the darkest times in the colony's twentieth-century history.

Although this period was the darkest in contemporary Guyanese history, it was also a period when Guyanese showed their best sides and gave a glimpse of what was possible in the future. In all communities across the nation, people of all ethnic groups protected members of other ethnic groups. The strike ended in July 1963 when the legislation for Industrial Relations Bill lapsed in Parliament.[61]

In October the second independence conference was held in London, and again there was deadlock. This time there was disagreement on the electoral system. As a result, the three parties (PPP, PNC, and UF) that attended the conference authorized the colonial secretary, Duncan Sandys, to make a decision on the type of electoral system to be used in the pre-independence election. He decided on Proportional Representation (PR). Cheddi Jagan was again outmaneuvered and left the conference angry.[62] The next elections were scheduled for 1964.

On Jagan's return to the colony, the PPP launched an anti-PR campaign, "The Hurricane of Protests." The PPP and PYO staged protests all over British Guiana. Among the slogans painted across the nation by the PPP were "No PR," "PR or Death," "We'll rather die than have PR," and "PR or CR." "CR" meant "cut rass"—a vicious form of beating.

In 1964 the violence escalated. In February the PPP-affiliated union, the Guiana Industrial Workers Union, launched a strike in the sugar industry that lasted for 161 days. According to Waters and Daniels, the goal of that strike was to "shift the colony's balance of power." The tactics used included intimidation, burning, and murder. At the time it was believed there was a Cuban hand in the violence. To counter the wave of terror, opposition unions formed "vigilance committees" with support of the US Central Intelligence Agency through the AFL-CIO. Based on interviews with Cuban intelligence operatives Domingo Amuchastegui and Osvaldo Cárdenas, Waters and Daniels concluded that there was indeed Cuban involvement in the terror tactics applied by Guiana Industrial Workers Union and its supporters during the strike.[63]

The violence continued to escalate. Persons were shot, had their throats slit, and their bodies mutilated. Women were gang raped. Homes were burned and people chased out of communities in which their families had lived for generations. Among the despicable acts of this period were the arson of the home of the Abrahams, in which eight persons perished; the bombing of the *Sun Chapman*, a passenger vessel owned by a PNC supporter, killing forty persons on the Demerara River, just below McKenzie; and the Wismar massacre, in which East Indians were beaten, gang raped, and killed. At the end of 1964, over two hundred persons had been killed and eight hundred injured as a result of 368 political/racial clashes. Thirteen thousand were refugees. There were 1,600 cases of arson, 226 explosions, 675 illegal discharges of firearms, and indictable offences increased by 100 percent from two thousand in 1961 to four thousand in 1964. As a result of this carnage and ignorance, a petition signed by Africans and Indians was submitted to the governor, Sir Richard Luyt, calling for the partitioning of the country.[64]

It was during this time that Guiana experienced the healing power of music. In 1964 Radio Demerara and British Guiana Broadcasting Service commissioned Fyrish, Corentyne–born Nesbit Chhangur, known as "The Singing Cowboy" because of his country and western singing style, to compose a song that would contribute to calming the society and nurturing peace. The song "Guiana Lament" was recorded at Radio Demerara on High Street. The melody was based on Marty Robbins's "Devil Woman." Chhangur used six verses to tell the story of the origins of the violence on "Tain public road," the scope and horror of the bombings, and the "barbarous deaths," and made a plea for "race with race work together as friends" in building a strong, free, and just Guiana.

During the height of the disturbances, the song was played as much as twenty-four times a day. Chhangur was born in Fyrish Village, Corentyne near Port Mourant in the early 1930s. During the 1940s he performed on the vaudeville circuit in shows arranged by Sam Chase. He also had a radio presence during the 1940s, winning *The Ovaltine Talent Show* (a.k.a. *Gong Show*) on ZFY, the local radio station. In the 1950s the guitar-playing, yodeling Singing Cowboy was a regular performer on *Berbice Calling*, a program produced and presented by Olga Lope-Seal on Radio Demerara.[65] To reinforce the message of "Guiana Lament," Chhangur followed up with the three-versed "Call to Guiana." The final verse pleaded with Guianese to forget race, pride, and recent past and work together side by side with "love and justice."

There were always hopes in the colony that there would be reconciliation between the PPP and the PNC. On October 27, 1964, Burnham made it clear at a public meeting that he was not entering into a coalition with the PPP.[66] Like previous elections, the election campaign of 1964 was "high powered and well organized." Among the innovations for this election were the "overseas vote," which permitted Guianese living abroad to vote, and the "proxy vote." The turnout was very high, 96.8 percent.[67] The PPP won 24 seats, the PNC 22, UF 7.

The PNC and the UF formed the coalition government that led the nation to independence in May 1966.

The governor had to issue a special Order-in-Council to oust Cheddi Jagan, who refused to resign after the election. The declared goals of the coalition government were to bring peace, address the unemployment problem (which stood at 30 percent), and seek financial aid from external sources. To address the first goal, the government "invited the International Commission of Jurists, to establish a Commission of Enquiry to deal with the racial imbalances in the security forces, the public service, and other government agencies. The Enquiry was also asked to look into Land Settlement Schemes and all other areas of government activity."[68]

To address the problem of unemployment, the government launched a series of Keynesian labor-intensive public works and raised the minimum wage from $3.04 per day to $4.00 per day. In the regime's first six months in office, "approximately six thousand persons were employed."[69] For the third goal, the coalition received substantial support from the governments of the United States, Canada, the United Kingdom, and the United Nations. Of these, the United States was the largest contributor.[70]

At midnight on May 26, 1966, 2nd Lieutenant Desmond Roberts raised the Gold Arrowhead at an impressive ceremony at the Queen Elizabeth II National Park, signaling the arrival of the independent nation of Guyana. One hundred and fifty-three years of British colonial rule came to an end and a fragile multi-ethnic, multi-religious state had emerged. Although the PPP boycotted the wider celebrations, Dr. Cheddi Jagan was present at the flag-raising ceremony and exchanged hugs with Linden Forbes Sampson Burnham, Esq., QC, Guyana's first prime minister. The new nation remained a member of the British Commonwealth, with Queen Elizabeth II as the symbolic head. Her Majesty's representative in Guyana was the Guiana-born governor general, Sir David Rose. During the crisis in 1953, he was head of the Special Branch of the British Guiana Police Force. He was also a respected tenor and sang regularly with the British Guiana Police Force Male Voice Choir. His father had been very active in the local music scene during the 1920s and 1930s, performing regularly at concerts.

There was much more to independence than raising the new flag. New national symbols were developed. These included the motto, coat of arms, and a national anthem. All of these were expected at that phase in the construction of nationhood and identity. Work on the development of these national symbols had started on February 1, 1962, when "the Legislative Assembly affirmed a motion by PPP Member of the Legislative Assembly Mohamed Saffee, to set up a Select Committee tasked with designing a national flag and coat of arms, composing a national anthem and selecting a new name for the colony."[71] This was in anticipation of a decision on independence to be arrived at during the 1962 independence conference in London.

It took many years to arrive at decisions of the symbols of nationhood. Deciding on the motto was the easiest. The new nation's motto was "One People, One Nation, One Destiny," which Brindley Benn had approved in 1958. The design for the national flag was approved in March 1966. An American citizen, Whitney Smith, then director of the Flag Research Center in Massachusetts, submitted the winning design. He had submitted the design to Jagan in 1960.

The story of the selection of the national anthem is very interesting. As Lynette Dolphin has detailed, Guyana was one of the few new countries whose citizens knew the words and music of their national anthem before the day of independence.[72] The route to that achievement started in 1960 when a special committee of the legislature invited submissions of lyrics for a national anthem. Two hundred and twelve entries were submitted. However, by 1962 no decision was made, so the Minister of Education and Community Development, C. V. Nunes, tasked the chairman of the National History and Arts Committee to move the process forward. Again, no decision was arrived at.

In 1965 there was urgency to select a national anthem, and Winifred Gaskin, then the Minister of Education in the PNC government, tasked the National History and Arts Council (elevated from a committee), under Lynette Dolphin to establish a public and transparent process to select a national anthem. In the same year, a new competition was launched and a small committee of "persons with broad literary and poetic backgrounds" was appointed for the task of selecting the anthem. This committee developed a set of principles to guide their work. The anthem was expected to be dignified, encourage patriotism, "be simple in conception that even a child could understand it," be singable in a rousing manner, and must project the special attributes of the nation. Further, it was expected that the national anthem would not make undue references to ideology, political party slogans, or names of personalities, avoid religious references, especially in denominational terms, and should not bear undue resemblance to other national anthems.[73]

Two hundred and sixty-six entries were received and, through a selection process, the number was winnowed down, first to forty and then to twelve, and finally to the winning submission—"Green Land of Guyana." The composer of the winning entry was Rev. Archibald Leonard Luker, the English teacher at the New Amsterdam In-Service Teachers Training Programme.

His lyrics speak to the geography and aspirations of the new nation and frame Guyana as a mother to whom the citizens need to pay homage and to protect. It reaffirms a value consistent in all sectors of the society: you must respect and make sacrifices for your parents, especially your mother; they sacrificed for you and you are expected to do that for them. This sentiment is summed up in the promise embedded in fourth and final verse: "Dear land of Guyana, to you will we give / Our homage, our service, each day that we live / God guard you, Great Mother, and make us to be / More worthy our heritage, land of the free."

With the selection of the lyrics, the next task was to select the music for the anthem. For this another public competition was organized. According to Lynette Dolphin, copies of the lyrics were circulated to Guyanese musicians at home and abroad. More than one hundred entries were received. Eventually, the pool was reduced to the entries submitted by William H. L. Pilgrim, Robert Cyril Gladstone Potter, and Valerie Rodway.

R. C. G. POTTER

COMPOSER OF THE GUYANA NATIONAL ANTHEM

Profile

BY

CLEVELAND W. HAMILTON

Figure 7.1. Robert Cyril Gladstone Potter. Photograph courtesy of Guyana National Library.

The final decision was an exercise in participation. A committee of one hundred persons representing schools, youth groups, religious organizations, and the political parties was established to make the choice. The principles of transparency, participation, and inclusiveness were clearly here. The process started with the recording of the three versions at the studios of Radio Demerara. A soprano, Evelyn John; a baritone, Stanley Ridley; a school choir, the Bishop's High School Junior Choir; and a military band, the British Guiana Police Force Band, recorded these versions. On the appointed day, the hundred-person committee gathered at the Government Technical Institute (GTI) at the corner of Woolford Avenue and Camp Street. Compton Pooran, the East Indian tenor, who we met in Helen Taitt's *The Future Is Bright*, was at that time the principal of the institution.

According to Lynette Dolphin, the atmosphere at the GTI was friendly and there was lively banter. There was excitement in the air as the committee members received their score sheets and the technicians from the Government Information Services stood by to play the recordings. The committee

Valerie Rodway (*Photo courtesy of Cicely Gouveia*)

Figure 7.2. William Rutherford Alexander "Billy" Pilgrim. Photograph courtesy of Guyana National Library.

Figure 7.3. Valerie Rodway. Photograph courtesy of Guyana National Library.

was doing a blind test, as they had no knowledge of the names of the composers. All they had were numbers. Based on the committee's evaluations, Potter's setting of Rev. Luker's lyrics was selected as the music for the national anthem.

Robert Cyril Gladstone Potter (1899–1981) was educated at Queen's College and had a substantial career as a teacher in primary, secondary, and tertiary institutions. Between 1948 and 1952, he was principal of the Guiana Teachers College. From 1952 to 1956 he was the colony's deputy director of education. In addition to his career in education, Potter was also a composer who specialized in setting poetry to music. Among his popular compositions in this vein prior to 1965 were "A Christmas Carol" (John Parris), "My Guiana Eldorado" (Lawrence), "Song of Hope" (P. Lawrence), and "Way Down Demerara" (J. R. Hutson).[74] His music for the anthem was hymnlike, as were most of the anthems of recently independent Caribbean nations. The composition was stylistically similar to the English hymns that dominated the hymnals of the Anglican and other mainstream Protestant denominations in the colony. With the selection of the lyrics and the music, radio programs such as *Broadcast to Schools* produced by the Ministry of Education, dedicated its twice-weekly singing program to teaching the new anthem. At midnight on May 26,

1966, when the Union Jack was lowered and Guyana's Golden Arrowhead was raised for the first time, symbolizing the birth of the new nation, the country knew the words and melody of the anthem and they sang it lustily!

All of the persons associated with the selection of the music for that national anthem were impressed by the high quality of the entries by William Pilgrim and Valerie Rodway. As a result, they were asked to submit alternative lyrics so that their compositions could be used as national songs. They did so and Valerie Rodway's composition became "Guyana the Free" and William Pilgrim's became "Salute to Guyana."

Among the international invitees to the independence celebrations was William "Billy" Pilgrim, who was at that time the program manager for the Jamaica Broadcasting Corporation.[75] The attention his anthem entry attracted and his visit to Guyana for the independence celebrations appears to have catalyzed his decision to return to his land of birth. After winning a scholarship to study music at the Royal Academy of Music in 1939, unlike Lynette Dolphin and his brother Philip he had not returned to British Guiana after graduation.

During World War II, Pilgrim joined the Royal Air Force and received an officer's commission. After the war, he graduated from the Royal Academy of Music and became a music teacher and for a period of time was a choirmaster in London. He also became a regular producer of programs on Caribbean cultural matters on the BBC Caribbean Service. In 1959 he left the BBC to take up the appointment as director of music with the Jamaican Broadcasting Corporation (JBC).[76] He was also the conductor of the JBC Concert Orchestra. His wife, Ester Olivegren, an accomplished concert singer, accompanied him to Jamaica where, in December 1966, she won the prestigious Roderick Jones Cup for singing.[77]

During his stay in Jamaica, Billy Pilgrim became very active in Jamaica's musical life, especially in the realm of classical and light classical music. He emphasized choral music and was also the musical director for the Jamaican Amateur Operatic Society. Under his leadership the society presented many Gilbert and Sullivan operettas and works by Noel Coward and Jean Anouilh. He also was engaged in using forms of popular music and novel packages to tell national stories. On May 30, 1967, the *Jamaica Gleaner* reported that William Pilgrim was leaving Jamaica to take up the appointment as public relations officer with the Demerara Bauxite Company (DEMBA). He exerted substantial influence on music in Guyana until he died in 2006.

From the special publication, *Guyana Graphic Independence Souvenir*, published on May 26, 1966, it appears that music was associated with three categories of activities: (a) ceremonial, (b) moments of affirmation, and (c) public celebrations. In addition to the official program, private citizens also contributed to the music that marked Guyana's independence. For example,

Vivian Lee produced the LP *Let's Celebrate Guyana's Independence* on the ACE label. The featured musicians on this album were Bumble and the Saints, Tom Charles and His Guyana Syncopaters, and Lyric Smith's Masquerade Band. This album was indicative of the state of popular music in the nation in 1966. The album not only reaffirmed Lee's entrepreneurial skills, it also captured the mood of the times and gave visibility to Guyanese folk music, especially masquerade and its derivative "the bhoom."

The electric guitar band Bumble and the Saints are the featured performers on side one of the album. The first track is an original composition titled "Independence Time." Next is a medley of three folk songs, "Sweet Madeline," "Satira Gal," and "Yalla Gal." The final track on side one is the instrumental "Kissing Bridge," another original composition. That track eventually became a theme song for Ron Robinson's morning show on Radio Demerara. The band, led by Colin "Bumble" Wharton, was multi-ethnic. According to Carlo Lachmansingh, the founding members of the band were Errol Lachmansingh (drum set), Carlo Lachmansingh (congas/bongos/timbales), Colin Wharton (lead guitar), Steve Busby (bass guitar), Aubrey Cummings (rhythm guitar), Trenton "Saggie" Jarvis (electronic organ), Celeste Milling (female vocalist), and Eustace Sealey (male lead vocalist). The owner of the band was Lionel Augustus Lachmansingh, the proprietor of a pharmacy on Regent Street opposite St. Barnabas Church—thus the name Bumble and the Saints.[78]

The first track on side two is "The Guyana Bhoom," performed by Tom Charles and the Guyana Syncopaters, one of the few remaining big bands in Guyana at that time. The bhoom was invented by Tom Charles and was inspired by the beat laid down by the bhoom drum of masquerade bands. It was to be Guyana's equivalent to Jamaica's blue beat and Barbados's spooge. "The Guyana Bhoom" is followed by two tracks by Lyric Smith and his Masquerade Band, "Independence Flounce" and "On Freedom Road." Lyric Smith excelled on the flute, presenting standard masquerade flute melodies with wonderful trilling and variations on Kwe Kwe folk songs such as "Gal, yuh glorious marnin' come" and "Madeline." The two tracks are spiced with the "toasts" expected from masquerade bands. One of these toasts—"Don't mind you call me a negro / Don't mind my toe is full of chigoe"—sums up what was probably subconsciously flowing through the minds of many Guyanese of African ancestry who saw independence as the final severing of the chains of slavery and colonialism that had dominated them for more than three hundred years.

The bhoom was an example of musical exchange and an effort of the part of Tom Charles to create a national sound for Guyana. By 1966 Trinidad had been established as the calypso capital of the world; Jamaica had mento, blue beat, and ska—the precursors of reggae; and in Barbados, Jackie Opel had launched the Spooge (Spouge) and attained regional popularity. In the psyche of many Guyanese, both musicians and non-musicians, a national dance and party sound was needed to go with the new national flag and anthem. It was a matter of pride and identity. This quest to find an original national sound would remain unachieved in the post-independence era. In the interim, Guyanese bands became excellent cover bands.

Bumble and the Saints was one of a growing number of electric guitar bands in Georgetown at the time of independence. Others included the Casanovas, which had accompanied Andy Nichols when he recorded "Parting Is Hard"; the Jokers; the Crystals; the Heart Breakers; Bing Serrão and the Ramblers String Orchestra; Combo 7; the Rhythmaires String Orchestra; and the Telstars. Most of these bands had lead vocalists; Winston "Pepe" Romalho was vocalist with Des Glasford's Combo 7 and Ted E. Jones with The Rhythmaires. Recorder gave them plaudits in the *Guiana Graphic Independence Souvenir* publication. Pioneering pop vocalists such as Mike Bacchus and Johnny Braff were members of the Heart Breakers. The dominant electric guitar band in New Amsterdam was the Vikings. During a Facebook conversation in November 2010, New Amsterdam–born musician and audio engineer Gordon Burnett observed that the Vikings, who "started in the early 60's and first appeared on shows like *Stars in the Making* were simply untouchable, as they won every competition they ever entered, locally and nationally."[79]

There was only one female-led band during this era, Nona Permaul and the Playboys. She was also the only female drummer in the colony. Those skills gained her the respect of the popular music fraternity. The band was popular nationally and internationally. In 2010 she reflected on her domestic and international career, which involved playing with Tito Puente and Ben E. King and included performing for Queen Juliana of the Netherlands and Britain's Queen Elizabeth II.[80]

Other than Tom Charles and the Syncopaters, the other big bands in Guyana in 1966 included George Accra and His Hot Shots, Nello and His New Luckies, Clem Thomas's Bongo Nights Orchestra, and Sonny Thomas and His Orchestra. There were also smaller brass and wind ensembles such as Charlie Knights and His Boptets. There were also a number of steel bands, including Club 59, Invaders All Steel Percussion Orchestra, Kaietukians, Pelcans Steel Band, Radiation Steel Band, and Starland Steel Band.

All of the popular music ensembles during the 1960s shared some common characteristics: they were adept at covering the popular music of the era, and they all followed a performance pattern that ended with a "bruk-up" piece. There were interesting variations on "covers." An example of a successful cover is "Suhani Raat" recorded by the Rhythmaires for their album *Rhythmaires International: From Kaieteur to Europe* in the mid-1960s. Guyanese have an extended association with "Suhani Raat." Their first encounter with the song was the version performed by Mohamed Rafi in the 1949 film *Dulari*, which was popular in British Guiana. An instrumental version was the theme song for Ayube Hamid's radio program *Indian Melody Album*, which had started in 1958 and was still serving the same function in 2008. The song's melody was haunting and was expressive of the sensuous Urdu lyrics of waiting and unrequited love.[81]

During the turbulent early 1960s, the popularity of Rhythmaires' version demonstrated the power of the song's melody to transcend racial barriers and offer the potential for racial peace and harmony. The recording has achieved iconic status among Guyanese and has been redone by several Guyanese musicians such as Terry Gajraj and Ray Seales.[82] When heard in the diaspora, especially the generation that came of age during the 1960s and older, the song has the ability to evoke pleasant feelings of identity and harmony among Guyanese of many generations—another example of "unisonality" from the Guyanese songbook.

The tendency to make cover versions and perform popular international music was also evident in the music produced by Indo-Guyanese bands. The repertoire of bands—such as the Corentyne's Lonely Bulls and the Dil Bihar Orchestra; the Star Rhythm Combo in West Coast, Berbice; and the Original Pioneers and Melody Makers of Georgetown—were dominated by music from Indian films and the vocalists strove to sound like Mohamed Rafi, Mukesh, Kishore Kumar, Lata Mangeshkar, or other Indian playback singers.

As we have seen from the days of the "practice dance," if not before, it has always been a tradition for Guyanese bands to play a "bruk-up" session at the end of a dance or party in public or private spaces. In the 1960s, in addition to playing the popular calypsos and road marches from Trinidad, special emphasis was placed on adapting Guyanese folk music, especially the folk music associated with the African experience in Guyana in Guyanese calypsos. An example of this trend was King Fighter's "Me Na Dead Yet." Similar tendencies were also appearing in performances by Indian musicians as they began to perform Chatini songs from Matticore/Dig Dutty and other folk songs sung with a mixture of Bhojpuri Hindi and Creolese.

The popularization and promotion of folk was the outcome of cultural nationalism honed in resistance to colonialism, as evident in de Weever's 1901 "Me Cawfee in de Marnin'," the song catching of Vesta Lowe, and (after 1957) the expressed policy of the governments of the PPP, which was continued under the PNC after they took office in 1964. Guyanese folk music was an important attribute of Guyanese nationhood and identity. There were other factors that contributed to expanding the space for folk music in the years leading up to independence. Folk music slowly became an integral aspect of the aesthetics of the state. In the early days, the sound of folk music at official functions sounded "Englishified," at term used by a music festival adjudicator to describe the rendition of a Guianese folk song by the British Guiana Police Force's Male Voice Choir.[83] Renditions by the Civil Service Association's Folk Choir and the Woodside Choirs during this period had similar sonics. What was afoot was a discourse and practice aimed at "elevating" folk music to the status of "good music."

A similar development had taken place with black music in the United States starting in the late nineteenth century. For some African American composers and arrangers, this was demonstration of achievement by "a small nation of people" since the abolition of slavery in 1867.[84] Not all black intellectuals agreed with the strategy of using European frameworks to legitimize black creativity. Some were very upset. As early as 1926, almost at the start of Harlem Renaissance, the African American poet and philosopher Langston Hughes, then a "young Turk," thought that the effort to "elevate" African American folk music such as spirituals, blues, and jazz to "high art" indicated a subconscious desire to be white and to further efforts aimed toward the deification of Western musical aesthetics. Provocatively, he recommended, "Let the blare of Negro jazz bands and the bellowing of Bessie Smith singing Blues penetrate the closed ears of the colored near intellectuals until they listen and perhaps understand."[85] The tension between musical exchange/syncretism and authenticity would remain a major tension in African American musical creativity. This tension was reenergized during the 1960s, as a result of the multi-dimensional struggle for civil rights by African Americans. African American popular music genres such as R&B, soul, rock and roll, and jazz put issues such as justice, fairness, leadership, obligation, ambition, and authenticity on the cultural agenda across the African diaspora in the Americas. The African American songbook for the 1960s was potent. As Sam Cooke noted in 1963, "A Change is Gonna Come."

In Guyana an influential voice in support of "authentic" folk was the BBC-trained radio broadcaster Wordsworth McAndrew. He questioned the prevailing manifestations of cultural domination and the cultural ambivalence of Guyana's "Englishified" cultural leaders. He refused to wear a tie on the job. He also preferred to wear sandals and slippers to work. He argued that ties and shoes were impractical in a tropical country and adhering to those styles was subscribing to colonial aesthetics. Beyond his resistance to dress styles inherited from the colonial era, McAndrew was passionate about all aspects of Guyana's multi-ethnic folk heritage. He was very public about this passion and used every opportunity, on the radio or in public talks, to call for action to preserve and promote the nation's folk traditions.[86]

Despite McAndrew's call for the celebration of all the folk expressions of multi-ethnic Guyana, what emerged in the days leading up to independence

emphasis on creole folk culture

and in the years following was the unfortunate tendency by state agencies to position African-based folk as the only authentic Guyanese folk expression. Part of this was opportunistic, as most of state functions were held in Georgetown. Another aspect was a function of the ethnopolitics that continued in Guyanese society after independence. Cheddi Jagan and the PPP boycotted many state events and this stance was reproduced by many members of the East Indian Guyanese community. As a result, African-derived folk expressions and related derivatives from across the Caribbean—calypso and later soca—became the sound of "official" Guyana. This aspect of the musical aesthetics of the state was described by sectors of the Indian Guyanese community as "black man music" and framed as carnal, vulgar, and of poor taste—reproducing a colonial stereotype that it was not respectable. At the same time, the urban-based East Indian elite also did not appear to wholeheartedly embrace East Indian folk music, especially the creolized "recent developments" and the rum shop songs, as these were continuing examples of backward "Coolie culture." The preference was to seek authenticity from India. The Indian High Commission in Georgetown obliged with Indian highbrow varieties.

Not only were there more electric guitar bands in Guyana at the time of independence, there were also changes in the range of instruments used by these bands. When Bing Serrão and the Ramblers started in the 1950s, the dominant instruments were mandolins, quartos, guitars, and the string bass. By 1966 bands were expanding the range of musical instruments. Some featured organs and vibraphones; others featured steel pans. By 1966 the Rhythmaires had introduced the Selmer Clavioline, a forerunner to the synthesizer; a Vox electronic organ; and a Hammond L100 organ.[87] The Rhythmaires' keyboard player, Wendell Bunyan, established himself as the nation's leading electronic keyboard player. Des Glasford added the vibraphone and the professional drum set to Combo 7. In addition, bands were also experimenting with Latin percussion instruments.

A survey in 2009 of the record collection at the Bertie Chancellor Music Library at the National Communication Network suggests that during the 1960s there was an upsurge in the recording and publishing of music in Guyana. Among the local record labels were Halagala, ACE, Cee-Jays, GEMS, and WOW. Central to this proliferation of local record labels were the efforts of entrepreneurs such as Vivian Lee (ACE), Al Seales (GEMS), recording technologies and technicians of the radio stations, especially Radio Demerara, and the private studios operated by Seales and Terry Nelson. Among the important radio-based audio engineers during the 1960s were George Benson, Denis King, Eustace Lovell, and Hulbert W. Clarke. George Benson was responsible for a number of pioneering recordings, among them *Sharp Steel* by Marsden "Patsy" Adams—the first steel band album to be recorded in British Guiana—and *760 Jazz*, a jazz album featuring Hugh Sam on piano, Maurice Watson on bass, Art Broomes on drums, and Harry Whittaker on saxophone. Prior to migrating to the United States, Denis King engineered seminal recordings by Johnny Braff and Mark Holder. When Denis King migrated to the United States, he had a successful career as a recording engineer and record producer with Atlantic Records in New York during the 1970s. Hulbert Clarke was the recording engineer of note on recordings by Lord Canary, Joy Thomas, the Mighty Kaieteur (the Drunk Man), Neisha Benjamin, Moses Josiah, Bumble and the Saints, Des Glasford, Chronicle Atlantic Symphony, Guyana Police Male Voice Choir, and the Pupil Teachers Choir. Until the late 1960s the practice was to make the recordings in Guyana and have the records pressed overseas.

One of the realities facing the PNC/UF coalition government in 1964 was a shortage of skilled manpower in various sectors of the soon-to-be-independent nation. One response was to recruit from the Guyanese and West Indian diaspora in the United Kingdom through a remigration scheme. Under this program, the government paid passage and provided duty-free concessions for persons who were returning to take up positions in the public sector. Members of the diaspora were also encouraged to return to establish private businesses. Those who participated were also provided with a number of incentives such as duty-free importation of equipment and materials and a tax holiday for a defined period. One person who took up that later opportunity was Terry Nelson, who at that time was a blue beat/reggae musician in the swinging London music scene.[88]

Nelson returned to Guyana just after independence and established Halagala Studios. His ambition was to expand the Guyanese music industry and promote a distinctive Guyanese sound through the Halagala label. In addition to a recording studio, he established the first record pressing plant in the nation. His quest for the distinctive Guyanese sound would lead to the creation of the "Afro-Indi beat" and the emergence of a number of singers such as Joyce Urmella Harris, Neisha Benjamin, and the Mighty Enchanter who pioneered this beat. These artists would make popular some East Indian creole folk songs such as "Benji Darling" and "Oh Maninja." His release of Neisha Benjamin's "Sandrowta" is considered "Guyana's original Chutney hit."[89] Guyana's Terry Gajraj has recognized the contributions of the Halagala label to the creation of contemporary chutney music.[90] India's Babla and Kanchan would later cover some of the music that Terry Nelson's label recorded and enjoy popularity with them in India and across the Indian diaspora in the USA and the UK—an example of musical exchange and the circulation of musical ideas.

Terry Nelson remained in Guyana until he died in 2009. At the time of his death he was the owner and operator of a television station in Beterverwagting on the East Coast of Demerara. As a performer he had a few hits. Despite the recognition given to him by Terry Gajraj, his life as a music maker in Guyana was difficult. He too experienced problems with gatekeepers at the local radio stations. The primary complaint was about the quality of the materials he used in his products. Economic conditions, including the small size of the domestic record-buying market, caused Nelson to recycle the vinyl used in the pressing of records. His large body of work did not enjoy commensurate airplay. As Ray Seales noted:

> To me, Terry Nelson was one of Guyana's music die hards. Guyana beat that man down, but he kept coming back. He really impressed me with his determination to succeed in the music business. When Terry first came back to Guyana, he opened at the First Federation Building on Croal St. This was a big to do, all of the big wigs were present to drink and toast Terry's return. Thru the years Terry became Omar Farouk the TV Station owner in BV. This man tried hard.[91]

Guyana's struggle for independence also inspired the international progressive community. A powerful example was the opera *The Sugar Reapers*, composed by the noted British communist composer Alan Bush. The opera was premiered in Leipzig, East Germany, at the new Leipzig Operahaus on December 11, 1966. In his review for the *Times* (London), Fritz Bennewitz described the opera as a story of true love between Johnny Lucas, a sugar worker of African ancestry, and Sumintra, a woman of Indian ancestry. It is also a story about family betrayal that climaxes when the police "burst upon the marriage ceremonies of Johnny, who has become a leader of his people, and his Indian bride." Bennewitz praised the musical scope of the opera—"the splendidly composed choral ensembles, big in scope and vigorous in rhythm." Also praised were the "highly singable solo arias [that] enable the principal characters to engage the sympathy of the audience in a manner that is as welcome as it is uncommon in modern opera." Alan Bush was commended for "his use of Indian and African folk music [which gave] the score a new freshness and flexibility."[92] One example is "Corentyne Kwe Kwe," based on the folk song "Janey Gal."

In addition to persistent economic problems, the new nation started its life with multiple unresolved border problems. Throughout the nineteenth century there were increasing tensions with Venezuela, Dutch Guiana, and to a limited extent Brazil over borders. Within three years of independence, Guyana would have three significant border problems that would test its fledgling military and diplomatic capacity. The Austrian geographer Richard

Schomburgk had traveled to British Guiana between 1840 and 1844 to resolve the border problem with Venezuela by producing a definitive map of the colony's borders. This did not suffice because, by the late nineteenth century, the United States had to pressure the government of Great Britain to submit to international arbitration on the boundaries between British Guiana and Venezuela. The decision that was handed down in 1899 was reluctantly accepted by Venezuela. The border remained a festering problem in relations between the two countries.[93] During the late nineteenth and early twentieth centuries there were Venezuelan military incursions into parts of the colony. Those incursions and threats of invasion must have left a mark in the consciousness of the citizens; in 1938 Joe Coggins invoked the invasion in his calypso "Bush Women Come to Town," in which he thinks that the crowds gathered in Georgetown were witnessing the "Spanish man-of-war" that had come to take over the country, and subsequently finds out that it was the bush women who had come to town for King George's coronation!

In 1962, just as it was becoming clear that British Guiana's independence was going to be a reality in the very near future, the Venezuelans declared that the 1899 arbitration award was null and void because Great Britain had bribed the arbitrators and thus denied Venezuela three quarters of British Guiana's territory. This claim set off a chain of diplomatic events leading to a status-quo agreement signed in February 1966 in Geneva. Under what was known as the Geneva Agreement, "no new claim or enlargement of an existing claim to the territorial sovereignty in these territories (of Venezuela and British Guiana) shall be asserted while this Agreement is in force, nor shall any claim whatsoever be asserted otherwise than in a Mixed Commission while that Commission is in being."[94]

Despite this agreement, in October 1966 Venezuelan forces invaded the newly independent nation of Guyana and seized half of Ankoko Island. Forbes Burnham, Guyana's minister of External Affairs and prime minister, sent a protest note to Venezuela seeking the "withdrawal of Venezuelan troops and the removal of installations they had set up on Guyana's territory."[95] After consulting with Dr. Cheddi Jagan, the leader of the opposition, he addressed the nation urging calm and advising that steps were being taken to retain the nation's integrity by peaceful means." According to Odeen Ishmael:

> Burnham's announcement immediately galvanized all Guyanese to condemn the Venezuelan action. A few hours after the broadcast, members of the Progressive Youth Organization (PYO) and the Young Socialist Movement (YSM), the youth arms of the PPP and the PNC respectively, mounted a large protest outside the Venezuelan Consulate General in Middle Street, Georgetown. In the course of this noisy demonstration, some of the protestors invaded the

compound and pulled down the Venezuelan flag from the mast and proceeded to burn it on the street.[96]

Prime Minister Burnham and Attorney General and Minister of State Shridath Ramphal immediately extended apologies to the Venezuelan consul general, Señor Aranguren. Guyanese residents in London held protests at the British Foreign Office and in front of the Venezuelan Embassy.

The border problem with Venezuela would remain unresolved for the remainder of the century. In 1968 the Cuban government pledged military assistance to the government of Guyana should it be attached by Venezuela. It appears that the Venezuelan territorial demands and aggression during the twentieth century, especially since 1960, are really part of its role as the policeman for the United States. This proposition has been offered as it appears that, whenever Guyana pursued a development ambition or a foreign policy initiative that ran counter to US interests in the hemisphere, there was a ratcheting up of Venezuela's demand for Guyanese territory. Venezuelan ongoing saber rattling and virulent claims for Guyanese territory inspired "Not a Blade of Grass," an anthem of patriotic defiance composed by Dave Martins in 1980.[97]

In 1967 there would also be problems with the neighboring Dutch colony Suriname over borders. The first indication of the problem came in early 1962. In June 1962 the Dutch government raised claim to the New River Triangle and hoped to have this resolved before independence was granted to British Guiana. There were also tensions as to the interpretation of the Corentyne River as one of the boundaries between the two European colonies. A 1962 conference between the Dutch and British governments failed to resolve the issue, so Guyana became an independent nation with an unresolved border problem with Suriname. In December 1967 a Surinamese survey team was expelled from the New River Triangle for being on Guyanese territory without permission. This expulsion created a diplomatic furor, and later that month it was agreed Suriname "would refrain from encroaching on Guyana's territory."[98]

The first general election after independence was held in December 1968. In that election, the PNC claimed an outright majority, bringing to an end the PNC/UF coalition. As the elections approached so did tensions between the UF and the PNC. Mr. Peter D'Aguiar, the first deputy prime minister and minister of finance, had started to express concerns about corruption and fraud in the public sector. The UF was able to demonstrate fraud in the 1968 elections, especially with the overseas votes from the United Kingdom.[99]

Sometime in early to mid-1969, the Surinamese military occupied the New River Triangle, constructed a military camp, and started to build an airstrip. This installation was found by a Guyana Defence Force patrol on August 19, 1969. After a skirmish, the Surinamese troops, who had opened fire on the GDF patrol, fled back to Suriname. Odeen Ishmael has noted:

The camp built by Suriname's armed forces on Guyana's territory was constructed as a military installation. It had underground bunkers especially constructed to protect against shell and mortar attacks and was equipped with towers and machine-gun emplacements. Maps left by the Surinamese revealed a plan to occupy the entire New River area with a series of military camps, with the camp serving as a base and supply headquarters. Judging from the personal effects and accommodation facilities left at the camp, it was estimated that there were between 50 to 55 men occupying it. They left behind a Caterpillar bulldozer, a jeep, an electric power plant, a mechanical water pump, power driven handsaws, a large refrigerator and well-stocked kitchens.[100]

Like the Venezuelan border problem, the Surinamese border issue would not be resolved by the end of the twentieth century. Diplomatic relations would improve between Venezuela, Surinam, and Guyana, but the border disputes would continue to be festering sores and hindrances to major economic and industrial projects for Guyana, such as the development of a hydropower complex in the Mazaruni District and the prospecting of oil in the Corentyne River. In December 1969 Guyana had to deal with another territorial problem, this time an attempt by ranchers in the Rupununi region, with Venezuelan encouragement, to secede from the new nation.[101] One of the "spoils of war" from the suppression of the Rupununi rebellion was a collection of musical instruments. According to one source, these instruments were used to form the GDF Frontline—an army ensemble that enjoyed national popularity during the 1970s and the early 1980s.

The border disputes made it imperative that Guyana strengthen its diplomatic presence globally. The electoral victory in 1968 provided the Burnham government with latitude to modify the constitution, establish a republic, and chart a new foreign policy aimed at diversification of the economy and international economic relations. On the diplomatic front, Guyana was playing a role in the construction of a successor organization to the West Indian Federation, which was dissolved in 1962. In addition to becoming the 118th member of the United Nations, Guyana was exploring membership in the Non-Aligned Movement and advancing plans to establish diplomatic relations with the USSR.

American support for Burnham continued after independence. In addition to development aid from the United States, which amounted to more than $US18.3 million in 1968, there was a small amount of direct investment from the US private sector in shrimping. One company, Guyana Seafood, with trawlers and cold storage facilities on the Georgetown waterfront, established close ties with Tiger Bay, a notorious urban ghetto, and contributed to sport and music in the new nation. Bill Brown, the manager of the company, was active as a boxing referee. One of the trawler captains, an African American from Mobile, Alabama, known as Tiny, is considered to have been responsible for introducing the R&B and blues music of Swamp Dogg to the society. In Tiger Bay, at bars such as Coloured Footprint, Red Lantern, and Maracaibo, coin-operated jukeboxes churned out Doris Troy and other US Top 40 hits as sailors and locals drank copious quantities of Guyanese rum and Banks beer.

The 1960s were dramatic times for Guyana. The nation experienced the pain and destruction of racial violence on a massive scale. As a result of a number of stratagems by the United States and the United Kingdom, British Guiana attained independence and the threat of a government dominated by the communist PPP was thwarted. This decade also witnessed the civil rights struggle of black Americans, and the soundtrack from black America resonated with the radicalized, nationalistic mindset that existed in Guyana in its early post-independence years.[102] In multiracial Guyana, songs such as "People Get Ready," "We Shall Overcome," "Say It Loud (I'm Black and I'm Proud)," "Respect," and "Respect Yourself" nourished Guyanese nationalism. Dashikis and Afros were popular among Guyanese of all ethnicities. The spirit of black power and resistance to apartheid was supported by Guyana. Guyana became known as a place where people who were struggling for the liberation of Africa and for promoting the dignity of African people were welcomed. By the end of the 1960s, Guyana was also taking its place as a promoter of African and Asian solidarity and had an active voice in the Non-Aligned Movement. Emblematic of this moment was the founding of the African Society for Cultural Relations with Independent Africa (ASCRIA) by Eusi Kwayana, formerly known as Sydney King. At the first general congress of the PNC after independence, Kwayana along with Valerie Rodway created the rousing "Party Battle Song."[103] The first verse identified the PNC as the institution that led Guyana to independence and created the conditions in which Guyanese were the "reigning masters of [the] land" from the "peak of Mount Rorima" to "the mark of Pointa Playa." The anthem called for unity and linked the Guyana struggle with those of the "sons and daughters of the continents of Earth." The concluding verse called upon all workers "in the factory, in the office" to "rally to the PNC . . . and crush the monster Poverty!"

In terms of popular entertainment, the shift from big bands to electric bands was palpable and the discotheque was becoming the primary venue for consuming international and domestic popular music. As 1969 drew to a close, tragedy struck. On November 10, 1969, while on an official visit to Whitehall Place, London, nine stories of scaffolding fell on Guyana's governor general, Sir David Rose's car and killed him. He had been identified to become Guyana's first president when the nation would become a republic in 1970.

8

The 1970s: "Making the Small Man a Real Man"

It was the best of times, it was the worst of times; it was the age of wisdom, it was the age of foolishness; it was the epoch of belief, it was the epoch of incredulity; it was the season of Light, it was the season of Darkness; it was the spring of hope, it was the winter of despair; we had everything before us, we had nothing before us; we were all going directly to Heaven, we were all going the other way.
—**Charles Dickens,** *A Tale of Two Cities*

The Guyana Independence Act of 1966 established a constitution that has been described as "a standard Westminster type of export constitution for newly independent countries."[1] According to Mohammed Shahabuddeen a former attorney general and minister of justice for Guyana, "[i]ts principal value at the time of its promulgation was that it was regarded as the formal instrument evidencing the attainment of independence."[2] The Independence Act also anticipated the creation of a republic and the replacement of the governor general by a president.[3] On February 23, 1970, Guyana became the Cooperative Republic of Guyana and remained a member of the Commonwealth. With the creation of the republic, Guyana "scored two historic firsts": it was the first republic in the Commonwealth Caribbean and "the first Cooperative Republic in the world."[4] The descriptor *cooperative* reflected an idea and practice that had been present in Guyanese society for more than a century—an idea associated with the burial societies organized by enslaved Africans and also with the informal saving tradition known variously as box money, box hand, throwing box, and kuttu-chit. This informal saving tradition was evident in both African and Indian Guyanese heritages.

The establishment of the Cooperative Republic not only acknowledged this heritage; it also signaled the launching of the PNC government's goal of using the "cooperative as the instrument for building a socialist society in Guyana."[5] At another level, republican status represented "a further step in the direction of self-reliance and self-confidence and historical rectification."[6] The decision to establish the Cooperative Republic of 1970 also paid homage to the Berbice Slave Rebellion, which was led by the enslaved African Cuffy on February 23, 1763, at Plantation Magdalenenberg up the Berbice River. It has also been suggested that the date was chosen as it was very close to Burnham's February 21 birth date![7]

The Honorable Arthur Chung, a High Court judge of Chinese ancestry, was elected by the National Assembly to be Guyana's first president for a six-year term. Under the new constitution the Judicial Committee of the British Privy Council was replaced by the Guyana Court of Appeal as "the final court of appeal for Guyana in all matters."[8] Other than those changes, the 1970 republican constitution maintained all the rights and institutions established under the 1966 constitution. The National Assembly remained the primary legislative body of the land. The offices of leader of the opposition and the ombudsman were retained. Statutory commissions established for the recruitment and promotion of public servants in the nation's civil, judicial, and police services were also retained. Under this new constitutional arrangement, the president was the titular head of state with few reserved powers; power resided in the hands of the prime minister and the National Assembly. In that equation, the charismatic and ambitious Prime Minister Linden Forbes Sampson Burnham was the dominant factor, who was able directly to influence the processes of national governance and many aspects of cultural life in the new nation.

One sector that felt this influence early in the life of the republic was the steel band community. Burnham was admitted to the legal practice in British Guiana on March 11, 1949. Among his early clients were ordinary urban working people. A few of them were steel band musicians who were charged with disturbing the peace and parading without permission. His cousin, Charwin Burnham, then a member of Texacans All Steel Percussion Orchestra and one of the pioneers of steel band music in Guyana, recalled that during a tramp he was charged with "leading an illegal procession."[9] Forbes Burnham was his lawyer and was able to get the case dismissed, as the police prosecutor was unable to show how someone who was playing a pan could at the same time be leading a band.[10] Many of the pioneers of the steel band movement were convinced that the police harassed them. Bertram DeVarell, who founded Tripoli Steel Band, Guyana's first steel band, and Dan Sandiford have confirmed that one form of harassment was the seizure of the steel pans and converting them to other uses. DeVarell recalls seeing pans seized from Tripoli Steel band being used as flowerpots in the police headquarters in Eve Leary.[11] DeVarell suggests that this treatment was based on the perception that British Guianese steel band men were "Bad Johns" and renegades who, like their counterparts in Trinidad, did not want to work and had a predilection for lives of crime. They were framed as neo-centipedes! Burnham felt that archaic colonial laws unfairly treated steel band men and masquerade bands. He also felt the same about the Obeah Suppression Law of 1851.

Newspaper sources suggest that by 1971, there were more than twenty-five steel bands in Guyana. This represented constant growth from 1949, when there were about ten. Despite this growth steel bands lacked resources, and there were concerns that the quality of pan music in Guyana was static and even declining. As early as 1958, the government of British Guiana gave a grant of $1,200 to the embryonic Steel Band Association to buy costumes for a special tramp during Princess Margaret's visit to the colony. Within a year the association folded; an effort made to resuscitate it in 1960 was unsuccessful. Premier Cheddi Jagan sent a national steel band to Cuba in 1963 in an effort to strengthen economic, political, and cultural ties.[12]

By 1971 the Guyana National Steel Band Association, the successor to the Steel Band Association, had been in existence for three years and Hamilton Green, then the Minister of Works, Hydraulics, and Supply was its president, with Derrick Jeffrey as the general-secretary.[13] Among the activities the association organized in collaboration with the National History and Arts Council were annual pan festivals. The keynote speaker for the 1971 Pan Festival was Prime Minister Burnham. He used this platform to issue an edict declaring public-sector support for steel bands in Guyana, declaring, "every Public Corporation and every business in which the Government has a majority shareholding will have a steel band under its sponsorship."[14] At that time, the government of Guyana was well on the way to becoming the nation's primary employer. Prime Minister Burnham further stressed, "Guyanese performance on the steel band demonstrated their ingenuity, creativity, versatility and their association with the Caribbean."[15] For Burnham the steel band was "indigenous," and the decision to have the public sector support steel bands was aimed at "fostering the cultural expressions of the people of Guyana."[16] The decision would resonate across the next fifteen years.

In 1971 the critic Jerry Daniel was not enthusiastic about national steel band festivals. He felt that it was just a form of copycatism, apishness unfortunately sanctioned by the National History and Arts Council. For Daniel, the national steel band festival was unnecessary borrowing and a shallow act of political grandstanding aimed at showing that Guyana was in the forefront of Caribbean unity. He argued that in promoting Guyanese musical creativity there should be investment not in the "pee-dee-leep, ling-pong boom-ping of Pan" but in the "goo-doo-dup-ch-h-h-ng of the Indian band, the chak-chak-dum of the Amerindians, the dum-doom-doom of the Santapee band, the dum-pe-dum of the Queh Queh and Shanto, the pliant of the Fado and the captivating dance forms of all these."[17]

Between 1971 and 1974, the People's National Congress government had to deal with persistent problems inherited from the colonial experience, in addition to encouraging creativity. Among the persistent problems were protection and defense of the national border; the need to diversify the economy and reduce dependence on the sugar industry; actualizing the potential of the hinterland; building and maintaining drainage and irrigation and transportation infrastructure; making education, health care accessible; the crisis of national identity, and the construction of national unity. There were also new challenges facing the Cooperative Republic of Guyana, including establishing an independent foreign policy and responding to the financial crisis caused by OPEC's decision to reduce oil production and the resultant price increases. In responding to the constellation of challenges, the government fostered a range of cultural activities that would directly affect the quality and direction of music in the nation. Among the initiatives that had long-term impact on Guyanese cultural life and especially music included integrating folk expressions in diplomacy; state ownership of broadcasting; the hosting of the Caribbean Festival of Arts (Carifesta) in 1972; the Guyana Festival of the Arts (GUYFESTA); and the introduction of Mashramani, the national celebrations to celebrate the anniversary of the founding of the republic.

In the early 1970s, Guyana's foreign policy has a number of strategic foci. According to Cedric Grant, "the centerpiece of these relations was Guyana's ties with its sister Caribbean countries as it considered these relations central to its national security, to its ability to respond to the territorial ambitions of two of its neighbours [Venezuela and Suriname], and to its realization of its economic potential."[18] To this end, Forbes Burnham, along with Vere Bird of Antigua, Michael Manley of Jamaica, Errol Barrow of Barbados, and Dr. Eric Williams of Trinidad and Tobago, played a major role in the establishment of the Caribbean Free Trade Association (CARIFTA) in 1965 and the Caribbean Community (CARICOM) in 1973.

Other aspects of the policy included active engagement in the Commonwealth through participation in Commonwealth heads of government summits; support for ideological pluralism through membership and active participation in the Non-Aligned Movement; "support for national liberation struggles [especially in Africa] to eliminate colonialism, occupation, and apartheid." Another important aspect was deepening Guyana's "involvement in the campaign for a new international economic order and working for closer economic co-operation among developing countries" (South-South cooperation).[19] As noted previously, a somewhat covert aspect of Guyana's foreign policy was support for the civil rights struggle in the United States, which included providing refuge for a number of black power advocates. Guyana's foreign service professionals were quite effective and Burnham was popular among the leaders of the Commonwealth and the Non-Aligned Movement; as a result, starting after independence, Guyana was host to many world leaders and other dignitaries. These visits provided opportunities to express the musical aesthetics of the state.

Guyanese music became evident in the cultural aspects of the protocol developed for welcoming these guests to Guyana and for entertaining them during their stay. The National History and Arts Council was responsible for organizing the welcoming ceremonies, which invariably included a masquerade band. Other musical elements to state visits included special concerts and ambient music for state receptions.

This period marked the start of an extended period of work on Guyanese folk music by Lynnette Dolphin, which would result in the production of *Bamboo Fire and Other Folk Songs of Guyana*, a now-iconic LP record, and two publications on Guyanese folk music, including *One Hundred Folk Songs of Guyana*, published in 1996. She completed the editing of *Zeerenggang Bai (Let Us Sing)*, an anthology of Amerindian songs, in January 2000, a month before she died.[20] The compilation remained unpublished as of 2014.

Bamboo Fire was a recording by the EMEL Singers— a choir Dolphin created in 1970 at the Government Secondary Teachers' Training Center, where she was the Visiting Tutor in Music. Hilton Hemerding (first guitar), Marilyn Hunte (second guitar), Khemraj Sooknarine (bongos), and Maurice Watson (double bass), provided accompaniment for the choir. The album featured eleven of the nation's popular folk songs: "Bamboo Fire," "Satira Gal," "Samangereh," "Auntie Bess," "Brown Boy," "Sancho," "Manin' Neigba," "Me Na Dead Yet," "Lily Gal and Carrie," "Itanami," and "Small Days." These songs were primarily African Guyanese in provenance. The album also signaled the start of the National History and Arts Council's sustained support for the recording of Guyanese folk music.

In addition to *Bamboo Fire*, the council also sponsored *Jane Engage and Other Popular Folk Songs of Guyana*, which was recorded by the Guyana Police Male Voice Choir, conducted by Sgt. Morris Watson. This album featured another twelve popular folk songs: "Jane Engage," "Dymodee," "Tell Myray," "Timba Bruck Ah Me Back," "Me Gat Wan Coal Pot," "Blue Coat," "Ooman Ah Dead," "Yuh Wake Me Too Soon," "Ten Tousan' To Wan," "Ting-A-Ling-A-Ling," "Congo Man," and "Nora Darling." Again the recordings privileged folk songs of African Guyanese provenance. Was this a deliberate policy? The answer is much more complicated that a simple yes or no! Part of the answer must recognize the large and popular folk music repertoire created by Guyanese of African ancestry. Other elements were probably unawareness of Creole Indian folk music by urban-based officials in the National History and Arts Council and continuing "cultural cringe" by Georgetown-based East

Indian cultural gatekeepers, who could have agitated for the inclusion of Creole Indian folk songs. The folk music research of Peter Kempadoo and Marc Matthews in 1972 would catalyze a change in attitudes to Creole Indian folk songs in Guyana—music born of the Guyanese experience since 1838.

Bamboo Fire and *Jane Engage* became useful gifts for visiting heads of state and other international dignitaries. In order to respond to the frequency of high-profile visitors, the council drew upon the Woodside Choir, the Civil Service Association Choir, the Police Male Voice Choir, and later the CARI Singers for performances of Guyanese folk music. The council also had a roster of East Indian musicians who were incorporated into state-sponsored cultural events. This roster included Masselall Pollard (sitar) and Ustad Ramdhani (dholak), whose repertoire was dominated by Indian classical and devotional music. These musicians were held in high esteem as instrumentalists with groundings in Indian devotional and classical traditions.

In addition to folk singing groups and the roster of East Indian musicians, the National History and Arts Council also had a roster of steel bands, string bands, and a small cadre of musicians who performed in the European classical tradition. The classical cadre included Dr. Olivia Ahyoung-Benjamin; Avis Joseph, GRSM; and Dr. Joycelynne Loncke—all formally trained at leading music institutions in the United States, the United Kingdom, and France. By 1972 the arts council was an active place. At its helm were Lynette Dolphin and Arthur Seymour, with over three decades of experience organizing large-scale cultural events. The council also published the journal *Kaie*. William Pilgrim, who had close relationships with the council since his remigration in 1967, described the council as "an unwieldy collection of some forty individuals from every conceivable cultural stratum in the infant country."[21] Pilgrim was referring to a high level of creative energy, sometimes conflicting, that was emerging from a multi-class and multi-generational conversation on the direction of Guyanese expressive culture. The council had become the articulator of the state's engagement in cultural life. This dynamism would be challenged in 1972 when Guyana hosted the first Caribbean Festival of the Arts (Carifesta).

Another possible explanation for the relative absence of East Indian folk/creole music in the recordings sponsored by the National History and Arts Council may be found in the society's musical taste as mediated by the music programming of radio stations in Guyana in the early post-independence era. In 1972 Ron Sanders, a young man of Indian ancestry, was appointed program manager of the Guyana Broadcasting Service (GBS), which had been launched on October 1, 1968, to replace the privately owned British Guiana Broadcasting Service (BGBS), a sister service of Radio Demerara.[22] When GBS was established the Ministry of Information administered it. In 1972 GBS became Guyana Broadcasting Corporation, a public corporation under the

Public Corporations Ordinance 1962. According to the ordinance, the corporation was autonomous and had the following functions: "(a) to ensure the provision in Guyana of . . . broadcasting and television services; (b) to ensure that adequate and comprehensive programmes are provided by the Corporation to serve the best interests of the public generally."[23]

Prior to the creation of GBS, there were no significant differences between the music policies of Radio Demerara and BGBS. According to Ron Sanders, "music [on radio in Guyana] was divided into two categories—Indian music and all others. Indian music was played in particular slots in the early morning and then in the early evening and in special programs on Sundays." Another practice that supported this programming design was brokerage, the practice of selling blocks of time to independent producers who produced programs and sold advertising. This approach to Indian music programming had a history stretching back virtually to the beginning of Indian programming on radio in Guyana and was "well supported through advertising on both stations." The sponsors of the programs were not only "Indian business places, but also from other businesses [that targeted Indian consumers]."[24]

When Sanders was appointed program manager, he instituted "a system of integrating popular pieces of Indian music into mainstream programming. His objective was to make music of all kinds universally appreciated in Guyana and to remove the racial distinction associated with 'Indian music.'"[25] He felt that this approach would "break down the prejudice associated with it, and that its appearance on mainstream programs would cause Indians to listen to non-Indian music as well."[26]

Reflecting on his music policy intervention in 2008, Sanders did not think that experiment was a success. He wrote:

> It seemed that Indians, at the time, preferred to listen to Indian music in slots reserved for it, and non-Indians appeared unable to attune their ears [to] the Indian sounds. I suspect that there would be a big difference in today's Indian music, which, under the influence of Bollywood, has become very westernized. But, at the time the music was traditionally Indian and the cross-over did not succeed. The objective [of the music programming policy] was to try to integrate in a post-independence Guyana, the cultures of the Guyanese people through exposure to the music enjoyed by the different races. Up to that point, music on the radio was a reflection of division not integration.[27]

So part of the problem was the "ghettoization" of Indian music on the air and resistance by the commercial sector and the audience to attempts to change this pattern. Habits are sometimes hard to change! This polarization contributed to the pervasive problem of intercultural ignorance.

In addition to efforts to bring diversity to music policy across the broadcast day, the leadership of the new radio service, feeling obliged to promote local musicians, opened its "limited recording facilities to local bands and insisted that recordings of their music be interspersed with other music in mainstream programmes." Guyana Broadcasting Service in the early 1970s was more aggressive than the still privately owned Radio Demerara in promoting folk and other genres of Guyanese music. Through programs such as *Countryside Gawf*, Wordsworth McAndrew helped bring the words and sounds of Guyanese folk to the Guyanese audience regularly. To produce folk-based programming effectively required field research and documentation. This resulted in collaborations with the University of Guyana, where the first wave of Guyanese "baby boomers" had joined faculties in linguistics, history, and sociology. Out of these collaborations came interesting content and important publications. An exemplar of this yield is *A Festival of Guyanese Words*, edited by John Rickford in 1978. The initiatives of government and state agencies to stimulate and promote indigenous and authentic music created an environment that encouraged private initiatives. Excellent examples of this response are Jarai Productions and the Yoruba Singers.

According to Peter Kempadoo and Marc Matthews, *jarai* is a Hindi word meaning to sow paddies by hand—to "broad cast." So the name of the private organization they founded in November 1971 was a pun—a spark of Guyanese wit. The goal of the organization was to use the mass media in the preservation and promotion of the nation's root cultures, "the Indo-Guyanese, the Afro-Guyanese, the Amerindian, the creole, and so on."[28]

Kempadoo and Matthews were "re-migrants." Peter Kempadoo, who returned to Guyana in 1970 from the United Kingdom was born in Port Mourant and was dark skinned. He was a Madrassi who grew up on the periphery of mainstream Hindu culture in Port Mourant. When Kempadoo returned to Guyana in 1970, he had spent almost two decades in the UK, where he had a career in print journalism and radio and television broadcasting. As a broadcaster, he worked for the BBC and Britain's Central Office of Information. Among his achievements in the United Kingdom was the publication of two of his novels, *Guiana Boy* and *Old Thom's Harvest*.

Marc Matthews also spent an extended period in the United Kingdom, where he was actively engaged in the performing arts and broadcasting. Growing up, Marc Matthews lived in many parts of Guyana, including Buxton, New Amsterdam, Fyrish on the Corentyne, and Georgetown. Marc attended Queen's College and was a member of the artistic circle that met at the Taitts' home; he was one of the "Woodbine Kids."[29] On his return to Guyana he joined the Guyana Broadcasting Service. He would eventually resign that appointment and join Kempadoo in the creation of JARAI. Together they made history. With an Uher reel-to-reel tape recorder, they traveled across coastal Guyana in Kempadoo's old Volkswagen van collecting Guyanese folk materials. They visited villages along the entire coastal plain, from Pomeroon to Crabwood Creek. The team produced radio programs for both Radio Demerara and the GBS. For Radio Demerara they produced *Our Kind of Folk*; *Express Yourself*; *We, the People*; and *Roots and Rhythm*. For GBS they produced *Rural Life-Guyana* and *Roundabout Guyana*.

Altogether, JARAI recorded over six hundred hours of folk materials, primarily folk music. This is one of the most important collections of Guyanese folk music recorded during the twentieth century. Of immense popularity were the songs that were recorded at Kwe Kwes, Cacakalays, "Jollifications," "Works," "Matticores," and Amerindian festivals. By August 1972 JARAI had released a collection of six EP records featuring twenty-four folk songs that represented ethnic, geographic, and stylistic diversity. Many of these recordings, such as the Indo-Guyanese folk songs "Dis Time Na Lang Time" and "Bengali Baboo," received extensive airplay and became national hits.[30]

"Dis Time Na Lang Time" struck a positive chord in the society, as it resonated with the optimism of the time. The song satisfied Vatuk's criteria for an Indian folk song of "recent origin": the melody was Indian and the language was Creolese. The song spoke to the changes that had taken place in Guyanese society. The song offered a list of positive changes in housing (verse 1), lighting and other in-home facilities such as potable water (verses 2 and 5), fashion (verses 3 and 4), love life (verse 6), and transportation (verse 8). The lyrics were unpretentious and memorable and the beat appealing, revealing the cultural exchange that had taken place between Africans and Indians living in proximity in villages along the Guyanese coast. The song's memorable chorus states: "Dis time na lang time / Dis time na lang time / Dis na deh before time."

The popularity of "Dis Time Na Lang Time" stimulated interest in hybrid Indo-Guyanese folk songs by the wider society, especially among younger urban populations. It was something new for them. As the liner notes for point out, "Dis Time Na Lang Time" "is a fine example of a creole song. Indo-Guyanese have plenty of these; they call them 'nonsense' songs and they do not care much to sing them in public, as compared with their Indian devotional and 'picture' songs'" (songs from movies). The national popularity of the song contributed to the end of that attitude and elevated Indian Guyanese creole folk songs to a proud place in Guyanese folk music.

By the mid-1970s, Betty of Non Pariel on East Coast Demerara along with "Dougla" Elsie and Kaytie (Kassri Narine) from Grove on East Bank Demerara were recognized as treasured members of the nation's folk community.[31] In Berbice, the popular exponents of this music were "Aunty Nylon," "Aunty Margaret," Maddie, Kumbley, Dukhney, and Sughany.[32] Throughout the 1970s, *"afro-indi and Blend beats"*

songs of this type became the vehicles that launched the Afro-Indi and Blend beats and propelled the careers of singers such as Neisha Benjamin ("Benji Darlin," "Romeo," "Oh Maninja"), Joyce Narmella Harris ("Banaras Baboo"), the Mighty Enchanter ("Dulari Betty," "Maughe wid me") and Daisy Panchu ("Awee gon build Guyana").

One of Neisha Benjamin's hits was "Oh Maninja."[33] In a 2005 article in *Sunday Stabroek*'s "Celebrating Guyanese Creative Personalities" series, Rakesh Rampertaub stated:

> In all of the folk literature to originate from the East Indians, there is almost no verse that is as poignant and famous as the chorus of *Oh Maninja*. Unwisely, as has been generally the case with East Indian writing not regarded as proper culture by the guardians of Guyanese literature, these lyrics have long been ignored. The song epitomizes the appalling realities of estate village life—of stark poverty, the rising cost of living, hard labour for little return, thriftiness, brutal estate management, and despair.[34]

Joyce Narmella Harris drew upon a traditional Matticore rhythm and melody to deliver "Banaras Baboo." The song told the story of lost love, specifically, some older Indian men "leffing dem ole gal and tek dem young ones." Terry Nelson produced the song on the Halagala label and described the blended style as the Afro-Indi beat.

The Mighty Enchanter, an African Guyanese calypsonian, was also a pioneer and active promoter of the Afro-Indi beat. His marriage to a Guyanese of Indian ancestry provided him with intimate access to Indian Guyanese cultural life. He was conversant with the tradition of Indian folk songs related to problems in inter-caste and interracial marriages in Guyana's Indian communities. For example, "Garam Masala" spoke to the problems of young East Indian women who had sexual relations with black men and had "dougla [mixed-race] children" in these communities. In the 1960s, King Fighter had a major international hit with the calypso "Come Leh we Go Sookie." In that calypso the African Guyanese, King Fighter, falls in love with Sookie, an Indian girl who is equally in love with him. However, she tells him before they can marry he must "consult Mooma and consult Papa." Unfortunately, Papa was conservative, and when approached by King Fighter he "pulled out two revolvers, causing King Fighter to take off like a donkey / not even jet plane could not catch [he]."

The Mighty Enchanter probed the issue of inter-caste and interracial love in "Dulari Betty." In this song, a Chamar (from the lowest caste) boy, "bounce up a girl named Dulari, and asked she to get marry." As in the case with Sookie, she advised that both of them go and ask her Bhouji (mother). Her mother was very disappointed with the presumptuous request and asks her daughter: "Ah wha you gon do wid am? / He na fit fuh go in de market! / So Dulari Betty what you go do with am?" Dulari does not accept her mother's rejection of her lover's request and states that, irrespective of her mother's feelings, "tomorrow she will get married!" Well, her mother "fly up in a temper and pick up a belna (rolling pin)" to attack the Chamar boy! At this point, Dulari Betty tells her mother if she touches the boy, it will be murder. Dulari Betty was prepared to protect her man and to love as she pleased!

Lord Enchanter also recorded "Mauj wid Me" on Halagala. The word *mauj* and the verb *maujing* are of Hindi origin and mean to have fun.[35] The word is often used to refer to a gathering of primarily East Indian males in rum shops or in homes (on verandahs or the "bottom house") to have fun—to "sport" (drink) and sing. Most of the songs sung during these informal gatherings were improvised and the instruments used were also improvised. The table-top and bottles and coins were the primary improvised instruments. Sometimes the dhantal, the dholak, and other percussion instruments were used.[36] In other situations a wider range of instruments could be introduced into the sport. In "Mauj wid Me" Lord Enchanter invites men and women—"Mamu and Mami to come and sing aloud." He also invites "Dulaha" and "Dulahin" to "take up their dholak and leh we mauj." He also calls upon a wide array of instruments—dhantal, mandolin, violin, maracas, canuri, tabla, and jaal— to participate in the music making. The music that comes from this mix is "sweet" and everybody is jumping from out of their seats "bring[ing] down the heavens right down to your feet is the sound of the Afro and Indi beat." He describes the Afro and Indi as the "hottest beat," the sound of a music that "does turn on the heat."

For Lord Enchanter, the Afro-Indi beat is the most important musical development in Guyana in the 1970s, as he declares "Ah we na want none Lopi [a beat promoted by Eddie Hooper], Ah we want we Afro and we Indi!" "Mauj with me" is not only melodically and rhythmically attractive, and a powerful example of musical exchange, it also provides insight into another aspect of East Indian life in Guyana—"sporting"/partying. And what was revealed was similar to what took place when other ethnic groups relaxed and recreated. Popular music was helping in some small way to make similarities evident to some sections of Guyana. Maujing generated a genre of music that has been described as "rum shop" songs in Guyana and Trinidad and Tobago and may be the origin of the "rum songs" that dominated chutney music in the late years of the twentieth century and the first decade of the twenty-first century.

The East Indian folk songs popularized as a result of the 1970s fieldwork of Kempadoo and Matthews did not fade away. These vital aspects of Guyanese musical creativity have remained alive at home and in the Guyanese diaspora.

Terry Gajraj, who at the start of the twenty-first century was described as Guyana's chutney ambassador, had his first major hit with a remake of "Bengalee Baboo," a "discovery" of the Kempadoo-Matthews fieldwork. The song was "originally sung by a musician from the Portuguese Quarter, Berbice, but was popularized by Elsie."[37] The importance of JARAI was not only in the widening of appreciation for Guyanese folk music; it made clear the importance of systematic collection and dissemination. This truth would not be lost on the National History and Arts Council, which established a Folk Research Unit led by Sister Rose Magdalene in the mid-1970s.

The increased interest in creolized Indian folk music was emblematic of wider interest in "things Guyanese," especially music. Interest was also heightened in African Guyanese folk music traditions. In this case there were twin efforts, one aimed at expanding the repertoire and the other at authenticity—"de-Englishifying" the already popular African Guyanese folk songs. After listening to the competitors in the folk song groups at the 1967 Guyana Music Festival, John Russell, the adjudicator, commented that the renditions were "too staid and a little too Englishified."[38]

Like some urbanized East Indians, there were many urbanized African Guyanese who experienced cultural cringe with what they called "country people" music. This attitude started to crumble in 1968 with the creation of the African Society for Cultural Relations with Independent Africa (ASCRIA) and in 1971 with the creation of the Yoruba Folk Group at the Kitty Community Centre.

The origins of the Yoruba Folk Group (or, as they are better known, the Yoruba Singers) are to be found in ASCRIA. David Hinds has described ASCRIA as an Africanist or black power organization that was co-founded by Eusi Kwayana in 1968, four years after Kwayana was expelled from the PNC for proposing the partitioning of British Guiana as a strategy for resolving the racial strife that had engulfed the colony in the early 1960s. One of the challenges facing Prime Minister Burnham in the early post-independence days was addressing the psychic scars borne by people of African ancestry in Guyana. Because of the ethnic composition of the nation, and the fact that East Indians could also claim similar scars, Burnham had to be tactful in his strategies to rectify the African condition. It is speculated that this task was outsourced to ASCRIA.

Among the goals of ASCRIA were "bolstering Afro-Guyanese pride,"[39] "collecting materials on the African Cultural presence [in Guyana] with a view the preserving and propagating [that heritage],"[40] and the development of a "Black or African diaspora consciousness" in the nation.[41] ASCRIA attracted membership from across the spectrum of African Guyanese. It was out of this "womb" that the Yoruba Singers was born in 1971. The group's initial repertoire consisted primarily of African Guyanese folk songs and the use of a limited range of instruments—drums and a flute made from the chromium-plated tubing used by A.H. & L. Kisson Ltd. to make the legs for kitchen tables.[42] Its repertoire, African-influenced dress style, and onstage confidence made the band very popular in urban and rural communities. Their music contributed to a "feel good" period for African Guyanese and helped many urban blacks overcome their "cringe" of the music of rural black people. As Alvin Thompson noted in 2006:

> [T]hey have traveled widely around the world and performed on a number
> of important occasions in the Caribbean, United States, Canada, Britain, and
> elsewhere.... They are said to have over 300 songs to their credit and numerous
> music albums. The Guyana government has awarded them the Medal of Service
> [circa 1990] for their outstanding contribution to the country's musical culture.[43]

By 1972 the Yoruba Singers were regular and popular performers at the Green Shrimp, a nightclub and performance space in Robb Street, near Camp Street, owned by Vic Green and Conrad "Shrimpy" Meertins. The African Guyanese folk idiom that the Yoruba Singers were proudly presenting began to also appear in the repertoires of many of the string bands—Combo 7, The Rhythmaires, and the Dominators. The African Guyanese folk song medley became de rigueur at the end of a fete. It began to complement the calypso "jump up" which typically ended fetes. There was a high level of cultural confidence afoot as the nation set out to welcome "Plantation America" to Carifesta 72.

The December 1971 volume of *Kaie*—the official journal of the National History and Arts Council—was titled "The Vision of Carifesta." Its first two articles provided the political and ideological ideas upon which the Caribbean Festival of the Creative Arts was to be organized. The article "Government Policy on Cultural Development in the New Guyana" referred to the meeting that Elvin McDavid, the twenty-seven-year-old Minister of Information and Culture, had with the National History and Arts Council in 1971 about the Caribbean Festival of Creative Arts (Carifesta). During that meeting, Minister McDavid stated that the government was "investing more than a million dollars in the cultural development of Guyana, partly in Carifesta, which would take place in 1972 and also in a cultural center." The goal of the investment was "to create an awareness of the Guyanese people in their own identity, to highlight the achievements and goals of the Guyanese nation and to create and enhance an appreciation ... of the patterns and forms of various aspects of Guyanese culture."[44]

Clearly much was expected from the council, as he stressed the society "must not come to view the National History and Arts Council as a group of well-educated people enjoying themselves."[45] This was more than a perception. In 1964 members of the leadership of the Cultural Committee of the PPP felt that the National History and Arts Council was an "elaborate top heavy" organization and that it was "doubtful whether it [could] do useful work" promoting the cultural activism required for building national unity and identity. According to the PPP document, the National History and Arts Council was perceived as being limited to organizational and administrative functions.[46]

The second article, "The Vision of Carifesta," traced the origins of the ideas behind Carifesta and highlighted the role that Caribbean intellectuals played in the development of those ideas. Prominent Caribbean intellectuals had met in Guyana on two occasions between 1966 and 1970: in 1966 to celebrate Guyana's independence and in 1970 to celebrate the new republic. On both occasions conferences were held to discuss the role of culture in Caribbean development and the obstacles being faced, and on both occasions Burnham opened the conferences and used those speeches to articulate his vision.

His speech to the 1966 independence conference had four themes. The first was that his government intended to create the conditions in which Caribbean artists will be recognized and celebrated by the region and not have to depend on migration to London for recognition. The second theme was to declare that his government was not seeking to exert control over artistic expression. His third theme was articulating his vision of the role of the Caribbean artist and the place of Caribbean aesthetics in Guyana's development. In this sphere he anticipated literature "inspired by the peculiar temperament of West Indians"; language informed by research into Amerindian languages; and paintings and sculpture "inspired by the tropical jungles of Guyana," "the beautiful waters of the Caribbean," and the forms of "our forefathers from the dim and distant past." The fourth theme was recognizing global context, especially the influential European forms. In his speech he acknowledged the influence of European form but warned against the slavish following of European trends.[47] Prime Minister Burnham concluded his speech with the hope "that every year beginning with the first anniversary of Independence, Guyana will be the venue of Caribbean Arts Festival, featuring Guyanese and Caribbean artists whose work in poetry, painting and sculpture project our dreams and visions and help to foster and develop a Caribbean personality."[48]

The annual festival of the arts did not materialize. However, on February 24, 1970, Burnham did return to the topic when he gave the opening address at the second conference that coincided with the introduction of the cooperative republic. In that speech he recognized that the dream of an annual festival had not materialized; however, he remained personally hopeful that such an event would be held annually "in the Caribbean, not necessarily confined to Guyana." This modification was tactical and probably responding to domestic concerns about the economy being able to bear the costs of hosting such events and regional concerns that Guyana was usurping too grand a role in the "growing" of the Caribbean community. In 1966 at the first conference, Burnham did offer a "dream of a Caribbean nation, 'instead of a group of islands masquerading as independent states and believing that they can survive in the twentieth century.'"[49]

This time around, concrete action emerged. The United Nations Educational, Scientific, and Cultural Organization (UNESCO) and the United Nations Development Program (UNDP) made technical and financial contributions to Carifesta.[50] It was agreed that the festival should have three core principles:

- It should be inspirational;
- It should be educational; and
- It should relate to people and be entertaining on a scale and in fashion that would commend itself to the general mass of people who live within and around the great gulf of sea existing between North and South America.[51]

Demonstrating its organizational and administrative confidence, the National History and Arts Council established the Carifesta Secretariat in November 1971, with Lynette Dolphin as director and Frank Pilgrim as public relations officer in the Office of the Prime Minister as Commissioner.[52] By December 1971 official invitations had been extended to twenty-five nations in the Caribbean and South and Central America.[53] To accommodate the delegations, Burnham issued a "directive . . . to erect [Festival City]—a hundred houses in the suburbs of Greater Georgetown."[54] Also by December 1971, the two-thousand-seat National Cultural Center was being constructed in D'Urban Back Lands in Georgetown. This was described as "one of the most exciting features of Carifesta."[55] The center was expected to include an auditorium and a theatre. The idea of building a cultural center had been around since the destruction by fire of the Assembly Rooms in the 1940s. In 1951 a foundation stone was laid at the old site (now the Bank of Guyana building). In his July 15, 1964, paper to the Cultural Committee of the PPP, Colin Moore argued for the "establishment of a cultural center where various forms of creative activity can take place—Drama, painting and sculpture exhibitions, prose readings and musical shows."[56] For Moore, the center would help promote national unity and the evolution of a national identity. The PPP Manifesto for the 1957 elections announced that the party would "work for the establishment of the Cultural Center in Georgetown."[57] However, the old location in downtown Georgetown was considered inadequate in the 1970s because of traffic noise.

In the early 1970s, the burning issue was about money to build a cultural center in Georgetown. The government took the decision to use all the money in the Indian Immigration Fund for this purpose. That fund had been established in the nineteenth century to pay return passage for laborers who had completed their contracts of indenture. Because many laborers did not return to India, there was a substantial amount in the fund. According to Rampersaud Tiwari, in 1968 the fund amounted to $G300,000.[58] The decision to use the entire fund to build "one grand national center" was controversial.[59] The Hindu organization the Maha Sabha declared that it was against the use of all of the funds for the purpose of building the center. In a press release the organization declared that the descendants of Indian indentured workers who lived in rural areas should not be "cut off from any benefit which might accrue by the proposed use of the fund." The organization noted "that the Indian community might not be totally opposed to a part of the fund being utilized for a national cause." The Maha Sabha, however, stressed that the proposed cultural center must provide opportunities for Indian music, dancing, and other cultural activities as much as for steel band.

Going beyond equity in programming, the Maha Sabha pointed out the need for cultural centers in the counties of Berbice and Essequibo. Conscious of the "strong feelings in this matter" by its members, the organization pledged to "leave no stone unturned to see that justice is done to the Indian cause" and the "issue is favorably settled."[60] The Maha Sabha's reaction was mild compared to others. As Sheik Sadeek observed, "The Mahatma Gandhi Organization wanted this [fund] spent solely on the Indian population, like on sugar plantation cultural centers."[61] The decision to spend the fund on the cultural center caused racial tensions that lay just under the surface of the society to erupt quite vocally. One outcome of this eruption was the recommendation that Indian Guyanese should boycott Carifesta. Many did. However, many others such as Raj Kumari Singh, the daughter of Dr. J. B. and Mrs. Alice Bhagwandi Singh and mother of the innovative choreographer and dancer Gora Singh, did not support the boycott.

The planners for Carifesta emphasized drama, music, dance, folk arts, sculpture and art, and literature. In the months leading up to Carifesta, Guyana was alive culturally. Venues such as the Theatre Guild and Green Shrimp in Georgetown, the Penguin Hotel in New Amsterdam, and the Crimson Bat in Linden (formerly McKenzie) hosted poetry readings and presentations that integrated dance, music, poverty, prose, and film. There was ongoing experimentation with the integration of music as steel pan, sitar, saxophone, and the various drums sought to find a new Guyanese sound. One impressive development was the Theatre Guild Quintet, featuring Keith Waithe (flute), Masselall Pollard (sitar), Roy Geddes (pan), Keith Joseph (bass), and Kishore Etwaroo (tabla and dholak).

Carifesta 72 was launched on August 25 and extended over a three-week period. Prime Minster Burnham gave the keynote speech at the opening ceremony. In that speech he reprised the history behind the festival, stressed the importance of cultural independence and nurturing Caribbean identity, and recognizing the contributions of "THE LITTLE MAN." Burnham's welcome was framed as being on behalf of the "little men of Guyana"—the persons who "worked night and day and without such sophisticated props as sedatives, who worked hour after hour in the sun and the dew; the carpenters, the plumbers, the masons and those who swept the tarmac" to make Carifesta possible. In his conclusion, he called upon the gathered artists, "whether they are painters or writers, dancers or sculptors" to "portray actively and accurately to the world . . . the culture of THE LITTLE MAN."[62] The emphasis on the term *little man* anticipated a significant policy shift in 1974.

The Guyanese calypsonian, Lord Canary (Malcolm Corrica), composed and recorded "The Carifesta 72 Calypso," the theme song for the festival. In his song, Lord Canary welcomed all of the official invitees (which by the start of the festival had been extended to include Chile) to the "stupendous occasion." The Shantonian "Guitar" Levans composed a special shanto for the festival, which was recorded by his son Rudy Levans. In "Carifesta Shanto," Levans and his son effectively used onomatopoeia to capture the sounds of the masquerade/tanga bands and steel bands that were expected to participate in the festival.

In addition to the official delegations, there were unofficial delegations from the United States, Canada, and the United Kingdom. More than two thousand tourists attended the three-week festival, which was presented at venues in urban and rural Guyana. Carifesta 72 was an exciting time and many Guyanese felt proud of their nation's status as host of the festival. The musical aspects of Carifesta 72 were expansive in terms of the genres presented and their interrelationships with dance and other performing arts. From Jamaica came the pulsating drumming of Count Ossie and the Mystical Revelations of Rastafari. This was the first time that many Guyanese had seen or heard this aspect of the expressive culture of Rastafari. On many evenings during Carifesta, the Guyanese who had traveled to Festival City would experience Nyah Binghis and other forms of Rastafarian expression. Sometimes the drummers from Surinam's Maroon communities would join the Rastafarians for impromptu drumming sessions. Beyond the novelty of some of the expressions, Guyanese were able to see similarities among the drums used by the Jamaicans and the Surinamese drummers and drums used by Guyanese of African ancestry. Guyanese were therefore able to recognize the survival of West and Central African drums and various "hands"—drumming patterns in the Caribbean and Guyana.[63]

Music was also heard on the streets of Georgetown as masquerade bands from St. Kitts-Nevis-Anguilla, Montserrat, and Guyana took their performances around the city. Here again, Guyanese saw stylistic similarities in the masquerade bands and were again able to make ancestral and regional connections. From Venezuela, Brazil, and Colombia came folk-based music in which Guyanese were able to hear connections with the Banshikilli music of the Arawaks and Caribs in Guyana. The delegation from Suriname included performers of Javanese and East Indian origins. The musical repertoire of Suriname's East Indian delegation included bhajans and other devotional music. Their instruments included dholak, sitar, dhantal, harmonium, and other instruments known among Guyanese of Indian ancestry. Here again, cultural similarity was evident.

Guyana's musical contribution to Carifesta 72 also included music in the European tradition. Ray Luck, now internationally recognized, gave a piano recital. He had achieved much since his appearance at the 1952 British Guiana Festival of Music. Ian Hall, at that time an organist at Westminster Abbey in London, gave an organ recital at St. George's Cathedral in Georgetown on August 31.[64] Hall's father was one of those Guyanese who had volunteered to serve in the British Royal Air Force during World War II. So, the diaspora was also evident during Carifesta 72.

Music was also integrated with other performing arts. This was most evident in the many memorable dance performances presented. For many Guyanese the most memorable was the performance by Jamaica's National Dance Theatre Company, led by Rex Nettleford. The performance was held in the unfinished National Cultural Center. The roof for the venue was not completed. In its place were coconut branches and tarpaulins, and the audience could see the starlight sky during the performance. This partly open roof enhanced the presentation by the Jamaican troupe of sixty, which included singers and musicians. Jamaican folk life exploded in pieces such as *Kumina*, *Jonkonnu*, and *Pocomania* that drew upon Jamaica's African traditions. Here again, Guyanese saw cultural similarities and made connections between those dances and the Cumfa and Kwe Kwe traditions in Guyana's African heritage. Many who saw the dance companies from Barbados, Brazil, Cuba, Haiti, Grenada, and Venezuela experienced similar epiphanies.

An informal Carifesta also took place during the three-week period, activities that were not planned by the National Secretariat. These informal events took place after the official shows and were held in a number of venues. One popular venue was the Green Shrimp, a relatively new nightclub/discothèque in Georgetown, operated by a re-migrant from London, Victor Green, and Conrad "Shrimpy" Meertins, a painter and a sculptor who was also a pilot with the Guyana Airways Corporation. Being new, the nightclub had a lighting infrastructure that included a range of colored gels, follow spots, fillers, and strobe lights. The venue also had a good sound system with multiple microphones, amplifiers, mixers, turntables, and speakers. In addition, the space was intimate and the proprietors encouraged creative experimentation.

About six months before Carifesta, the proprietors hosted a poetry reading session featuring Marc Matthews, Vibert Cambridge, Gordon Carrega, Derrick Jeffrey, and Roy Green—members of "the Commune." This launched regular weekly sessions. Almost immediately, the sessions began to incorporate dance and music—all types of music—folk, jazz, Indian, and classical. The core of the music ensemble that emerged at the Green Shrimp included Art Broomes on drums, Compton "Camo" Williams on steel pan, and Abdulla Omawale on saxophone. Omawale was one of a number of African Americans who came to Guyana during the 1970s, claiming refugee status. During the three-week Carifesta period, guest performances were given at the Green Shrimp by many artists, including Jamaica's Louise Bennett, Toots Hibbert, and Carl Bradshaw; Barbados's Edward Braithwaite; and Robin Dobru from Surinam.

One of a series of radio programs produced by JARAI Productions was *Carifesta Khondi*, moderated by Peter Kempadoo. This series explored similarities among of the folk traditions of the countries participating in Carifesta 72. The final program featured Henry Josiah, Raj Kumari Singh, and "Guitar" Levans as guests. The aim of the program was to reflect on Carifesta 72 and look to the future. The guests agreed that the festival was a success. For Josiah, the festival reaffirmed his "Caribbeanness" by showing him how connected he was culturally with the wider Caribbean. However, all of the participants identified shortcomings like inadequate planning and sometimes poor coordination. As a result, some performers from rural areas were unable to participate at urban venues.[65]

The panelists also felt there was need for improvement in the quality of Guyana's performing arts. Attention was drawn to the quality of Guyana's folk musical *All Kinds of Folk*, which was held at the National Cultural Center on August 25 as the "Guyanese Welcome to Carifesta Guests." The panelists felt that compared to other folk music-based presentations at Carifesta, such as those from Jamaica, Brazil, Trinidad, and Haiti, *All Kinds of Folk* lacked professionalism and revealed the absence of training.

Scripted and produced by Frank Pilgrim, the public relations officer in the Office of the Prime Minister, *All Kinds of Folk* came across as a public relations piece, pandering to Prime Minister Burnham's ego and promoting some of his pet projects such as the Hinterland Road Project, which was launched after independence in 1966 aimed at building, by self-help, a road from Mahdia to Lethem. The model at work was probably based on Marshal Tito's tactic of using volunteers to work on large-scale development projects in the rebuilding of Yugoslavia after World War II. From Tito's perspective, having Serbs, Croats, and the other ethnic peoples of Yugoslavia work together on those projects would help forge national unity and develop national identity. Observers have suggested that Forbes Burnham, who had visited Yugoslavia prior to his return to British Guiana in the 1940s, had similar aspirations with the road project.

The panelists of *Carifesta Khondi* also expressed concern about the level of mimicry that was evident among Guyanese pop singers during the festival. One panelist commented on the use of American accents by the singers who seemed oblivious to the time, place, and orientation of the festival. Regrets were also expressed about the visible absence of Indian Guyanese in the audiences and as performers. This suggests that the boycott campaign was effective. In terms of looking toward the future, the panelists and the moderator emphasized the need for adequate planning, training, and ensuring the active participation of communities in future cultural development. Henry Josiah suggested that the organization of an annual or biannual Guyana Festival of the Arts (Guyfesta) might help rectify the problems identified and lay the foundation for relevant cultural development.[66]

Carifesta 72 did have benefits for Guyana. The nation's profile rose within the Caribbean community, and Guyana deepened its role in the development of the Caribbean integration movement. The festival also revealed the need for a robust infrastructure to execute the task of cultural development. It was evident that the work involved more than being able to organize festivals. There were the crucial tasks of training, research, and actively contributing the development of national identity and national cohesiveness. By 1975 the National History and Arts Council had launched the National School of Dance, the National Dance Company, and the Burrowes School of Art. Two other schools were envisaged, a School of Drama and a School of Music. All of these schools were expected to fall under the umbrella of the Institute of Creative Arts.[67]

Carifesta 72 also suggested the need to focus effort and resources on the common man. There was also more than a subtle hint that the prime minister appreciated having his ego stroked by the performing arts.

According to Shahabuddeen, the political leadership of the republic remained dissatisfied with the 1970 republican constitution as much of the old colonial order still remained. He amplified, "mere political emancipation is worth little unless the internal public order is reconstructed to ensure social and economic justice for all."[68] The result was the most dramatic change in governance of the society in the twentieth century. The changes were initiated in 1973, when the PNC declared itself to be the paramount societal institution, with the government being subordinate to the party.

In December 1974, on the tenth anniversary of the PNC in government, Prime Minister Burnham articulated a new vision for Guyana in his historic Declaration of Sophia speech. In that speech he declared that the PNC was a socialist party committed to establishing socialism in Guyana according to Marxist-Leninist principles and laid out a plan and strategy for national development. To that end, the party articulated a new constitution that included the constant pursuit of national self-reliance as one of the party's "objects." Other "objects" included the following: (a) securing and maintaining though the practice of co-operative socialism, the interests, well-being, and prosperity of all the people of Guyana; (b) pursuing commitment to the Socialist ideal and, more particularly, ensuring that the people of Guyana own and control for their benefit the natural resources of the country; (c) providing every Guyanese the opportunity to work for and share in the economic well-being of the country and ensuring that there is equality of opportunity in the political, economic, and social life of the country; (d) motivating the people of Guyana to improve, by their own efforts and through the Party, the communities in which they live; (e) working for the closest possible association of Guyana with her Caribbean neighbors and maintaining a link with international organizations and agencies whose aims and objectives are consistent with those of the People's National Congress.[69]

By the time that declaration was made, Guyana had already established diplomatic relations with the USSR (1970), East Germany (1972), the People's Republic of China (1972), Cuba (1973), and the Democratic People's Republic of Korea (1973). Guyana was also an active supporter of the African liberation struggle. On the domestic front, the government of Guyana had nationalized the sugar and bauxite industries and owned other key sectors of the economy. Education was free from "nursery to university," and a range of projects were introduced to "feed, house, and clothe" the nation. At the same time, a number of institutions were established with the goal of decolonizing and reorienting society. Among these were the Guyana National Service and the Ministry of National Development. The efforts to build socialism had a chilling effect on US-Guyana relations. By 1974 economic assistance from the USA to Guyana had dropped to $US0.2 million, from US$18 in 1968.

The declaration by the PNC of its socialist goals, its support for anti-imperialist forces, and its nationalization program led to a period of "critical support" by the PPP. Halim Majeed, a former aide to Forbes Burnham, has stated that this support was the direct result of decisions taken at the 1975 meeting of Latin American Communist parties held in Havana, Cuba, which was attended by Dr. Cheddi Jagan. At that meeting the general secretary of the Communist party of Uruguay, Rodney Arismendi, and Carlos Rafael Rodrigues, the vice president of Cuba, along with other influential members of the Cuban Communist party persuaded "Dr. Jagan that the PPP must adopt a realistic position vis-à-vis the PNC or be 'left out in the cold.'" Further, Jagan was advised that his support for the PNC had to be public.[70] On his return from Cuba, Dr. Jagan declared that the PPP "would shift from non-cooperation and civil resistance to one of 'critical support.'" He is also reported to have concluded that there existed in Guyana the possibilities for a real breakthrough in Guyana's social, economic, and cultural development based on anti-imperialism and socialist foundations. Majeed also observed that Dr. Jagan thought that Guyana had the "possibilities of truly becoming a second Cuba."[71]

For Burnham, reorientation in attitudes and values were necessary because of the accidents and fictions created by history, especially the fiction about class in Guyana. His views on class were most clearly articulated in the various debates associated with the establishment of the Guyana National Service (GNS) in the early to mid-1970s. For example, during the debate on the State Paper on the National Service on January 9, 1974, he referred to the negative legacies of the colonial era, especially the ideology of racial superiority and the practices of "Divide et rege"—divide and rule.[72]

The Guyana National Service (GNS) was to be one of the institutions that would help to undermine those fictions and accidents of history by eradicating racial and class divisions, nurture the "true spirit of self-reliance," and foster the "attitudinal skills" to contribute positively and confidently to Guyana's social, cultural, and political revolution—in essence, the development of "a citizen who places nation above self."[73] In the parlance of those times, the primary goal of the re-orientation programs was to bring about "attitudinal metamorphosis."[74]

The GNS was to be inclusive and cater to the entire society. However, National Service was to be compulsory for Guyanese students who were planning to attend or were already attending tertiary educational institutions in Guyana or abroad on government scholarships. During the 1970s, the government of Guyana awarded over two thousand scholarships for students to study a range of disciplines including music in Canada, the UK, USA, and in the Soviet Bloc.[75] All tertiary-level students, along with volunteers, became members of the Pioneer Corps and served a one-year stint on a number of GNS Centers, the first of which was established at Kimbia on the Berbice River in 1974. The curriculum on these centers included "training in Co-operativism [Co-operative socialism]; agricultural training (theoretical and practical); industrial skill training; craft training; cultural training; training to understand the values of the Co-operative Republic; Pioneer training; Para-military training and calisthenics."[76] Music was an important element in cultural training.

At the inception of the Guyana National Service, Rajkumari Singh was appointed director of the Mobile Theatre and Culture Corps (MT&CC), with the rank of captain. Her son Gora, an India-trained choreographer, in a series of articles in the state-owned *Guyana Chronicle* had articulated a vision of the cultural direction for the new revolutionary society. His argument was anchored by four concepts that were popular during that period—"cultural revolution," "ideological art," "cultural aggression," and "neo-colonialism." Gora Singh argued that the revolution that was taking place in Guyana was multidimensional and had to be built upon a cultural revolution, one that transformed attitudes and values. He saw "ideological art" as an important vehicle in this transformation: "The Ideological Art of Guyana is music, song, dance, drama, etc., reflecting Socialist policies and ideals in keeping with the development thrust of our country."[77] This orientation was necessary to inoculate the society against "cultural aggression" and to prevent "neo-colonialism." For Singh, "Ideological Art" had to be technically competent and demanded high levels of discipline; the Guyana National Service Mobile Theatre and Culture Corps embodied these ideals. The music that emerged spoke to the nation's aspirations and demonstrated musical exchange.[78]

One of the most popular songs, although not necessarily the most liked, in Guyana during the mid-1970s was "I Want to Build"—a song that emerged from the Kimbia Center. The story of that song must begin with the first staff trainee course, which started in February 1974 in Georgetown, and its transfer to the Kimbia Training Center, Berbice River, in May. The staff trainees were the cadres that would become the first leaders at the GNS center level. From this early moment, "ideological art" was practiced. In the realm of music, the goal was to move away from "the hard rock stuff and the unimaginative imitating of the foreign message."[79]

The MT&CC was a touring troupe that traveled "the length of Guyana always seeking out new talent, dance steps and musical expression to refine and incorporate in their portfolio." This action was referred to as "turning raw expression into dance and song." By the mid-1970s, the MT&CC was considered "second to none with their representations of ideological art."[80] Revolutionary songs were important assets in their educational arsenal. The first song to emerge from the experience was "I Want to Build," composed by GNS staff trainees in 1974. A spirit of optimism and passion is evident from the song's first verse: "I want to build this land that belongs to me / Plant on this land to build our economy / Leave for our children a future that will be free / From all types of props and leaning dependency."

Many Guyanese also associate the three-verse "I Want to Build" with the first GNS Great March—a feat completed by 280 pioneers who marched a distance of 160 miles from Kimbia Centre to the National Park in 1975, and a nod to Chairman Mao's Long March and *The Little Red Book*. In the early 1970s, several varieties of socialism contended in Guyana. The song became a crossover hit with the Dominators, a popular party band, recording two versions in 1976.

By the end of 1975, the Guyana National Service had established centers at Papaya, Tumatumari, Konawaruk, Itabu, and New River. Songs were also created at these centers. Among them was "New Guyana Man" composed by Corpswoman Gillian John. That song told the story of the founding of Papaya Centre in the Northwest District, near Matthews Ridge, "Beneath the Imataka / Where papaws once grew wild." In the final verse we are told that at Papaya Training center, pioneers had an opportunity learn "All the skills and foot drills / To make a new Guyana Man."

Rector Schultz, a respected guitarist, was a member of the Culture Corps. Schultz, along with Ganesh Persaud, a pioneer, composed "The Pineapple Song." That song was inspired by a special work project cleaning an overgrown pineapple field at Tumatumari.[81] At the same location Schultz also composed the instrumental "Rocks, Rapids, and Rhythms," inspired by the journey up the Potaro River from Rockstone to Tumatumari. "The Pine Field Song" was Schultz's first work song. He later composed "The Cane Field," which referred to a period when GNS staff, pioneers, and members of the public service were called upon to harvest sugar cane because the Guyana Agricultural Workers Union (GAWU), a union controlled by the PPP, had called a strike in 1977 that lasted for 135 days.

At Kimbia, Schultz worked with Maurice Watson, Rajkumari Singh, Daisy Panchu, and Gora Singh on compositions such as "The Cotton Song," "Macadingo," "Ahwee Gon Build Guyana," "Wuk Comrades," and "Steamer Day." "The Cotton Song," composed by Rajkumari Singh, was not only a testimony to the staff and pioneers who re-introduced cotton to Guyana; it was also a tribute to the enslaved Africans who had grown it before. As the first verse reminded: "Long time ago is slaves plant cotton in Kimbia / Now free Guyana Pioneers a them planting / Now free Guyana Pioneers a them picking / Planting and picking cotton in Kimbia."

The reintroduction of cotton was seen as not only contribution to clothing the nation; it was also seen as an export crop. As an article in the *Sunday Chronicle* of December 14, 1975, reported, "Guyana will export its first shipment of cotton after 70 years."[82] "Ahwee Gon Build Guyana," an Afro-Indi-flavored composition by Daisy Panchu in 1975, predicted "with National Service we will change Guyana." "Wuk Comrades," composed by Maurice Watson, a Kneller Hall–trained musician, who was seconded/on loan from the Guyana Police Force Band, exhorted the pioneers and staff "to sing a song to make the wuk feel light."

Guyanese folklore was also evident in the songs composed by pioneers and staff in the GNS hinterland centers. "Macadingo," also composed by Maurice Watson, referred to the resident ghost at Kimbia. "Steamer Day," another Maurice Watson composition, was inspired by Major Pelham V. Van Cooten, who was responsible for signing the leave passes that permitted pioneers and staff members to spend "bush leave" off the center. The song's chorus pleaded: "Sign me leave pass fuh go home / Mister Van Cooten / We wan' go home fuh see ah we family." Sgt. Terry Blackman composed "We are building.," the lyrics of which summarized the optimism among the pioneers: "We are building this land that we love / With the forests and the creeks / Agriculture as our means / We can make it—Yes Comrades we can't lose."

The optimism of the first years of the Guyana National Service was also a function of the leadership of its founding director general, Norman McLean. Collectively, the songs encapsulated important moments in the development of GNS, memorialized personalities, and described the experiences of pioneers. In 1981 Colonel Desmond Roberts, the second director general of the GNS, initiated a project to make recordings of the songs that emerged from the first years of the GNS. The result was the LP *I Want to Build.* [83] At that time Maurice Watson was Guyana National Service's director of music. Watson was a versatile musician with experience in pop, jazz, and military music. He was a member of the legendary Rhythmaires during the recording of "Sohanni Raat." He was the bassist on the memorable album *Jazz 560* with Hugh Sam, Art Broomes, and Harry Whittaker. He was also the director of the Guyana Police Force Male Voice Choir when they recorded *Jane Engage*, the LP of Guyanese folk songs. In 1985 Watson returned to the Guyana police force as director of music after Superintendent Barney Small retired.

The GNS album is an important cultural artifact from Guyana's period of socialist experimentation. It reveals a deliberate attempt to bring together the nation's racial communities to create cultural products that transcended particular identities. It is also an invaluable record of the spirit of the times and a clear example of the continued use of music as a vehicle for national mobilization.

The Guyana National Service was not the only entity in the now expanding military and paramilitary services (collectively known as the uniformed services) creating music to support the ideological changes in the society. By 1975 the Guyana Defence Force Band Corps had four distinct formations— the Corps of Drums, the Military Band, the Steel Band, and the String Band. The origins of the Corps of Drums are to be found in the defunct Volunteer Force. [84] The Military Band was established in 1972 under the command of Warrant Office Grade 1, Ronald Harrison Bennett, the bandmaster of the Berbice Junior Band, which was the name given to the No. 7 Volunteer Band from New Amsterdam after it was dissolved.[85] The core of the Military Band came from the Berbice Junior Band. Other members of the band came from the Corps of Drums and the Steel Band. In late 1972, Captain A. "Sonny" Ault became the band's director of music. By 1973 the Band Corps launched a successful nationwide recruitment initiative. As a result, there was rapid growth of the Band Corps and the creation of a "formidable Military Band, which went on to provide the Force and the civil population with both martial and entertaining music. The unit's membership climbed to a record strength of one hundred and twenty (120) which included eight (8) females."[86]

The Guyana Defence Force Steel Band was formed in 1970 from pan players who were already in the force.

> The Steel Band was led by Ex Corporal Archie McAllister. The members of both the Steel Band and the Corps of Drums were then trained on second instruments (Bugle, Pan or Drums) and would merge for engagements, which enabled the Corps of Drums to field a large Band for parades and the steel band to meet required strengths for out-door performance and competitions. This created multidimensional instrumentalists who provided the foundation for the future establishment of the Military Band.[87]

The nucleus of Guyana Defence Force's String Band was established in 1974 when four members led by Andrew Jackson were posted to the Band Corps. GDF World-Wind String Band was created in October 1975 and immediately received "high acclaim both nationally and internationally." In 1982, the band's name was changed to the GDF Front Line Band.[88] As the director of music of the GDF Band Corps, Capt. Sonny Ault established himself as the primary composer of military music in the nation in the post-independence era. This was a deliberate act; the goal was to rid the Guyanese military of music from the colonial period. He composed regimental music for all of the Army Corps.[89] This led to the dramatic expansion of nation's martial music repertoire, a field of musical creativity pioneered by Clem Nichols in the 1920s.

The Guyana Police Force Band continued to present public concerts. In the 1970s its repertoire reflected the orientation articulated by the PNC and featured more folk music, calypso, and other music from the Caribbean.[90] The Guyana Prison Service and the Guyana Fire Brigade also had steel bands. At times, all of the music units of the uniformed services would get together as the Massed Band to provide the music for major ceremonial events. However, the GNS was the most active proponent of ideological art.

What the Guyana National Service was doing musically in the hinterlands, the People's Culture Corps was doing in the urban and rural areas. Headquartered in Sophia, this organization was an arm of the People's

National Congress and operated out of the fused offices of the Ministry of National Development and the office of the general secretary of the People's National Congress. There is limited documentary information on this group. However, the group was multi-ethnic and included a range of performers including calypsonians such as El Cid and the Mighty Chief. Sub-sets of the People's Culture Corps included the Maha Sabha Culture Corps and the PNC Breakthrough Steel Band. The signature strategy of the People's Culture Corps was the political skit, which incorporated music, dance, and drama. There were a number of other state-sponsored cultural initiatives aimed at promoting decolonization and socialism during the 1970s. Of these the most significant was the introduction of the Guyana Festival of the Arts (Guyfesta) in 1975.

The National History and Arts Council organized the first Guyana Festival of Arts in 1975. The theme for the multi-sectored festival, which started on September 12, was "My Community, My Nation." The goal of the festival was to find new ways to identify, appreciate, and promote the creative arts needed for "the realization of the new Guyana man." Shirley Field-Ridley, now the minister responsible for culture (the third since independence) and a leading ideologue of the PNC, summed up the Guyfesta task in her "Message" published in the booklet to commemorate the inaugural festival: "the cultural revolution has started, we have seen the transformation of our economic way of life, our attitudes are changing, our approach to identifying, appreciating and promoting our creative arts must change."[91]

The aims and objectives of the Festival of Arts were:

- To encourage active participation in the several branches of the arts by Guyanese of all ages endowed with creative potential;
- To identify individual talents in these arts which should be nurtured and brought to full development through the Institute of Creative Arts, the education arm of the National History and Arts Council;
- To expose Guyanese residents in all regions of the nation to the valuable experience of viewing cultural manifestations of quality in their own regions;
- To help improve the quality of life of Guyanese wherever they may live;
- To foster a sense of national identity, pride, and unity; and
- To develop an awareness of the heritage of the past and the potential of our Creative Arts to strengthen the growth of the Guyanese nationality.

According to Lynette Dolphin, the chairwoman of the National History and Arts Council, "the festival . . . attracted nearly eighteen hundred entries."[92] A. J. Seymour described Guyfesta '75 as a "smaller sister to Carifesta '72." For him,

Table 8.1
Certificate of Excellence awarded for music at Guyfesta '75 by category

Musical Category	Number of Certificate of Excellence
Instrumental Group	29
Instrumental Solos	31
Vocal Group	37
Vocal Solos	44
Total	141

Source: Guyafesta '75. Georgetown, Guyana: National History and Arts Council, n.d.

Table 8.2
Certificate of Excellence awarded at Guyfesta '75 by Regional Centers
[IG = Instrumental Group, IS = Instrumental Solos, VG = Vocal Group, VS = Vocal Solo]

Regional Center	IG	IS	VG	VS	Total
Anna Regina	–	–	2	–	2
Bartica	1	–	1	1	3
Corriverton	–	3	4	7	14
Georgetown	21	24	14	11	70
Lethem	–	–	4	2	6
Linden	1	3	2	2	8
Matthew's Ridge	2	–	2	8	12
New Amsterdam	2	1	8	5	16
Uitvlugt	2	–	1	2	5
Victoria	–	–	1	4	5
Total	29	31	37	44	141

Source: Guyafesta '75. Georgetown, Guyana: National History and Arts Council, n.d.

the value of the Guyfesta "was that it encouraged a decentralized approach to artistic and cultural development."[93]

Five categories of the creative arts were showcased: visual arts and crafts, dance, drama and verse speaking, music, and creative writing. Unlike the Guyana Music Festival, there were no prizewinners. In lieu of prizes, "more than 600 certificates of Merit and Excellence were awarded." The decision not to award prizes was based on the idea that competitions were unhealthy in this stage of the nation's cultural development. The aim was to identify talent for education and training. According to the published records, 141 Certificates of Excellence were awarded for music in 1975. Tables 8.1 and 8.2 provide the details.

Unlike Carifesta 72, Indian Guyanese did not boycott Guyfesta '75.[94] There were also many "discoveries" at Guyfesta '75. Among them was Chuck Gerard, the New Amsterdam–born folk singer then residing in Lethem. According to Ken Crosbie, his style was fresh and his standards were considered world-class.[95] Unfortunately, the economic downturn that the Guyanese economy experienced as a result of the OPEC decisions and other domestic factors ended the Guyfesta experiment after 1977. Avis Joseph, who participated as a judge in the Guyfesta experiences, has concluded that the Guyana Festivals of the Arts were effective in identifying and promoting Guyanese musicians during the time they took place.[96] Joseph, who graduated from the Royal College of Music in 1975, like Philip Pilgrim, Lynette Dolphin, and Billy Pilgrim was a winner of the prestigious scholarship to study at the Royal College of Music.

The Guyfesta experience also came in for its share of criticism, especially from members of an older generation of African Guyanese nurtured in the culture of respectability with its commitment to English cultural values. It has been argued that the removal of competition in the field of music led to the loss of standards. One of the consequences of Guyfesta was the suspension of the Guyana Music Festival in 1975. The Guyana Music Teachers' Association had organized that festival biennially since 1952. The Guyana Music Teachers' Association's records state that declining economic conditions led to the suspension of the festival.[97] Individual members and other observers of Guyana's musical environment during the period of "cultural re-orientation" indicated that the Guyanese political directorate felt that the organizing philosophy of the Guyana Music Festival, especially the emphasis on competition, was not compatible with the "cultural revolution."

In addition to Guyfesta, the public sector was also exploring other strategies to develop more relevant responses to the demands of the political directorate. The tendency toward centralization was amplified in the processes of national governance during this era. There were sycophantic responses to the dictates of the Kabaka—the political directorate dominated by L.F.S. Burnham. Some government ministries followed the pattern of the Ministry of National Development and organized their own "Culture Corps" to promote their work and highlight their contributions to national policy.

Mashramani, the annual celebrations of the republic, became more centralized and directed by the Ministry of National Development. These celebrations began to feature special concerts to commemorate the birthday of Burnham. Many of these concerts took the form of musicals, and the National History and Arts Council produced most of them. The first of these musicals, *A Pride of Heroes*, was held in 1977 at the recently completed National Cultural Center. Also during the mid-1970s, the National History and Arts Culture introduced a number of initiatives that were intended to democratize the National Cultural Center, which had appeared to be giving preference to highbrow cultural events, emphasizing the "good music" of the colonial era, and was alienating significant elements of urban black people. The person tasked with the democratization project was Malcolm Corrica (Lord Canary), who had been elected a Member of Parliament for the PNC and appointed by Forbes Burnham as a Minister of State in the Ministry of Education and Culture. Among Minister Corrica's initiatives was a series of concerts by popular musicians from the private sector. These concerts, known as CC Varieties, would become frequent events during the late 1970s and early 1980s.

By 1979 the National History and Arts Council was upgraded to the Department of Culture in the Ministry of Education, Social Development and Culture. For the International Year of the Child 1979, the department published, for use in schools, George W. Noel's *Sing! Guyana's Children.*[98] The songs in the collection were "To Serve My Country," "We Joinin' Di G.N.S.," "Farmerman," "I Love My Country," "Youths Are Important to Guyana," "Guyana Is a Paradise," "The Country of My Birth," "To Build Our Nation," "A Better Life," "Treat All Guyanese Equal," and "Love and Unity." These songs were originally composed for three musical plays. George Noel was born in Buxton and was a trained teacher who had served in many rural and hinterland communities.[99]

The seemingly unbridled power of Prime Minister Burnham; the declaration of the paramountcy of the PNC; the increased centralization of all aspects of the state; and deteriorating economic conditions, caused in part by the oil crisis, galloping national debt, and IMF conditionalities, led to increasing opposition and resistance. Music played an important part in the resistance led primarily by the Working People's Alliance (WPA) and the PPP against Burnham and his government. Although Burnham was not the head of state by law, he was the de facto maximum leader.

The PNC and its supporters were not the only entities using entertainment formats to promote ideological messages, motivate members, and influence the wider society. In 1974 a new source of political opposition emerged in Guyana: the Working People's Alliance (WPA). Its leadership included Eusi Kwayana, Moses Bhagwan, Dr. Clive Thomas, Brindley Benn, and Dr. Walter Rodney. To the WPA, Burnham was a dictator and the PNC was "the single biggest obstruction to Guyana's progress."[100] Music was an important weapon in the WPA's anti-Burnham arsenal. The repertoire included national patriotic songs, hymns, reggae anthems, folk chants, international protest songs, and original compositions. In *Dangerous Times: The Assassination of Dr. Walter Rodney*, Gabriehu gave an example of the use of national patriotic music when he reflected on a WPA meeting in Bourda Green. According to his recounting of the moment, electricity to that location mysteriously went out at the same time as "one hundred and eighty brawny, Afro-Guyanese men" began to advance menacingly on the meeting. Of these, ninety were policemen armed with revolvers and "a two-foot hardwood baton." The other ninety men were members of the House of Israel and some were also dressed as policemen. Walter Rodney was at the microphone when the power went out, and on seeing the approaching men, he "appealed to the crowd to remain calm." Other WPA activists repeated this call. Andaiye's response was to raise the first bars of Guyana's best known patriotic song, "Song of Guiana's Children"; the crowd joined her in asserting solidarity in the face of violence through the song's chorus: "Onward, Upward may we ever go / Day by day in strength and beauty grow / Till at length the each of us may show / What Guyana's sons and daughters can be."

According to Kwayana, hymns and hymnlike songs were also used, and one of the popular ones was Max Romeo's reggae anthem "Let the Power Fall on I," which sought deliverance, justice, and peace.[101] Songs from other struggles, such as "Shaheed," a Muslim freedom song from pre-independence India, were also used. Topical pop songs such as John Lennon's "Give Peace a Chance" and Bob Marley's "Rastaman Chant" were also part of the repertoire of resistance. "Rastaman Chant," which "predicted" the fall of Burnham's Babylon, was particularly popular. In addition to songs, call-and-response street chants, particularly those led by David Hinds, were particularly memorable. For Kwayana, one of the most effective was "Ah who shame? Burnham shame!"[102] A number of WPA activists, including Walter Rodney, would be killed. Their deaths would be enshrined in "People's Power," the song of the WPA; composed by Eusi Kwayana, it called upon Guyanese to "take the fight for freedom into every street / every hill and village / where the people meet."

For this song, the melody, rhythm, and language would not be European in origin but reggae from Jamaica. This was an indication of a generational shift and changing musical tastes in Guyanese society. Jamaican reggae music in the 1970s had evolved "from a relatively nonconfrontational cultural expression to one that openly challenged the dominant sociopolitical system [in Jamaica]."[103] Those attributes, along with the ethos of Rastafari, had spilled over and taken root in Guyana by the end of the 1970s, despite concerted efforts to reorient society to building a new Guyana man and the construction of cooperative socialism.

Starting in the 1950s, the People's Progressive Party had incorporated music in its political work. The party had many cultural groups. Among these was the choir of the Women's Progressive Organization (WPO), established in the 1950s, and the Workers Stage, created in 1977. A review of the various songbooks of the PPP reveals a repertoire that included national patriotic songs, folk songs, special party songs, and international songs.

In 1977 Gail Teixeira, who had recently returned from Canada, sought permission from the PPP's central committee to develop a cultural group made up of members of the Progressive Youth Organization (PYO) and the WPO. Teixeira visualized the group playing an important role in mobilizing resistance against the PNC. Permission was granted and the Workers Stage troupe was born. According to Teixeira, the Workers Stage expanded the party's existing musical repertoire by writing new songs. Among the important composers were Brijmohan, Narvin Chandarpal, Vibert DeSouza, and Gail Teixeira. Lord Enchanter, who was known for his commitment to Afro-Indi musical fusion, was a member of the PPP and also participated in the work of the Workers Stage.

By the late 1970s there was solidarity among various elements of the political opposition in the resistance against the PNC government. This solidarity was evident in cultural activities associated with public political actions. The Workers Stage, along with groups aligned to the Working People's Alliance, were active in the protests. These groups used music, especially folk songs and chants, to encourage urban and rural Guyanese to keep up the struggle. Two members of the Workers Stage, Gail Teixeira and Frank Anthony, would in the future become Ministers of Culture, Youth and Sport.

During social crises people seek escape, relaxation, and clarification of the ambiguities in the environment. The Guyanese private sector responded to the need for escape and relaxation. From advertisements in the weekend editions of the national newspapers, it appeared that every major hotel in the urban areas had a disco during the 1970s. There were discos at the Pegasus, Tower, Park, Belvedere, and Woodbine hotels in Georgetown. In New Amsterdam, there was a discothèque in the Penguin Hotel. Among the new discothèques in Georgetown were the Penthouse, Dog and the Bone, Green Shrimp, Friends, Xanadu, and the Evil Eye. Traditional exclusive clubs such as the Georgetown Club, the ethnic associations, lodge halls, and bars also became venues for dancing and "partying." By the 1970s Linden (formerly McKenzie), Rose Hall, Corriverton, and Anna Regina had either been designated towns or had started to acquire urban attributes, and they too had their share of nightclubs and discothèques. Other styles of partying evident during the 1970s included the house fete (immortalized in Lord Canary's "Down at the Bottom Floor"), the Wednesday "Big Girls" picnic, the "2-10s," the "2-2s," the "after-lunches," "picnics," and the ever-popular steamer excursions.

The music to satisfy this "partying" demand came from a number of sources. The discos had resident DJs, and on occasion radio personalities such as Pancho Carew and Matthew Allen moonlighted as DJs at discos. Business dictated that most of the discos would at some time hire one of the many "party" bands. In this context emerged bands that were categorized as "social" or "roots." "Social" bands were those that were primarily urban and played at upscale venues and catered to the "sophis[ticated]" clientele. "Roots" bands, such as Mischievous Guys, catered to the working class. They were the inheritors of the "practice" and their clientele were considered to be the lineal descendants of the "centipedes." The social bands aimed for respectability and the roots bands were considered representatives of "reputation"—the loud and the raucous. But like all things musical, the boundaries between "social" and "roots" bands were porous. The porosity was a function of the personalities associated with the bands.

The upcoming examination of the interrelated biographies of a few musicians and entrepreneurs—coupled with commentaries by journalists on the "culture beat" during the 1970s—are offered to provide perspectives on musical life outside the musical environment dominated by the demands of the partisan politics that was pervasive in the early post-colonial 1970s.

In the 1970s Aubrey Cummings was a full-time working musician and was associated with all of the major "social" bands and "roots" bands of the decade.[104] He performed for every sector of the society—the "sophis" upper class and the "roots"—experienced changes in instrumentation, made recordings of original music, toured internationally, and migrated in pursuit of his career. Cummings was a guitarist and vocalist with the Dominators until 1972, when he left with Telstars International to tour Brazil. Since the 1960s, Brazil had been welcoming Guyanese musicians and musical groups. No definitive reason has been offered to explain this; however, it is plausible that Guyanese musicians were welcomed because of their ability to sing in English and so satisfy the increasing number of English-speaking tourists flocking to Rio, Sao Paulo, and other destinations in Brazil. In the Bertie Chancellor Library at the National Communication Network, there are a number of recordings by Guyanese musicians who migrated to Brazil. Among these are Bobby MacKay, Ev Manifold, and Minerva Daly. Unfortunately, there are no accessible records of the work that Reggie Simpson did in Brazil during the 1960s. Simpson, who died in Brazil, was Guyana's leading steel band arranger before migrating to Brazil.

When Cummings returned to Guyana in 1975, he was ready for another engagement with popular music in Guyana. His next band was the well-equipped Music Machine. According to Cummings, "We had the best of equipment."[105] The entrepreneurs behind this new band were Vic Insanally, Butch Parmanand, and Pancho Carew—a popular DJ with the Guyana Broadcasting Service.[106] The band rehearsed at Insanally's Church Street and Camp Street home. The other members of the band included Colin Aaron, George Reid, and King Souflantis. The band had solid string and brass sections. A new generation of the Guyanese "big band" had arrived! The Music Machine was also the first band since Combo 7 to pay its members monthly salaries. The band lasted only about six months; however, the musicians earned themselves "big reputations." After the Music Machine, Cummings joined the After Dark Movement, which is credited with being the first band in Guyana to perform the music of Earth, Wind and Fire. For a period, the After Dark Movement was the resident band at the Pegasus Hotel on Saturday nights. The Pegasus at the time was Guyana's newest and most exclusive hotel.

On October 10, 1978, Cummings joined the exodus from Guyana and migrated to Barbados. He took with him the Yamaha twelve-string FG 230 box guitar given to him by Roland Phillips, who was carving a name as a broadcaster, innovative musician, and folk singer who celebrated hinterland themes. In Barbados, Cummings established an active musical career as guitarist and vocalist. He recorded the regional hit "A Flower Named June," which was followed by "Think I Am in Love," "Analie," and "Children of Sanchez." He never returned to Guyana and died in Barbados in 2010.

Another biography that helps in the exploration of music emerging from the private sector during the 1970s is that of Derry Etkins.[107] Commentators who have concluded that some of Guyana's boldest steps in cultural development took place in popular music during the first two post-independence decades always include Derry Etkins in that discourse. Born in Plaisance, a rural village on the East Coast Demerara about ten miles outside of Georgetown, Etkins grew up in a musical family. His father sang with the All Saints Boys Choir in New Amsterdam. His mother was a schoolteacher, a music teacher, and a mezzo-soprano. There was a piano in his home. Etkins was also influenced by the soundscape of Plaisance—sounds of the birds in the backdam, masquerade bands, steel bands, Cumfa drumming, and bhajans. His siblings also played music: two younger brothers played steel pans and drums in high school.

Etkins's foray into popular music started in 1968 at Queen's College, where he was a co-founder of the Q.C. Syncoms. Bold and confident, the band entered the 1968 music festival and won the instrumental and percussion competition. Its next step was a Christmas concert performed on Yamaha instruments loaned by Utility Store on Water Street. The loan, negotiated by Etkins, included an organ, two amplifiers, and a drum set. The band's festival victory and performance at the Christmas concert gave it credibility. As a result, Rupert Cheong offered the band access to the instruments used by the now defunct Dominators and rehearsal space in the band room in Brickdam, Georgetown. By this time, Etkins had migrated from bass to organ. As the arranger for the Q.C. Syncoms, he resisted any tendency to play tunes as they sounded on original recordings. He was "bucking" the copycat system.

In September 1970 Etkins graduated from Queen's College and joined the Graduates as organist. He has described the Graduates as a "weekend band." So he was able to take a "day job" at the National Insurance Scheme (Guyana's

Social Security scheme). In 1973 Etkins joined the Telstars along with Aubrey Cummings and toured Brazil. For Etkins it was a successful and confidence-boosting trip. After the Brazilian tour, the band travelled to Barbados and recorded the important LP *Orbiting*. The tour to Barbados opened other avenues for Etkins. For the next three years (1973–76), he worked in Barbados, performing with the Outfit, Wendy Allen and the Dynamics, and the Tropical Islanders. In 1976 Etkins was invited to Canada. There he spent eighteen months with the road band Ashiba, whose members included Marleen Curtis, Kimberly Curtis, Tyrone Clarke, and the Guyanese singer Aubrey Mann. Etkins by this time had established "cred" on the keyboards. With Ashiba he played five keyboard instruments—organ, synthesizer, clavinet, Fender Rhodes, and string ensemble. This exposed him to the world of electronic music. These were challenging, pre-MIDI days and the instruments had no digital memory, so the player had to be very dexterous.

Etkins returned to Guyana in 1978 and pursued formal music training. Between 1978 and 1983, he studied music with Sybil Husbands and Edith Pieters, emphasizing composition and arranging. During this period he composed *64* and *Jig Saw*, two piano pieces. At the end of his training with Edith Pieters, he was certified as a music teacher.[108] He also joined Solo Sounds International, a large multi-instrument band owned by Neil Chan.

Neil Chan was one of the significant music entrepreneurs in the early post-independence era. In addition to Solo Sounds International, Chan was also the owner of Xanadu, a popular upscale discothèque. He grew up in the Lacytown area of Georgetown during the 1940s and 1950s and was exposed to the musical ferment taking place in this urban working-class ward during that era. He was part of the early steel band "action," playing an energetic role in developing costumed bands for tramping. As a young man, he along with Billy Moore, Neville Rose, Willie Wright, and Ev Manifold were members of the standard-setting Billy Moore and the Four Lords. In addition to being a supporter of music, he was also a businessman, specializing in the import trade. In the early 1970s he was appointed the first director of the External Trade Bureau (ETB), which was responsible for the importation of most of Guyana's food and other commodities. Given the politics of public-service appointments, it could be concluded that Chan was aligned with the PNC. However, he was also strong-willed and somewhat self-centered and therefore resisted the constraining cultural orthodoxy that came from Congress Place, the headquarters of the PNC.

Chan felt that Guyanese music should be dynamic and reflective of the changes taking place internationally, especially in the United States. This meant that the best contemporary instruments and sound equipment had to be used and the music had to be original. It was in this context that Solo Sounds

International emerged. Like Combo 7 and the Music Machine, Solo Sounds International also paid its members a regular monthly salary. Although Chan owned and operated Xanadu, he did not believe that Solo Sounds International's music should be cloistered in that venue. By the late 1970s he was active in creating large public entertainment events for the increasingly stressed-out society. His mission was to "Nice up Guyana!" *Smile Guyana* was one such event. Part of this mission included bringing in international musicians, particularly acts from Trinidad and Tobago. It was through Neil Chan's efforts that Guyana was able to see a new generation of calypsonians from Trinidad such as David Rudder, Tambu, and Shadow and hear the experimentations that were taking place in Soca. By the end of the 1970s, Solo Sounds International was the band that was in demand by the state sector. Because of this visibility, Neil Chan and Solo Sounds International exerted significant influence on popular music in Guyana during the 1970s and the early to mid-1980s.

With Solo Sounds International, Etkins began to experiment with the incorporation of indigenous beats and rhythms. The masquerade influences of his early childhood began to infuse his music and can be heard in compositions and arrangements such as the theme music for the *Smile Guyana* project, "Coconut Broth," "Roots Walk," and "Plaisance Backdam." Those compositions introduced the "fish beat" and celebrated Guyana's racial and ethnic heritage. The results of Etkins's experimentation are to be found on the LP *Solo Sounds International*—a limited-edition LP of original compositions. Despite the creative space available with Solo Sounds International, Etkins, like Cummings and so many other musicians, migrated. The environment was stressful for them.

Many performers and entrepreneurs took their cues from the state sector. "Local Dish," a calypso by El Cid (Sydney Prince), is a good example of this tendency. In this calypso, El Cid supports the PNC government's decision to ban the importation of a range of foodstuff, declaring, "I like me local, local dish" and proceeds to celebrate the "Local, local fish" and the "local, local dishes like pepper pot and metagee." Tony Harrop's "Nationalize the Bauxite" was a song that supported another PNC government decision. Terry Nelson's Halagala label released an LP titled *Socialist Explosion*. As mentioned earlier, the Dominators covered "I Want to Build," the theme song of the Guyana National Service.

The list of Guyanese making records during the 1970s is impressive. Maybe they were influenced by Brook Benton's guidance in 1962 on how to make a hit record.[109] Male musicians outnumbered females by a ratio of 4 to 1. Of a 2,733-unit sample of the Guyanese music created during the twentieth century, approximately 45 percent were composed and recorded during the 1970s. The predominant theme of these recordings from the 1970s was love in its many dimensions—love found; love lost; partying; and commentary on topical issues, including alcoholism, Jim Jones and the People's Temple, corruption, and rural-to-urban migration. Neisha Benjamin's "Benji Darling," Gordon Bevan and the Young Ones' "The Wonderful Sound," and Alan Liverpool's "My Head in a Whirl" are examples of songs in the "love found" category. Examples of "love lost" are Lionel Abel's "Lonely Man," Sammy Baksh's "To Be Lonely," Tony Ricardo's "Margie," and Eddie Hooper's "Where Are Your Friends Now?" "Party Time," "Georgetown Hustle," and "Boogie Gonna Get You" are examples of "partying" songs. The topical issues songs included the Mighty Kaieteur's "Drunk Man," which focused on alcoholism; Eddie Hooper's "Country Girl," commenting on rural to urban migration; "Who Kill Jim Jones" and "Jonestown Express," addressing the People's Temple catastrophe; and "Dishonest Cop" and "Political Gangsters," on the rise of corruption in the society.

The Yoruba Singers' output maintained focus on the folk ("Massacuraman," "Bird Pepper," "G.O. Go," and "Yoruba Man"). Hilton Hemerding, Roland Philips, and Alan Khan composed music in a neo-folk style and celebrated the hinterland and the flora and fauna of Guyana. Hemerding's "Going up the Potaro," "Tumatumari," "Song of the Pork knocker," "Kurkubaru," and Philips's "Ode to Kamarang," "Waramadong," and "The Land Where I Was Born" are exemplars of this tendency in Guyanese popular music during the 1970s.

The music created during the 1970s has become an important element of the soundtrack of Guyana during the twentieth century. In the first decade of the twenty-first century, many of these recordings have iconic status—they are the obligatory "oldies" that populate the playlist at Guyanese parties at home or in the Guyaspora. Songs such as "My Love Is Not Retail" (Satch Persaud), "Sharon, Sharon" (Mark Bryan), "Party Time" (Glen "Family" Teach), "Take Warning" (Eddie Hooper), "Margie" (Tony Ricardo), "Local Dish" (El Cid), "Lonely Man" (Lionel Abel), "I Think I Am in Love" and "A Flower named June" (Aubrey Cummings), "Set My Heart at Ease" (Rita Forrester), "Lost, Lonely and Helpless" (Pamela Maynard), and "By My Side" (Sammy Baksh and Barbara Sookraj) are among the more popular recordings found on compilations of Guyanese music from the 1970s. Aligned with this musical productivity was the growth in the number of domestic recording labels. Many musicians who had "cut their teeth" on local talent radio shows such as *Teensville* and *In Search of a Star* created their own labels.

In addition to the large output, there was ongoing musical exchange. Ivor Lynch, the Kitty-born and raised singer and music producer, incorporated the tassa and dholak rhythms and other Indian Guyanese beats that he learned from Joe Taylor, a Guyanese of African ancestry. Joe Taylor was considered an expert on Indian drum rhythms in the Kitty/Campbellville/Subryanville area.[110] Eddy Hooper was introducing the Lopi. Terry Nelson pushed the

Afro-Indi beat. Harry Whittaker encouraged a Guyanese free-style jazz. The Mashqi and other rhythms joined the bhoom of the 1960s as examples of a multiracial people seeking a distinctive national sound.

There were other streams of popular music in Guyana during the 1970s. Undoubtedly, one of the most influential streams came from Jamaica. Since the late nineteenth century, there had always been a Jamaican musical presence in Guyanese society. The bands of the Royal West Indian Regiment contributed to the circulation of popular and folk music around the West Indies. It was through this circular route that "Sly Mongoose" came to British Guiana and de Weever's "Me Cawfee in de Marnin'" went to Jamaica. In the 1950s Mento recordings such as "Hill and Gully Rider" attracted regular airplay on Radio Demerara, no doubt a function of the music policy of the regional broadcaster—Rediffusion International, which owned stations in Jamaica, Barbados, Trinidad, and British Guiana. Throughout the 1960s, Guyanese enjoyed blue beat, rock steady, and ska hits such as "My Boy Lollipop" by Millie Small, "Guns of Navarone" by the Skatalites, and "Israelites" by Desmond Dekker. By the early 1970s Guyanese were ardent consumers of reggae, a new development in Jamaican popular music. Singers of soft reggae such as Ken Lazarus, Ken Booth, Dobbie Dobson, Boris Gardner, John Jones, John Holt, Pluto Shervington, and bands such as Tomorrow's Children and Byron Lee and the Dragonaires popularized this new genre of Jamaican music in Guyana.

In February 1970, Jamaican musicians had eight singles on Guyana's Top 10 charts. Of these, six were by Ken Lazarus: "Tonight" (#1), "Monkey Man" (#3), "No More Heartaches" (#5), "Hello Carol" (#7), "Happy Heart" (#8), and "How Can I Love You" (#9). The other two were by Roy Shirley ("Flying Reggae," #2) and Boris Gardner ("Love Can Make You Happy," #6). "Cissy Strut" (#4) by the Meters and "Love at First Sight" (#10) by Sounds Nice were the other two.[111] By the 1970s Guyana became a major destination for Jamaican performers, and Jamaica's *Daily Gleaner* often carried stories about these tours.[112] For example, on March 12, 1971, the newspaper carried a photograph, captioned:

> Ken Lazarus dances with Mrs. Forbes Burnham, wife of the Prime Minister of Guyana on the occasion of Guyana's "Republic Eve Ball" which took place recently on the grounds of the Prime Minister's Residence in Guyana. Ken Lazarus and Tomorrow's Children who are at present touring the Caribbean, performed at this ball which was one of their engagements during their one week stay in Guyana.[113]

Ken Lazarus was so popular in Guyana that, at one time in the early 1970s, he was "reportedly selling more records in Guyana than Tom Jones and Engelbert Humperdinck combined."[114]

By 1975 the sound of the "Jamaican invasion" shifted from the mellow "lovers reggae" of Ken Lazarus, Ken Booth, Boris Gardner, and Pluto Shervington to the hard realism of Burning Spear, Bob Marley, Big Youth, Yellowman, and assorted "rude boys." This music was sharply focused on social, economic, and political injustices. Although composed in the Jamaican context, the lyrics and sentiments resonated across the Caribbean and around the world. The purveyors of this "conscious reggae" were primarily Rastafarians who wore their dreadlocks with pride and dignity. As *The Story of Jamaican Music* states, this was the period when "Natty [sang] Hit Songs." These artists drew attention to the poverty and abuse still being experienced by people of African descent in the Plantation America and placed the blame for much of it on the "politricks" practiced by the corrupt cliques that ran post-independence societies. Songs such as Bob Marley's "No Woman No Cry" and Jacob Miller's "Tenement Yard" spoke to the unacceptable conditions of the ghettos that persisted in the Caribbean. In Guyana the equivalent could be found in Tiger Bay, Albouystown (All Man Town), and Charlestown. Leroy Smart's "Ballistic Affair," Max Romeo's "War Ina Babylon," Willie Williams's "Armageddon Time," and Junior Murvin's "Police and Thieves" provided details on the violent consequences of these oppressive conditions. Burning Spear reminded the world that solutions to the contemporary problems could be found in the words of "Marcus Garvey."

By the late 1970s the Rastafarian philosophy and its associated lifestyle—Ital (vegetarianism) and the smoking of marijuana—had taken root in Guyana. The lifestyle was apparent among the unemployed and dispossessed and some of the more cosmopolitan sectors of the society, especially those who had studied or lived in the UK, Canada, and the United States. Guyanese consumers of "conscious reggae" were multi-ethnic. It was from this multi-class and multiracial community that the Working People Alliance drew its support and sympathizers.

With its insider language, conscious reggae altered Guyana's soundtrack, contributing to the sharpening of an "us against them" tension in society. The ruling class in Guyana felt that the music and the associated lifestyle were subversive. The police harassed Rastafarians and would on occasion shear their locks for even the slightest perceived infractions. Earlier in the 1970s, various agencies of the government of Guyana began to censor various aspects of popular culture. In 1972 a ban was placed on showing kung fu, sex, and horror movies in Guyana.[115] Earlier, in 1970, Carl Austin, the commissioner of police, promised to prosecute persons playing music with "lewd and indecent" lyrics.[116] These interventions in popular culture influenced the playlists of the state-owned radio stations, and many conscious reggae songs were banned.

But the radio stations were not the only medium for airing music in Guyana during the 1970s. By 1975 component stereo sets had become more widespread; more Guyanese were buying records, and reggae was very popular with the urban record-buying public. What was banned on the radio was played in nightclubs, on jukeboxes in bars, in private homes, on portable "boom boxes," and from the giant speakers at "bubbles" (public dances). Guyanese remained current with all the changes taking place in reggae music and Rastafarian fashion. Red, green, and gold—the colors of "Ites"—and "khaki suit and ting" became fashion statements and "skanking" the popular dance. The Jamaican invasion left an indelible mark on Guyanese cultural life, even influencing Guyanese vernacular vocabulary and way of speaking. The Jamaican invasion was responsible for the emergence of the "roots" music tradition that would play an important role in the development of Guyanese political, social, and cultural consciousness during the 1980s and throughout the remainder of the twentieth century.

Charles Knights, LRSM, ARCM, noted that for music to grow in a society four groups must interact: composers, performers, audiences, and critics.[117] In the 1970s Guyana had an active group of newspaper columnists who regularly commented on music in the press and on the radio—the "critics." Among this group were Humphrey Nelson, Rashid Osman, Basil Hinds, and Roddy Fraser. By the mid-1970s all of these critics were employed by the *Guyana Chronicle*, the state-owned and dominant national newspaper. None of these columnists wrote with the technical flair and competence that Clef demonstrated during the 1950s. Most were enthusiastic and cast a discerning eye and ear across the range of musical events taking place during the 1970s. Humphrey Nelson, Fraser, and Osman were the most prolific. Their work provides special insight into the ideological, popular, and formal aspects of Guyanese music of the decade.

Joseph Leonard Humphrey Nelson's writings seemed to have two themes. The first was the need to increase the airplay of compositions that promoted the nation's heroes, especially his 1970 composition, "O Martyr, O Martyr, To Cuffy We Sing," which adulated Cuffy, the enslaved African revolutionary who in 1763 led an uprising against the Dutch in Berbice.[118] The second theme addressed his concerns about what he perceived were anti–local music tendencies among gatekeepers at the state-owned radio stations. In the latter effort he was reprising the concerns expressed by Al Seales in the 1950s and contemporaneously by Terry Nelson. In a series of articles, Humphrey Nelson focused on impediments to the promotion of Guyanese music on the radio station, including inferences that "the unfair, wicked, and ruthless form of malpractice—PAYOLA—may be evident in Guyana's radio stations."[119] His analysis of the playlist of *Guyana's Morning Programme* on Radio Demerara revealed such a preponderance of popular music from the United Kingdom that he suggested dropping that word Guyana from the program's title. James Sydney, a member of the management at Radio Demerara during the 1970s, agreed that there were indeed inducements that "encouraged" the station to play certain records. He was of the opinion that record jobbers from Trinidad and Tobago who serviced the Rediffusion stations in Barbados, Trinidad, and Guyana used some sort of payola in their business practice. During a 2012 Facebook conversation, Ray Seales, the son of Al Seales, the owner of GEMS Records, wrote of a personal experience he had with the restrictions placed on Guyanese music by Radio Demerara:

> I produced "LONELY MAN" and "Theme From Babylon" by the Mischievous
> Guys in 1973 on a GEMS/EKO label. I knew if the radio station found out it was
> from GEMS it would not be played. My way out of the blackball was to take
> and make music from our subculture popular in the streets of GT. These were
> Guyana's biggest selling 45 rpms. The subculture supports their own just as I
> expected. The radio station eventually caught on and sent Pancho Carew to beg
> me for a copy. My father before tried to be anonymous by using many labels other
> than GEMS, like . . . EKO, POSH, JET but world-wide he will always be GEMS the
> inventor of CARIBBEAN CARNIVAL.[120]

As a columnist during the 1970s, J. L. H. Nelson was seen as self-serving, using his articles to push his private causes. However, he was also caught up in the spirit of the times and dedicated to the reorientation of society. He was not unique in his belief that music had an important role to play in the education of the nation, especially during tough economic times.[121] Nelson's work as a columnist shone a light on structural problems faced by Guyanese musicians and, through statements such as "the ship of existence in which local recording musical artistes are sailing will sooner or later sink," drew attention to the underlying crisis faced by musicians during the early years of the 1970s. Nelson must also be recognized as one of the composers to launch the "odes" for Odo and Cuffy genre. Other "odes for Odo" included "In Burnham's Garden" by Evelyn John, "Oh Burnham Boy" (Doreen Thomas), "Strongman Cuffy" ("Guitar" Levans), and "Tribute to Our Leader" (Mighty Smoker).

Roddy Fraser's columns focused on many aspects of the popular music scene in Guyana during the 1970s—performers, musical consumption, steel band, calypso, and soca. His columns were invariably based on firsthand experiences. As a result, he left a valuable historical record. His piece on "JB [juke box] fete music" is an example of this mode of partying in Guyana in the mid-1970s: "JB fete music is divided into three segments. The first segment lasting up to about 11:30 p.m., may be hard rock, swinging reggae, soul and calypso. The second segment, the strongest, is a mixed bag of local tunes, old and new.

The third is the regular oldies from abroad bringing the fete to a close."[121] The article also provided a list of the Guyanese music that was popular among jukebox operators in the mid-1970s:

> Johnny Braff's 'Read it Over,' 'Neville,' and 'It Burns Inside' (both old and new version) . . . The Yoruba Singers, 'Black Pepper' . . . The Dominators' 'I Want To Build' . . . Eddy Grant's 'Hello Africa' . . . Mark Holder's 'Music Turns Me On,' 'Today, Tomorrow, and Always,' . . . 'Someone' by Czerina Ali . . . Lionel Abel's 'Lonely Man' . . . Eddie Hooper's 'Passing Memories' and 'Where Are Your Friends Now,' . . . Halagala's production of 'In the Ghetto' . . . 'Tribute to Our Leader' by the Mighty Smoker . . . Harry Whittaker's Saxful of Harry is in demand . . . and is likely to remain so for a long time . . . Others include King Fighter's 'Big Banana' and Jerry Jackson's 'Desperately.'[123]

Fraser also loved to rank Guyanese musicians and musical groups, publish biographies, and provide updates on Guyanese musicians overseas. He tended to use annual retrospectives to identify the "Top 5" in a number of genres. At mid-decade, he identified the Yoruba Singers as the Band of the Year for 1975. Harry Whittaker, who received the Medal of Service (a national award) in 1975, was declared the Musician of the Year for 1975. Among the other musicians identified as deserving of recognition in 1975 were Hector Bailey France, the lead guitarist with the Graduates Combo, and three female vocalists—Patricia Arthur, Lady Monica, and Czerina Ali. He declared Czerina Ali the Female Vocalist of the Year.[124] Flautist, Keith Waithe; saxophonist with the Dominators, King Souflantis; and David Chester, saxophonist with the Jet Stars Combo from Linden, were also identified as outstanding musicians in 1975.[125] Sammy Baksh, Compton Hodge, Eddie Taylor, and Otis Goodluck were identified as the outstanding male vocalists.[126] Fraser also ranked calypsonians. For him the top calypsonians in 1975 were King Fighter, Eddie Hooper, Lord Canary, Calypso Joy, El Cid, Lady Guybau, Calypso Stella, the Mighty Kaieteur, Mighty Panther, Mighty Serpent, and the Mighty Smoker.

He wrote valuable biographical articles on many of Guyana's leading musicians of the 1970s, among them Harry Whitaker, Monica Chopperfield, Sid of the Slickers, Noel Adams, and Derry Etkins. In "The Whittaker Genius," he examined Harry Whittaker's career and his contribution to the development of jazz in Guyana.[127] His examination of Monica Chopperfield (Lady Monica, Lady Guybau, and later Lady Guymine) placed her in the context of a constellation of critically acclaimed male and female Guyanese singers from the forties and fifties—Annie Haynes, Lloyd Brandt, Doreen Gravesande, and Billy Moore. He focused attention on her long career and the fact that her style was unique and that she was not a "copy-cat" singer.[128] Sid, the leader of the Slickers, was identified as a musician and bandleader who demonstrated tenacity and versatility—attributes that made him, by the 1970s, a musician who had been successful for more than three decades.[129] The pianist, Noel Adams, who in the 1970s worked with Radio Demerara, was celebrated as a talent scout and as a composer.[130] The article on Derry Etkins reported on the musician's progress in Canada and was emblematic of the interest that Fraser and others maintained about what was happening with Guyanese musicians in the diaspora.

Through his articles on Guyanese artistes overseas, such as his piece on Derry Etkins, the Guyanese reader was able to follow the careers of many Guyanese artists who were working overseas. His February 1, 1976, article in the *Sunday Chronicle* spotlighted the career of Tony Ricardo, who had left Guyana in 1969 to become a member of the Troubadours—the band that accompanied the world famous calypsonian the Mighty Sparrow. Since then he had become very popular across the Caribbean and had toured Canada and the United States.[131]

He also wrote articles examining what was happening with steel band music in Guyana. In his review for 1975, he identified the Pegasus Soundwaves, Guybau Invaders, Demtoco Silvertones, and Chronicle Atlantic Symphony as the nation's top four steel bands. He also drew attention to the Eldorado Steel Band of Lodge, the Police Steel Band, the Guyana Defence Force Steel Band, the P.N.C. Breakthrough Steel Band, and the Mobilizers Steel Band of the Ministry of Cooperatives and National Mobilization as bands that impressed him. He singled out the Mobilizers as one of the few bands with female players who "interchange on the various pans and do so with the maximum of skill as their male counterparts."[132] For him the Chronicle Atlantic Brass and Steel Orchestra exemplified the benefits of discipline and hard work: "The high standards of artistry produced by the Chronicle Atlantic today is [*sic*] not something that can be achieved easily. It certainly took them long hours of experiment and actual performance to mould that sound and style of theirs."[133]

Underneath his chronicling of the music scene in Guyana and his biographical work on Guyanese musicians, Fraser had two concerns: the exploitation of Guyanese musicians and the unfortunate tendency for Guyanese musicians to be "copy-cats." His article "Musicians should buy their own instruments" was occasioned by the sudden breakup of the Telstars because of what Ray Seales, a member of the band, described as "extreme exploitation." In examining that exploitation, Fraser surveyed the development of popular music bands in Guyana in the post–World War II era and noted that, in recent years, investors in bands had grown to dominate the music. He situated the change in band management with the advent of the string bands. He noted that Combo Seven and the Rhythmaires "started on a cooperative basis which worked well." However, "younger musicians, who wanted to get on the bandstand, created the system which led to downfall by allowing a fabulous percentage to anybody who could purchase instruments for them to play, and installing the same person as manager." This, Fraser contended, facilitated "the whole machinery of exploitation"—musicians became the hired hands of band owners/managers.[134] Fraser felt that musicians could only eradicate that form of exploitation and abuse if they owned their own instruments.[135]

"Copycatism" was another one of Roddy Fraser's pet peeves. A June 1974 article captures his abhorrence; he observed that many Guyanese musicians were "living on lazy street, all waiting for the next big foreign hit record to come along for them to slavishly copy." He described this as "a sickening symptom" which "creates stagnation in the creative flow."[136]

Not merely critical of the copycatism, Fraser was expressing concern about what was happening with the quest to develop a truly Guyanese sound/beat, especially the failure to consistently experiment with the range of "roots" beats. In his review of the 1970s, he identified several of the short-lived attempts:

[In] 1971 outstanding groups like Combo 7, Melons and the Syncopaters, all working hard towards developing Tom's creation of the Bhoom, a musical idea intended to be a national beat . . . Somewhere around that same period Jean Daniels created some exciting moments with her own brand of folk singing . . . Nesha Benjamin pioneered the Afro-Indi beat . . . The Linden Fascinators big band made up of unique strings and brass started revolution in music bringing about a new flair based on Latin pop sequence. . . . The Yoruba Singers were moving very rapidly towards a pure cultural direction. They brought fresh fever on the scene.[137]

He bemoaned the fact that nothing was sustained, and hoped that the 1980s would be better. In an obligatory tip of the hat to domestic politics, he expressed the belief that "the Socialist trend our Government is taking will provide maximum benefit for our creative artists."

Despite regular and justified criticism from local critics, for Billy Pilgrim the pop sector was the most creative sector in Guyanese music during the twentieth century.[138] And musicians felt that way also. In 1978 the Guyana Association of Musicians (GAM) was formed with the aim of establishing "a $1.5M modern recording studio to cater for the needs of all local artistes." They took their step in that direction in February 1978, when an account was opened at the Guyana National Cooperative Bank.[139] Alas, this did not bear fruit!

As a critic, Rashid Osman's "beat" tended to be highbrow, covering the formal music scene and accompanying official Guyanese cultural delegations when they traveled overseas. Although not a musician himself, he exhibited competence with the vocabulary of music in his writing. Osman had his feet in three cultural camps. He was of Indian ancestry, had African in-laws, and appreciated European classical musical forms. In addition to writing for newspapers, he also hosted classical music programs on the radio stations.

An examination of his body of work during the 1970s shows him to be a sensitive observer of the wider cultural environment. This attribute was most evident in his review of the poorly attended 1973 Guyana Music Festival. He wondered if the poor attendance was a function of "the controversial general election [held a week earlier] which swept the People's National Congress into the Parliament with a two-thirds majority." He wondered if "the hectic election campaign" caused the public to ignore the fact that the adjudicator was Ray Luck, the first Guyanese ever to have that distinction. Some members of the society did not support Luck's selection as the adjudicator—a manifestation of doubt in the ability of Guyanese to do things formerly done by Caucasians. As Osman noted: "When it was announced that Ray Luck was coming to be the first Guyanese adjudicator at the local festival, there was some doubt in certain quarters about the concert pianist's suitability for such a role."[140] Osman's article revealed how successfully Ray Luck rose to the task:

> His performance over the past two weeks has, however, quieted those who thought the idea a bad one. He approached his work with thoroughness rare among the breed he represented and, in many cases his adjudication turned out to be music lessons for grateful competitors and thrilled audiences. His work on opening night was somewhat flawed as he sought to put into words, for the benefit of the layman, criticisms drawn from his considerable expertise.[141]

An influential discourse among the political elite questioned the relevance of the music festival to the new nation. Osman was sensitive to this discourse and zeroed in on one of the deficiencies of the 1973 Music Festival—the absence of Indian music. He cogitated:

> Clearly, the strongest contention against the Music Festival in Guyana being truly relevant is the complete absence of Indian music on the programme. In this pot-pourri of a nation, where more than 50 percent of the population is of Indian descent and where Indian music is enjoying a new wave of popularity, the exclusion of this genre of music from the festival is hard to understand.[142]

That absence is probably one of the reasons the festival was suspended after 1973.

Through Osman's articles, Guyanese were able to read about the performances of Guyana's delegations at influential international festivals such as

Carifesta 76 in Jamaica, Festac 77 in Nigeria, and Carifesta 79 in Cuba. These festivals were important planks in Guyana's public diplomatic initiatives. For Carifesta 76 he reported on Ray Luck's brilliant performance in Philip Pilgrim's *Legend of Kaieteur*, the "fine showing" of the Yoruba Singers, and the accomplishments of the Trevini Dance Troupe (Philip McLintock, Marilyn Hall, Malcolm Hall, and Donna Ramsammy) and the Chuck Gerard trio.[143]

The Legend of Kaieteur at Carifesta 76 was an exercise in musical cooperation between Jamaica and Guyana. This was no doubt a function of the status Billy Pilgrim had as a musician in both societies and the close relations that existed between Forbes Burnham and Jamaica's Prime Minister Michael Manley. According to the *Jamaican Gleaner*, *Legend of Kaieteur* was "disappointingly attended." Harry Milner's review considered the poor turnout "strange and particularly sad," as Jamaicans performers were actively involved.[144] For example, the Jamaica School of Music's eighty-strong choir was augmented by 160 additional voices for the performances.[145]

The Yoruba Singers won a silver medal in the Carifesta 76 Song Contest with their rendition of "Zamin Let Your Culture Reign." The winner was Trinidad and Tobago's Mighty Chalkdust with his calypso "Chain of Strength," an appeal for Caribbean unity. The other four finalists were from Haiti, Jamaica, Mexico, and Surinam.[146]

In 1977 Guyana participated in Festac 77, The Second World Black and African Festival of Arts and Culture, held in Lagos, Nigeria. The government of Guyana loaned Carifesta 72 Commissioner Frank Pilgrim to Nigeria to help with the planning for Festac 77. As a result, several features from Carifesta 72, such as the Festival Village and the staging of shows in rural areas, were evident at Festac 77.

Guyana's delegation to Festac 77 included Hamilton Green, then Minister of Cooperatives and National Mobilization, the "Singing Member of Parliament" Malcolm Corrica (Lord Canary), the Harry Whittaker Combo featuring Keith Waithe and Art Broomes, and the Chronicle Atlantic Steel and Brass Orchestra (CASBO). From Osman's articles, it is clear that the Guyanese delegation made a significant impression at the festival.[147] According to Malcolm Hall, who attended the festival, "the hit of the festival was the Chronicle Atlantic Steel and Brass Orchestra."[148]

As a result of the political developments in Guyana and a number of other "push" and "pull" forces, the Guyanese diaspora grew in the 1970s. During this period there was a shift in the geography of the diaspora. As UK immigration laws became more restrictive, immigration laws in Canada and the United States became more liberal, and Guyanese began moving in substantial numbers to those nations. By the end of the 1970s, New York and Toronto had joined London as key centers of the Guyanese diaspora. Guyanese in London had access to music from many Guyanese musicians. Rannie Hart, Mike McKenize, Iggy Quail, Ivan Chin, and Frank Holder were "representing" in jazz circles. Neville Marshall-Corbin, who performed as Sol Ray, had a vocal style that caused him to be dubbed "the British Nat Cole." A younger generation had already placed a powerful stamp on British pop music by the 1970s. This younger generation of Guyanese musicians included Eddy Grant, who was the leader of the Equals. Guyanese musicians also had influential roles in bands such as Aswad and Cymandie. In Sweden, Douglas Harper, who in the 1940s and 1950s had enjoyed jam sessions in British Guiana with Valerie Rodway, James Rodway, Iggy Quail, and Robert Frank, emerged as Sweden's leading jazz pianist.

In New York, Guyanese musicians were the core of the Brass Construction and important members of the Salsoul Orchestra. In Canada, David Campbell, Names and Faces, and Dave Martins and Trade Winds were Guyana's musical ambassadors. Residing in Vancouver, Campbell established himself as one of Canada's leading folk singers and an important voice of the First Peoples of the Americas. His songs "Cabacaburi Children" and "No Not Columbus" were anthems of pride. In Toronto, Dave Martins and the Trade Winds, a pan-Caribbean band, ruled the roost at We Place, the definitive Caribbean nightclub. Martins composed and recorded songs that questioned the state of Caribbean identity. Among the popular recordings in this vein were "Copycats," "Caribbean Man," and "Where Are Your Heroes." Another Trade Winds trademark was to push the boundaries of "double entendre" with songs such as "Honeymooning Couple," "Wong Ping," "You Can't Get," "Mister Rooster," and "Sleepy Willie." As a result of much success in this category, by the end the 1970s, Dave Martins and the Trade Winds had more records "banned" from airplay in Guyana than any other contemporary artist from the Caribbean. Despite these bans, the band's records were very popular in private circles and remained best sellers into the first decade of the twenty-first century. Martins also composed a number of songs that responded to the nostalgia that the Guyanese diaspora experienced. Songs such as "Boyhood Days," "Come Back Again," and "West Indian Alphabet" spoke about the good old days and times of innocence.

Also in Canada was Names and Faces, a band that was "one of Guyana's most popular bands." According to a December 18, 1975, *Guyana Chronicle* article, the popularity of Names and Faces in Canada was "growing apace." The band featured Reggie Paul, Deryck Paul, Patrick Rego, Len Hone, Carlton Rampersaud, and Godfrey King.

Guyana also had a diaspora in the Caribbean. King Fighter, who now lived in Grenada, was part of that Caribbean diaspora.

A relatively buoyant economy during the first half of the 1970s encouraged the creative developments mentioned above. In 1974 and 1975, Guyana earned substantial profits from exports, especially sugar. According Tyrone Ferguson, "Export earnings more than doubled between 1973 and 1974, rising from G$288m to G$600m and increased by over 40 percent in 1975 over 1974 to record G$858m."[149] As a result, in 1975 Guyana boasted one of the highest foreign currency holdings in the Caribbean. However, by 1976 the economy started to decline rapidly as the prices of sugar, rice, gold, diamonds, and bauxite dropped on the world markets. In addition, the Venezuelan crisis became shriller and Guyana's relations with the United States deteriorated. Both developments were no doubt directly related to the "Socialist thrust" and the nation's alignment with the Soviet Bloc.

To complete the picture, the Oil Producing and Exporting Countries (OPEC) increased the price of oil. As a result, Guyana had to spend increasing amounts of GDP on oil imports. In 1970, Guyana's oil import bill was G$23m, which represented 8 percent of the value of total imports and was equivalent to 9 percent of export earnings. By 1979 this had increased to G$230m and represented 29.3 percent of imports and 31.2 percent of export earnings.[150] As a result, Guyana had to borrow money for capital works and current accounts from international financial institutions such as the World Bank, the International Monetary Fund, the Inter-American Development Bank, private commercial banks, and through bilateral agreements from Barbados, Canada, China, Cuba, France, Trinidad and Tobago, the United Kingdom, and the Soviet Union, among others.

Loans from the international financial institutions carried with them harsh "conditionalities," in the development jargon of the period. For example, in 1978 an IMF loan of US$6.25m required that the government of Guyana reduce government expenditure; impose wage restraints; progressively eliminate subsidies for a range of foods, such as rice and flour; and increase the prices for utilities such as electricity, telecommunications, and ground and air transportation.[151] That level of borrowing put Guyana on the road to becoming the country with one of the highest per capita debt burdens in the developing world. In 1979 Guyana's external debt totaled G$507m and the servicing of this debt was equivalent to 15.8 percent of the country's earnings from the export of goods and services. In 1985 it amounted to $G769.8 million and required 70.8 percent of the earnings from the export of goods and services.[152] This was the cost of creating the new Guyana man!

The economic downturn led to a number of stringent economic measures, among them wage and salary freezes, compulsory saving schemes, and further restrictions on the importation of foodstuffs. The importation of wheat flour was banned! The economic conditions galvanized opposition forces against the increasingly autocratic rule of President Burnham. These political actors contended that the PNC government was fraudulent as a result of a pattern of rigged elections. There was broad-based resistance to the 1979 referendum to modify the republican constitution of 1970. Despite protest and disapproval from sectors of the society that hitherto supported Burnham, the PNC garnered more than 75 percent of the vote and was able to adopt a new constitution, which led to the installation of Linden Forbes Sampson Burnham as Guyana's first executive president in 1980. Like all post-independence elections, the referendum was perceived as fraudulent.

At the end of the 1970s, many of the grand dreams did not materialize and the "small man" was, in some sectors, probably worse off than at the start of the decade. National caloric intake dropped. Burnham acknowledged that the Feed, Clothes and House program had failed. He would also later regret making a decision to scrap the national railroad system in 1971.[153] In addition, democracy was compromised in Guyana.

In February 1980, Blackman's Public Relations Agency produced a special issue magazine with the sub-title *A Review of 10 Years of the Republic of Guyana*. Carl Blackman, the editor of the state-owned *Guyana Chronicle* and a close friend of Forbes Burnham, was also closely associated with the Blackman's Public Relations Agency. The magazine's foreword noted that the nation was not celebrating its tenth anniversary with any "smugness or illusions about our achievements." It reflected on the past ten "tumultuous years" in which there were "signs of hope and progress amid the disappointments and setbacks." The foreword and a majority of the articles in the publication identified a list of external forces responsible for the "bludgeoning" the nation experienced during the 1970s. On the list were increases in the price of oil and falling prices for Guyana's primary export commodities—sugar, bauxite, and rice. There was no reference to the concerns about and resistance to the increasingly autocratic practices of Forbes Burnham's governance; the cost of decolonization; or Burnham's failure to engage the Guyanese people on a strategy for import substitution, rather than arbitrarily imposing bans on foodstuffs such as flour. The foreword declared that 1970s was a "testing decade," as "ten back-to-the wall years," and concluded that as a result of the draconian import substitution regime, Guyanese learned to eat what they produced and "not to seek or expect speedy solutions." The foreword predicted: "Future generations will read about our blackouts and 'Guylines' of the Seventies and thank us for bequeathing to them what will surely be by then, one of the most viable nations of the developing world."[154]

Blackman was reflecting on a multi-dimensional decade, one marked by substantial decolonizing efforts aimed at building national pride and projecting national identity in domestic and international spheres. Bold steps also marked the decade in economic independence through the nationalization of the bauxite and sugar industries. Similarly bold steps were taken in the ideological sphere, through active engagement in advancing Caribbean regional integration, declaring commitment to socialism and establishing diplomatic relations with the Soviet Bloc. The decade also saw the reemergence of autocratic and repressive dimensions to the Guyanese political fabric, last experienced during the heyday of British colonial rule. The many social, economic, and political problems, including the killing and arbitrary imprisonment of members of the opposition, contributed to a very stressful Guyana. These developments accelerated migration to the Caribbean, Canada, the United States, Venezuela, and Brazil. It was a decade of hopes, failures, and many forms of violence. It was indeed the best of times and the worst of times.

9

The 1980s: Long Live the
President—The President Is Dead!

President Forbes Burnham has been compared to Machiavelli, Napoleon, and Caesar Augustus. Like Caesar, he recognized the importance of public entertainment as a vehicle for the citizenry to let off steam, for diverting attention, for mobilizing the society in times of crisis, and the "promotion of a political regime."[1] In 200 BC, Juvenal described entertainment as one aspect of the *panis et circenses* (bread and circuses) formula politicians used to gain and maintain popular support in Rome. In British Guiana, the colonial governors incorporated public entertainment in their governance practices through networks of influence nurtured by patronage. This tradition was not lost on Forbes Burnham and the leadership of the PNC. At the start of the 1980s they had to deal with a welter of daunting social, economic, and diplomatic problems. The quality of life declined. According to the Caribbean Conference of Churches at the start of the 1980s, "life-expectancy fell, crude death rate rose and inflation was at 50%."[2]

According to the Guyanese psychiatrist Dr. Horace Taitt, almost one-third of the Guyanese population had some psychiatric problem—but the majority was not aware of it. The major public health problem was alcoholism.[3] HIV/AIDS was also establishing its deadly presence in society. Declining levels of production and unfavorable world prices for Guyana's primary exports sugar, bauxite, and rice had a disastrous impact on the national economy. The American invasion of Grenada, along with increasingly shrill threats from Venezuela on the unresolved border issue, were stressful variables in the environment. The economic, political, and social crises accelerated migration, both legal and illegal. Between 1976 and 1981, approximately 72,000 persons—one-tenth of the population—emigrated, primarily to Canada, the United States, the Caribbean, and Guyana's continental neighbors Venezuela, Brazil, Surinam, and French Guiana. This outflow took with it many of the nation's most experienced managers, entrepreneurs, and creative artists, including musicians.[4]

Forbes Burnham would have read about Augustus, his ideas, and the zeit-geist of those times from texts by Horace (*Odes*), Virgil (*Eclogues, Aeneid*), and Livy (*Ab Urbe condita*) during his study of Latin at Queen's College. He must have also read Augustus's official biography *Res Gestae*. From these readings he must have developed an appreciation of the challenges faced by Augustus and some of the elements of his style of leadership.

Augustus was a title bestowed on Octavian, the great nephew and adopted son of Julius Caesar. The title, which means "the Revered One," was in recognition of his achievements as a soldier and as a statesman. It was only one of the many titles bestowed on him for the role he played in ending the years of civil war that dominated Roman life after the assassination of Julius Caesar. Augustus was also recognized by the Roman Senate for his contributions to laying the foundations for the expansion of the Roman Empire and the flowering of Roman arts, drama, letters, science, and architecture. He was also known as *pater patriae* (Father of his Country).[5] For fifty years (43 BC–14 AD) he was a "maximum leader," his influence pervasive across the then known world. His influence has lasted for centuries. The name of month August is a testimony of his continuing presence.

By 1980 it was clear that Linden Forbes Sampson "Odo" Burnham did not object to being framed as Guyana's *pater patriae*. Growing up, Forbes Burnham would also have been aware of the colonial governor as a leadership model and his deployment of entertainments in governance. As a young progressive in post–World War II Europe, he was aware of the apparent efficacy of national governance dominated by strong leaders and centralized command. Yugoslavia's Marshal Tito was of special interest.

Under Burnham's leadership the state had a range of assets to execute the *panis et circenses* tradition. The state controlled the nation's calendar of events. By 1980, the nation's calendar of holidays, festivals, and anniversaries provided the framework on which to organize and influence "entertainments." The New Year provided the moment to establish the focus or slogan for the year. For example, in 1980 the focus was on the tenth anniversary of the republic. 1982 was the "Year of Defence." In 1983, the slogan was "The Will to Survive."[6] These rhetorical devices focused political and cultural life for the year. Depending on the year, Youman Nabi, the Islamic festival, was also celebrated in January. The primary celebrations in February were the birthday of Forbes Burnham and Mashramani, the anniversary of the republic. Again, depending on the year, the Hindu spring festival of Phagwah could be held in either February or March. Similarly, the Christian holidays of Good Friday and Easter Monday could be celebrated in either March or April. May 1 was Labor Day. Also celebrated in May was the anniversary of independence and Youth Week. Co-op Week was celebrated in June and on July 1; CARICOM Day was a national holiday. Freedom Day, celebrating the emancipation of enslaved Africans, was held on August 1. Also in August was the National Exhibition, and the Congress of the People's National Congress was held biennially. Agriculture Month tended to be held in late September or early October. The Islamic feast day Eid-ul-Azah was commemorated in September. Deepavali—the Hindu Festival of Lights—was celebrated in November or December. The highlights for December were the Christian festivals of Christmas Day and Boxing Day. Throughout the 1980s, special emphasis was given to the celebrations to mark the republic's anniversary. A central element in the Mashramani celebrations was the special concert to mark the birthday of President Forbes Burnham. The event was always held at the National Cultural Center.

The state also owned and controlled the primary venues, had the power to influence content, the capacity to "mobilize" the citizenry to attend these entertainments, and if necessary, use the primarily state-owned transportation system to get the audience to the venues. It can be said that *panis et circenses* remained an important element in Forbes Burnham's political strategy until his death on August 6, 1985. Janus-like, this strategy afforded a number of benefits and contributed to a number of drawbacks. Among the benefits of the strategy were increased collaboration among the controllers of the nation's cultural assets; increased collaboration among the nation's creative personnel; a heightened level of innovation in some areas of the performing arts; and improved technology to support the performing arts. The strategy also helped identify and nurture creative talent, as it contributed to progress in the development of national aesthetics in many areas, including music. Other benefits, during the crisis dominated 1980s, included opportunities for social release and diversion.

As will be presented below, there were many negative drawbacks to *panis et circenses*. These state-sponsored entertainments became venues for regurgitating undigested ideology, much of it was stilted, forced, and unnatural—attributes that undermine the credibility of any genre of expressive culture. As we shall see, this requirement to imbed socialist rhetoric and party propaganda contributed to the decline of many musical and theatrical genres, especially calypso and drama. In addition, because of pervasive self-censorship and the fear of offending President Burnham, criticisms in the state-owned media of the public entertainments were nonexistent or muted. It is felt that this ultimately led to the acceptance of mediocrity and the resultant decline of standards. This chapter will explore both the positive and negative dimensions of *circenses* in Guyana during the 1980s. It must also be noted that a few sectors of the society remained somewhat insulated from this strategy.

Mashramani is derived from an Arawak word meaning a celebration after a successful cooperative venture, such as fishing, hunting, preparing a field, reaping produce, or building a home.[7] The term was first used in Jaycees of McKenzie (later renamed Linden, after Linden Forbes Sampson Burnham) to describe the activities organized to celebrate Guyana's independence in 1966. According to Jimmy Hamilton, the celebrations were modeled on Trinidad's Carnival. In 1970 the word was appropriated for the celebrations to mark the birth of the Cooperative Republic of Guyana in 1970.

By 1980 Mashramani was the preeminent national celebration, funded primarily by the state and organized by a government bureaucracy, which drew upon the colonial centenary celebrations template. The monthlong celebrations tended to have three discrete aspects: the ceremonial, the festive, and mass mobilization. The ceremonial aspect included the flag-raising ceremony and the National Awards. The flag-raising ceremony was typically held at the Queen Elizabeth II National Park; however in 1985, it was held for the first time at the Square of the Revolution—a site located near to The Residence, home of President Burnham and the Presidential Secretariat and dominated by Philip Moore's monument commemorating the 1763 Berbice Slave Rebellion.[8]

The festive aspects had roots in the colonial centenary celebrations and the "festivals" organized for National History and Culture Week, and was increasingly influenced by Trinidad's Carnival. Among the key elements were the Calypso Monarch competition, the National Steel Band competition, the Costume Bands and Float Parade, and Indian music competitions. Other festive elements included the president's birthday concert and, starting in 1980, the Mass Games. The primary mass mobilization event was the People's Parade. In addition, openings of prestigious development projects were always timed to coincide with the Mashramani celebrations. For example, in 1980 the tenth anniversary of the republic, the Textile Mill,[9] the second phase of the Upper Demerara Forestry Road, the Abary Sluice of Mahaica-Mahaicony Agricultural Scheme (MMA), and a wood-based light industrial complex at the Guyana National Service Center at Tumatumari on the Potaro River were opened.

A number of state-controlled or -influenced agencies and organizations were involved in the execution of Mashramani. The organization of this central event at the start of the 1980s provides an insight into the internal workings of the PNC and the influence of the party on the governance of society. Among the members of the 1980 National Mashramani Committee were Rudy Bishop, Pandit Gowkarran Sharma, and Robert Corbin. Bishop was the leader of Chronicle Atlantic Inc., a beneficiary of Burnham's 1971 dicta on steel bands. Bishop also represented the Hamilton Green wing of the PNC. At the start of the 1980s, Green was a member of the general council of the PNC, Vice President for Public Welfare, and president of the Guyana Steel Band Association. Bishop and Green were responsible for the National Steelband Competition. Pandit Gowkarran Sharma, head of the faction of the Maha Sabha that supported the PNC, was in charge of the Indo-Guyanese Music Competitions. The Department of Culture was really the subordinate agency, primarily responsible for the president's birthday concerts, until this responsibility was transferred to the Hamilton Green faction in 1984. By 1982 it was clear that Robert Corbin, the Minister of National Development, led the organization of Mashramani.[10] Corbin had power to influence the outcome of the Calypso Monarch competition and the scope of the Costume and Float Parade.

At the start of the 1980s, Guyana had a number of internationally recognized calypsonians. In the preceding years, Lord Canary (Malcolm Corrica) had joined King Fighter (Shurland Wilson) and Lord Coffee as a Guyanese calypsonian with a place in Trinidad's pre-Carnival calypso tents. In 1980, Lord Canary, now a minister within the Ministry of Education, cancelled his contract to sing in the Kingdom of Wizards Calypso Tent in Trinidad to become the Convener of the Calypso Caravans for that year's Mashramani.[11] Instead of static calypso tents as in Trinidad, the Guyana Calypsonians Association, in collaboration with the Central Mashramani Committee and the Department of Culture, organized calypso caravans that, starting in January, toured Guyana and signaled the start of the Mash season.

In 1980 two caravans were organized—the Original Caravan and the Creole Caravan. That format continued for the remainder of the decade. Initially, the National Youth Band, founded by Eddie Rogers, retired director of Music of the Guyana Police Force Band,[12] and the People's Culture Corps—an arm of the Ministry of National Development and the office of the general secretary of the PNC—provided musical accompaniment for the caravans. Accompanying the caravans was an important source of income for bands during the 1980s. By the mid-1980s, Solo Sounds International and the Yoruba Singers dominated that market. The East Coast (EC) Connection, led by Burchmore Simon, joined them in the late 1980s.[13] An attempt was made in 1982 by Terry Nelson (now known variously as the Big Bossman or Omar Farouk) of Halagala Records to create an additional caravan. He called his caravan the AFI Tent with the declared intention of promoting calypsos with the Afro-Indi beat.[14] The idea did not fly—it was probably ahead of its time!

The annual Mashramani calypso competition, whose lineage can be traced to Vivian Lee's annual calypso competitions, continued to be the primary calypso event in Guyana throughout the 1980s. At the start of the decade a new crop of calypsonians arrived on the stage. These included the Mighty Rebel, De Iatolah, Durant, Sonnet, Madam Tumbler, Mighty Offender, and Wicked Pertaub, a Guyanese of Indian ancestry.[15] They joined older performers that included Lord Canary, the Mighty Chief (an Amerindian calypsonian and pioneer of the Calymari beat),[16] Groucha, Smoker, Intruder (also known as "32"), Spurwing, Lady Stella, Lady Guymine, Chet Etkins, Dreamer,

Enchanter, Thunder, and El Cid.[17] The number of new calypsonians, including female calypsonians, increased yearly throughout the decade. Of the forty calypsonians involved in the 1981 Calypso Caravans, eight were first-time participants—Wildfire, Lady Matamba, Lady Explainer, Young Guymine, Traveler, Kendingo, Mighty Colly, and Maishee.[18] Also in 1981, the female calypsonians declared their intention to dominate and capture the Mash Calypso Crown. The most vociferous of the female calypsonians were Lady Guymine and Lady Matamba.[19]

Like Trinidad's Carnival, associated with the calypso competition was the road march competition, with the prize going to the calypso played by most of the bands participating in Costume Bands and Float Parade. Berkley "Lee" Huston released "Freeway" as a road march tune for 1981. The song was nationalistic and referred to the annual invasion of Guyana's calypso space by foreign calypsonians such as Arrow, Shadow, Kitchener, Crazy, and Nelson, and his intention to break that pattern and declaring that Guyanese were now self-reliant and no longer depended on imported calypsos for road march tunes.[20] By February 1981 Lee Houston's "Freeway" rose to Number 7 on the Guyanese Top 20 charts.[21]

In 1983 Lady Guymine won the calypso crown with "Babylon." It was an unpopular decision, as the crowd favorite was "Disappointing System" by Mighty Rebel. The Mighty Rebel shared second spot with Guyfesta discovery Chuck "Chuckman" Gerard, whose calypso was "They Don't Care."[22] What was obvious in the 1983 calypso competition was the use of the art form to protest the contemporary situation in Guyana. This traditional role of calypso in the West Indies was criticized by the Guyanese historian P. H. Daly in an article in the state-owned newspaper: "It was noticeable that many of the calypsos were political protests against shortages of food items in this country. That represented the perversion of the calypso to political purposes and as an art it should not have identified itself as partisan."[23]

Daly was turning a blind eye to that fact that calypsonians had always been commenting on politics in Guyana and that there was evidence that efforts were being made to have calypsonians sing in praise of Burnham and the PNC. Those efforts came across as contrived and were neither credible nor entertaining. As we will note below, the Mighty Rebel lost the calypso crown on several occasions because his calypsos always tended to be critical of the government and the post-colonial ruling class. He was awarded so many second places during the 1980s that he was known as "PS"—Permanent Second.

Despite the impressive increase in the number of calypsonians participating in the annual event (they got paid to participate), the manipulation of the calypso tradition by the PNC had a negative impact on the quality of calypso. Despite superficial comments about improvement in the quality of calypsos, newspaper columnists and cultural commentators such as Lionel Smith, Leon Saul, and Quintyn Taylor lamented the decline of the art form, although they did not appropriate blame or identify the cause.[24] In 1980 Reginald Frederick, who performed as Prins Solomon, ventured in that direction when he concluded that most of Guyana's calypsonians were not "real calypsonians" as they only centered their minds on "narrow themes of local subjective politics and Mashramani." He also noted that although some of them had good voices, they "were not professional enough." He also criticized musical arrangements and the "last minute rush to get things done" and called for longer periods of rehearsals prior to participating in national competitions.[25] Unlike Trinidad, Guyana did not have the infrastructure to support calypso making and performance during the entire year. As implied above, Prins Solomon's criticisms were justified and partially explained by the fact that the bureaucrats from the Ministry of National Development, who were responsible for executing Mashramani, were insensitive to the importance of sustained training and development in the performing arts. The ministry's interest was getting bodies on the road to deliver the circuses.[26]

In the 1980s, the National Steel Band Competition held during Mashramani was the nation's premier annual steel band activity. For most of the 1980s, the Chronicle Atlantic Brass and Steel Orchestra (CASBO) and the Bauxite Industry Development Corporation (BIDCO) Invaders dominated the competition. This was the result of a decision by Roy Geddes in the late 1970s to retire the DEMTOCO Silvertones from national competitions. The sponsorship of steel bands by the public sector ensured that there were many bands, most of them full-time units. This stability in the steel band environment also supported the performing of complex works from the repertoire of classical music popular in Guyana. There was a rivalry between conductors and arrangers, with Desmond Fraser pushing the Chronicle Atlantic and the Young Entertainers into ever more complex arrangements and Billy Pilgrim and Cecil Bovell doing the same with BIDCO Invaders. The test pieces for the national competitions and the repertoire presented during international tours also reflected this confidence. In 1983 the test piece was Hugh Sam's 1958 prize-winning composition *Fantasia on Three Folk Song*. During their 1980s tour of the Soviet Union, CASBO performed Tchaikovsky's *1812 Overture* in Moscow and received critical acclaim. In addition to stability, innovation, and experimentation, the national steel band competition also had the benefit of competent adjudicators. Among the judges during the 1980s were Olivia Ahyoung Benjamin, Avis Joseph, Patricia Smith, Frank Pilgrim, Godfrey Proctor, and Compton "Camo" Williams.[27]

The Costume Bands and Floats competition defined Mashramani Day, February 23. On this day, a spectacle of costumed bands and floats accompanied by bands playing popular music paraded through the streets of Georgetown en route to the National Park, where judges made decisions on the best band, the best float, the king, the queen, and the road march. The roots of costume band parade can be traced back to the Christmas masquerade traditions, religious processions, Labour Day parades, route marches, decorated bicycles and cars, steel band tramps, "Festival," and Trinidad's Carnival. The costume bands and floats were valuable barometers of the state of the nation's psyche. The themes reflected preferred national ideas; costume materials reflected the state of the economy; and the musical accompaniment reflected the state of calypso and popular music. During the 1980s participation had to be induced. Because of economic conditions, most potential revelers could not afford to purchase their costumes, as was the practice in Trinidad and other places in the Caribbean with carnival traditions. In Guyana during the 1980s government ministries, public corporations, and other entities of the public sector in most cases provided costumes. This resulted in the perception that participation was based on the provision of costumes free of charge. Costume bands and float parades were not only held in Georgetown. Similar events were held in other regional centers along the coastal plain during the almost monthlong Mashramani celebrations. In some cases, the kings and queens and representative "sections" of the winning bands from Georgetown traveled to other urban centers and rural areas to participate in the local costume band and float parade. In the tough economic conditions of the 1980s, many citizens saw the event as an expense that could be ill afforded. For some Guyanese of Indian ancestry, it was another experience of exclusion and another manifestation of "Blackman culture." For many, it was a family day and a day to relax and enjoy the circus.

One result of Guyana's economic woes and its increasing isolation in the West was to "diversify its foreign policy" and establish relations with the Communist world, including the Democratic People's Republic of Korea (DPRK). From the land of the autarchic Juche idea, Guyana appropriated the mass games,[28] performances of coordinated gymnastics usually presented in an arena, invariably in front of a "background of card-turners occupying the seats on the opposite side from the viewers."[29] For President Forbes Burnham these games provided another vehicle to promote group cohesiveness, discipline, strength, unity, and order. In addition, mass games also provided another channel to promote government policy and ideology—it was a good propaganda device!

Like other initiatives to promote socialism, mass games were not welcomed by the wider society. Criticisms and resistance came from many sources— teachers, parents, and the opposition press. However, the state's propaganda machinery promoted it. In January 1980 as rehearsals were in full swing for the first mass games, Quintyn Taylor and other writers in the state-owned *Guyana Chronicle* declared that "mass games are here to stay" and predicted that "mass games will be a household word."[30] The first Mass Games in Guyana was presented on February 23, 1980, at the National Park in Georgetown, and Quintyn Taylor used his favorite phrase "resounding success" to describe the event.[31] By May 1980 a version of the event featuring 216 students from Demerara, Berbice, and Essequibo was presented at Albion Sports Complex as the culminating event for Youth Week 1980. According to Leon Saul, "Mass Games [scored] another first."[32] In an invited comment after the first games, Kim Il Nam, the leader of the mass games team from the People's Democratic Republic of Korea, declared that "Guyanese children are really quick to grasp."[33] The execution of the mass games reflected the growing strength of Guyana/DPRK relations. In 1984 Kim Il Sung was awarded the Order of Rorima, Guyana's highest national award.

By 1981 Guyanese had developed enough confidence to put their own stamp on the imported the art form. The 1981 Mass Games lasted for "105 minute non-stop" and were described as "engrossing, well-done . . . colorfully costumed and a success." The presentation used eleven chapters to tell an encapsulated story of the nation's development, from the indigenous peoples up to the new constitution. Like the first mass games, the Guyana Police Force Band presented the music for the display. During the second the chapter the music was "a medley of Afro-American spirituals and Guyanese folk songs, including 'Nobody knows the trouble I've seen,' 'Joshua fit the battle of Jericho,' 'When the saints go marching in,' 'Sitira Gal,' 'Sweet Madeline,' and a masquerade tune." The music for the first chapter reflected Amerindian rhythms. According to a reviewer of the 1981 display, "it was easy to feel proud."[34]

The 1982 mass games took its theme from the slogan for that year: The Year of Defence. A sub-theme was the depiction of Guyana's multiracial identity. Patricia Smith, the director of music in the Mass Games Secretariat, composed the music for the 1982 games. She had returned to Guyana in April 1981 after completing a degree in music education at Boston Conservatory on a government of Guyana scholarship. Her compositions drew upon the repertoire of music from Guyana's musical heritage. One of the pieces she "sampled" was Elgar's "Pomp and Circumstance Military Marches, Op. 39." She grew up in post-independence Guyana and was unaware of the association of that composition with the nourishing of British imperialism. She was aware of its place in the American context where she studied and matured. It was the music of achievement. However, she was working in socialist Guyana and was advised by Ranji Chandisingh, then vice president and Minister of Education during a rehearsal for that year's mass games, to immediately take the Elgar sample out as it was associated with British imperialism and offended official sensibilities.

To allow such an ideologically incorrect message to be disseminated would have been a personal affront to President Burnham. With editing done and Chandisingh saving his skin, Vanessa Cort, a journalist with the *Guyana Chronicle* described the event as "impressive and memorable."[35]

The 1983 mass games were described as "a triumph for Guyana's Children." More than three thousand children participated. The focus was "paying tribute to President Forbes Burnham." Superlatives were again used to describe the event. Sase Parasnath, a journalist with the *Guyana Chronicle*, declared the mass games of 1983 as the "Best Ever Mass Games." The dominant music was Guyanese folk music, arranged by Pat Smith and presented by the Guyana Police Force Band under the baton of Assistant Superintendent Maurice Watson.[36] The theme for the 1985 mass games was "Our Heritage, Our Youth"—a tribute to the International Youth Year. The music for 1985 was based on "old school songs." With the death of Forbes Burnham in 1985, the death knell was sounded for the mass games. Its demise in 1990 was not really mourned, as it was resisted from its inception because of its coercive nature and the blatant propagandistic function. Ian McDonald summed it up when he observed, "Mass Games, perhaps, but Mass Views I certainly hope not."[37]

The tradition of organizing a special celebration around Forbes Burnham's February birthday started in 1967. Initially, these were fund-raising events for the PNC and tended to be dinners. However, with the opening of the National Cultural Center, these birthday celebrations became moments for major musical theatre, and William Pilgrim, then director of music in the Department of Culture, played a pivotal role in reawakening a genre that Helen Taitt had pioneered during the 1950s. Pilgrim had substantial experience in musical theatre; for many years he directed Gilbert and Sullivan operettas in Jamaica.

In addition, by 1980 Guyana had the infrastructure and a critical mass of technical talent to support musical theatre. There was the National Cultural Center, which in 1980 had its audio infrastructure upgraded. In terms of human resources, Monty Blackman had returned from Croydon College in the United Kingdom where he was trained in lighting design and production management. Robert Narain, who had worked in London's West End as a director, was also in Guyana. His skills in choreography were complemented by the talent in the National Dance Company. Billy Pilgrim's sister Cecile Robinson, along with Daphne Rogers, had substantial experience as costume designers. A number of artists such as Dudley Charles, Keith Agard, George Simon, and others were capable as set designers. The National Cultural Center also had a cadre of enthusiastic support staff. Further, there was an energetic performing arts community to draw upon: Chronicle Atlantic Steel and Brass Orchestra (CASBO); The Theatre Guild;[38] the Woodside, Police Force, and Hallelujah Choirs; and similar groups. The administrative capacity of the Department of

Culture under Lynette Dolphin provided the organizational glue needed to present a major piece of musical theatre in Guyana during Mashramani.

The 1980 presentation, titled *The Purchase*,[39] was written and composed by Billy Pilgrim and directed by Robert Narain, set in 1839 and based on the true story of recently emancipated Africans who formed a proto-cooperative and purchased Northbrook Estate on the East Coast of Demerara and renamed it Victoria.[40] The musical was sponsored by the Parliamentary Group of the PNC. The show was declared a "resounding success."[41] Duanne Schultz, one of the lead singers from the Chronicle Atlantic Steel and Brass Orchestra, was the lead female vocalist.

In 1981 Pilgrim produced *The Yard* for the president's birthday presentation. *The Yard* was described as a musical fantasy, "set in a low-income community somewhere in Le Repentir, and revolved around the central character, Aunt May, a matriarch with a built-in resistance to change." Pilgrim again composed original music; singers were drawn from the Woodside and Police Choirs; and Daunne Schultz was again the featured singer."[42] From this show came the hit "Let Us Co-operate," with the affirmative chorus and conclusion: "Can we do it? / Yes we can." Rashid Osman gave the show mixed reviews. He felt the incorporation of various musical styles—blues, American musical theater, disco, African and Indian—were laudable but the story dragged.[43]

In 1982 the traditional variety concert format was used for the president's entertainment and the best Guyanese entertainers were put on display, including the National Dance Company performing Robert Narain's *Linden Lights* and Orestes Nejca's *Advance*. The combined Police and Woodside Choirs presented what Rashid Osman described as a particularly saccharine version of Valerie Rodway's "Oh Beautiful Guyana." The Chronicle Atlantic Steel and Brass Orchestra, conducted by Desmond Fraser, presented Tchaikovsky's "1812 Overture" and Duanne Schultz was again the featured soloist. Her performance of "Best Years of Your Life" was singled out for praise.[44]

The Mashramani celebrations for 1983 were extra special as they celebrated Forbes Burnham's sixtieth birthday and his thirtieth year as a parliamentary politician. The 60th Birthday Concert was a reflection on his life. Although not consciously paying homage to Helen Taitt, stylistically, the dominant orientation of the concert was the integration of visual and performing arts. The show was described as "visually splendid." The set was designed by the artists Keith Agard and Dudley Charles. Cicely Robinson and Daphne Rogers were the costume designers. Performers were drawn from the National Dance Company, Guyana Youth Singers (originally Redeemer Youth Singers conducted by Edith Pieters) with Pat Cameron as the MC.[45]

The return of musical theatre and the emergence of "big" theatre at the National Cultural Center for the president's birthday triggered competition.

From sectors of the PNC there were expressions of concern about the "bourgeois" domination of this genre. Some sectors of the PNC, like some members of the PPP Central Committee in the 1960s, did not have confidence in the ideological vigor of the cadre that managed culture in Guyana. In the 1980s, the terms *bourgeois* and *bourgeoisie* were bandied about loosely and directed against persons who were not ideologically fervent, may have come from the older so-called "respectable" and privileged urban families, and may have been of fair complexion! Billy Pilgrim was defined in some quarters as "bourgeois." In 1984, responsibility for the President's Birthday Concert was turned over to the Chronicle Atlantic Brass and Steel Orchestra, led by Rudy Bishop. For this occasion, the group presented *The Rebellion*, written and directed by another Guyfesta "discovery," Kwesi Ojinga.

The show focused on the 1763 Berbice Slave Rebellion, which started on February 23 of that year.[46] The production also coincided with the 150th anniversary of the abolition of enslaved Africans in the British West Indies. All of the talent—the actors, musicians, singers, and dancers—for the production came from the CASBO organization. According to Rashid Osman, the production was uneven; the lines that Ojinga created for the white Dutch colonists "were overdrawn and silly."[47] *The Rebellion* contributed to the examination of the abolition of slavery and its place in the construction of the modern Guyanese nation that was being planned by the Guyana Commemoration Commission (GCC) for an August 1984 launch. The 1985 birthday presentation was the play *The Inheritance*. This CASBO production also harkened to another moment in Guyana's history: the Rupununi Uprising of 1968, when a group of ranchers attempted to secede from the newly independent nation. Like *The Rebellion*, *The Inheritance* was written and directed by Kwesi Ojinga. Rashid Osman criticized the play for being flawed and inordinately long.[48]

Despite the widely held and justifiable perception that the president's birthday concerts were moments for propaganda, indoctrination, and vulgar adulation, these concerts were examples of innovation and provided a valuable opportunity for training and confidence building. Ironically, these programs at the National Cultural Center popularized and democratized theatre in Guyana. These performances also made the National Cultural Center an entertainment destination for ordinary Guyanese.[49]

The first state-sponsored Indian bands competition was held during Mashramani 1980. In time the event would expand and became the Indian Music Competition. The initial event was sponsored by the Ministry of Home Affairs and was coordinated by Mannie Hanif. There was participation by bands from Berbice, Demerara, and Essequibo, reflecting the popularity of music by Indian orchestras. The Dil Bahar Orchestra represented the Corentyne coast. The Blairmont Estate Orchestra represented East and West Bank Berbice and

New Amsterdam. Representing Upper East Coast Demerara and West Coast Berbice was the Vidyarty Orchestra. The Originals represented Lower East Coast Demerara and East Bank Demerara. The Subha Ka Tara Orchestra represented West Demerara and East Bank Essequibo. Representing the Essequibo Islands and the Essequibo Coast was the Merrytones Orchestra.[50]

At the start of the 1980s, the Merrytones Orchestra was among the most popular of Indian bands. Vishnu Persaud, a music teacher with Grade III passes in the Royal School of Music External Examinations, started the band in 1970s. The band "migrated" to Georgetown in 1976 as a result of work at Diwali fairs, other festivals organized and celebrated by Guyanese of Indian ancestry, Mashramani competitions, and regular gigs. In addition, the band was actively engaged in accompanying singers. For example, the band "supplied background music to records made by Mighty Enchanter and Joyce Ormella Harris." The band also supplied background music and appeared in Vivian Lee's film *If Wishes Were Horses*. The band also had crossover appeal, serving as the opening act for Guyanese diaspora artists Dave Martins and the Trade Winds and the Dennis DeSouza Trio when they toured Guyana.[51]

As mentioned recently, by 1982 the Indian Bands Competition was expanded to become the Indian Music Competition. The coordinator for this expanded competition was Pandit Gowkarran Sharma, leader of the Maha Sabha and a leading member of the PNC. There were five bands in the national finals that year: Dil Bihar, Merrytones, Prakash Orchestra, Pioneer Orchestra, and Subha-Ka-Tara. Male and female singers competed in Sentimental, Creole, and Taan categories.[52] The Indian Music Competitions were held in Albion, Port Mourant, and Lusignan and other major Indian communities. The Indian Music Competitions served to establish the fact that there was another dynamic aspect to music in Guyana. It became a contested site with the political directorate providing patronage and attempting to appropriate it for political ends. For example, in 1986 the Maha Sabha Culture Corps band was formed under the auspices of the Ministry of National Development. Their first show was held on August 8, 1986 at the Liberty Cinema in Georgetown—the premier venue for Indian cinema in Guyana, especially the Bollywood genre.[53]

Throughout the 1980s, the announcement of national awards was an anticipated event during Mashramani. Following a trend that started in the 1970s, when Lynette Dolphin received her first national award, musicians were among the visible recipients in the 1980s. Guyana's national awards are hierarchical. At the apex is the Order of Excellence; this is followed by the Order of Rorima; and third is the Order of Service, in which there are three levels: the Cacique's Crown of Honour (CCH), the Golden Arrow of Achievement (AA), and the Medal of Service (MS).[54] Table 9.1 provides a partial list of musicians who received national awards between 1970 and 2000.

Table 9.1

Partial list of musicians who received National Awards between 1970–2000 according to rank of award

Name	National Award	Year of Award
Lynette de Weever Dolphin	OR	1982
William R. A. Pilgrim	CCH	1981
Celeste Dolphin	CCH	1988
Dr. Joycelynne Loncke	CCH	1991
Dr. Ray Luck	CCH	1992
Valerie Rodway	CCH	1996
Rajcoomarie Singh	AA	1970
Ruby McGregor	AA	1971
Dave Martins	AA	1982
Albert Bumbury	AA	1988
Edith Pieters	AA	1988
Roy Geddes	AA	1996
Lillian Dewar	MS	1973
Maselall	MS	1974
Gobin Ram	MS	1975
Harry Whittaker	MS	1975
Gora Singh	MS	1976
Augustus Hinds (a.k.a. Bill Rogers)	MS	1976
Rudy Bishop	MS	1978
Hilbert Eddie Hooper	MS	1979
Yoruba Singers	MS	1981
Vernal Jones (a.k.a. Little Jones)	MS	1982
Ramdhanie	MS	1982
Cecilia Clementine Boody	MS	1982
Monica Chopperfield (a.k.a. Lady Guymine)	MS	1982
Cedric Williams	MS	1983
Janet Hunte	MS	1986
Princess Sinclair	MS	1986
Mahadei Roopchan (a.k.a. Celia Samaroo)	MS	1991
Malcolm Corrica (a.k.a. Mighty Canary)	MS	1992
Daphne Scott	MS	1992
Woodside Choir	MS	1993
Mohan Nandu	MS	1993

Source: E. Vic Persaud, Protocol Advisor, Office of the President, Guyana, December 2012.

Beyond Mashramani, during the 1980s the decolonization and socialist program of the PNC government was evident in every sector of the society, and this dominance influenced musical development. This domination was evident in the way the National Cultural Center was operated, in the musical policies and practices of the uniformed services, in the music policy of the radio station and in foreign policy. Although showing some degree of independence, the private sector's engagement with music in Guyana during the 1980s was also influenced by the decolonization and socialism paradigm.

As indicated above, the National Cultural Center (NCC) became a major site for the performing arts during the 1980s. For a period during the late 1970s, it appeared as if the center was on the path of becoming a white elephant, as the acoustics were poor, and the programming was perceived as highbrow and elitist. So in 1980, in preparation for President Burnham's 60th Birthday Concert, the entire audio system was upgraded and a program was launched to democratize the venue. Malcolm Corrica (Lord Canary), a Minister of State in the Ministry of Education, was responsible for coordinating the project. The first venture in that direction was the *Cultural Center Varieties* series of concerts, popularly known as *CC Varieties*.

The *CC Varieties* series was announced in January 1980 with the declared aim of "providing year-round entertainment and promoting Guyanese talent."[55] From the start, it was clear that the series was guided by the nation's vaudeville heritage. The first *CC Varieties* presentation was held on March 30, 1980. It was a true variety show and revealed its vaudeville ancestry as it incorporated popular song, classical song, magic, dramatic poetry, dance, a mystery guest, and "a new talent discovery" component. The house band for the first season, which ended in 1982, was the band of the People's Culture Corps. The series seemed to have lacked enthusiastic support from the leadership of the Department of Culture. Minister of State Malcolm Corrica was not taken seriously by the post-colonial cultural elite who led the Department of Culture. As a calypsonian with rural roots, he did not have the gravitas to seriously guide the cultural direction of society. He faced a number of virtually insurmountable barriers with the design and execution of his efforts to democratize the National Cultural Center through the *CC Varieties* series. Despite the limited success of Corrica's efforts, the National Cultural Center was "democratized." Throughout the 1980s the NCC was the site for theatrical and musical innovations by non-state actors. By the end of the 1980s, the religious community also began to be active users of the venue, presenting increasing numbers of gospel music shows. The Hallelujah Group, aligned with Reverend Moon's Unification Church and led by the Guyanese-born Italian-trained soprano Ester Burrowes, used this space for most of the 1980s. Ester Burrowes was the daughter of E. R. Burrowes, the Barbados-born pioneer of art education in

Guyana. Her repertoire included African American spirituals. We will return to this group later when we discuss the interactions between religion and music in Guyana during the 1980s.

The economic crisis required the government of Guyana to enter into emasculating relations with the IMF and other Bretton Woods organizations who imposed "conditionalities" on the scope of national governance. Despite the conditionalities imposed by the IMF on Guyana, such as the need to reduce the size of the uniformed services, during the 1980s Guyana had the highest per capita expenditures on its military among developing countries.[56] The militarization of the society—a function of the border problems; the need to provide employment; a strategy for imposing discipline and order; and to project the coercive power controlled by the PNC—was one of the most visible developments in Guyanese society since independence.

By 1980 Guyana had men and women in uniform in the Guyana Defence Force, the Guyana Police Force, the Guyana National Service, the Guyana People's Militia, the Guyana Prison Service, the Guyana Fire Brigade, and the National Guard Service. In addition to the roles of defending the nation's territorial integrity and serving as a mechanism for imposing discipline in society, during the 1980s the uniformed services, especially the Guyana Police Force, the Guyana Defence Force, and the Guyana National Service was responsible for keeping national and patriotic music alive. Like the former British Guiana Militia Band, the bands were the primary sites to learn to play woodwind, brass, and other instruments and at the same time earn a living.

The bands of the uniformed services took their cues from the prevailing political environment. During the 1980s the repertoire of the Guyana Police Force Band was "Caribbeanized" under its bandmaster and director of music, Superintendent Barney Small. He gave calypso, reggae, and soca higher visibility in the band's repertoire. The Guyana Police Force band also began to turn a blind eye to members of the band performing with commercial bands. When the British Guiana Militia Band became the British Guiana Police Band in 1957, members of the band were prohibited from playing with commercial ensembles. The shift in the 1980s was acknowledgment of the inadequate salaries being paid to band members. During the 1980s, as a result of a massive recruitment project, the size of the Guyana Defence Force Band under Major Sonny Ault grew dramatically.[57] In addition, new music was composed for all the army's units—purging it of the music associated with colonialism, imperialism, and neo-colonialism.[58]

During the 1980s the Guyana National Service took a number of initiatives aimed at promoting creativity, training in music, and supporting Guyana's diplomatic efforts. One of the most important Guyanese recordings in the 1980s was the GNS LP *I Want to Build*, released in 1980. This album was released as part of the service's sixth anniversary celebrations.[59] The record-ing was done at the National Film Center and pressed at West Indian Records in Barbados. The project was initiated by Colonel Desmond Roberts in 1979. The album, which featured twelve songs, was to be the first in a series, and was recorded on a monaural system at the Film Centre (a gift from West Germany). The twelve songs were composed during the period 1974 to 1976. Collectively, the songs encapsulated important moments in the development of GNS, memorialized personalities, and described the experiences of pio-neers. In 1980 Superintendent Barney Small retired from the Guyana Police Force and joined the Guyana National Service with the rank of major, and was tasked with establishing a music institute at Camp Cocos—the former Belfield Girls' School, a reformatory established in the 1920s. The institute was envisioned as the training center for all of the disciplined services.[60] This ambition did not materialize on the scale that was anticipated because of the declining economic conditions and Small's declining health.

Since 1963, when the PPP government sent a steel band to Cuba on a thank-you tour, Guyana has used steel bands in its diplomacy. During the 1980s the Guyana National Service contributed to this tradition. In 1985 the GNS sent Warrant Officers Winston Roberts and Roy Geddes to Tanzania to establish a steel band and train Tanzanian players. Roberts was a member of the New Opportunity Corps and Geddes was a member of the Special Service Corps. In Tanzania they worked at Tanzanian National Service's camp at Buhemba about a thousand miles from Dar-Es-Salaam. They were well received.[61] What Roberts and Geddes did in Tanzania, Calvin Whyte did in Cuba. During the 1980s Guyana contributed to the global diffusion of steel bands.

Like the Guyana Police Force and the Guyana Defence Force, the vari-ous musical ensembles of the Guyana National Service performed in public spaces. GDF's Frontline Band was an exceptionally popular party band during the 1980s. Individual musicians such as Sam Bennons and Abdulla Omawale from the Guyana National Service were recognized as innovators. Bennons, the New Amsterdam–born leader of the GNS Steel Band, was recognized a virtuoso steel pan player (a pannist). The level of his skill was captured for posterity on the GNS LP. Abdulla Omawale, an African American refugee, was an accomplished saxophonist who, along with Harry Whittaker from the Guyana Police Force Band, contributed significantly to the upsurge in the popularity of jazz in Georgetown. Also during the 1980s, all of the bands of the uniformed services provided a soundtrack for the musical aesthetics of the state and would be joined to create the Massed Band and perform at func-tions of high national significance.

The state also exerted direct influence on the organization and orienta-tion of radio broadcasting in Guyana. On July 1, 1980, Radio Demerara and

GBS ceased to exist and in their place emerged GBC 1 and GBC 2. This move reflected a new orientation, expressed in the following mission statement: "To produce through the broadcast media programme material which recognizes our cultural diversity and advances our national, social, economic, and political objectives through information, education and entertainment programming for both the urban and rural areas of Guyana."[62] According to Leon Saul, the mission statement would reorient radio programming with its urban, "city folks" bias to one that was more national and multiracial in orientation. GBC 1 would emphasize the rural and GBC 2 would concentrate on general programming. Radio in Guyana during the 1980s was under mandate to play more music by Guyanese and even restrict music from countries with which there were diplomatic tensions. For example, in the early 1980s during a chilling of relations with the United States, an edict was issued by the Ministry of Information to edit Salsoul Orchestra's "Xmas Medley" and remove the section that featured "God Bless America." The irony was that there were Guyanese musicians on the recording. This kind of political decision exacerbated the challenge of finding adequate content to satisfy even the limited broadcast day. During the 1980s radio generally started around 5:30 a.m. and ended at midnight. The program *Towards the Dawn*, sponsored by the Joint Services Secretariat, extended the broadcast day to 2:00 a.m. on Fridays and Saturdays.[63]

Guyanese recordings, particularly those recorded and pressed in Guyana, continued to have quality issues and this led to problems with the gatekeepers of the Guyana Broadcasting Corporation, which had inherited some of the biases of the past. In addition to the structural problems, Guyanese musicians during the 1980s also had contractual problems. More and more musicians complained of being "robbed" by producers.[64] In addition, there were increasing concerns about piracy and the failure of radio stations to pay royalties to local musicians. Despite these challenges, a number of Guyanese singers, such as Elroy Bentick ("Glen Family Teach"), Mark Bryan, Bunny Morian, Alan Feidtkou, Nicky Porter, and Compton Hodges, recorded songs that were popular in Guyana and some Caribbean markets.[65]

The government's relationship with radio broadcasting during the 1980s was heavy-handed. For example, in the effort to decolonize Guyanese society, there was an effort to de-emphasize Christmas, and this resulted in a very limited playlist of Christmas music in 1981. This raised public concern to the extent that the state-owned *Guyana Chronicle* published an article bemoaning the small amount of Christmas music being aired and indicating that there are rumors that certain songs are not to be aired. The columnist argued:

> It is rumoured that only certain Christmas selections are to be aired, that's fair
> enough, but most of us do not have enough of what it takes to have a really bright

and cheerful Christmas. The only "cheer-er upper" is to have those cheerful little Yuletide airs, that we're so accustomed to at this time of the year. So come on, GBC, pour out those Christmas sounds. Let us have a ball this season, as those small doses won't do.[66]

The state-owned print media also contributed to the musical direction of the society by featuring weekly columns on the Top 20 and other current popular music hits. The state-owned *Sunday Chronicle* regularly published the lyrics for popular English-language and Hindi Filmi songs. Hindi film lyrics were published in the column *Indian Song Corner*. A popular columnist during the 1980s was Dee Jay. His columns gently focused attention on deficiencies in the musical scene or dropped hints on important developments. For example in the December 25, 1982, column Dee Jay noted:

Superstar Eddy Grant of Guyana plans on settling down in the land of the Flying Fish (Barbados). Already Studio equipment has been shipped to the tourist resort.

It seems Coach House (the UK-based Recording Studio) will operate in these parts. Eddy's first "LIVE" recording *Eddy Grant LIVE AT Notting Hill* is already on sale throughout the Caribbean and across the world.

It features among some of his former recordings and two new tracks, *Cockney Black* and *Curfew*—Haven't heard it on the local stations but will be listening out for this latest addition to the popular ICE Label series where the slogan reads, "Everything on ICE is Nice."[67]

For many Guyanese this was the first inkling of a major development that would have a transforming effect on music in the Caribbean. There were many rumors why the studio was not being set up in Guyana. One had it that government of Guyana wanted majority shares in the enterprise—as was the economic orthodoxy in Guyana at that time. In an interview with Eddy Grant in 2004, he denied this, saying that the major reason for locating the studio in Barbados was Guyana's lack of infrastructure, especially reliable electricity. Even before independence in 1966, the nation's electricity supply was unreliable.

Although the government of Guyana dominated the cultural environment and influenced the direction and scope of music, they were not the only players. Local entrepreneurs, the diplomatic community, and Christian denominations were also engaged. During the 1980s, the private sector increased investments in record stores and the promotion of live performances, especially jazz concerts by local musicians and concerts by international acts.

By the 1980s there were more people with access to music playback technologies. The major department stores and the consumer electronic stores were importing the major brand names like Phillips, Sony, and Sansui. The government established Guyana Radio & Electronics Company (GRECO) to assemble component sets at a factory in the historic village of Victoria during this decade. Going with the proliferation of music playback technologies was the expansion of the distribution of recorded music. The audiocassette joined the phonograph, and this nourished the expansion of music stores in urban and rural Guyana. Among the top music stores during the 1980s were Affonso's Modern Record Store, Mohamed Radio and Electronics Ltd, Mayfair Musical Center, Pioneer Record Bar, and Matt's Record Bar at Guyana National Trading Corporation (GNTC). These establishments responded to the ethnic and taste realities of the marketplace. For example, the Pioneer Record Bar specialized in Indian music. In 1982 the top selling LPs at Pioneer were *Suhaag, Disco Deewane, Nikaama, Kaala Patthar, Muqaddar, Skandar, Dhan Daulat, Dream Girl, Midnight, Jhoota Kahin Ka, Qarbani* (English), *Duniya Meri Jeb Mein,* and *Khatta Meetha.*[68] Mayfair also offered a wide selection of Indian music—religious, sentimental, and hot and spicy, along with "English" cassettes.[69] Affonso's and Matt's stock was more diversified and included country and western, pop, R&B, soul, calypso, soca, reggae, golden oldies, and Guyanese nostalgia. This did not mean that Guyanese and other performers earned much income from these sales. In the 1980s cassettes became a significant platform for music distribution; this launched the problem of piracy, which helped further undermine the income of Guyanese recording artists.

Promoters found a niche catering to those who longed for the swing era songbook. So, the 1980s saw the continuing popularity of jazz shows, with the Savannah Suite at the Pegasus, the Penthouse Skyline Disco, the Guyana Legion, and the Public Service Sports Complex emerging as important venues on Sunday afternoons. Harry Whittaker on alto sax dominated the scene. Among the other popular performers were Duce Jeffrey (tenor sax), Roddy Fraser (tenor sax), Art Brooms (drums), Richard Robinson (drums), Patrick Whittaker (alto and tenor sax), Rector Schultz (bass), Adrian Van Sertima (guitar), Alston Hall (organ), Ivan Knights (drums), Charlie Agard (bongos), Jake Canterbury (bass), and Noel Adams (piano). In addition to the instrumental standards such as "Take the A Train" and others from the Duke Ellington songbook, there were vocalists at the jazz concerts. Lady Monica (Lady Guymine), Patricia Arthur, and Compton "Coody" Hodges were among the popular vocalists. Braving questions of class and decorum, returned music scholarship winners Avis Joseph and Patricia Smith also "jammed." The jazz concerts were recognized as a space for the "older generation" to congregate.[70]

International musicians continued to come to Guyana during the 1980s. These performers were sponsored by private investors or were part of the public diplomacy of embassies in Guyana. Performers sponsored by private investors were primarily calypso, soca, reggae, and chutney/Bollywood artistes. Artistes who came as part of the public diplomacy of embassies tended to be in the classical sphere.

The Mighty Sparrow maintained his connection with Guyana throughout the turbulent 1980s. His first visit for the decade was in March 1980. According to Leon Saul, Sparrow was at his "effervescent best" during his performance to more than sixteen hundred fans at the National Sports Hall. His show included hits from yesteryear and contemporary ones. Lady Guymine, who had joined his calypso tent in Trinidad during the 1980 Carnival, and the Mighty Rebel also performed in the show.[71] A year later Sparrow was back again with his band the Troubadours, comedian Bill Trotman, and Elvina "the sexy dancing star." Neil Chan's Solo Productions was the primary investor in this category of international performer. Among the calypsonians and cutting-edge soca artistes that his organization brought to Guyana were Charlie's Roots featuring David Rudder, Shadow, Laro, Arrow, Blue Boy, Singing Francine, Calypso Rose, Crazy, and Robin Imamsha. These artistes were contemporizing calypso and soca and also provided some respite for a weary and stressed society.

Yellowman, John Holt, Gregory Isaacs, Sister Nancy, D.J. Fathead, and Roots Radics Band were some of the popular Jamaican acts that came to Guyana during the 1980s. As was now standard practice, Guyanese performers were featured as warm-up acts. For example, Family Teach, Revelation, Mark Bryan, Cannon Ball, Yoruba Singers, King Fighter, and others were opening acts for shows by Yellowman and John Holt.[72] Sometimes the Jamaican acts failed to live up to expectations and came close to being failures, as was the case with the Yellowman and John Holt shows in 1981 and 1982 respectively. In the case of Yellowman, the audience wanted to hear the full versions of his hits such as "Mr. Chin," "Pon de Line," and "Getting Married in the Morning" and not a medley of those hits.[73] In the case of the John Holt show he was upstaged by the Yoruba Singers.[74] Despite these shaky starts, reggae music established an unassailable foothold in Guyana's musical psyche during the 1980s and continued to influence music in Guyana throughout the remainder of the century and into the first decade of the twenty-first century.

The international visitors also included leaders in the Bollywood tradition and regional chutney groups. In September 1980 the "undisputed queen of Indian play-back singers Lata Mangeshkar" visited Guyana and performed at urban and rural venues—the National Cultural Center, the National Park, and the Albion Sports Complex.[75] H. Gobind presented other singers from India in *The Mama Dey and Tun Tun Show* with performances in Georgetown, Leonora, and Albion in the Corentyne. As was now standard practice, "local musicians and singers" joined the performers from India.[76]

In October 1982 Babla and Kanchan visited Guyana.[77] They had been experimenting with western music and later had hits covering Arrow's soca anthem "Feeling Hot, Hot." Also targeting the Indo-Guyanese audience was *Bee Wee Solid Gold*, a show promoted by Sri Yoogeandra of Top Rank Promotions featuring the BWIA National Indian Orchestra of Trinidad and Tobago. Harry Mahabir, who was described "as taking music to new heights blending Indian and Caribbean rhythms," conducted the band.[78] Built into to the show was a competition between the National Indian Orchestra of Trinidad and Tobago and Guyana's Superstars—reminiscent of the regional clashes during the swing band era.[79] The Guyanese performers on the show included Celia Samaroo and Joyce Ormella Harris. Subsequently, Samaroo and Harris toured Trinidad and Tobago, Surinam, New York, Canada, and the United Kingdom with National Indian Orchestra of Trinidad and Tobago and established themselves as leading exponents of the new chutney genre of music. Like Bollywood music, chutney was popular in multiracial Guyana. Chutney music with its creolized rhythms and lyrics was accessible to the wider society— musical exchange had taken place. Tours of Guyana by chutney leaders from Trinidad and Tobago continued throughout the 1980s. In December 1988 Rani Dasrat Persaud Food Products presented the then monarch of chutney, Sundar "Soca" Popo, in a number of shows in Georgetown, Albion, Hampton Court, Lusignan, and Enmore. Guyana had become an important destination in the Indo-Caribbean musical circuit.

Public diplomacy is recognized as the use of soft power, such as the performing arts, by one country to win the "hearts and minds" of citizens of another country or to demonstrate solidarity with a country. The public diplomatic activities of embassies in Georgetown contributed to musical life in Guyana during the 1980s. Their efforts introduced diversity and in some cases energized genres that were dying because of migration and inadequate training facilities. Guyana had a diversified diplomatic community and, as is standard practice, each embassy endeavored to win the "hearts and minds" of the people of Guyana. The cultural exchange agreements with Guyana provided the framework for the presentation by international musicians. Some countries such as the USA, India, Cuba, and the Democratic People's Republic of Korea had active programs. Others such as the Soviet Union had little musical presence, primarily because of language and style. Even so, a troupe of "first class" Georgians from the USSR put on a number of variety concerts in June 1980.

Despite the chilly relations between Guyana and the United States during the early to mid-1980s, the United States maintained engagement through cultural collaborations between the United States embassy and Guyana's Department of Culture. Through these collaborations urban Guyanese were exposed to many musical genres. One such collaboration was a concert and workshop by the jazz-rock musician Chick Corea.[80] According to a promotional piece by Tangerine Clarke of the *Guyana Chronicle*, Chick Corea and his group would introduce a "new type of music—fusion—to Guyanese people." The pre-concert workshop was well attended. Guyanese wanted to maintain cultural linkages with the United States, despite the rhetoric of the PNC and the government.[81] Roddy Fraser's article on the Corea visit concluded that it was "a pleasure to have an artiste of Chick's caliber to visit the Republic of Guyana."[82]

Another USIA-sponsored performer was the African American soprano Brenda Rucker-Smith. Guyana-born Patricia Smith and Marilyn Dewar, along with US-born Stanley Sisskin, accompanied Rucker-Smith at the concert held on October 6, 1982 at the National Cultural Center. Also appearing in the concert was the Woodside Choir conducted by Billy Pilgrim.[83] In 1985 the Berklee College Rainbow Band toured Guyana. In addition to giving performances in Georgetown, the Berklee band also toured New Amsterdam. The New Amsterdam show was dedicated to the memory of Harry Whittaker, who had died earlier that year. The band featured the trombonist Phil Wilson, who had performed with Jimmy Dorsey, Woody Herman, Louis Armstrong, and Herbie Hancock.[84] Like Corea, the band held a workshop for Guyanese musicians. The band also performed at Public Service Sports Complex, as mentioned recently a popular venue for Sunday afternoon jazz concerts.[85]

Some observers of Indian cultural life in Guyana have suggested that the Indian High Commission has tended to privilege "highbrow" Indian musical and dance aesthetics. They have also argued that this orientation has contributed to the further marginalization of creolized Indian expressions by Guyana. The Indian High Commission in Georgetown operated the Indian Cultural Center and this primary vehicle for its public diplomatic work tended to be directed primarily to Guyanese of Indian ancestry.

The public diplomatic activities of the socialist bloc in Guyana during the 1980s could be categorized as demonstrations of solidarity. Starting in 1981, there were increases in cultural exchanges between Guyana and Cuba as they strengthened their political alliances. In 1981 the Cuban funk group Pello [el] Le Afrokan participated in Mashramani.[86] The Cuban musical presence was very visible during events organized to commemorate the 150th anniversary of the abolition of slavery in 1984. The engagement of the Democratic People's Republic of Korea was most evident in the mass games.

Among the consequences of the economic and social crisis in Guyana during the 1980s was increased religiosity. As a result, certain ecstatic rituals and experiences associated with Kali, Cumfa, and evangelical Christian worship became increasing popular. These ecstatic rituals and experiences are rooted in belief systems that explain life's vicissitudes as the result of evil and demonic forces that can be exorcised by the intervention of benevolent and retributive deities. In the case of Kali, it was the Maha Kali—the Black One—the Hindu goddess who destroyed ignorance and helped those who strove for knowledge and enlightenment. In Hindu mythology, Maha Kali was the destroyer of the demon Raktabija. Kean Gibson has described Cumfa as a syncretic and retributive religion developed in Guyana. This religion also holds that personal crises were the result of work of negative forces and that participation in a Cumfa ritual was an important requirement in resolving the crises. According to Gibson, the Cumfa ritual includes prayers and offerings to a hierarchy of deities. These deities reflected the state of the power hierarchy in Guyanese society and were indicative of cultural exchange.[87] The evangelical Christian denominations such as the Assemblies of God held the view that the Satan was the cause for the range of crises individuals were experiencing in Guyana, and only through accepting Christ as the Savior would these problems be resolved.

Music had a central role in the liturgy of Kali, Cumfa, and many of the evangelical Christian denominations. In Kali Mai Pujas, there were melodic chants and intoxicating rhythms played on the Tapu drum. Some participants in Kali Mai Pujas entered into trance states. For Cumfa rituals, there was a mixture of English hymns; African drumming, with several specific "hands" being used for certain moments in the ritual; and the music of the "ole time" band—bass, drum, saxophone, and guitar. Little Jones's band from the East Coast was an exemplar of this type of band. A participant who had a Cumfa "work" done would have had a successful experience when he or she entered into a trance state.

Evangelical Christians, such as the Assemblies of God, incorporated large choirs and well-equipped bands in their frequent services. The success of a new branch of the church was dependent on the quality of the new church's band. "Bappy" Roopchand, a Hindu, was once hired by a new church in Kitty to start the church's band. Roopchand was a popular musician who had performed with many popular bands, including the Maha Sabha Culture Corps. He brought to the church the ability to draw upon a range of popular musical genres—rock, soul, country and western, reggae, calypso, soca, and chutney.[88] Music in the church was to encourage feeling good. It was about taking back what Satan stole.

The evangelical Christian movement in Guyana was also a prominent promoter of music. Many of the churches were affiliated with denominations in the United States; as a result there were many crusades during the 1980s. African American singers presenting concerts of Negro spirituals and songs of inspiration were *de rigueur* during these crusades. For example, in September 1980 Myrtle Hall, who sang with Billy Graham, was the featured singer with the Anis Shorrosh crusade in Guyana.[89] In addition to crusades featuring international singers, Guyanese evangelical churches also held gospel concerts at prime venues such as the auditorium at Queen's College, the City Hall, and the National Cultural Center. The concerts tended to feature the church's choir and band and guest performers. These Sunday afternoon concerts were efforts at rehabilitating the concert tradition that was popular in urban and rural Guyana during the twenties, thirties, forties, and fifties.[90]

The Hallelujah Group International had a special place in music making in Guyana during the 1980s. The group was an active arm of Reverend Sun Myung Moon's ultra-conservative Unification Church in Guyana. After the Jonestown mass suicides in 1978, the organization was viewed with some skepticism. However, despite that reality, the group led by Barbara Burrowes—a "medium" since 1965, who studied opera in Italy—became active and influential in Guyana's musical space.[91] The group had a varied repertoire, were well trained, and attempted complex and challenging works. Among the group's productions were *God's Trombones*—an iconic African American gospel musical; *Easter Showcase*, which featured classical music, Afro-Caribbean rhythms and excerpts from the Broadway hit *The Wiz*;[92] and *Harmony*, described as a dazzling variety show carefully combining gospel, pop, jazz, modern classical, and folk.[93] Most of the group's major productions were held at the National Cultural Center. By the middle of the decade, the organization, which was created to attract "young people into the faith," had started to wane.

By the end of the 1980s, it was evident that the evangelical Christian denominations were important sites for music education and performance in Guyana. But it was not only the evangelical Christians that were incorporating new musical genres into the liturgy. Guyanese composers, such as Brother Pascal Jordan, S.J., were changing the tone, tempo, and rhythm of the liturgical music of Catholicism in the Caribbean by composing hymns in folk, reggae, and calypso styles. That innovation was in response to the changing cultural realities in the Caribbean and an effort by the church to attract the young and make church going more attractive.[94]

Kali, Cumfa, and some evangelical Christian denominations provided solace and hope for many Guyanese during the crises of the 1980s and reinforced the role of religion as an important societal institution. Among the ideologically fervent, this was a retrograde development—a decline into ignorance. For leaders of the traditional Christian, Hindu, and Islamic religions, these developments were seen as aggressive, because they were all losing members to the triune—Kali worship, Cumfa, and evangelical Christianity.

As a result of dramatic increases in migration, the Guyanese diaspora grew dramatically during the 1980s. Many musicians were among the migrants. Like other categories of migrants, the major pull factor was work. Some musicians such as Reginald Francis (Prins Solomon) found employment on cruise ships serving the Caribbean.[95] Others sought their chances in the rough and tumble of New York, Toronto, and London.

Reports on the achievements of Guyanese musicians living overseas were regularly reported in the press. This was a favorite theme in the columns of Roddy Fraser ("The Music Man") and Dee Jay ("The Music Scene"). Early in the decade Fraser had penned a report on New York–based Mickey Daniel, who was known as "Mickey D" before he migrated. Fraser gushed about Mickey D's latest "disco LP," which featured two tracks. Side A featured "Obeah" and "The Witch Woman" and Side B was titled "You Make Me Feel This Way."[96] In his column Dee Jay reported the international chart-topping successes of Eddie Grant, Randy Muller, and Raphael Cameron. During the 1980s Eddie Grant had huge hits such as "Do You Feel My Love." Randy Muller's Brass Construction was a major act in the North American music industry with several hits.[97] Raphael Cameron's "Magic of You" was among the top 10 selling records in the USA during 1980s.[98] Former Radio Demerara engineer Denis King joined Atlantic Records and was the recording engineer on many of the hits by Muller and Cameron. Muller and Cameron were also actively associated with Skyy and Salsoul Records, an influential R&B label, and producers of the influential Salsoul Christmas LP.

Another source of information about what was happening to Guyanese musicians in the diaspora came from interviews visiting Guyanese musicians gave. Among the Guyanese returning home during the 1980s were Pamela Maynard,[99] James Smartt, King Souflantis, Vesta Lowe, Dr. Ray Luck, and Dave Martins, who was an annual visitor. In addition to profiling their achievements, the visiting Guyanese musicians tended to give a performance, offering encouragement and providing pointers to budding musicians and to those contemplating departure. Pamela Maynard's message was, "Guyanese are some of the best and if given the scope and encouragement needed, can succeed."[100]

Prior to migrating to Trinidad in 1972 to join Sparrow's band, the Troubadours, James Smartt was the leader of the Syncopaters. In 1980 he was still living in Trinidad. In an interview with columnist Fraser, he stressed the importance of the perseverance needed to succeed in the international music scene. According to Fraser, many of Guyana's musicians did not have that attribute.[101] Smartt encouraged the younger generation to develop musical competencies and to reject the "copycatism trend of musicianship that is existing on the local scene."[102]

King Souflantis's message was about the importance of training. He described the Guyana Police Force Band as the only music education institution in Guyana and the place where he developed his musical vocabulary.[103] Dave Martins and the Trade Winds were regular visitors to Guyana during the 1980s and their 1981 recording of "Not a Blade of Grass" mobilized Guyanese resistance to Venezuela's claims to Guyanese territory. The song became a highly popular rallying song in Guyana and across the Guyanese diaspora. In 1982 Martins was awarded the Golden Arrow of Achievement, a national honor "for distinguished service as a musician and composer."

During the 1980s Dr. Ray Luck, who had established an international reputation as a concert pianist, academic, and music festival adjudicator visited Guyana. In 1982, Luck gave the inaugural concert on the National Cultural Center's new Steinway grand pianoforte, a gift from the Georgetown Chapter of the Lions Club. The purchase was based on advice from Luck. This instrument was seen as a major contribution to piano music in Guyana.[104] In 1992 he was appointed a Member of the Order of Service of Guyana and awarded the Cacique's Crown of Honor for outstanding musical achievements. In 2008 he was appointed the US State Department's artistic envoy to the Caribbean.[105] Another notable visitor to Guyana in 1982 was Vesta Hyacinth Lowe.[106] She had migrated to the United States during the 1960s, having found it difficult to find pensionable employment in the public service.[107] This time around she was feted by the urban musical elite.

Sir Lionel Luckhoo, who was active as a politician during the turbulent 1950s and was Guyana's High Commissioner to London during the 1960s and 1970s, joined the ranks of commentators on music during the 1980s, on occasion using his column "Lionel Luckhoo's Viewpoint" to comment on aspects of Guyanese culture. During the early 1980s, he regularly commented on the state of music. His March 16, 1980, column was titled "If this be music—stop!" He ranted against disco music, calling it noise. He decried the popularity of Donna Summer and called for a return to "Old music"—the old masters, operas, operettas, and classic ballads such as "Night and Day," "Smoke Gets in Your Eyes," and "What a Difference a Day Makes." He reminded his readers, "[William] Congreve was certainly not thinking of Disco music when he wrote, 'Music hath charms to soothe the savage beast to soften rocks and bend the knotted oak.'"[108]

In addition to criticizing prevailing popular music tastes and harping for the "good old days," Luckhoo and other cultural critics also commented on other trends and tendencies in the music environment. Roddy Fraser asked the question, "Where have all the singers gone?" That article commented on the virtual absence of a group of pop singers who shone during the 1970s and seemed to have world-class potential. "Where," he asked had "Satch Persaud, Sammy Baksh, Compton Hodge, Barbara Canterbury, Evelyn John, Patricia Arthur, Neisha Benjamin" gone? He wondered if they had lost faith in themselves or if they had "run into trouble with promoters?" He offered a few potential reasons: excessive financial expectations by the artists; lack of organizational skills; and the absence of recording infrastructure. As he put it, "some of our local recording stars have asked for huge sums of money to perform at home, yet these same people went abroad and sold themselves cheaply to promoters." He also commented on the need for artists to organize themselves to ensure proper marketing and management:

> Our singers have got to do more in terms of organizing themselves. There is
> an old saying "Only those who help themselves shall get help." But some artists
> just sit and wait for a call. They are content to do this because they might have
> released a good record months ago and the radio station play it daily so they feel
> that is good enough to bring about other things. Wrong attitude. It can end up in
> a bad dream.

Fraser said that the improvement of recording facilities at the National Cultural Center and the introduction of ten-track recording facilities at the Halagala Recording Company were important infrastructural developments that should help.[109] The cultural critics of the 1980s shied away from stating the truth that Guyanese popular music quality at all levels—composition, performance, recording, and distribution—was generally mediocre. This failure was emblematic of the society at that time. There was heavy self-censorship and fear about telling the king and his courtiers that they were naked.

Until the 1980s little scholarly work was done on music in Guyana. Among the pioneers in this field were Percy and Serena Braithwaite with their publications on Guyanese folk music during the 1960s.[110] In the 1980s scholars such as Dr. Joycelynne Loncke and Olivia Benjamin started to publish occasional articles in the state-owned press. Dr. Loncke's article "African Survivals in the Music of Guyana" was emblematic of that new development.[111] Olivia Ahyoung-Benjamin's writings focused on the importance of music education in the primary school system.[112]

President Forbes Burnham died on August 6, 1985. He had bestridden Guyanese society for the first half of the 1980s, and the impact of the decisions of this maximum leader remained evident throughout the remainder of the decade. President Desmond Hoyte's primary task was to deal with the economy. He rapidly distanced himself from the ideological framework of the Burnham era. This was quickly seen in his decisions to lift the bans imposed on certain types of imported foodstuffs, return to the free market, and build bridges with the West.[113] In December 1988 the Hoyte administration introduced the Economic Recovery Programme, which reopened relationships with the IMF.[114] The emerging economic relations also demanded changes in national governance. In August 1986, on the first anniversary of his presidency,

Hoyte articulated the core planks of his administration: (a) a society based on law, tolerance, and humanity; (b) the economy; and (c) foreign policy.[115]

President Hoyte's engagement with Guyanese cultural life was not as direct as that of President Burnham. His touch was light. He recognized that *panis et circenses* was costly and the return was marginal. For him the task was to put society on a solid economic foundation. This did not mean that he was disengaged with Guyanese cultural life. As the head of state, he served as the patron for important musical events, such as the *Songs of the Spirit* concert, which featured the Ohio University soprano Dr. Maisha Hazzard, accompanied by Patricia Cambridge (née Smith) at the National Cultural Center in 1985 to end the period of mourning for President Forbes Burnham.[116] He was also the patron of the concert to commemorate the first anniversary of the passing of President Burnham.[117] Hoyte also began the task of repurposing The Residence, former home of the late President Burnham. In 1986 President and Joyce Hoyte hosted a Carol Recital at the Residence. He never moved into that building. The carol recital featured the Princesville Orchestra, the Guyana Police Choir, and Hugh Sam.[118] President Hoyte's focus and legacy would be establishing the Guyana Prize for Literature.

International Monetary Fund (IMF) conditionalities demanded reduction of state expenditure. So, from 1988 the paradigm for Mashramani shifted from being primarily state-funded to a profit-making/cost-recovery course. The diet of bread and circuses ceased to distract the population by the end of the decade. There were too many pressing problems in the environment. The good musicians were leaving the country. Generally, the quality of musical product in the country declined. Bunny Alves concluded "the pause button was pressed."

The 1980s was not a great decade for European classical music in Guyana. The decolonization project of the earlier era and the musical content required for *panis et circenses* did not help the cause. There were few original compositions in this genre. Among the meager output were Olivia Benjamin's two arrangements of Cleveland Hamilton's poem *Give Us This Land*[119] and Hugh Sam's 1988 composition to commemorate the 150th anniversary of the emancipation of enslaved Africans in British Guiana.[120] By the end of the decade there were few if any Guyanese compositions on the local hit parade.[121]

10

The 1990s: "Dessie, You Wrong!
Dessie, You Wrong!"

The dominant themes in the discourse on Guyana during the early months of 1990 were economic recovery, divestment, privatization, "national dialogue," and free and fair elections. There were many contributors to this discourse: international actors, including diaspora groups such as the Association of Concerned Guyanese; and domestic participants including the Patriotic Coalition for Democracy, which in 1990 comprised the PPP, the WPA, the Democratic Labour Movement, the People's Democratic Movement, the National Democratic Movement, the United Force, and the United Republic Party.[1] According to international commentators such as the Washington, D.C.–based Council on Hemispheric Affairs, Guyana's economic performance was so poor during the 1980s that it was "rapidly catching up with Haiti as being the poorest nation in the hemisphere."[2] 1989 was considered to have been a particularly devastating year. Unemployment rose, and incomes declined as result of massive devaluation of the Guyanese dollar. Table 10.1 shows the devaluation of the Guyana dollar compared to the US dollar between 1985 and 1991.

In addition to the devaluations, the caloric intake of the poorer sectors of the society was "estimated to be only 89 percent of that recommended by nutritionists."[3] The percentage was considered lower for rural women and children. Further, the reliability of the nation's infrastructure reached new lows, with continuous electricity and water outages in urban and rural areas resulting in widespread public dissatisfaction. The Hoyte government's response was an economic recovery plan that included liberalizing the economy, including the divestment and privatization of state-owned industries, companies, and properties. Despite efforts at liberalizing the economy, the inflow of foreign investment was slow. The international community joined the opposition forces in Guyana in demanding free and fair elections and respect for human rights as prerequisites for their participation Guyana's economic recovery. As early as January 1986, leaders of CARICOM had made it clear to President Hoyte during a special meeting on the island of Mustique that failure to create a more

Table 10.1			
Value of one US dollar compared to one Guyana dollar 1985–1991			
1985	1987	1989	1991
$4.25	$10.00	$33.00	$125.00

Data Source: US Library of Congress. Available online at lcweb2.loc.gov/frd/cs/guyana/gy_glos.html

democratic space in Guyana, including allowing a free press and holding of free elections, could result in Guyana being expelled from the community.[4] That would have been a disgrace, given Guyana's pivotal role in the founding of the community.

United States Senator Edward Kennedy also added his voice to the issue when he too called for free and fair elections.[5] In his reply to Kennedy, President Desmond Hoyte announced that he had indicated to Dr. Jagan that he would do three things in time for the next elections: "(1) abolish the overseas votes; (2) abolish the postal votes; and (3) restrict drastically the proxy votes."[6]

Where the international community did engage immediately was through the provision of food aid to alleviate the dietary crisis. The United States and Guyana signed a US$4 million agreement under the PL480 program, which permitted the importation of 24,000 metric tons of wheat.[7] The government of France donated US$1 million worth of powdered milk.[8] The Canadian government provided Cdn$35 million to Guyana. That represented 29 percent of approximately $Cdn120 million in debt relief to the Commonwealth Caribbean—the former British West Indies—with whom the Canadians had significant historic ties. There was an element of *quid pro quo* in the Canadian decision, as a number of Canadian mining companies, such as Omai signaled their intentions of investing in gold mining in Guyana's hinterland, provided there were indicators of democratization of the political sphere. Between 1993 and 2005, when Omai ceased operations in the Potaro region, the Canadian-owned company extracted more than 3.7 million ounces of gold and was responsible for the first cyanide spill in Guyana's history.[9]

Undoubtedly, the key issue was the rehabilitation of the political space in Guyana, which included the holding of free and fair elections. After the elections in 1985, which were considered rigged, the Patriotic Coalition for Democracy (PCD) was established to agitate for free and fair elections. According to Cheddi Jagan, the coalition included parties from the "extreme left to the extreme right."[10] Internal disagreements on power sharing and the composition of a government, should the PCD defeat the PNC at the pending general elections, led to the dissolution of the PCD. The specific issues that led to the unraveling of the coalition included who was going to be the coalition's presidential candidate and the number of seats to be allocated to the PPP. However, almost immediately upon the breakup of PCD, Guyana Action for Reform and Democracy (GUARD) emerged, led by Samuel Hinds. According to Jagan, Hinds did not go along with the maneuverings that led to breakup of the PCD and was supportive of an alliance to challenge the PNC at the next elections. This led to the creation of PPP/Civic in 1991.[11] A parliamentary effort to rehabilitate the political environment was launched in 1989. This initiative was termed the National Dialogue and was based on a motion introduced in Guyana's Parliament by Eusi Kwayana, the Working People's Alliance Member of Parliament. The motion called "for a National Dialogue of all social forces." It was passed unanimously by the National Assembly.[12] There was hope that the Guyana political crisis could be resolved by Guyanese initiatives. According to Kwayana, "the rulers [President Hoyte and the PNC government] went back on their word, altered the terms of the proposed dialogue and caused it to fall apart. Instead of a homegrown solution resulting from deep and frank, plain talking conversation, there was a change of scene. Enter President Jimmy Carter in October 1990. The conversation was overtaken by negotiation."[13] Out of these negotiations came changes in the election law and speculations about early elections.

The elections took place in 1992 and music played a significant role in the campaigning. Altogether, eleven political parties contested the general elections that were held on October 5, 1992.[14] According to contemporary press reports, the PPP leadership arrived with "blaring party jingles" and the party's theme song "Back in Demand"—a chutney-flavored local tune—to make its formal registration at the Elections Commission's office.[15] The same report noted that the WPA arrived with much shouting and the ringing of a bell. The WPA's symbol was the bell and its theme song was "Ring de Bell," a rapso anthem by Trinidad's Brother Resistance. The PNC's theme song for the 1992 general election was the soca anthem "Follow da Leader" by the Trinidadian duo Nigel & Marvin.

Special songs were also created to position the presidential candidates. From the PPP songbooks came "We have decided to follow Cheddi."[16] The PNC's presidential song was "Desmond!" The Mighty Rebel's 1991 Mashramani calypso "Don't sing bout that" served to synthesize the PNC record in office. The calypso had a catchy melody and infectious beat and provided a list of failures and negatives associated with the PNC—the lack of transparency in the privatization of public corporations and state-owned properties; escalation of the cost of living brought about by the Economic Recovery Programme; corruption by senior officials; the proliferation of ganja and cocaine trafficking; increased sexual deviance, including bestiality; and the increasing number of persons with mental health problems. According to Gail Teixeira, the popularity of "Don't sing bout that" was also a signal that the society was ready for change.[17] The election, which was declared "free and fair" by observers from the Commonwealth and the Carter Center, was won by the PPP.[18] On October 7, 1992, President Desmond Hoyte accepted the results of the poll and started the process of handing over the government to Dr. Cheddi Jagan.[19] Dr. Jagan is reported to have concluded that the PPP may have control of the government but did not control the bureaucracy and there were immediate efforts to replace PNC-era personnel. One area that felt this tension was the Department of Culture.

In 1959 Jagan had scribbled a note about the role of the artist in society: "it was the artists' role to mobilize and lead the society." How did the PPP operationalize this idea on its return to office after twenty-eight years? In-depth interviews with three ministers responsible for culture from 1992 to 2000 are used to answer that question.

Dr. Dale Bisnauth, an academic, a Canadian Presbyterian minister, and a member of the Civic group (the PPP coalition partner in government since 1992), was appointed Minister of Education and Social Development in the new government. He held that office from 1992 to 1996. Dr. Bisnauth grew up on the Essequibo coast and got his primary education at Dartmouth, a predominantly black village. Prior to returning to Guyana in the 1980s he had lived in Trinidad, Jamaica, and Barbados.

Dale Bisnauth inherited a ministry that for almost a decade was led by Deryck Bernard, who was also an academic and an enthusiastic musician. He was a member of the Woodside Choir and was committed to Guyanese folk music. Bernard joined the PNC government as a technocrat during the Hoyte regime. He felt that a crucial variable in Guyana's national development strategy must be folk music. He argued that Guyana's folk music traditions, as distinct from the music of its colonial elite and popular music, held the capacity to build trust and civic cooperation, attributes necessary for the development of social capital, the key ingredient needed for equitable and sustainable development in Guyana. For him social capital was necessary to give the society the capacity to cope with "churn," develop the infrastructure of collaboration, and nurture "gardening" capacity. The extract below is from a paper he presented to the conference Soundscapes: Reflections on Caribbean Oral and Aural Traditions, at the University of the West Indies, Cave Hill, in July 2005.

> *Churn* is the degree of dynamism and radical change in a society. Inherent in this concept is the capacity of a society and economy to cope with change, instability and innovation.... *Infrastructure of collaboration* is the ability of people to work together for a common purpose in groups and organizations. *Gardening* is the capacity of a community to engender growth as opposed to the constant foraging

as in "hunting and gathering" for sources of ideas and the inspiration for development. It refers to the degree to which the development models are indigenous, local resources and capital mobilized, and the extent to which development is a passive or active process.[20]

From this emerged a range of programmatic aspirations, including the collection and preservation of Guyanese folk music, incorporating the study of folk music in the education system, and making folk music accessible in contemporary styles and formats so that they "can again be sources of identification and pride."[21] However, severe economic conditions, including IMF conditionalities, did not allow for implementation during his tenure in office.

In August 2009 Dr. Bisnauth acknowledged inheriting a vibrant policy framework from Deryck Bernard, whom he described as one of Guyana's transformative figures. He also identified the three core tasks that dominated his tour of duty as Minister of Education and Social Development. These tasks were: (a) responding to cultural snobbery, (b) encouraging cultural cosmopolitanism; and (c) resisting extremist elements within the PPP who wanted to eradicate "Blackman culture and music."

According to Dr. Bisnauth, "One of the first things we had to do when we took office in 1992 was to address the problem of cultural snobbery." This problem had many dimensions. One referred to the ongoing valorization of the music of what Deryck Bernard called the "music of the colonial elite—a combination of western classical music, the related sacred music of the established Christian churches and the related functional music such as military music performed by the police and [military]." This music was primarily urban and alienating for rural Guyanese, especially those of Indian ancestry. In racially polarized Guyana, these genres were seen as a "Blackman thing," "a Burnham thing," as Guyanese of African ancestry had demonstrated competence as composers, conductors, and instrumentalists. Guyanese of African ancestry were also framed by Indian ethnic extremists as a people who were deracinated—a people who had lost all of their culture and were mere parrots of the colonial experience and not worthy of emulation. This orientation was ingrained in the rhetoric of PPP field workers in their exchanges with their electoral base, especially in the Corentyne. As a result, there was active resistance to accepting the dignified or lively styles of music created by Guyanese of African ancestry.

For Bisnauth, the scope of the reality manifested itself during a large meeting in Port Mourant about a week before the 1992 elections. There it was decided that the national anthem would be sung before the start of the meeting. He claimed that, of the entire audience, only two persons seemed to know the words of the national anthem. He considered this a sad experience! Many rural Guyanese of Indian ancestry did not learn the national anthem, as it was a "Blackman thing and you don't need to know this." This situation demanded that the ministry take special efforts to push national and patriotic songs in rural areas.

This experience was an eye opener for Bisnauth. It reflected a deep and complex problem that was exacerbated by the rancor and polarization of post-independence politics. He was of the opinion that Guyanese politicians seemed programmed to keep fighting "somebody" after independence. There was no politics of consensus building and this led to the cultural parochialism that was evident in Port Mourant. Similar conclusions could be drawn about the cultural perspectives of many urban Guyanese of African ancestry. Not many of them were able to appreciate the range of Indian musical expressions in Guyana. Bisnauth felt that, twenty-six years into independence, correcting that reality was one of the core tasks of his ministry.

Dr. Bisnauth was also aware of the musical exchanges that were taking place in the Guyanese musical landscape, despite various parochialisms. As he was aware of the Caribbeanization and spread of chutney, he was also aware of the increasing Christianization of rural Indians and the modification of the rhythms of some of the hymns to cater to this new audience. He was cognizant of the exchange that was taking place between chutney and soca. He was also conscious of the Indian duo Babla and Kanchan "picking up the Matticore thing" and circulating it globally. He was also conscious of the potential of music to break down stereotypes. For this task he built upon the infrastructure that was in place. Increased emphasis was placed on patriotic and folk music in the programs produced by Broadcast to Schools. In this case, deliberate efforts were made to incorporate the music of Guyana's Indian heritage, which unfortunately, tended to be absent in these programs.

The task of expanding the musical repertoire had an impact on the musical aesthetics of the state, as bands such as the Guyana Police Force Band and the Guyana Defence Force Band began to incorporate Indian melodies into their repertoires. Another effort at encouraging cultural cosmopolitanism was the publication of Lynette Dolphin's *One Hundred Folk Songs of Guyana* in 1996 as part of the activities to celebrate the thirtieth anniversary of independence.[22] This collection may have been the first state-funded publication to include Amerindian (Ackawaio) and Indian folk songs. These efforts at expanding the nation's musical consciousness revealed the pent-up resistance to "Blackman music" that existed in influential sectors of the PPP. Dealing with the latter was probably the most significant challenge Dr. Bisnauth had to respond to.

According to Dr. Bisnauth, there were extremist elements within the PPP who wanted to impose a rigid, basically racial view on Guyanese cultural life and to eradicate "Blackman music" from the society. The demand was for a complete transformation of the musical aesthetics of the state. Some elements felt that the primarily black staff of the Department of Culture were not progressive, were anti-PPP, and should be replaced. Another group argued that folk songs such as "Sitira Gal" and "Ganja Mani" were degenerate, antisocial, and racist and should be banned from public presentations. This position was clearly a contradiction, as for almost four decades those songs had been part of the PPP's repertoire and were featured in the songbooks published by the PPP.[23]

At the center of the challenge was the demand to get rid of Mashramani, as it was too closely associated with the late President Forbes Burnham. Dr. Bisnauth's ministry was now responsible for executing the celebration through the National Commemoration Commission, an entity originally established in 1984 to commemorate the 150th anniversary of the abolition of slavery. President Jagan wanted to emphasize independence and move some of the activities associated with the republic to the independence anniversary. According to Dr. Bisnauth, he and other members of the Cabinet felt that "Mash was a "People's thing! . . . It was too much a people's thing and it could not be destroyed." The argument was not accepted enthusiastically and the approach was to minimize the celebration. Dr. Bisnauth reported that one year there was no flag-raising ceremony. The "Mashramani problem" would continue to exist for the duration of Dr. Bisnauth's tenure. Starting under the Hoyte presidency, there were substantial reductions in the allocation of state funds for the Mashramani celebrations. The state of the economy dictated that. Under President Jagan's government this practice continued. Mashramani became a political football, with the PNC organizing parallel Mashramani celebrations. The management of Guyana's cultural life during the early years of the PPP's tenure was tense.

In his quest to develop "cultural cosmopolitanism" in Mashramani, Bisnauth got himself into hot water because of a statement that he claims was taken out of context. At a Mashramani planning meeting, he asked the folk researcher Lakshmi Kallicharran to develop a strategy to encourage participation by Indian villages in Mashramani as one got the impression that Mashramani was a "Blackman thing." The press reported that he described Mashramani was a "Blackman thing." According to Bisnauth, that was a misrepresentation of what he actually said. His statement created a storm in the racially charged atmosphere of the times. Hamilton Green, the Mayor of Georgetown, described Bisnauth's remarks as reactionary and polarizing in continuing to frame the expressive culture of urban Guyanese of African heritage as coarse, vulgar, and disreputable.[24]

Irrespective of his quest to expand participation in Mashramani, he received lukewarm support from the PPP field workers. According to Bisnauth, "The PPP did not promote the thing vigorously among their constituency! The plan was to move national festive celebrations to Independence." Despite the political drama, Mashramani continued and remained an important site for expressing Guyanese musical culture. In 1993 the Mighty Rebel won the calypso competition with "Dessie Yuh Wrong, Dessie Yuh Wrong." This calypso "expressed" the late President Burnham's chagrin with Desmond Hoyte for losing the 1992 elections to Cheddi Jagan and the consequences of that for the nation.[25]

In 1994 Cheddi Jagan reflected on the achievements of his government at the halfway mark of its first tour of duty. He noted that his government had responded to the political, economic, and social challenges inherited from the Hoyte regime. He also pointed out that his government was seeing some progress in "the cultural field." The conversion of the Residence, the former home of Prime Minister and President Burnham, into Castellani House for "the benefit of the arts" was a major gesture.[26]

Paralleling this development at Castellani House, the government was actively engaged in restructuring the management of culture in Guyana. This action was actually initiated by the previous government; in 1992 the international consulting company Peat Marwick submitted a report recommending the creation of an autonomous Ministry of Culture. Minister Bisnauth did not have to deal with the controversial mass games, as the last one was held in 1990 under the title "A Rainbow." The music for this final venture was composed by Assistant Superintendent Cecil Bovell, the director of music of the Guyana Police Force Band, with a special choir organized and conducted by Edith Pieters.[27]

On March 6, 1997, President Cheddi Jagan died in Washington D.C., from the massive heart attack that he had suffered three weeks earlier. Within a year, elections were held and the PPP won the election with 55.26 percent of the vote. However, the PNC alleged substantial electoral fraud and related irregularities. The PNC went to court and obtained an order prohibiting Janet Jagan from being sworn in as Guyana's first female and foreign-born president. Janet Jagan's swearing in as president took place in a controversial manner. She famously threw away the court order prohibiting her from being sworn in. The allegations of substantial electoral fraud and the aftermath of her swearing in were destructive. Desmond Hoyte pledged to make the country ungovernable and initiated a campaign of civil disobedience—the "slow fire, more fire campaign." This campaign was captured in Lord Canary's calypso "Slow Fire." It was not until the CARICOM-brokered Herdmanston Accord of January 17, 1998, that some modicum of peace returned to Georgetown. The accord developed an agenda for moving forward. This included commitment to political dialogue, an external audit of the election results, constitutional reform, and elections in 2001 instead of 2003.

Under Janet Jagan's presidency, the Ministry of Culture, Youth, and Sport was established and Gail Teixeira—the granddaughter of Major Henwood, the last director of music of the British Guiana Militia Band—was appointed as the first minister. This was the first time in Guyana's history that an autonomous ministry responsible for culture was established. The ministry's ancestry could be traced back to the National History and Culture Committee that was established in 1958 and morphed through five decades from the National History and Arts Council, to the Department of Culture, to the Ministry of Culture, Youth, and Sport.

The orientation of the new ministry was articulated in Sections 5.5, 5.6, and 5.7 of the PPP's manifesto for the 1997 general election.[28] Specifically, the ministry's goal was to support and promote a development strategy "that was people-oriented . . . culturally relevant and culturally-based." Gail Teixeira brought a rich body of experience as an activist to the appointment. She grew up in Georgetown, and studied dance with Ivy Campbell and art with Ben Chinapen. She was an immigrant to Canada at age fourteen; studied political science in Canada; developed a love for jazz there; became an activist in the pro-PPP Association of Concerned Guyanese; remigrated to Guyana in 1977; and became Cheddi Jagan's personal secretary, a member of the PPP's central committee, and a co-founder of the Worker's Stage. Prior to her appointment as Minister of Culture, Youth, and Sport, she was Minister of Health in President Cheddi Jagan's 1992 cabinet.

It was with this background that Gail Teixeira assumed the leadership for the Ministry of Culture, Youth, and Sport. Her team included Keith Booker, who was appointed as the permanent secretary. Prior to that appointment, he was a lieutenant colonel in the Guyana National Service and was responsible for folding the service into the new ministry. In addition to the directions articulated in the 1997 PPP manifesto, Teixeira had to deal with the harsh realities of ethnic relations and the unsettled question of Mashramani.

During a August 2009 interview, she declared that she loved Mashramani, supported the concept behind it, and believed that the annual festival could catapult Guyanese expressive culture to higher levels and be a thing of pride for Guyanese.[29] Her thrust was to get more people involved and hype the festival as a Guyanese thing and not a Burnham or Hoyte thing. She was attuned to the lovers of Mashramani, the persons who brought their families out along the route, who wanted a bigger and more inclusionary Mashramani. From 1998, Gail Teixeira became a visible part of Mashramani. On Mashramani Day, she would be at the front of the Costume Bands and Float Parade.

But it was not an easy project as the parade continued to be a site for political protests. For many years after 1992, the PNC would join the parade and disrupt it by pulling elements of the parade to Congress Place, the headquarters of the PNC, instead of entering the National Park. There was a certain amount of back-channel communication taking place between the Ministry of Culture, Youth, and Sport and the PNC on saving and growing Mashramani. The general quest was to minimize the possibility for violent confrontations and encourage positive engagement. The message was the need to throw political polarization out of the window for one day. She offered the conclusion that by the end of the twentieth century, Mashramani had become more inclusive as there was more private-sector participation, the Evangelical churches were entering troupes, and Guyanese of Indian ancestry were now very visible in the Mash Day parade—"Wining fuh so!"

Despite the survival of the festival, there were ongoing concerns about the musical quality of the calypsos. Assistance was sought from Trinidad's Carnival Development Committee to help with that challenge. Guyanese calypso content and themes continued to be topical. For example, in 1998 the dominant topics were Janet Jagan as president of Guyana, and the 1997 post-election violence. The winning calypso that year was Lord Canary's "Deh Talking 'Bout Woman." According to a contemporary report, this calypso

> pointed out the peculiarities of women and the important role they played in [Guyanese] society. During his rendition, three females came on stage to portray the different roles women adopt in society. The first was attired in a suit, carrying a briefcase. She looked like a superb professional lady. Then a pregnant woman came, and later, one who mimicked President Janet Jagan joined them to aid Canary's presentation.[30]

The runner up was Lady Tempest's "Why de Fighting So," which commented on the violence that followed the 1997 elections. Her second entry in the competition was "Big Up Guyana," which sought to promote racial unity by having dancers presenting "choreography [that] blended African and Indian techniques." Young Bill Rogers earned the third spot with his calypso "JJ's [Janet Jagan] Race and Poor Elections." Rogers's second entry was "One Race the Human Race," like Lady Tempest's "Big Up Guyana" a call for racial peace. A majority of the calypsos created for Mashramani 1998 commented on the race crisis and pleaded for national unity. By 1998 a separate Mashramani Secretariat was established, which, like the Central Mashramani Committee under the PNC, exerted influence on the content and orientation of calypso. Following a practice that had become popular in other aspects of Guyana's political culture, calypsonians developed a code of conduct informed by the 1998 Racial Hostilities Act.[31] The act stated:

A person shall be guilty of an offence if he willfully excites or attempts to excite hostility or ill-will against any section of the public or against any section on the grounds of their or his race:

(a) by means of words spoken by him in a public place or spoken by him and transmitted for general reception by wireless telegraphy or telegraph;

(b) by causing words spoken by him or some other person to be reproduced in a public place from a record; or

(c) by means of written (including printed) matter or pictorial matter published by him.[32]

Several strategies were adopted to improve the quality of calypso during the 1990s. In addition to help from the Trinidad and Tobago Carnival Commissions, the Junior Calypso and Soca Monarch competitions were established. Further, calypsonians from the Guyanese diaspora in the United States such as D'Ivan and John "Slingshot" Drepaul became regular participants.

Gail Teixeira pointed out that it was recognized that improvement in the quality of calypso and other genres of popular music in Guyana depended on establishing a sustainable and accessible music education system. This called a coherent music policy for rehabilitating and expanding the state-funded music education infrastructure in the nation's school system, providing support for persons and organizations that produced and distributed music, and supporting music appreciation through non-formal and informal strategies.

Gail Teixeira, like Deryck Bernard, felt that the content of the state-funded music education in Guyana was too Anglicized. She had strong views on a strategy for changing that. A May 23, 2000, memo titled "Music Development: Discovery and Preservation," to Major Ault, formerly director of music for the Guyana Defence Force, now the director of music in the Ministry, gave a hint of her strategy and related environmental tensions, particularly the "philosophical differences" between them. In that memorandum she identified four pressing tasks in the music sphere that she expected him to address. These included conducting an inventory of musical instruments still in use in Guyana; field research, especially in rural and hinterland communities; establishing training programs; and creating new music and strategies for propagating this creativity. This approach, she wrote, will be the "genesis of a new and distinctly Guyanese music, through creative and 'revolutionary' arrangements."[33]

That memo appears to be the synthesis of an extended period of discourse about the place of music in Guyanese society and a strategy for systematically integrating various musical traditions. Other elements in Gail Teixeira's philosophical orientations included creating space for all aspects of Guyanese musical expressions, widening the range of participants in the dialogue on the place of music in Guyanese society, undermining and destabilizing musical practices that reinforced racial and gender stereotypes, and encouraging and nurturing research and scholarship. This was a new paradigm. It required changing the path and direction of the management of cultural development in Guyana. It did not mean throwing out the European traditions and foundations. It meant creating new spaces for Guyanese expression and resuscitating what was dying because of the lack of state support due to the economic crisis since the 1980s, such as steel pan! It also meant giving space to hitherto marginalized or paternalized forms of creative expression, especially Amerindian languages, music, and dances.

The execution of this philosophical orientation and the PPP's manifesto required collaboration across many governmental agencies, including the Ministry of Education. This unfortunately did not go as smoothly as was anticipated. During the August 2009 interview, Teixeira, then a minister in the office of the president with responsibility for governance, recalled a series of meetings she and her permanent secretary held with the Ministry of Education about re-introducing music and physical education in the national primary education system. The guiding theory anticipated benefits such as better self-concept and inculcating the importance of teamwork. Specifically, she was of the opinion that music in the curriculum from the nursery grades would help children hear better, develop better coordination, and do better in mathematics. The task was to introduce students to sound!

Minister Teixeira claimed that the vision was derailed by the Ministry of Education's stance that such an intervention would require specialized equipment. There was resistance to the idea of using folk games and locally produced and indigenous instruments, particularly flute, drum, and other percussive instruments as core instruments. According to Minister Teixeira, the Ministry of Education resisted this approach and continued to privilege the piano. According to Teixeira, "the idea fell flat on its face. It was a downer!" The "older" Ministry of Education appeared to put in place many bureaucratic roadblocks.[34]

Despite those challenges, Teixeira managed to advance many aspects of the PPP's manifesto. She was able to rehabilitate and reposition Mashramani as the premier national cultural festival and potentially the primary site of Guyanese musical expression. She was also gave the Ministry of Culture, Youth, and Sport a credible national profile for which she credits her permanent secretary, Lt. Col. Keith Booker, M.S. Further, she expanded the range of participants engaged in the discourse on the form and direction of music in Guyana. As expressed in the earlier cited memo, Minister Teixeira envisioned expanding the place of the drum in Guyanese society, and in this task she encouraged experimentation and depended on experimentation by Garfield Benn and Colgrain Whyte, the pan technologists. Her commitment to drums was manifested in the quest to establish a national drum orchestra—one made up of all the types of drums evident in Guyana. Such an ensemble participated in Carifesta 9 that was held in Surinam in 2006. Simply stated, she launched "new days" and was aware of the approaching impact of the new electronic environment in a more liberalized economic environment.

Over the twentieth century, several technologies influenced the production, distribution, and consumption of music on Guyana. Of these the more obvious ones were phonographs and gramophone (1910s), radio broadcasting (1920s), "talkies" (sound cinema) (1930s), recording studios (1950s), jukeboxes (1950s), transistor radios (1960s), stereo sets (1970s), and television (1980s). In the last decade of the twentieth century a range of digital technologies, especially the computer, exerted significant influence on the development of musical talent and the production and delivery of Guyanese music. A brief exploration of the work of Bunny Alves, Burchmore Simon, and Walter "Wally" Frazer between 1991 and the end of the century illuminates this development.

Bonny Alves, who has been described as "the under-celebrated Guyanese music pioneer," was born in Agricola on the East Bank of Demerara.[35] He pioneered the production of music videos in Guyana, which by the end of the twentieth century was an important channel for the distribution of Guyanese music in Guyana and around the world. Bunny Alves's first venture into this field took place in 1991 when he produced the "first music video to be recorded, filmed and edited in Guyana."[36] This was the live recording of "I Feel Good," performed by Charmaine Blackman accompanied by Pete's Caribbean Fusion. Between 1991 and 2009, he produced more than a hundred music videos and numerous television jingles and commercials using original music. The music videos have received airplay in the Caribbean, Europe, Canada, the United States, and Africa.[37]

Alves brought a musical sensibility to these digital productions. Prior to his ventures in the digital sphere, he was a member of the Yoruba Singers for almost two decades and had established national and regional credibility as a composer and musical innovator. He came to public attention in 1985, when his compositions "Let's Talk It Over" and "I Feel Good," performed by Toni Barry, were awarded first place at the Song Contest of the Guianas. With that victory he became the "only home-based Guyanese to win an international song competition."[38] His arrangements for the Mighty Intruder's "Steel Band Man," "Lilawatee," and "Way Mi Lila Gone" resulted in victories in the Mashramani Road March competitions in 1987, 1988, and 1989 respectively.[39] He also had success arranging "Talking about Education," which won the Regions Calypso Competition in 1987.

In 1995 Alves formed the production company SSignal. His long association with the Yoruba Singers influenced his musical aesthetics and led to
experimentation with "Kwefo" (the merging of Kwe Kwe and other folk music
styles). Like the bhoom, the experiment did not attract sustained public support. In the process of developing his body of work in the digital domain,
Alves has promoted the career of Charmaine Blackman, one of Guyana's
important female singers of the 1990s. She was featured in a majority of the
music videos and feature films produced by Alves. By the end of the decade
that collaboration had resulted in more than thirty-eight music videos, fifteen
CDs, numerous international tours, and stints of employment on cruise ships.

At the end of the twentieth century, Alves had not developed a robust enterprise. His primary challenges were coping with illegal duplication (piracy)
and developing the capacity to participate in the global distribution system.
So, despite interest in his work in Guyanese diaspora, which in the 1990s was
approaching 750,000, he was unable to exploit this potential market. Burchmore Simon would address the issue of international distribution.

Burchmore Simon wore many musical hats during the post-independence
years. He was a bandleader, a practicing musician, a music teacher, a record
producer, and eventually the owner of Kross Kolors—a full-service music
company. Burchmore Simon started his music education at the age of six with
Mrs. Fox, a music teacher in his home village of Buxton, East Coast Demerara. She was one of many music teachers in this historic Guyanese village.[40]
Burchmore followed the traditional route and studied music up to Grade
VIII under the curriculum of the Associated Boards of the Royal College of
Music. In addition, he studied music in high school and was trained as a music
teacher by Edith Pieters. After his formal music education, he joined Golden
Grove Secondary School as head of the Music Department.[41]

In 1984, he formed the E.C. (East Coast) Connection—a band of musicians from villages on the East Coast of Demerara.[42] According to Simon, "we
were the country boys." When the E.C. Connection was created, the only other
bands on the East Coast were Sid and the Slickers and Terry Nelson's Stax 5
from Beterverwagting. In 1985, the dominant party bands in Guyana were the
Cannon Balls, Mingles, Solo Sounds International, Pete's Caribbean Fusion,
and the Yoruba Singers. These bands controlled the musical landscape and
it was the ambition of the new band "to represent the East Coast and break
the dominance the Georgetown bands had [on the lucrative East Coast party
scene]."[43] In time, the E.C. Connection dominated that East Coast party scene
and became one of the backup bands in the national Mashramani calypso
competition.

As a "roots" party band, E.C. Connection's repertoire was primarily popular
music. What distinguished the band was the fact that it tended to perform

original compositions. In 1991 the band travelled to Surinam to record its first album. From that album came "Number One Lady" and "Where Did the Children Play?" Both compositions attracted domestic and international attention. As Simon reflected in 2009, both "Rudy and Eddy Grant wanted to do something with 'Number One Lady' as it was such a good song."[44]

As early as 1986, Simon was thinking about life beyond the E.C. Connection. In that same year he registered a company with the name Kross Kolors. The goal of the company was to become producers and marketers of E.C. Connection's music nationally and internationally. The idea remained dormant for a decade until the company started to produce jingles for radio and television. According to Simon, the name Kross Kolors reflects his belief in racial integration and his adherence to the creed "Love your neighbor as you love yourself." He described the use of the "K" in the spelling as a gimmick to make the company distinctive.

Throughout the 1990s, a majority of the radio and television jingles aired in Guyana were produced in Trinidad and Tobago. Like Bunny Alves, it would be in this arena that Burchmore Simon would establish himself as a music producer in the digital age. Also like Alves, his clients came from the private and public sectors. In the beginning, his studio was his kitchen table, a laptop computer, and a four-channel Midi mixer. The move to a formal studio was the result of investments in the E.C. Connection by King Solomon, a Guyanese entrepreneur with East Coast roots. The investments were originally aimed at improving the sound of E.C. Connection to ensure that it had the capacity to produce music of international quality. The equipment acquired also included a thirty-two-channel (Macie) mixer. Immediately after the equipment was acquired, the band broke up and the new equipment had to be repurposed. It became the infrastructure for the Kross Kolors Recording Studio. Kross Kolors' first project was in gospel music. The product was Miriam Williams's *Vision of Excellence: The Beginning*. A fifteen-track compilation CD featuring fourteen of Simon's soca-inflected compositions and fourteen of Guyana's leading musicians of that period, followed *Vision of Excellence*. Simon used the compilation CD to establish his signature production and marketing strategy.

Simon's production portfolio was not limited to the gospel and soca genres. In time it was expanded to include folk, chutney, jazz, soul, comedy, world beat, alternative soca, and alternative reggae. Kross Kolors' first formal venture in the folk genre resulted in the CD *Korowka: Folk Guyana Style* (ca. 1998). This CD was produced in collaboration with the former Minister of Education, Deryck Bernard, who was at that time the musical director of Korowka, the twenty-person folk-song group within the Woodside Choir. *Korowka* was one of the initiatives Bernard took to make folk music accessible in contemporary styles and formats so that they "can again be sources of identification and pride."[45] In the Arawak language, "Korokwa" means "to remember."[46]

The production of *Korowka: Folk Guyana Style* was a challenging exercise for Kross Kolors as the studio was small—no more than 108 square feet. The choir had to be divided into two groups; each group recorded tracks, and then Simon and Bernard "stitched the two parts" together. The CD immediately attracted critical acclaim and popularity. The fourteen recordings included a mixture of thirteen traditional and folk style Guyanese compositions and one Barbadian folk style item. *Korowka: Folk Guyana Style* was to be the first of a series of productions on Guyana's folk music traditions. Deryck Bernard's untimely death in February 2008 brought that ambition to a halt. By the end of the twentieth century, Kross Kolors had developed a complex music business with a secure e-commerce portal and an A&R unit with most of Guyana's top soca and chutney artists on its roster.

The 1990s saw artist development as a key activity and one of the successful innovators in this field was Wally Frazer's Vizion Sounds Promotions. Walter Frazer re-migrated to Guyana in 1995 and started Vizion Sounds Promotions, at 85 Robb Street, Georgetown, as a label aimed at covering all styles of music and producing and promoting local talent in all genres of music. The first step in that direction was the signing of First Born in 1997.

First Born—an a cappella group of Rastafarians— first impressed its presence on the Guyanese musical consciousness in 1997, as a warm-up act during a Vizion Sounds–promoted concert featuring the Jamaican reggae singers Freddie McGregor and Dennis Brown at the National Park in Georgetown. The group's performance was so impressive that Vizion Sounds immediately offered them a contract and Dennis Brown offered to do a guest spot on their first recording that was to be made in Jamaica. Prior to their trip to Jamaica, the group did further training in voice and harmony with Russell Lancaster and Edith Pieters.[47] In 2000 Russell Lancaster still spoke excitedly about his initial encounter with Troy, Steve, Trion, Commo, Lambi, Shawn, and Anthony who were all "first borns."[48]

The group's debut recording was the single "Repatriation Time," which featured Dennis Brown. The song, recorded at Leggo's Studio in Kingston, Jamaica, was militant and optimistic. It called for people of African ancestry to "step up!" It also called upon the wider society to develop positive visions; seek education, especially history; and avoid the dangerous lifestyles. The CD, *Exodus Chapter XIII Verse 2*, followed the single. The CD featured fourteen tracks and was a deeper and more incisive explication of the vision and sentiments of "Repatriation Time." The recording of the debut CD attracted some of Jamaica's best musicians. Dean Fraser was the musical director. In 1999 the group won the Best New Artist and Best Album Awards in Guyana. Since 1997

First Born has become an important part of the Caribbean consciousness reggae community and has toured extensively.

By the end of the decade, Vizion Sounds had an active roster of Guyanese and international reggae artists. In 2006 Vizion Sounds installed a US$10 million state-of-the-art recording studio in Georgetown.[49]

The initiatives by Bunny Alves, Burchmore Simon, and Walter "Wally" Frazer, especially their demystification of digital technologies, contributed to the reawakening of Guyanese musical productivity. By the first decade of the twenty-first century there were at least six recording studios in Guyana.

Throughout the 1990s a number of Guyanese musical icons passed on. These included Harry Whittaker (d. 1991), Norman Beaton (1994), Al Seales (1995), Tom Charles (1999), Pancho Carew (1999), and King Fighter (1999). Short biographical pieces by Letroy Cummings on Harry Whittaker (1991), Ras Michael on Al Seales (1997), Ray Seales on Al Seales (2009), Francis Farrier on Tom Charles (1999), Angela Fox on King Fighter, and G. I. Chapelle on Pancho Carew (1999) have emerged. However, full-length biographies for these and other Guyanese music icons are needed.

That Guyanese musical icons would pass from the stage was inevitable. What was uppermost in the minds of the Guyanese musical community, especially in the diaspora, was that they should not be forgotten, or merely eulogized in death. There was a call to recognize and celebrate these icons during their lifetime. One step in that direction was by Winston Ewart Smith ("Sir Wins"), who organized the Guyanese Musicians and Entertainers Association's Hall of Fame.[50] Among the first persons to be inducted into the Hall of Fame were Tom Charles (leader of the Syncopaters Orchestra) and Albert Seales (leader of the Washboards Orchestra). Others inducted in 1990 were Monica Chopperfield (Lady Guymine), Ferdinand Eversley (pianist and saxophonist Washboards Orchestra), Ivor Hendricks (drummer, Washboards Orchestra), Alvin Frank (pianist, Washboards Orchestra), Eddie Rogers (former bandmaster, Guyana Police Force Band), and Irma V. Smith-Dixon (soprano, Sonny Thomas Orchestra).

On August 12, 1992, the Department of Culture organized at the National Cultural Center a tribute concert for Alyce Fraser Denny, who had died in the United States in 1988. In addition to performances by the members of the classical music community, a bronze bust was unveiled.

The need to recognize Guyanese musicians became even more acute in the early years of the twenty-first century, when several died in destitution. Had it not been for the contributions of Rudy and Eddy Grant, iconic personalities such as Billy Moore and Richard Noble would have been buried in unmarked paupers' graves in some unknown place in Guyana. It was this situation that

Table 10.2							
Distribution of Hugh Sam's classical compositions 1952–2006							
1952–59	1960–69	1970–79	1980–89	1990–99	2000	2001–2006	
23	5	4	16	58	78	95	

Data Source: Hugh Sam, "Hugh Sam printed compositions (Finale)," an unpublished document prepared by Hugh Sam, September 3, 2006

stimulated the series "Celebrating Our Creative Heroes" by Vibert C. Cambridge and the Wordsworth McAndrew Awards by the Guyana Cultural Association of New York in 2003.

Meanwhile, in the diaspora, Guyanese musicians continued to be productive and influential. Eddy Grant had established himself as a world-class performer, producer, and studio owner; Ray Luck was appointed a cultural ambassador for the United States; Dave Martins was recognized as the conscience of the Caribbean; and Loris Holland had earned international recognition, including a Grammy, as a composer of television scores and producer of hits for Mary J. Blige, Mariah Carey, Lauryn Hill, and Whitney Houston.

During the 1990s, Hugh Sam was Guyana's most prolific composer of music in the classical style. One hundred and thirty-six of his compositions were printed during this period. Between 1952 and 2006, 279 of his compositions were printed. Table 10.4 contains a distribution of his printed compositions between his first in 1952 and last in 2006.

Sam migrated to the United Kingdom in 1967 and studied piano and harmony at the Guildhall School of Music. In the early 1970s he again migrated to the United States, where he earned a B.A. in music composition from the Manhattan School of Music. This period of formal study partially explains his reduced productivity between 1960 and 1979. Prior to leaving British Guiana, Sam won acclaim for his composition, including first prize for *Fantasia on Three Guianese Folk Songs* during the first National History and Culture Week in 1958. Sam continued to draw inspiration from Guyanese and Caribbean folk songs and national airs. In this process, he was doing what Bach, Bartok, Chopin, Dvorak, Mozart, Ravel, Tchaikovsky, and others did—celebrating their nation's folk music traditions!

There are Guyanese musicians in the diaspora who were actively engaged in their community's musical life. Some of them have attracted critical acclaim and earned impressive awards, including Emmys, in many genres of music—pop, gospel, chutney, soca, reggae, and classical.[51] The overarching point is that at the end of the twentieth century, Guyana had world-class musicians living in the diaspora, and one of them, Eddy Grant, headlined the BBC's

Millennium Ring Bang Concert held on December 31, 1999, which was seen by a global audience of over one hundred million! Other performers in that concert included Guyana's Yoruba Singers and Charmaine Blackman. In 2007, the government of Guyana issued a set of postage stamps celebrating Eddy Grant and declaring him "Guyana's Superstar"!

11

Findings and Conclusions

This book aims to explore the dynamics of the intersection of national-level governance and the creation, production, distribution, and consumption of music in multicultural Guyana during the twentieth century. *Governance* in this book is used to mean the institutions created and the practices, tactics, and processes used by governments and their allies to achieve policy goals that advance their interests. By necessity, the concept had to engage those excluded and marginalized elements of society who sought, through various means to participate in the process of deciding on national policies and in the implementation of those policies. As stated before, during the twentieth century Guyanese society experienced three distinct eras of governance: (a) the period of matured colonialism (1900–53); (b) the period of internal self-government (1953–66); and (c) the post-colonial era (1966–2000). The last period could be subdivided into the PNC era (1966–92) and the PPP era from 1992.

Across all three eras, Guyana has faced a range of persistent problems which have demanded the active engagement of the state. Among the seemingly intractable problems have been racial and ethnic polarization; anti-democratic practices; persistent poverty; inadequate infrastructure; inequitable access to resources for self-actualization; and unimaginative government bureaucracies. On occasion it has been suggested that what was needed was a Napoleon type of leader to resolve these persistent problems. Throughout the twentieth century, Guyana has had a succession of strong personalities who used charisma and power in ways that have been described by terms such as autocratic and dictatorial. In the post-independence era those terms have been used to describe Linden Forbes Sampson Burnham, Desmond Hoyte, Cheddi Jagan, Janet Jagan, and Bharrat Jagdeo. Similar terms were used to describe the governors of the colonial era.

Across the twentieth century the musical demands of an active state exerted substantial influence on musical life in the society. This influence came from the state's demand for music's ceremonial, mobilization, propaganda and strategic-communication roles, including the provision of entertainment through "bread and circuses," and indirectly through various forms of patronage such as duty-free and other tax incentives, sponsorship of events, and performance contracts. Those sectors of the society that were excluded or marginalized from the process of national governance have across the twentieth century drawn upon their musical assets to call for accountability, to shine spotlights on corruption and inefficiency, and to express their frustrations and aspirations. The practices of governance exerted disproportionate influence in the dynamic processes related to the creation, production, distribution, and consumption of music in Guyana during the twentieth century.

In addition to the overarching goal of exploring the dynamics of the intersection of governance and the creation, production, distribution, and consumption of music in multicultural Guyana, subsidiary questions that this book has sought to explore include:

- What was the range and nature of Guyanese musical creativity during the twentieth century?
- What factors contributed to the musical environment that blossomed, bloomed, and unfortunately wilted in Guyana during various moments during the twentieth century?
- What institutions and organizations contributed to this dynamic?
- What were the various forms of musical interaction in the process?
- What were the consequences of this musical dynamic for stratified Guyanese society?

Irrespective of the style of governance that obtained in the society, Guyanese demonstrated competence and confidence in composing and performing multiple genres of music across the twentieth century. The Guyanese soundscape became increasingly cosmopolitan, especially in the influential urban areas. Without a doubt, composition, performance, and consumption reflected the political tenor of the times.

The psycho-political orientation for most of the era of matured colonialism was to demonstrate that the British were the best; privilege the ideology of white supremacy; promote loyalty to the Crown; and operationalize "new imperialism." The British ruling class in the colony had the ideological state apparatus and the musical assets to support that psycho-political project—a raft of sacred and secular compositions. Global economic, political, and cultural developments of the mid-1920s, including agitation by the subordinated classes in British Guiana for self-determination, occasioned shifts in music policy. Local creativity began to be accommodated.

This shift was evident in the music that the ruling class drew upon for public and private consumption. The music for the ceremonial aspects of the colony was primarily martial and instrumental, drawn from an imported repertoire. By the 1920s British Guianese, of which Clem Nichols of the British Guiana Militia Band is an exemplar, were composing instrumental martial music in the British style and winning recognition at international events such as the British Empire Exhibition at Wembley in 1924. His "Dear Demerara" is an example. By the start of the twentieth century, British Guianese were also beginning to compose sacred songs and secular art songs based on Western musical styles. An example is Smellie's anthem "For the Lord Jehovah."[1]

The colonial ruling class and their allies also demanded music for relaxation and recreation. This realm was also dominated by imported music to support the fox trot, gavottes, two-steps, waltzes, the Charleston, the Lindy Hop, and other popular dances of the early decades of the century. Although the record is not clear on compositions by British Guianese in this realm, it is clear that Guianese musicians were more than competent performers of those genres of popular music composed outside of the colony.

But imported music and local derivatives were not the only compositions in the colony's soundscape during the era of matured colonialism. By the start of the twentieth century, there was a body of local songs, by now anonymous composers, which by their popularity questioned the orthodoxy of new imperialism. These songs drew upon African musical traditions, including the use of praise/blame/ridicule song traditions, spoke about the conditions of disadvantage, and inspired a discourse on self-determination and a localized patriotism. Peter de Weever's "Me Cawfee in de Marnin'" is of that heritage. As the century progressed, local geography, flora, and fauna became embedded in the proto-nationalist discourse that was emerging to counter the dominating British ethos. By the 1930s this localized patriotism—as expressed in Bryant's "The Song of Guiana's Children" and Cossou's "My Native Land"—was coopted in now shifting patterns of matured colonial governance. The efforts at modification in the musical aesthetics of the state did not reflect adequate changes in national governance, and Bill Rogers and the vaudevillians kept the pressure up.

World War II not only hurried political change in British Guiana; it also tilted the tenor of the soundscape. The presence of American troops in the colony consolidated and expanded the American musical aesthetics present in the colony. By the early decades of the twentieth century many American genres, including Negro spirituals were present in Guyanese society. The presence of the Negro spiritual is associated with the late-nineteenth-century tour by the Tennessee Jubilee Singers with Madame Sissieretta Jones—the Black Patti—and the subsequent accomplishments of the British Guiana–born soprano Alyce Fraser. The war years brought Sousa, Broadway, and swing to the forefront, and Guianese musicians continued to demonstrate confidence in performing popular works from the American repertoire. By the end of

World War II, Guianese musicians had developed such confidence that they began to demonstrate versatility in jazz. In the early postwar era, the Guianese swing bands that blossomed and composers such as Harry Whittaker and Al Seales created a body of compositions including "Cool Dive" and "Bion Calypso" that are now enshrined as Guyana's jazz standards.

Paralleling these World War II developments in popular music were activities in the "classical" sphere, which drew upon Guyanese poetry to nourish other streams of domestic composition—the tone poem and the art song. Of special significance is Philip Pilgrim's *The Legend of Kaieteur*, based on A. J. Seymour's poem of the same name. That choral fantasy has been recognized as one of the few classical compositions to come from the Anglophone Caribbean during the twentieth century. Among the first things that Lynette Dolphin launched on her return to British Guiana at the end of World War II were the British Guiana Music Teachers' Association and the Schools' Music Festival. Both initiatives attracted ruling-class support as they were founded on a theoretical framework that believed that musical competence and appreciation were key strategies for equipping Guyanese for a more self-determined future. The initial repertoire for these interventions, especially the Schools' Music Festival, were considered too foreign, and the organizers were encouraged to seek more domestic and culturally relevant materials. This was the context that triggered other poem-based compositions such as R. C. G. Potter's "Way Down Demerara" (1951) and "My Guiana, Eldorado" (1952); Francis Percival Loncke's "My Guiana" (n.d.); and Valerie Rodway's "Hymn for Guiana's Children" (1956), all of which are now enshrined as national songs of Guyana.[2] By the end of World War II, Guianese were demonstrating creativity in all genres, including Taan. The nationalist spirit was not muted. The destination as an independent nation was clear.

The early 1950s brought profound change to the colony's body politic. Universal adult suffrage and the 1953 electoral victory of the multiracial People's Progressive Party put the colony on an irreversible road to independence, and this demanded and resulted in shifts in the musical landscape. The compositions emerging out of this period to political independence in 1966 revealed growing levels of musical exchange and confidence to create in any of the musical many genres that were part of the nation's multicultural heritage. In the classical sphere, Hugh Sam ("Fantasia on Three Folk Songs," 1958), Valerie Rodway ("O Beautiful Guiana," 1962), and Patricia Loncke ("The Kiskadee," 1964) not only demonstrated confidence with European styles, they celebrated Guyanese idioms. Tom Charles drew upon "Cumfa, Que Que, the shanties and other British Guiana folk idioms" in his 1959 LP *Fete for So!!!*[3] During the racial violence of the early 1960s, Nesbit Chhangur drew upon the country and western style to deliver "Guyana Lament" with its call for calm and racial reconciliation. Andy Nichols and Johnny Braff appropriated sentimental rock and roll, R&B, and soul to speak to a generation though hits such as "Parting Is Hard" and "It Burns Inside." Hilton Hemerding's "O Guyana" shifted the composition of national songs from variations on Anglo-hymn styles to the more up-beat neo-folk style in 1966.[4]

The politics of the post-independence era was characterized by efforts at decolonizing the Guyanese mind and fostering "attitudinal metamorphosis." The governance practices were dominated by a "vanguard party"—which, despite the rhetoric of "consultative democracy," "worker participation," and "regional decentralization," did not advance good governance as decision-making was not transparent, human rights were not always respected, corruption was rampant, and the national bureaucracy was not effective. The politics of this era deemphasized European and other "bourgeois and decadent" musical genres and encouraged the local. The state and its multitude of agencies adopted several strategies to encourage and promote Guyanese musical creativity. Among the initiatives were state sponsorship of steel bands; Guyfestas and Cultural Center Varieties which sought to identify talent; state-sponsored ensembles such as the CARI Singers, People's Culture Corps, and the Maha Sabha Culture Corps; the musical arms of the uniformed services (the Guyana Police Force Band, the Band Corps of the Guyana Defence Force, the Mobile Theatre and Culture Corps of the Guyana National Service, the steel bands of the Guyana Prison Service and the Onderneeming Boys School); the president's birthday concerts; and musical competitions associated with Mashramani. The yield from these state-sponsored initiatives included a series of iconic recordings such as El Cid's "Local Dish," the LP recordings *Bamboo Fire* and *I Want To Build*, and the emergence of Cali-Mari—a fusion of calypso and Mari Mari pioneered by Neville Calistro, "the Mighty Chief," an Amerindian musician from the Pomeroon and a former member of the People's Culture Corps.

Out of this political climate came deliberate efforts at integrating the musical flavors of Guyana's African, European, and Indian heritages. The Theatre Guild's Quintet featuring Masselall Pollard on sitar, Etwaru Kishore on tabla, Keith Waite of the Guyana Police Force Band on flute, Keith Joseph on upright bass, and Roy Geddes on steel pans was a bold move in this direction. Here the emphasis was on blending classical traditions, especially Indian ragas with African rhythms, European and Caribbean instruments, and Caribbean sensibilities. Terry Nelson's efforts at launching the Afro-Indi beat gave this creative possibility national airing and paved the way for the subsequent popularity of chutney. As the Mighty Enchanter declared in "Come Maugh wid Me," it was the Afro-Indi beat that was the best beat! For him, the bhoom, the Lopi, and the other experiments in finding a distinctly Guyanese beat was not getting the nation on its feet!

Despite the decolonization exhortations, the music of the fete and the nightclub was closely connected with the musical products manufactured for the global Top 100 marketplace. The party bands in Guyana competed to see which one could best copy the industrial, formulaic original product. A joke that still circulated in 2012 contended that some bands copied so effectively that they even included the scratches, hisses, and pops that may have been present on the disc that they listened to during rehearsals. Newspaper columnists bemoaned the blight of "copycatism." This seeming contradiction was the stimulus for creativity and a number of ensembles such as the Dominators, Telstars, and the Yoruba Singers rejected copycatism and created original music that drew upon domestic flavors.

The state-sponsored efforts to promote music to support decolonization were also seen as manifestations of a dictatorial and a racist regime—dictatorial in that it represented the top-down vision of President Burnham being executed by a predominantly African People's National Congress, which by 1972 had declared itself the primary societal institution. The traditions of resistance were mobilized against the PNC starting in the mid-1970s, and new music was created and international music appropriated in the anti-Burnham/PNC resistance. The resistance, coupled with economic decline, led to what has been described as a pressing of the pause button on Guyanese musical creativity. In its place emerged Jamaican-derived roots music. When the People's National Congress was voted out of office in 1992, it was replaced by the predominantly East Indian People's Progressive Party. An immediate consequence was the required introduction of Indian musical elements into the musical aesthetics of the state. The Guyana Police Force Band began to incorporate Indian melodies in its repertoire at public events. After internal tensions surrounding the domination of the public sphere by "Blackman music," the new regime settled down to a variant on bread and circuses, facilitating the promotion of dance hall music and the rehabilitation of steel band. By the end of the twentieth century, expansion of the Christianization of East Indians resulted in emergence of chutney gospel as a popular element in the society's repertoire of sacred music. An example of this genre is Anil Azeez's "In Jesus, Me Can't Die."[5]

To summarize, during the twentieth century Guyanese composed music in a wide range of genres. Table 11.1, based on a convenience sample of 2,000 units of Guyanese twentieth-century music, provides a typology of the dominant and related sub-genres.

Songs made up approximately 94 percent of this sample.[6] Singing has been Guyana's dominant form of musical expression. The fact that songs have dominated the Guyanese soundscape may be indicative of the nature of the society during the twentieth century. As an oral society, songs were important

Table 11.1

Partial List of dominant genres and sub-genres of music composed by Guyanese during the 20th and early 21st centuries

Dominant Genre	Sub-Genres
Classical	Art Songs, Concertos, Marches. Musical Theater, Operas, Symphonies, Tone Poems, Taan
Folk	African Creole folk (e.g., Kwe Kwe), Amerindian folk music, Indian Creole (e.g., Chatini), Masquerade, Work Songs, Shanties, Neo-folk
Pop	Bollywood, Country and Western, Funk, Hip Hop, Jazz, R&B, Rock, Soul
Caribbean and Latin	Bion, Bossa Nova, Calypso, Cha Cha, Mambo, Reggae, Soca, Steel band
Fusion	Afro-Indi, Afrugu, Banshikili, Bhoom, Bion, Calymari, Chutney, Chutney-Soca, Foja, Kwefo, Lopi, Masqui
Religious	Bhajans, Christian liturgical, Gospel, Chutney-Gospel, Hymns, Quesada
Ideological	Party political songs, National and Patriotic songs

Source: Personal collection, and from a list provided by Dr. Paloma Mohamed from her 2006 dissertation "Communicative Power and Social Change in the Caribbean: The Cases of Guyana and Trinidad and Tobago" (University of the West Indies, Faculty of Social Sciences, Department of Behavioural Sciences, St. Augustine, Trinidad).

vehicles for cultural transmission, identity maintenance, social mobilization, and vocalizing resistance.

Instrumental music in Guyana, especially in the classical realm, was composed primarily for the piano and could be considered a barometer on the state of musical literacy in the society. Herman Snijders and Joycelynne Loncke included Clement Nichols (1896–1962), Philip Pilgrim (1917–1944), Valerie Rodway (1919–1970), William Pilgrim (1920–2006), Joyce Ferdinand-Saunders (1923–), and Hugh Sam (1934–) in their list of the major composers of classical music for the pianoforte in the Guianas during the twentieth century.[7] The audience for these compositions, especially the more complex compositions, has been limited to the musically literate. However, compositions in this genre tended to be more accessible when they were variations on folk song melodies. In the latter case, Hugh Sam, Joyce Ferdinand, and to some extent Valerie Rodway may have been the most accessible classical composers during the twentieth century. A similar dynamic obtained for instrumental popular music. Pop instrumentals based on folk melodies, a folk song, or special venues were popular as those attributes made interpreting easy. This may explain the success of "Kissing Bridge" by Bumble and the Saints or "Rudy's Delight" by Rudy and the Roosters.

During most of the twentieth century, the piano dominated musical creativity in urban and rural musical communities. By the second decade of the twentieth century, the piano was pervasive. In addition to being an important instrument for family recreation, the piano was a special piece of furniture in some homes as an indicator of upward mobility. As a result of this diffusion, the piano became the foundation instrument for music education, and because of its melodic, harmonic, and dynamic range became the primary instrument to accompany church and school choirs. In Indian Guyanese musical communities, the harmonium was one of the dominant musical instruments.

Brass and woodwind were the instruments of the military and the Salvation Army. Those were among the few institutions that trained Guyanese on those instruments. After World War II the steel pan became a popular instrument and maintained that status until the 1980s, when state sponsorship dwindled as a result of the failing economy. The fundamental instruments in Guyana for most of the twentieth century were drums. The making of these instruments and learning to play them were an important part of cultural transmission and a site for innovation. Across the twentieth century Guyanese of all ancestral origins played drums from hollowed-out tree trunks, barrel staves, puncheon drums, and various lengths of PVC pipe. In addition, a wide range of membranes from goatskin to X-ray film were used in making these instruments. The calendar of folk events and religious activities provided the venues where the older generation mentored and trained the younger generation in the many "hands" of drumming. In the hinterland, the drum had a central role in religious and celebratory events. In predominantly African villages, Kwe Kwe and Cumfa ceremonies were important teaching and learning sites. In Indian villages the mandir was the key location for learning to play the dholak, dhantal, cymbals, and harmonium. By the end of the twentieth century "Teacher" Raghunandan and the Primo Brothers had established drum-making establishments, and along with Buxton Fusion had created private schools to train the next generation of drummers. Other percussive instruments in the society included maracas/shak shak, dhantal, and "iron." Among the hinterland communities, the carapaces of beetles were strung together to make rattles. In Indian communities it was not unknown to find ghungroos made from bottlecaps. With the arrival of electrified instruments, the guitar became popular in the 1950s and thereafter. From the 1970s, the increasingly portable electronic keyboard appeared and became a popular instrument in Guyanese music making.

The term *production* is used here to refer to the mechanical and industrial processes used in moving musical creativity to more permanent platforms—sheet music, phonographs, audiocassettes, CD/DVD, and on servers for Internet download. It involves the application of technology and the aesthetics of sound. The process also incorporates distribution of the finished production to consumers. Government policies—including tax and incentives regimes, access to recording facilities, legal regimes regulating the operation of record stores, and the protection of intellectual property—determined the production and distribution of music in Guyana. The recording studio established at Radio Demerara in 1957 was a function of a deal between Rediffusion International, a London-based company, and the British government on the development of commercial broadcasting in the West Indies after World War II with the aim of bringing broadcasting to "Her Majesty's loyal subjects in the West Indies."[8] The specifics for the British Guiana operations were refined in an agreement with the government of the colony. Like Radio Jamaica, Rediffusion Barbados, and Radio Trinidad, Radio Demerara had a monopoly of the broadcast spectrum and by extension the advertising market. For this privilege Radio Demerara relayed approximately 22 hours of BBC programs per week and provided the government of British Guiana with ninety minutes of time daily.[9] About 55 percent of Radio Demerara's programming came from imported recorded music. A 1957 Rediffusion publication describing its music programming practices of the West Indian network noted:

> Much of the current ephemeral popular music come from the United Kingdom, many popular music recordings of a more lasting character from the U.S.A., a country which has made a long study of producing recordings expressly for broadcasting purposes and designed to facilitate program compilation. Through the activities of its subsidiary, International Library Services Ltd., the Rediffusion Group has, for some time past, been in a position to provide recordings of this specialized type. More serious musical recordings are generally obtained from the United Kingdom.[10]

Radio Demerara's music programming was augmented with "programmes of local interest." This category of programming included in-studio performances featuring "singers, instrumentalists, comedians, vocal groups and choirs, calypso singers, steel bands . . . dance orchestras, police and militia bands," and local talent shows.[11] The goal behind the "programs of local interest" was to increase listenership and increase advertising revenue. To support the production of local musical content, Radio Demerara's production facilities in the early 1950s included "a concert studio capable of staging shows on a considerable scale and accommodating a studio audience of 80; while there were two smaller general purpose studios."[12] These studios were built according to "modern designs" and incorporated "the latest techniques in layout and acoustic treatment."[13] With this policy framework and production and distribution infrastructure, Radio Demerara dominated music making and the formation of musical tastes in the colony. As we discussed in an earlier chapter, Vivian Lee was able to use brokerage practices to bring some diversity to what was a conservative Anglo-American musical palette. Visibly absent were the musical tastes and expressions of the working class.

Al Seales sought to correct this when he established General Electrical and Musicians Service (GEMS) in the late 1940s. Seales was not the beneficiary of special incentives from the government of British Guiana. He did not broker any deal or reach any agreement with the colonial government. His equipment was limited to recording technologies. He had the ambition of establishing a pressing plant. However, according to Ray Seales, that ambition did not materialize because the authorities "said he wasn't qualified to run a boiler operated machine."[14] Further, as was said earlier, GEMS experienced problems with the gatekeepers of musical taste at Radio Demerara. Despite those barriers, GEMS with its house band the Caribbean All Stars, featuring Basie Thomas, Al Seales, Harry Whittaker, "Bongo" Charlie, and Rector Schultz, went on to create a distinctive and unmatched sound that attracted regional calypsonians and made his products marketable in the wider Caribbean and around the world through arrangements with Melodisc Records in the United Kingdom. One recording, "Melvina" by Norman Beaton, reached the top of the Trinidad hit parade during the 1950s.[15] When the gatekeepers at the local radio station kept GEMS recordings off the air, Seales partnered with the franchise holder for Selectomatic jukeboxes in British Guiana, and GEMS recordings reached audiences in restaurants, cake shops, and restaurants—popular venues with working people. King Cobra sang the praises of this technology in his calypso "Selectomatic Juke Box."

Al Seales sold his 45 rpm recordings to the DJs who operated the jukeboxes. By the 1950s jukeboxes had become popular music delivery systems at dances and private parties in in British Guiana. The diffusion of radiograms and record players also created a market for GEMS recordings. By the 1960s, the size of a record collection, like the brand of radiogram or the size of the speakers, was a status symbol. By establishing Guyana Radio and Electronics Company (GRECO), the radio and stereo assembly plant at Victoria Village on the East Coast Demerara, the government of Guyana supported one aspect of the music distribution equation—access to playback technologies.

The re-migration scheme, aimed at repatriating Guyanese and Caribbean nationals, was also a site where government policy affected music production. Terry Nelson was a re-migrant when he established Halagala in the early post-independence era. All participants in the re-migration scheme enjoyed some benefits. Those who came back to work in the public sector got their passages to Guyana paid and were granted duty-free importation of personal effects, domestic appliances, and personal motor vehicles. Those who came back to enter into the private sector received a number of incentives such as the duty-free importation of equipment and supplies and a tax holiday. Terry Nelson enjoyed those benefits. Halagala was established as a full-service recording business—recording studio, pressing plant, house band, A&M services, and a sales outlet. In Nelson's case the size of the Guyanese market, his production aesthetics, and his product mix did not make for a winning business model. He too had problems with the gatekeepers in the radio system. Unlike Al Seales's GEMS, Nelson's Halagala was never able establish a presence in the wider Caribbean. He was, however, able to capitalize on the increasing number of Guyanese who wanted to "cut a record" for vanity reasons. In the process, Halagala pioneered the Afro-Indi beat, a precursor of chutney music in Guyana. By the end of the twentieth century, Nelson had gotten out of the recording business and had migrated to low-watt commercial community television.

Eddy Grant's presence in Barbados is testimony to the significance of policy-driven environments and reliable infrastructure in locating music industries. Grant is proud of his Guyanese heritage. He is a sophisticated businessman. When he was making his decision to relocate to the Caribbean from the UK in the 1970s, he had to be aware of the nationalization policies of the Government of Guyana and the unreliability of Guyana's electrical power supply. Those realities did not encourage decisions to locate a cutting-edge recording facility in Guyana. Further, in the competition to attract businesses, Guyana was unable to compete with the incentives offered by Barbados. So Blue Wave Studios and ICE Records were established in Barbados. The rest is history. Blue Wave Studios and Ice Records transformed Barbadian music and are directly responsible for the sustained level of high-quality popular music in Barbados. It was not until the 1990s and the advent of digital technologies that ambitions to establish full-service music production facilities were rekindled in Guyana. By the end of the twentieth century and the first decades of the twenty-first century, the PPP government had started to offer a range of tax incentives aimed at nurturing and supporting music production in Guyana. The digital age has removed the need for specialized pressing plants. The only pressing plant in Guyana during the twentieth century was the one operated by Terry Nelson's Halagala Studios.

The production of records is only one aspect of the process. An equally important step is distribution. Here again, radio played an important role in bringing new products to the attention of the public. Over the history of radio broadcasting in Guyana, there have been concerns about radio's role as the nation's musical gatekeeper and allegations of payola or restrictions based on

Figure 11.1. Music cart in Georgetown. Photograph courtesy of the author.

ethnicity or class. As has been noted recently, radio broadcasting was not the only distribution mechanism in Guyana during the twentieth century. The gramophone, the jukebox, and later the radiograms, stereo sets, tape recorders, and portable CD and MP3 players became important distribution mechanisms. The commercial sector introduced hire-purchase packages as early as the 1920s to encourage the purchase of gramophones so as to encourage and sustain the sales of records. The arrival of tape as a distribution device, especially audiocassette tapes, introduced a new technology for the distribution of music in Guyana—illegal duplication, or piracy. At the end of the twentieth century, piracy was institutionalized in Guyana and was even recognized in some government quarters as a legitimate form of employment. The music cart became an important vehicle for the marketing of pirated music. Figure 11.1 is a photograph of a music cart in Georgetown.

In summary, government policies and the state of the national infrastructure, especially the supply and delivery of power, exerted significant influence on the nature and scope of music production and distribution in Guyana during the twentieth century. This reality did not give Guyana a robust production and distribution infrastructure, and as such Guyana has been unable to produce music products of consistent quality.

For the centenary celebrations in 1931, W. McDavid wrote an article titled "The Progress of Music in British Guiana." In that article she observed, "it is not given to all to excel as composers or as performers of music, but where the power of expression is limited, there may be considerable development in the appreciative faculty."[16] The contexts in which Guyanese have consumed music across the twentieth century have demonstrated the scope and depth of the society's "appreciative faculty." Throughout the twentieth century Guyanese consumed music in a number of contexts and for a number of purposes. Music helped make work easier. Music was part of the passage of life—birth, puberty, marriage, christenings, and death. Music released tensions and resisted oppressive political contexts. The portable technologies such as the transistor radio, 8-track and cassette tape formats, CD, and MP3 players made music portable. Music was consumed in homes, on the road, in churches and temples, in bars, cake shops, nightclubs, cinemas, rice-bonds, and in minibuses. Music launched fashion statements and contributed to the vernacular language. Music consumption varied by time of the day, day of the week, and season of the year. In the process, music created the soundtrack for each generation of the twentieth century.

The type of music consumed in Guyana was an important indicator of generational taste and a valuable indicator of intergenerational tensions. The rock and roll fan of the 1950s and 1960s could be a rabid hater of hip hop and dance hall at the end of the century! Musical tastes could also be indicators of class identity and aspirations. At the end of the twentieth century, there was a category of music known as "oldies," the perennial favorites from the "golden age" of radio broadcasting that are essential ingredients in any Guyanese party at home or in the diaspora. "Oldies" are popular across race, class, and generational lines.

The recent exploration of the dynamic of music production, distribution, and consumption in Guyana during the twentieth century would be incomplete without attention to the consequences of those dynamics at the societal, community, and individual level. What follows are conclusions about those consequences. Despite the various ideological orientations that determined the governance of Guyanese society during the twentieth century, even governmental efforts to impose musical tastes, Guyana remained a sonically open society. The nation's soundscape was cosmopolitan. From this soundscape came ideas about rights, justice, lifestyles, and aspirations for material and spiritual goods. This musical amalgam created a powerful social force in Guyanese society.

What have been the consequences of the interplay of governance and the creation, production, distribution, and consumption of music in a society with a constellation of persistent problems over the twentieth century? Did music reinforce the superiority complexes generated by the dominant ideologies that have flavored the orientation and practices of national governance during the twentieth century? Did music undermine the inferiority complexes and cultural cringe associated with the history of colonial and imperial domination? Did music contribute to the development of the cultural cosmopolitanism required for envisioning and nurturing an inclusive and just future for the multi-ethnic nation? Did the potential for musical exchange materialize—and if so, what has been the yield? Answers to these questions must be sought at the macro-social, community, and individual levels.

The term *macro-social* is used here to refer to the entire society. Across the twentieth century there has been evidence of the ruling class and their allies using music as a tool in formal, non-formal, and informal educational contexts to manufacture consent and as a device to inculcate certain beliefs, attitudes, and behaviors. This practice was evident during the three periods considered in this book, and has resulted in the creation of a body of patriotic music that has been important as building blocks in expressing Guyanese identity. "The Song of Guiana's Children," "My Native Land," and "O Guiana" are examples from this repertoire that can ignite a feeling of nationality over the particulars of ethnicity. In addition to patriotic songs, national policies and governance practices also stimulated musical creativity in multiple genres, including innovations that emerged from exchanges among the nation's multiple musical heritages. Afro-Indi, the bhoom, Caly-Mari, and the Lopi are examples that suggest musical exchange.

The repertoires of the military and other state-funded ensembles and the music policies of radio in Guyana since World War II exposed the Guyanese society to a wide range of international musical expressions: the European classical canon; American spirituals, standards, jazz, country & western, rock and roll, and soul; British pop; mambo, cha cha, salsa, and Indian film music. Through the end of the twentieth century, the signature tunes for important radio programs were derived from European and American classical canons. The theme music for the major prime time newscast was Holtz's "Jupiter"; Sousa provided the theme for the daily sportscast. Guyanese have more than passing awareness of African-derived music, especially Caribbean and Latin American variants. Guyanese can be erudite in a conversation on the history of calypso or the development of reggae.

Music has served as an important asset in projecting Guyana in the international arena. In the 1920s the British Guiana Militia Band's performance at Wembley established it as one of the best military bands in the British Empire. Those were important bragging rights. In the late colonial period and the early post-colonial era, Guyana used the steel band as an important plank in its public diplomacy. In 1963 the PPP sent a steel band to Cuba, and during the 1970s the PNC sent pannists/pan technologists to Tanzania and Cuba to establish steel band ensembles in those countries.[17]

Across the twentieth century, the various players in the governance of the society have, in an inconsistent manner, invested and deployed national assets in the promotion and encouragement of music in Guyana. These investments range from subventions to church and schools, support for the schools music festivals, and national festivals of music during the colonial era. In the era of internal self-governance, the National History and Culture Week festivals were another investment. The post-colonial era brought not only an expanded range of events but also changes in qualitative orientation. Of special significance was the replacement of the regular, competitive national festival of music with Guyfesta, a national event in which competition was replaced by recognition of participation. Engagement replaced critical evaluation and this had an unintended consequence—the decline in musical literacy and declines in competence.

Wider national policy and political practices also influenced music in Guyanese society. The social and economic crises that started in the mid-1970s amplified the relationship between macro-level policy and musical culture. One of the consequences of this economic and social crisis has been dramatic increases in emigration and the loss of skilled manpower. The loss of Guyanese with competence in all musical genres has had a negative impact on music making in Guyana. A limited range of musical instruments were used in music making in Guyana at the end of the twentieth century. At the end of the twentieth century, there was one violin teacher in Guyana. Another result of emigration has been the loss of musical memory; many childhood lullabies, school yard songs, national songs, masquerade chants/toasts, and the ancestral folk repertoire can be lost unless there is some systematic intervention. Because of the massive departure of the Guyanese starting in the early 1960s and accelerating since the late 1970s, Guyana has lost the benefits of music criticism. So there is little if any informed discourse on musical aesthetics and experimentation. This has indubitably slowed down the potential of musical exchange and experimentation in all genres of music.

At the end of the twentieth century, despite the world-class status of individual Guyanese musicians living in the diaspora, there is the pervasive opinion that during the twentieth century Guyana did not produce any enduring internationally popular music genres. There is no Guyanese equivalent to reggae, dancehall, soca, mambo, meringue, bachata, or zouk. The international popularity of reggae, dancehall, and soca has benefitted the economies and national identities of both Jamaica and the twin island republic of Trinidad and Tobago. According to dancehall music scholar Sonja Stanley Niaah, "[in 1999], Jamaican music generated more than 1.2 billion in US dollars, and in 2000, estimates of overall worldwide earnings from exports of reggae music went as high as 2.5 billion US dollars."[18] The names of the soccer teams that represented Jamaica and Trinidad in the World Cup tournaments in 2006 and 2010 were "Reggae Boyz" and the "Soca Warriors," respectively. Reggae and soca have become powerful public diplomacy assets, winning hearts and minds around the world for Jamaica and Trinidad. Reflecting on the engagement of Guyanese governments with Guyanese musical life, former President Janet Jagan concluded that the PPP government and all governments of Guyana in the post-independence era had not invested enough in music.[19]

The term *community level* can be used to refer to ethnic, gender, or geographic formations. In all of these categories it is possible to discern a number of consequences. In multi-ethnic Guyanese society, musical achievement generated ethnic pride as it demonstrated ethnic achievement. Despite internal class divisions, the achievements of Philip Pilgrim, Alyce Fraser, Rudolph Dunbar, Ken "Snakehips" Johnson, Lynette Dolphin, Bill Rogers, and Eddy Grant, among others, on the international stage were sources of pride for Guyanese of African ancestry. Similar pride was derived by East Indians from the achievements of the Mootoo Brothers, Bal Gangadur Tillack, Rosemary Ramdehol, Terry Gajraj, and other musicians of Indian ancestry. Among the Portuguese, the achievements of Frank Brazzao, Gun Fernandez, and others also generated ethnic pride. Ray Luck's achievement as a world-class pianist and adjudicator was of immense pride for Guyanese of Chinese ancestry. David Campbell's recognition as an important musical voice of the First Peoples of the Americas has been the source of pride for Guyanese of Amerindian ancestry. The musical creativity of Basil Rodrigues, the Mighty Chief along with the Calistro Band, and Guy Marco have been influential voices celebrating Amerindian achievement in Guyana. There are some musicians such as Dave Martins (a Guyanese of European ancestry) whose achievements in the post-independence era have served to generate national pride more than for a specific ethnic sector of the society. In actual fact, there has always been this ambivalence between ethnic and national pride associated with the achievements of Guyanese musicians.

Musical achievement is also the source for gender pride. Throughout the twentieth century it was women who were the cornerstones for music education in Guyanese society. Starting with Mrs. Cassell's work in the early decades of the twentieth century, urban and rural women have been the nation's principal music teachers. Nell Kerry (née Brown), E. McDavid, Ruby McGregor, Millicent Joseph, Edna Jordan, Lynette Dolphin, Vesta Lowe, Mrs. Fox, Sister Vanessa, Edith Pieters, Joyce Aaron, and Janet Hunt are just a few of these women whose efforts contributed to the development of performance techniques and music appreciation. It was primarily women who led in the creation and management of crucial national institutions such as the British Guiana Music Teachers' Association, the British Guiana Festivals of Music, and the National History and Arts Council—institutions that have exerted substantial influence on the musical directions of the society.

It is at the level of the geographic community—the county, village, and settlement—that we see the important role that music has played in preserving and transmitting Guyana's multicultural musical heritage and generating regional pride. There was always a musical competitiveness among the more urbanized counties of Demerara and Berbice. The virtual clean sweep by Berbice of the major prizes at the first British Guiana Festival of Music was a major moment in Berbician pride and directed the nation's attention to the musical talents from Berbice. This musical competitiveness was also evident in other genres of music. Musicians and orchestras from Berbice, such as Bal Gangadur Tillack and the Dil Bihar Orchestra have exerted dominance over Indian music in Guyana. The massive Essequibo has been the nursery for the folk shanties associated with the work of harvesting Guyana's hinterland resources; the flora, fauna, and geographies that have inspired patriotic musical compositions; and the indigenous genres, Banshikilli and Caly-Mari.

At the level of villages and settlements where face-to-face communication and similar patterns of interpersonal communication dominates, music has been central to community life in Guyana across the twentieth century. Music played an important role in cultural transmission. It is in the villages and settlements, through Mari Mari, Kwe Kwe, Cumfa, Matticore, Yags, and other events that the rhythms, melodies, and memories were passed on from one generation to another. In some villages an individual musician may embody many of the musical traditions of that village. For example, in Kitty Village on the East Coast of Demerara, there was Joe Taylor, the Village Crier, who was described as being versatile on all drums. He was the core of the village's masquerade band and the preferred tassa drummer for Dig Dutty ceremonies. Most villages had a musical ensemble to support rites of passage and support relaxation.[20]

Ethnomusicologists point out that in the dynamic process of creating sound that is socially accepted as music, a range of benefits accrue to musicians, and among them are prestige and status. Across the twentieth century, music has provided a space for Guyanese to seek distinction and gain prestige in many genres of music. Some did it well and earned national and international accolades. Some Guyanese musicians attained iconic status and received colonial and, later, national awards for their contributions to music. In the post-independence period, the government of Guyana awarded a few scholarships for Guyanese to study music overseas. For those beneficiaries, the opportunity to study overseas improved technique and widened musical vistas.

As it is in all societies influenced by European traditions, music in Guyana during the twentieth century was influenced by ruling-class patrons.

The individuals, institutions, and processes associated with the governance of Guyana across the twentieth century intentionally and unintentionally exerted substantial influence on music. In the post-independence era, the state and its charismatic leaders became the most active patrons. This had a number of consequences, among them expectations that the state would subsidize all aspects of music, including ensuring sustained employment. This expectation and dependency had negative consequences, as it nurtured an attitude among some musicians that they had already mastered their craft and had nothing more to learn. Further, it contributed to the jettisoning of critical appraisal and the tendency to "applaud" every effort as an achievement—a function of the reluctance to offend. These factors, coupled with the loss of music teachers, contributed to the lack of progress of Guyanese music during the latter decades of the twentieth century.

Despite efforts at censorship and control, Guyanese musicians demonstrated the capacity to shine the spotlight on the dark corners of the society and, in the process, call for accountability and demand effective and efficient use of the nation's scarce resources. Musicians, especially those emerging from the dominated sectors of the society, demonstrated that the dominated sectors of society are capable of demanding participation in defining the present and imagining the future. These attributes will be important ingredients in the construction of a democratic and caring twenty-first-century Guyana.

Music will continue to have a crucial role in Guyana's social, political, and economic life in the twenty-first century. Despite the above-mentioned lack of progress at the end of the twentieth century, Guyana has a range of assets to build a positive musical future. Among them is a young population that continues to demonstrate musical inquisitiveness. There is also the persistence of a number of institutions that have historically piloted musical development in the society. These include churches and other religious bodies, which encourage and support the acquisition of musical competencies. The evangelical denominations, especially the Assemblies of God, are particularly active. In the 2008 song competition sponsored by Guyana Telephone and Telegraph (GT&T), six of the top ten winners came from evangelical denominations, including the Assemblies of God.

In addition to the bands of the Guyana Police Force and the Guyana Defence Force, the Guyana Music Teachers' Association and the Woodside Choir are other examples of the persistence of institutions committed to promoting musical competence. Despite migration and other factors that have depleted their ranks, these organizations have remained active and, in the early decades of the twenty-first century, resuscitated the Guyana Festival of Music. The Center for Communication Studies at the University of Guyana introduced a course in cultural journalism in 2010, and this can ultimately contribute to the revival of music criticism. There is need for professional critics with the capability to offer a theory-based assessment of Guyanese musical creativity, as there is also the need for informed consumers.

In recent years, the private sector has contributed to the resuscitation of musical life in Guyana. Banks, such as the Republic Bank, since 2006 have sponsored the annual Mashramani steel band competition and sponsored workshops by leading international performers. Other companies have invested in recording studios and have kept the important "impresario" tradition alive by promoting concerts that feature major international artists, especially performers of popular genres such as hip hop, reggae, dancehall, and soca. The public sector, recognizing the ongoing importance of entertainment, has invested in the infrastructure to support the distribution of music in the future. The National Stadium at Providence, East Bank Demerara; the world-class stage built for Carifesta 2008; upgrades at the National Cultural Center; and the increased studio and field production capacity of the National Communication Network are examples.

The philanthropic and diplomatic communities are contributing to Guyanese musical life. The Tina Insanally Foundation was established to promote music education among poor and underserved communities in urban and rural coastal Guyana. The diplomatic community contributes by bringing in musicians as part of their public diplomatic efforts. The Indian High Commission's Indian Cultural Center is an important education and training site for Indian musical traditions in Guyana. The United States embassy has an active music program, one element being the annual visit by a military band to be part of the embassy's July 4th celebrations. By the end of the twentieth century, these annual visits included master classes and workshops for musicians in Guyana's uniformed services. As China and Russia expand their economic presence in Guyana, their use of music in their public diplomacy may also expands.

Migration patterns have always influenced musical life in Guyana. This dynamic continues. Since the last decade of the twentieth century, there has been an explosion of gold mining in Guyana's hinterland. This has attracted large numbers of Brazilian miners, who have established operations in the hinterland and support institutions in urban and rural communities. One consequence of this development is musical exchange. Request programs on the local radio station are already featuring fojo music and influencing Guyanese musicians such as the Calistro Band, led by Neville Calistro (the Mighty Chief), who in 2011 released a CD of fojo-influenced music.

Guyana's diaspora has been a vital variable in the nation's musical life. Successful musicians over the century—Alyce Fraser-Denny, Rudolph Dunbar, Rannie "Sweet Lips" Hart, Ken "Snakehips" Johnson, Dave Martins, Terry

Gajraj, Eddy Grant, and Dr. Ray Luck—have stirred national pride and served as models. Musicians in the Guyanese diaspora have also been vectors for new musical ideas and techniques. At the start of the twenty-first century, the musical expertise resident in the Guyanese diaspora is phenomenal and, based on ongoing conversations on social media sites, there is substantial interest in developing partnerships with musicians in Guyana.

The tradition of active government engagement in music making has cultivated an orientation that expects the public sector to play a pivotal role in facilitating music making, especially in providing employment. The future of music in Guyanese society cannot be left solely to the public sector. The development of music in Guyana demands a national partnership. In the new relationship, the public sector must partner with other societal entities to ensure the provision of adequate, quality music education that is accessible to all Guyanese. This would increase the quality of musical performance and ensure that the society respects the intellectual property rights associated with the creation of music, specifically curbing of piracy and the payment of royalties for music played on the state-owned and private radio and television outlets.

The partnership must also be multidimensional. The academic community must encourage more writing about Guyana's musical history and support the study of ethnomusicology. The participatory methods demanded for both of these academic fields will enrich Guyanese historiography as it will have to seek out and give voice to sectors of the society that have been hitherto muted or silent. This will contribute to making Guyana's collective history more nuanced and accessible.

One of the challenges facing contemporary multi-ethnic Guyana is addressing the problem of pervasive ignorance of the collective history. Understanding this history will reveal a common humanity and contribute to the undermining and exorcising of racial myths and stereotypes that have retarded progress and national development. Among the works that call for immediate attention are biographies of musicians and musical families. The current ethnomusicological work being conducted by Gillian Greaves-Richards, Rohan Sagar, and Deo Persaud must be complemented and expanded. The partnership to encourage and nurture music development in Guyana must also promote composition in all genres of music. It is passing strange that Guyanese have not yet developed a compositional tradition based on its rich bird songs. Guyana's song birds are as melodious as those expressed in Heitor Villa-Lobos' *Uirapurú* (The Organ Wren), Leopold Mozart's Cuckoo in *Kindersymphonie,* or Olivier Messiaen's *Oiseaux Exotiques.*

Responding to these challenges and opportunities requires an enlightened, enabling environment and effective coordinating mechanisms. The trend in this direction was evident under Deryck Bernard's tenure as Minister of

Education and has been consolidated since 1992 through the creation of a discrete Ministry of Culture and the articulation of a number of national cultural policy drafts.

In 2006 Dr. Frank Anthony was appointed Minister of Culture, Youth, and Sport. During his tenure, he has supervised or supported a number of initiatives that could have a positive impact of music in Guyana in the future. These have included revising the national cultural policy in 2008, the staging of Carifesta X in 2008, and the return of the Guyana Music Festival in 2009. For Carifesta X, the Ministry of Culture, Youth, and Sport established the National Steel Orchestra—a first step in the rehabilitation of steel band music in Guyana. The National School of Music was established in November 2011.

It is hoped that this contribution to the story of musical life in twentieth century Guyana provides a platform for deeper and more robust explorations of music in Guyana and its role in articulating Guyanese pain, achievements, and aspirations.

Notes

Preface and Acknowledgments

1. For further details see "Obituary—William Rutherford Alexander Pilgrim (August 27, 1920–April 17, 2006)," in *Sunday Stabroek*, April 30, 2006. Available online at guygenbiosociety .blogspot.com/2007/12/william-rutherford-alexander-pilgrim.html. Accessed May 1, 2011.

2. The Philip Pilgrim Memorial Harp was the most prestigious award granted "to a candidate who passed in Grade 6 to the Diploma of the Associated Board of the Royal Schools of Music . . . and who, in the examiner's opinion, possesses outstanding musicianship." Guyana Music Teachers' Association, *50th Anniversary Souvenir Brochure* (Georgetown, Guyana, 1998, 7 & 26).

Introduction

1. For further details see "Obituary—William Rutherford Alexander Pilgrim (August 27, 1920–April 17, 2006)," in *Sunday Stabroek*, April 30, 2006. guygenbiosociety.blogspot .com/2007/12/william-rutherford-alexander-pilgrim.html. Accessed May 1, 2011.

2. The Philip Pilgrim Memorial Harp was the most prestigious award granted "to a candidate who passed in Grade 6 to the Diploma of the Associated Board of the Royal Schools of Music . . . and who, in the examiner's opinion, possesses outstanding musicianship." Guyana Music Teachers' Association *50th Anniversary Souvenir Brochure*. Georgetown, Guyana, 1998. 7, 26.

Chapter 1

1. R. H. Major (transl. and ed.). *Letters of Christopher Columbus, with Other Original Documents Relating to his Four Voyages to the New World* (London: Hakhyt Society, 1961).

2. For details on the Amerindian presence in early Guyana, see W. Edwards and K. Gibson. "An Ethnohistory of Amerindians in Guyana." *Ethnohistory*, Vol. 26, No. 2. (Spring, 1979): 161–75; Denis Williams. *Ancient Guyana*. Kingston, Jamaica: Ian Randle Press, 2005; and Hazel Woolford, "Climate change and the movement of people to Guiana," *Stabroek News*, April 8, 2010, available online and accessed August 6, 2011. At the end of the twentieth century, there were nine ethnic groups among the Amerindians in Guyana: Ackawaio, Arawak, Arekuna, Carib, Macushi, Patamona, Wai Wai, Warrau, and Wapishana.

3. For details on this history see Vere T. Daly, *A Short History of the Guyanese People* (London: Macmillan, 1993).

4. Walter Rodney. *A History of the Guyanese Working People, 1881-1905* (London: Heinemann Educational Books, 1981), 1.

5. See Sir Walter Raleigh, *The discoverie of the large, rich and bewtiful Empire of Guiana.* London, 1596; also D. W. Meinig, *The Shaping of America: A Geographical Perspective on 500 Years of History. Volume 1: Atlantic America, 1492-1800* (New Haven: Yale University Press, 1986), 40–41.

6. See Mellissa Ifill, "Creating and solidifying African ethnic identity in Guyana," in "History This Week," *Stabroek News*, September 23, 2010. www.stabroeknews.com/2010/features/09/23/creating-and-solidifying-african-ethnic-identity-in-guiana/. Accessed September 23, 2010.

7. Rodney, *A History of the Guyanese Working People*, 3.

8. Brian Moore, *Cultural Power, Resistance and Pluralism: Colonial Guyana 1838–1900* (Montreal and Kingston: McGill-Queen's University Press and University of the West Indies Press, 1995), 93–94.

9. Eric Williams, "The Historical Background of British Guiana's Problems." *Journal of Negro History* 30, no. 4 (October 1945): 357–81.

10. The slave trade ended in 1808. However, an illegal trade continued throughout most of the nineteenth century to Cuba and Brazil.

11. For details on indentured workers from Africa and the British West Indies, see Barbara P. Josiah, "After Emancipation: Aspects of Village Life in Guyana, 1869–1911." *Journal of Negro History* 82, no. 1 (Winter, 1997): 105–21. For references to immigrants from Malta and Germany, see Richard Schomburgk, *Travels in British Guiana 1840-1844, Volume 1.* Translated and Edited by Walter E. Roth (Georgetown, British Guiana: Daily Chronicle, 1923), 18–29.

12. Carl A. Braithwaite, "The African-Guyanese demographics 1838–1988." In Granger, et al. (eds.), *Themes in African-Guyanese History.* Georgetown: Free Press, 1998.

13. Tina Ramnarine, *Creating Their Own Space: The Development of an Indian-Caribbean Musical Tradition* (Jamaica: University of the West Indies Press, 2001).

14. For further details on Pidgin-English, see "Tower of Babel" in Robert McCrum, Robert MacNeil, and William Cran, *The Story of English* (London: Penguin, 2003), 215–19.

15. For a substantial discussion of this practice, see Dena J. Epstein, *Sinful Tunes and Spirituals: Black Folk Music to the Civil War* (Chicago: University of Illinois Press, 1977), 7–17.

16. See Roger D. Abrahams and John F. Szwed, *After Africa: Extracts from British Travel Accounts and Journals of the Seventeenth, Eighteenth, and Nineteenth Centuries concerning the Slaves, Their Manners, and Customs in the British West Indies* (New Haven: Yale University Press, 1983), and Trevor Burnard, *Hearing Slaves Speak* (Guyana: Caribbean Press, 2010) for reports on the presence of African musical instruments, including the banjar in eighteenth-century Guyana.

17. B. Moore, *Cultural Power, Resistance and Pluralism*, 93–94.

18. Peter Manuel. *East Indian Music in the West Indies: Taan Singing, Chutney, and the Making of Indo-Caribbean Culture* (Philadelphia: Temple University Press, 2000), 22–23.

19. Ibid., 8.

20. Tina K. Ramnarine, "Brotherhood of the Boat: Musical Dialogues in a Caribbean Context." *British Journal of Ethnomusicology* 7 (1977): 2.

21. Monica Schuler, *Alas, Alas, Kongo: A Social History of Indentured African Immigration into Jamaica, 1841-1865* (Baltimore: Johns Hopkins Press, 1980).

22. *Jhaji Bhai* = shipmate.

23. See B. Moore, *Cultural Power, Resistance and Pluralism*, 244–53.

24. For further details on this topic see the various publications on the Portuguese in Guyana, especially Mary Noel Menezes, *The Portuguese of Guyana: A Study in Culture and Conflict* (India: self-published, ca. 1992).

25. See Moore, *Cultural Power, Resistance and Pluralism*, 265.

26. Clem Seecharan, *Muscular Learning: Cricket and Education in the Making of the British West Indies at the End of the 19th Century* (Kingston, Jamaica: Ian Randle, 2006), 2.

27. See M. Shahabuddeen, *Constitutional Development in Guyana 1621-1978* (Georgetown, Guyana: self-published, 1978).

28. James Rodway, *Hand-book of British Guiana* (Georgetown, British Guiana: Columbian Exposition Literary Committee of the Royal Agricultural and Commercial Society, 1893), 17–18.

29. Anthony Kirk-Greene, *On Crown Service: A History of HM Colonial and Overseas Service 1837–1997* (London: I. B. Tauris, 1999), 10.

30. Other nineteenth-century governors: Sir Benjamin d'Urban (1831–33), Sir James Carmichael Smyth (1833–38), Sir Henry Barkly (1849–53), Sir Francis Hicks (1862–85), James Robert Longden (1874–77), Sir Henry Turner Irving (1882–87), and Viscount Gormanston (1888–93).

31. For a discussion on the "dignified and efficient," see Walter Bagehot, *The English Constitution* (Oxford: Oxford University Press, 1929).

32. Thomas August *The Selling of the Empire: British and French Imperialist Propaganda, 1890–1940* (Westport, CT: Greenwood Press, 1985), 2.

33. For details, see Emília Viotti da Costa, *Crowns of Glory, Tears of Blood: The Demerara Slave Rebellion of 1823* (Oxford: Oxford University Press, 1994).

34. Earl Grey, "On the population of the Colony of British Guiana, as Enumerated on the 31st of March, 1851. Being the substance of a dispatch from Governor Barkly, presented to the Society of the Right Hon. Earl Grey, Her Majesty's late Secretary of State for the Colonies." *Journal of the Statistical Society of London* 15 (September 1852): 234.

35. H. Kirke, *Twenty-five Years in British Guiana* (Westport, CT: Negro Universities Press, 1970), 4–5.

36. Ibid., 193.

37. Richard Schomburgk, *Travels in British Guiana 1840–1844*, Vol. 1. Walter E. Roth, ed. and transl. (Georgetown: Daily Chronicle, 1923), 43.

38. For an exploration of the importance of "high society balls," see B. Moore, *Cultural Power, Resistance, and Pluralism*, 32–33.

39. Ibid.

40. John A. McKenzie, *Propaganda and Empire: The Manipulation of British Public Opinion, 1880–1960* (Manchester: Manchester University Press, 1984), 29–31.

41. John Graziano, "The Early Life and Career of the 'Black Patti': The Odyssey of An African American Singer in the Late Nineteenth Century." *Journal of the American Musicological Society* 53, no. 3 (Autumn 2000): 562.

42. Kirke, 48.

43. For further information on Winkle and the company slaves of the Dutch West Indian Company, see Alvin Thompson, *Unprofitable Servants: Company Slaves in Berbice, Guyana 1803-1831* (Barbados: University of the West Indies Press, 2002).

44. A Landowner, *Demerara after Fifteen Years of Freedom*, 68.

45. For details on the role of enslaved Africans in humanizing the coastal regions of Guyana, see Rodney, *A History of the Guyanese Working People*, 1–18.

46. Randy M. Browne, "The 'Bad Business' of Obeah: Power, Authority, and the Politics of Slave Culture in the British Caribbean." *William and Mary Quarterly* 68:3 (July 2011): 451–80.

47. Calculations based on www.carolynjewel.com/historical/costs.php. Accessed June 22, 2011.

48. Based on William N. Arno's *History of Victoria Village, East Coast, Demerara* (Georgetown: self-published, ca. 1964).

49. A communal village had the following characteristic: there was a common title for all proprietors. For further details, see Cecilia McAlmot, "Remembering the Village Movement: A Significant Afro Guyanese Achievement," in "History this Week." *Stabroek News*, September 29, 2005. Available online at www.landofsixpeoples.com/news503/ns5092950.htm. Accessed September 4, 2014.

50. Barbara P. Josiah, "After Emancipation: Aspects of Village Life in Guyana, 1869–1911." *Journal of Negro History* 82, No. 1 (Winter 1997): 110.

51. See Lynette Dolphin, *One Hundred Folk Songs of Guyana* (Guyana: Department of Culture, Ministry of Education and Cultural Development, 1996), 53.

52. See Clem Seecharran, *Sweetening Bitter Sugar: Jock Campbell, The Booker Reformer in British Guiana 1934-1966* (Jamaica: Ian Randle, 2005).

53. See, for example, Walter Roth, *Additional Studies of the Arts, Crafts, and Customs of the Guiana Indians: With Special Reference to Those of Southern British Guiana* (Washington: Smithsonian Institution, 1929).

54. William Hilhouse, *Indian Notices* (1825; Georgetown, Guyana: National Commission for Research Materials, 1978).

55. See E. M. T. Moore, "Random Remarks on Social Music." In Marion Rockcliffe and Joseph Waterton Jackson (eds.), *British Guiana Woman's Centenary Effort 1831–1931* (Georgetown, British Guiana: Daily Argosy, 1931), 80–84; W. McDavid, "The Progress of Music in British Guiana." In Rockcliffe and Jackson, *British Guiana Woman's Centenary Effort*, 90–91; and P. M. de Weever, "The History of Music: 1831–1931." *Daily Argosy*, October 1931.

56. E. M. T. Moore, "Random Remarks on Social Music," 81.

57. Ibid., 83.

58. Ibid., 81.

Chapter 2

1. Sir Walter Joseph Sendall (March 27, 1898–December 25, 1901), Sir James Alexander Swettenham (December 25, 1901–September 26, 1904), Sir Frederick Mitchell Hodgson (September 26, 1904–July 5, 1912), Sir Walter Egerton (July 5, 1912–April 15, 1917), and Sir Wilfred Collet (April 15, 1917–April 4, 1923).

2. Thomas August, *Selling the Empire* (Westport, CT: Greenwood Press, 1985), 65.

3. Kimani S. Nehusi, "The Causes of the Protest of 1905," in Winston McGowan, James G. Rose, and David Granger (ed.), *Themes in African-Guyanese History* Georgetown: Free Press, 1998), 251–76.

4. The exemption was made under the Swettenham Circular issued in 1904 and was not withdrawn until 1933.

5. From e-mails.

6. Roy Heath, *Shadows Round the Moon* (London: Collins, 1990), 50. "Coming down" was akin to the loss of status/demotion during slavery. For further discussion on demotion during slavery, see B. W. Higman, "Population and Labor in the British Caribbean in the Early 19th Century." In Stanley L. Engerman and Robert E. Gallman, (ed.), *Long-Term Factors in American Economic Growth* (Chicago: University of Chicago Press, 1986), 605–40.

7. Nehusi, "The Causes of the Protest of 1905," 251–76.

8. For a comprehensive examination, see John M. McKenzie, *Propaganda and Empire: The Manipulation of Public Opinion, 1880–1960* (Manchester: Manchester University Press, 1984).

9. See Jeffrey Richards *Imperialism and Music: Britain 1876–1953* (Manchester: University of Manchester Press, 2001).

10. Brian Moore, 116.

11. According to "Octave" in *Guyana Police Force Magazine* (1972), the band was established on August 22, 1858, under the authority of Ordinance No. 21 of 1858 M.G.O. 37. Alfred Edward Zealley and J. Ord Hume, "British Guiana Militia Band," in *Famous Bands of the British Empire* (London: J. P. Hull, ca. 1925), 51, state the band was formed in 1860, "four years after the formation of the Demerara Militia, which was brought into existence as a result of the riots of 1856."

12. For more on the Portuguese bands, see the various publications on the Portuguese in Guyana by Sister Mary Noel Menezes.

13. Steve Garner, *Ethnicity, Class, and Gender: Guyana 1838–1985* (Kingston, Jamaica: Ian Randle, 2007), 65.

14. Zealley and Hume, *Famous Bands of the British Empire*, 31.

15. Octave, "The Band Moves On." *Guyana Police Force Magazine* (1972): 101.

16. Other bandmasters between 1860 and 1920 included 2nd Lieutenant C. H. Sherns; Dr. Otto Becker; C. R. Friecke, Esq.; John Miller, Esq.; and G. Horner, Esq.

17. "The B.G. Militia Band: Lady Visitor's Appreciation." *Daily Argosy*, October 7, 1917, 7.

18. See Brian Moore, 261, and Menezes, *The Portuguese of Guyana*, 123–36.

19. *Christ Church Bazaar* (December 1, 1912): 1.

20. "Grand Concert and Dance by the Demerara Symphony Orchestra," *Daily Argosy*, September 7, 1919, 1.

21. "British Guiana Musicians' Band: Moonlight Concert in the Gardens," *Daily Argosy*, September 7, 1919, 4.

22. Brian Moore, *Cultural Power, Resistance and Pluralism, 1838–1900*, 54.

23. *Daily Argosy*, September 1, 1912, 6.

24. For example, "Dance Practice Assault," *Daily Argosy*, December 25, 1912, 8.

25. Juanita De Barros, *Order and Place in a Colonial Society: Patterns of Struggle and Resistance in Georgetown, British Guiana, 1889–1924* (Montreal: McGill University Press, 2003), 91.

26. Ibid.

27. F. Van Sertima, "Christmas in Georgetown." In *Scenes and Sketches of Demerara Life* (Georgetown, 1899).

28. Lynette Dolphin, "Introduction." *One Hundred Folk Songs of Guyana* (Georgetown: Department of Culture, 1996).

29. Heath, *Shadows Round the Moon*, 13.

30. See Judith Roback, "The White-Robed Army: An Afro-Guyanese Religious Movement." *Anthropologica* 16: 2 (1974): 233–68.

31. Dolphin, *One Hundred Folk Songs of Guyana*, 4.

32. Pugagee Pungus (G. H. H. McLellan), "Mudland Songs and Bajan Red Legs," *Daily Chronicle*, Sunday, January 9, 1938.

33. The lyrics are from Lynette Dolphin.

34. Nehusi, "The Causes of the Protest of 1905," 251–76.

35. en.wikipedia.org/wiki/Frederick_Mitchell_Hodgson. Accessed October 14, 2011.

36. Ibid.

37. Ashton Chase, *A History of Trade Unionism in Guyana, 1900–1961* (Georgetown, Guyana: self-published, 1964), 27.

38. Rodney, 193.

39. Rodney, 190. Reflect on the autonomy of workers in organizing labor in the integrated sugar industry.

40. See Nigel Westmaas, "Revolutionary Centennial: Guyana's 1905 Rebellion." Available online at Solidarity www.solidarity-us.org/node/1139/print. Accessed September 18, 2007.

41. Contemporary newspaper reports referred to the use of "drums and pipes" suggesting the appropriation of Scottish instruments or were referring to drums and fifes.

42. Hazel Woolford, "The Origins of the Labor Movement." In Winston McGowan, James G. Rose, and David Granger (ed.), *Themes in African-Guyanese History* (Georgetown, Guyana: Free Press, 1998), 277–95.

43. E-mail from Hazel Woolford to author, October 19, 2010.

44. See "Scheme to Develop British Guiana," *New York Times* (May 17, 1914).

45. For further details see Glenford Howe, *Race, War and Nationalism: A Social History of West Indians in the First World War* (Jamaica: Ian Randle, 2002); Cedric L. Joseph, *The British West Indian Regiment 1914–1918* (Georgetown, Guyana: Free Press, 2008).

46. *Daily Argosy*, July 4, 1915, 7.

47. Ibid.

48. For a substantial discussion on the health conditions that led to rejection, see the chapter "Military Selection and Civilian Health" in Howe, *Race, War and Nationalism*, 59–71.

49. See Howe, *Race, War and Nationalism*. See also Caribbean Online—Routes to Roots: World War One and the British West Indies Regiment. commonwealth.sas.ac.uk/carib_web/wwi.htm. Accessed September 27, 2007. See also Cedric Joseph, *The British West Indian Regiment 1914-1918* (Georgetown, Guyana: Free Press, 2008).

50. Caribbean Online—Routes to Roots: World War One and the British West Indies Regiment.

51. Ibid., 6.

52. "London College of Music Examinations: Ursuline Convent Successes," *Daily Argosy*, September 5, 1916, 8.

53. "Royal Academy of Music: Local Examinations in Georgetown Next Year," *Daily Argosy*, December 2, 1917, 5.

54. "Trinity College of Music (Local Examinations)," *Daily Argosy*, August 4, 1918.

55. See J. Graham Cruickshank, *Notes on the History of St. Andrew's Kirk, Demerara* (Georgetown, Demerara: Estate of C. K. Jardine, Deceased, 1911), 34.

56. *Daily Argosy*, October 2, 1915, 6.

57. See newspaper advertisement "Opening of New Organ," *Daily Argosy*, September 7, 1913, 1.

58. From an interview with Charles Knights, LRSM, February 17, 2008.

59. Edgar Mittelholzer, *A Swarthy Boy* (London: Putnam, 1963), 59.

60. Based on an interview between the author and former New Amsterdam resident Alfred Bone, February 5, 2008.

61. *Daily Argosy*, December 7, 1917, 1. For further details on the academy, see "Melisma Academy of Music and Dancing: To Be Opened Next Year," *Daily Argosy*, December 7, 1917, 2.

62. *Daily Argosy*, November 7, 1915, 1.

63. In 2003 the song "Manuelita," performed by Lovey's Trinidad String Band, was included in the US government's inaugural "Top-50" list of recordings to be preserved in perpetuity by the Library of Congress. For further details see "Trini music band on US Govt. Top 50 list" by Terry Joseph, 3 February 2003. www.trinbagopan.com/forum/webbbs_config.cgi/noframes/read/134.

64. See the advertisement "Thrilling Martial Music," *Daily Argosy*, May 5, 1918, 1.

65. See the advertisement for "War Songs" and "Columbia Grafonolas," *Daily Argosy*, November 3, 1918, 6.

66. According to the *Daily Argosy*, December 25, 1914, 4, the Vagabonds, a Pierrot troupe, introduced the first complete vaudeville show in British Guiana in December 1914.

67. "Great Fire in Georgetown," *Daily Argosy*, December 23, 1913, 4, 5.

68. See chapter 1 in this book for earlier discussion on Kwe Kwe. Also see youtube.com/watch?v=QNxphGjKAnM for a reflection on Kwe Kwe by Mama Vanessa, a legendary Kwe Kwe tutor from Ithaca, West Coast Berbice.

69. Peter Manuel, *East Indian Music in the West Indies: Tän-Singing, Chutney, and the Making of Indo-Caribbean Culture* (Philadelphia: Temple University Press, 2000), 5.

70. Ibid., 8–9.

71. For further details on "bruk up" sessions see Vibert Cambridge, "Rector Malcolm Schultz: Making Music from Canje Creek to New York," in the series "Celebrating Our Creative Personalities," *Sunday Stabroek*, May 16, 2006. landofsixpeoples.com/news402/ns4051611.htm.

72. For a detailed exploration of Cumfa and Kwe Kwe, see Kean Gibson, *Comfa Religion and Creole Language in a Caribbean Community* (New York: State University of New York, 2001).

73. See Amerindian Languages Project, *An Introduction to the Akawaio and Arekuna Peoples of Guyana* (Guyana: University of Guyana, 1977), 18–19.

74. For further details see Sr. Mary Noel Menezes, "Amerindian Music in Guyana." *Arts Journal* 1, no. 2 (March 2005): 95–99.

75. Amerindian Language Project, *An Introduction to the Akawaio and Arekuna Peoples of Guyana*, 21–22.

76. See Rohan Sagar, "Banshikilli: The Music of the Spanish Arawaks of Moruca, Guyana." Unpublished paper in author's possession and DVD (ca. 2007); and "Chants in the Rainforest: An Essay on the musical traditions of the Amerindian people of Guyana." Unpublished paper in author's possession (Georgetown, Guyana, August 17, 2009).

77. Garner, *Ethnicity, Class, and Gender*, 72.

Chapter 3

1. en.wikipedia.org/wiki/Wilfred_Collet. Accessed November 25, 2011.

2. Ibid.

3. Harold Lutchman, *Patronage in Colonial Society: A Study of The Former British Guiana* (Georgetown: Critchlow Labour College, 1976), 5.

4. For extended discussion of the politics of accommodation, confrontation, and nationalism, see Maulana Karenga, *Introduction to African American Studies* (Los Angeles: Kawaida, 1982).

5. Ibid., 25.

6. Document I.O. L/E/7/1254-J. & P. 5169/1919, encl. No. 4 (Indian Office and Library) cited in Clem Seecharan, 39.

7. Clem Seecharan, *India and the Shaping of the Indo-Guyanese Imagination 1890s–1920s* (Leeds: University of Warwick and Peepal Tree Books, 1993), 13.

8. Ibid.

9. Ibid., 15.

10. See en.wikipedia.org/wiki/History_of_the_Indian_National_Congress. Accessed September 4, 2014.

11. See Wikipedia article "Indian Independence movement: en.wikipedia.org/wiki/Indian_independence_movement. Accessed March 22, 2008.

12. Seecharan, 11.

13. Ibid., 21.

14. Ibid., 93.

15. Ibid., 27.

16. Ibid., 72.

17. *Daily Argosy*, September 21, 1921.

18. "The Beleaguered." In *The Boylston Club Collection of German and English Four Part Songs* O. Ditson (ed.) (Boston: Oliver Ditson, 1895), 35–39. Available online.

19. See Ashton Chase, *A History of Trade Unionism in Guyana 1900 to 1961* (Guyana: self-published, reprint 2007), 249. Although a copy of that songbook was not accessible during the writing of this book, it could be speculated that "The Beleaguered" was part of that collection.

20. From Vibert Cambridge, "Music and Working People in Guyana During 20th century Guyana," paper presented at Critchlow Labour College, Georgetown, Guyana, on December 3, 2007.

21. Mary Noel Menezes, R.S.M., *The Portuguese of Guyana: A Study in Culture and Conflict* (Gujarat, India: self-published, ca. 2004), 79.

22. Ibid., 101.

23. F. Van Sertima, "Christmas in Georgetown." In *Scenes and Sketches of Demerara Life* (Georgetown, 1899).

24. *The Portuguese of Guyana*, 135.

25. Ibid.

26. "Miss E. Elcock's Musical Success: Wins Sir Wilfred Collet's Trinity College Medal. Donor's Tribute to Teacher," *Daily Argosy*, June 3, 1927, 6.

27. *Daily Argosy*, September 30, 1931, 4.

28. *Daily Argosy*, December 5, 1920, 6.

29. "B.G. Musical Society," *Daily Argosy*, June 5, 1921, 7; *Daily Argosy*, May 2, 1926, 1.

30. "Leeward Island Relief: Concert by Music Lovers' Club," *Daily Argosy*, November 4, 1928, 6.

31. See for example, "Annual Musical Recital," *Daily Argosy*, September 3, 1922, 1.

32. Shilling Concerts and Concert Parties were fund-raising methods. In these contexts, the public pledged money to have certain performers sing.

33. See, for example, *Daily Argosy*, December 25, 1928, 7.

34. See Heath, *Shadow Around the Moon*.

35. *Daily Argosy*, May 6, 1923.

36. For details on the his role in educating enslaved Africans and his association with the 1823 slave revolt in Demerara, see Emilia Viotti da Costa, *Crowns of Glory, Tears of Blood: The Demerara Slave Rebellion of 1823* (Oxford: Oxford University Press, 1994).

37. *Daily Argosy*, December 25, 1930, 4.

38. Details available at en.wikipedia.org/wiki/British_Empire_Exhibition.

39. *Daily Argosy*, April 8, 1923, 5.

40. From the score "Mighty Kaieteur (British Guiana)," composed and arranged by Clement E. N. Nichols, L/CPL British Guiana Militia Band, and published by the Commissioner of the British Guiana Pavilion, Wembley. The 1925 copyright was held by J. A. Barbour James. The score is available at the British Library (Call Number h.3829.k. (38).

41. From the score "Beautiful England" composed and arranged by Clement E. N. Nichols, L/CPL British Guiana Militia Band, and published by the Commissioner of the British Guiana Pavilion, Wembley. The 1925 copyright was held by J. A. Barbour James. The score is available at the British Library (Call Number h.3829.k. (36).

42. For further details on J. A. Barbour James, see various references in Jeffrey Green, *Black Edwardians: Black People in Britain 1901-1914* (London: Frank Cass, 1998).

43. Ibid.

44. See Vibert Cambridge, "Hubert (Bert) and Edward (Eddie)—The Rogers Brothers and Musical Giants," in the series "Celebrating Our Creative Personalities," *Sunday Stabroek*, February 29, 2004. Available online at www.landofsixpeoples.com/news401/ns4022922.htm. Accessed January 8, 2012.

45. See Vibert Cambridge, "Vincent De Abreu: A Pioneer," in the series "Celebrating Our Creative Personalities," *Sunday Stabroek*, April 20, 2003. Available online at landofsixpeoples .com/news303/ns3081711.htm. Accessed January 8, 2013.

46. *Daily Argosy*, July 3, 1927, 8.

47. Theo, "Matter for Investigation," *Daily Argosy*, November 1, 1925, 12.

48. *Daily Argosy*, August 3, 1930, 12.

49. Colonel E. Woolmer, DSO, of Messrs. Curtis Campbell & Co., H. P. C. Melville, Jas Smith, Manager of Plantation Rose Hall, and Jas Bee, Manager of Plantation Albion.

50. *Daily Argosy*, November 6, 1927, 7.

51. Kirke, 48.

52. Juanita De Barros. "Metropolitan policies and colonial practices at the boys' reformatory in British Guiana." *Journal of Imperial and Commonwealth History* 30: 2, (2002): 1–24.

53. Ibid.

54. *Daily Argosy*, December 25, 1926, 7.

55. *Daily Argosy*, December 4, 1927, 4.

56. Ibid.

57. For further details, see: chevalierdesaintgeorges.homestead.com/Burleigh.html www
.artsongupdate.org/Articles/DvorakBurleigh&ArtSong.htm. Accessed January 8, 2013.

58. *Daily Argosy*, July 29, 1931, 5.

59. "Friday Night at 8:30 by Special Request Madame Anita Patti Brown." *Daily Argosy*,
January 29, 1930, 1.

60. "Adios British Guiana," *Daily Argosy*, August 4, 1929, 1.

61. Radio Static, "Weekly Radio Review," *Daily Argosy*, December 30, 1928, 9, 14.

62. "Local Broadcast Service," *Daily Argosy*, July 25, 1928, 8.

63. "Local Broadcast: Station V.R.Y, To-Night's Programme," *Daily Argosy*, May 24, 1930, 24,
announced that it was broadcasting, between 7 and 8 o'clock, a service from Smith's Memorial
Church.

64. "Music Lovers Orchestra Broadcast on the 5th," *Daily Argosy*, June 5, 1930, 6.

65. "'Talkie' Films," *Daily Argosy*, March 26, 1930, 4.

66. See the advertisement "Monday Night at 8:30 'Broadway Scandals,'" *Daily Argosy*, April
6, 1930, 1.

67. See, for example, an advertisement by the Colonial Transport Department in *Daily
Argosy*, July 2, 1922, 1.

68. *Daily Argosy*, December 31, 1925, 8.

69. *Daily Argosy*, April 2, 1921.

70. *Daily Argosy*, November 26, 1930, 5.

71. *Daily Argosy*, April 6, 1924.

72. "The Ruimveldt Tragedy: Tact and Patience by the Military," *Daily Argosy*, April 6, 1924,
1–3.

73. "TRAGEDY," *Daily Argosy*, April 4, 1924, 5.

74. "Lessons of the Week," *Daily Argosy*, April 6, 1924, 8.

75. For further details on Critchlow's letter, see *Daily Argosy*, April 6, 1924, 1, 3. The extract of
the song is from "When wilt thou save the People?" composed by Ebenezer Elliott in 1850; the
melody is "Commonwealth" by Josiah Booth (1852–1929). This provides insight into the music
that Critchlow was drawing upon, in the early days of the labor movement in British Guiana.

76. *Daily Argosy*, April 6, 1924, 5.

77. Letter to the editor in *Daily Argosy*, April 8, 1924, 8.

78. Melissa Ifill, "Federating the British West Indies," in the series "History this Week," February 14, 2002. Available online at landofsixpeoples.com/news602/ns2021455.html. Accessed
January 8, 2013.

79. For additional information see Roderick Roy Wilson, *Report of the British Guiana Commission* (London: HMSO, 1927).

80. James Rose, "The Coming of Crown Colony Government," in McGowan, Rose, and
Granger, *Themes in African-Guyanese History*, 296–326.

81. Ibid., 317.

Chapter 4

1. See Karl Galinsky, *Age of Augustus* (Cambridge: Cambridge University Press, 2005).

2. Among the books published were Norman Cameron, *The Evolution of the Negro* (Volume 1); *Balthasar, Guianese Poetry: Covering the 100-year period 1831–1931*; a reprint of J. Graham Cruickshank, *Black Talk*; Aloysius de Weever, *Geography of British Guiana and the West Indies*; and A. R. F. Webber, *Centenary Handbook of British Guiana*.

3. "Centenary Carnival," *Daily Argosy*, October 4, 1931, 1.

4. For further discussion on "unisonality" and "unisonance," see Benedict Anderson, *Imagined Communities* (London: Verso, 1983), 145.

5. "Berbice Programme," *Daily Argosy*, October 11, 1931, 7.

6. "Celebrations in Berbice," *Daily Argosy*, October 14, 1931, 5.

7. Ibid.

8. For further details on Rev. M. A. Cossou, see Petamber Persaud, "Preserving our literary heritage: National Songs, Part three," *Guyana Chronicle*, March 2, 2008.

9. "My Native Land," in *Ten National Songs of Guyana*, Lynette Dolphin (ed.) (Georgetown, Guyana: National History and Arts Council, Ministry of Information, 1969).

10. "Centenary Celebrations," *Daily Argosy*, October 9, 1931, 7.

11. "Centenary Beauty Contest," *Daily Argosy*, October 4, 1931, 1.

12. "1931 Beauty Queen," *Daily Argosy*, October 14, 1931, 5.

13. "The Beauty Contest," *Daily Argosy*, October 18, 1931, 7.

14. "1932 Beauty Contest," *Daily Argosy*, May 24, 1932, 1.

15. "The History of Music, 1831-1931," *Daily Argosy*, October 18, 1931, 7.

16. "Combined Choirs to Sing," *Daily Argosy*, October 17, 1931. See also "Combined Choirs at Providence," *Daily Argosy*, October 20, 1931, 5.

17. "School Children's Entertainment," letter to the editor, *Daily Argosy*, October 16, 1931.

18. "Centenary Committee," *Daily Argosy*, October 18, 1931.

19. See "Government Notice" dated June 29, 1934, signed by P. W. King, Colonial Secretary (ag), published in *Daily Argosy*, July 1, 1934.

20. *Daily Argosy*, July 3, 1934, 1.

21. Ibid.

22. "A Splendid Volume," *Daily Argosy*, July 31, 1934.

23. Franz Fanon addressed this theme in *Black Skin, White Mask* (New York: Grove Press, 1967).

24. "Negro Progress Convention: 'The Third Step,'" *Daily Argosy*, August 3, 1934.

25. See Robert Moore, "Colonial Images of Blacks and Indians in Nineteenth Century Guyana," in Bridget Brerton and Kevin A. Yelvington (ed.), *The Colonial Caribbean in Transition: Essays on Postemancipation Social and Cultural History* (Jamaica: Press of the University of the West Indies, 1999), 126–58.

26. "One Hundred Years," *Daily Argosy*, July 20, 1934, 5.

27. For further details see Brian Moore, *Cultural Power, Resistance, and Pluralism*.

28. Percy E. Armstrong, "There's Gold in Them Thar Hills!," *Daily Argosy*, January 5, 1937. See also "British Guiana Consolidated Shares," *Daily Argosy*, January 17, 1937 and "Ousting the Pork-Knocker," *Daily Argosy*, January 19, 1937, 6.

29. Ralph Fitz Scott, "Shout All Guiana," BCD 16623-1/26. Accompanied by chorus and Charlie Smith and His Demerara Lucky Strike Orchestra.

30. "Re-organizing Rice Industry," *Daily Argosy*, January 16, 1937, 6.

31. "Great Future for British Guiana," *Daily Argosy* January 16, 1937.

32. "Excursion to Surinam," *Daily Argosy*, January 1, 1937, 1. "Trinidad Carnival Excursion," *Daily Argosy*, January 5, 1937, 1.

33. "Home of Truth and Beauty," *Daily Argosy*, February 20, 1937.

34. "Pure Water Supply Scheme for Georgetown," *Daily Argosy*, January 5, 1937.

35. See the editorial "Assisting Ourselves," *Daily Argosy*, January 5, 1937.

36. "Pure Water Supply Scheme for Georgetown."

37. "City Centenary Celebrations," *Daily Argosy*, January 10, 1937

38. "City Centenary Music," *Daily Argosy*, February 6, 1937, 7. Neither the lyrics nor the music for M. E. Bayley's winning composition were available at the time of writing.

39. "Centenary Cabaret Night," *Daily Argosy*, February 14, 1937, 1.

40. From *Who's Who In British Guiana*, 1945–1948.

41. For a discussion on contemporary European propaganda techniques, see Steven Luckert and Susan Bachrach, *State of Deception: The Power of Nazi Propaganda* (Washington: United States Holocaust Museum, 2011).

42. "The Coronation: Local Preparations," *Daily Argosy*, May 6, 1937.

43. "Ceremony Heralded In," *Daily Argosy*, May 12, 1937.

44. "Ceremonial Parade at Eve Leary," *Daily Argosy*, May 13, 1937.

45. "British Guiana Honours: Four Places Awarded," *Daily Argosy*, May 13, 1937.

46. "Coronation Music Festival," *Daily Argosy*, February 28, 1937.

47. "New Year Message to East Indians," *Daily Argosy*, January 6, 1937.

48. "Indian Musical Heroes Anniversary," *Daily Argosy*, May 1, 1938.

49. Details on the hymn were not available at the time of writing this book.

50. "East Indian Centenary Celebrations," *Daily Argosy*, May 6, 1938.

51. Ibid.

52. Ibid.

53. See "Indian Music for Centenary Celebrations," *Daily Chronicle*, March 6, 1938.

54. For further details on the Mootoo Brothers, see Vibert Cambridge's article in "Celebrating Our Creative Personalities" series in *Sunday Stabroek*.

55. *Daily Argosy*, Friday, May 21, 1937, 6.

56. See "Indian Music for Centenary Celebrations," *Daily Chronicle*, March 6, 1938.

57. "Endless Vibrations," *Caribbean Beat* 69 (September/October 2004).

58. Based on interview with Roger Hinds (Young Bill Rogers) in Georgetown, Guyana, July 31, 2007. See also Roger Hinds, *Bill Rogers* (Georgetown: Carifesta X Secretariat, 2008).

59. Gordon Rohlehr, *Calypso and Society in Pre-Independence Trinidad* (Port-of-Spain: Gordon Rohlehr), 144.

60. Pugagee Pungus, "Mudland Songs and Bajan Red Legs," *Daily Chronicle*, January 1938.

61. Ibid.

62. See Appendix 1 for a partial list of the shantos recorded by Bill Rogers in November 1934.

63. Augustus Hinds, "Bhagee." In "Shantos by Bill Rogers." *Forward Guyana* (A magazine to commemorate the Cooperative Republic of Guyana), February 23, 1970, 28.

64. Rohlehr, *Calypso and Society in Pre-Independence Trinidad*, 144.

65. Ibid., 142.

66. See "Peggy Dearie," 178 in *West Indian Rhythm: Trinidad Calypsos on World and Local Events Featuring the Censored Recordings—1938-1940* (Hambergen, Germany: Bear Family Records, ca. 2000). See also From Richard Noblett, "Lord Caresser in Guyana," 179–80.

67. Roger A. Hinds ("Young Bill Roger"), *The Life and Works of Bill (Bhagee) Rogers and the Origins of Shanto Music in Guyana* (Georgetown, Guyana: Carifesta Secretariat, 2008), 10.

68. See Vibert C. Cambridge, "The Muttoo (Mootoo) Brothers Calypso Orchestra," in the series, "Celebrating Our Creative Personalities," *Sunday Stabroek*, August 3, 2003. Available online at www.landofsixpeoples.com/news303/ns3080312.htm Accessed January 11, 2013.

69. Roger A. Hinds, 85.

70. For further details see *A History of Trade Unionism in Guyana 1900 to 1961*, 85–93.

71. Roger A. Hinds, 78.

72. Ibid.

73. For a discussion on this, see Emilia Viotti da Costa, *Crowns of Glory, Tears of Blood: The Demerara Slave Rebellion of 1823* (Oxford: Oxford University Press, 1994); and see also Martin Carter's poem "After One Year," in which the lines "Old hanging ground is still green playing field / smooth cemetery proud garden of tall flowers" make reference to the venue.

74. *Daily Argosy*, May 4, 1938.

75. *Daily Argosy*, February 28, 1937.

76. *Sporting Chronicle* (Trinidad), February 28, 1937.

77. See Vibert C. Cambridge, "Ken 'Snakehips' Johnson," in the series "Celebrating Our Creative Personalities," *Sunday Stabroek*, May 29, 2003. See also "Ken 'Snakehips' Johnson: Swing and the Black Atlantic," *North Star E-Journal*: Special Edition 2006. www.nsjournal.com/ken3 .html.

78. "For One Night Only," *Daily Argosy*, August 8, 1935.

79. "New Star of the Jazz World," *Daily Argosy*, May 6, 1939.

80. *Daily Argosy*, February 26, 1939.

81. "President Roosevelt Thanks Song Writer," *Brooklyn Times*, February 4, 1934, and reprinted in *Daily Argosy*, March 28, 1934, 4.

82. See *Women's Progressive Organization: 50 Years of Glorious Struggle for Women's Rights, Democracy and Social Progress. Part 1, 1953-1964* (Georgetown, Guyana: Women's Progressive Organization, 2003), 4.

83. For details on this incident, see Ashton Chase, *A History of Trade Unionism in Guyana 1900 to 1961*, 87–90.

84. Ibid.

85. Bridget Brereton and Kevin A. Yelvington (eds.), *The Colonial Caribbean in Transition: Essays on Postemancipation Social and Cultural History.* Jamaica: University of the West Indies Press, 19–21.

86. *A History of Trade Unionism in Guyana*, 94.

87. Ibid.

88. Brereton and Yelvington, 18.

89. Ibid.

1. Denis Williams, "Guiana Today." *Kyk-Over-al* 2, no. 9 (December 1949): 9–10.

2. Stetson Conn, Rose C. Engleman, Brian Fairchild, *United States Army in World War II—The Western Hemisphere: Guarding the United States and Its Outposts* (Washington: Center of Military History, United States Army, 1964), 354.

3. See "U.S. Bases in British Guiana." *Daily Argosy*, January 3, 1941.

4. *Guarding the United States and Its Outposts.*

5. Cheddi Jagan, *The West on Trial* (Berlin: Seven Seas, 1980), 80.

6. Ibid., 83.

7. Denis Williams, "Guiana Today."

8. "Recruitment for Royal Air Force." *Daily Argosy*, January 3, 1941.

9. For further details, see Vibert Cambridge, "Cy Grant: Doing it his way" in "Celebrating Our Creative Personalities," *Sunday Stabroek* (April 18, 2004). Available online at www.land ofsixpeoples.com/news402/ns4041814.htm Accessed February 27, 2012.

10. See "Annual Distribution of Music Certificates and Prizes." *Daily Argosy*, January 25, 1941, 8.

11. Al Jolson entertains US troops in Georgetown, British Guiana—"the new Jolson was born." ("Entertaining the Troops Overseas.") Available on-line at www.dinesp.fsnet.co.uk/ enterta.html. Accessed April 28, 2002.

12. E-mail from Erica Gomes (née Henwood) to the author October 21, 2008.

13. Ray Seales, "The Making of Guyanese Popular Music." www.gems-av.com/themakingof popguyanesemusic.htm. Accessed March 2, 2009.

14. Julia M. H. Carson, *Home Away from Home: The Story of the USO* (New York: Harper & Brothers, 1946), xi.

15. See Steven High, "The racial politics of criminal jurisdiction in the aftermath of the Anglo-American 'destroyers-for-bases' deal, 1940-1950." *Journal of Imperial and Commonwealth History* 32:3: 86.

16. See "U.S.O. Has First Dance." *Daily Argosy*, May 28, 1942, 8, for the complete list of "persons who kindly consented to as Patrons and Patronesses."

17. Harvey Neptune, "White Lies: Race and Sexuality in Occupied Trinidad." *Journal of Colonialism and Colonial History* (2001). Available online. Accessed October 24, 2008.

18. Carson, *Home Away from Home*, 142.

19. Helen Taitt, *My Life, My Country*, 16.

20. Ibid., 19.

21. Paul Blanshard, *Democracy and Empire in the Caribbean* (New York: Macmillan, 1947), 132. Also cited in Harvey Neptune, "White Lies: Race and Sexuality in Occupied in Trinidad." *Journal of Colonialism and Colonial History* (2001). Available online. Accessed October 24, 2008.

22. Helen Taitt, *My Life, My Country*, 18.

23. For details on the workings of a brothel during this period, see Godfrey Chin, "Best Little Whorehouse," in Trev Sue-A-Quan, *Cane Ripples: The Chinese in Guyana* (Vancouver: Cane Press, 2003), 180–82.

24. From recordings done at Albion Estates, August 2007.

25. Ibid.

26. This theme of racial prejudice during World War II was also explored in Rogers and Hammerstein's *South Pacific*.

27. For further details see www.calypsoworld.org/noflash/songs-1.htm. Accessed March 1, 2009.

28. Melissa Ifill, "Federating the British West Indies," in the series "History this Week," *Stabroek News*, July 19, 2003. Available online at landofsixpeoples.com/news303/ns3071225.htm. Accessed January 11, 2013.

29. For a valuable analysis of this period, see Cary Fraser, *Ambivalent Anti-Colonialism: The United States and the Genesis of West Indian Independence, 1940-1964* (Westport: Greenwood Press, 1994).

30. See *Daily Argosy*, September 5, 1943, 1; *Daily Argosy*, September 26, 1943.

31. For further details on the Muttoo Brothers, see Cambridge, "The Muttoo/Mootoo Brothers Calypso Orchestra."

32. For the complete lyrics, see *West Indian Rhythm: Trinidad Calypso on World and Local Events Featuring the Censored Recordings—1938-1940* (Hambergen, Germany: Bear Family Records), 240.

33. Seecharran, *Sweetening Bitter Sugar*, 54.

34. From Jagan, *The West on Trial*, 18–19, cited in Seecharran, *Sweetening Bitter Sugar*, 406.

35. See Manuel, *East Indian Music in the West Indies*, 35. See also chapter 2, "The Development of Local-Classical Music," 15–56. The author is indebted to Peter Manuel for this section of this chapter.

36. See Manuel, *East Indian Music in the West Indies*, 25.

37. Ibid., 35; and from a telephone interview with Jawaharlal Tillack (son of Bal Gangadhar Tillack) on October 8, 2006.

38. From interview with Jawaharlal Tillack, 2006. The interview was conducted by the author and the tape of the interview is in his possession.

39. For further details see entry in Wikipedia at en.wikipedia.org/wiki/Bal_Gangadhar_ Tilak. Accessed November 11, 2008.

40. See "He Came! He Sang!! He Conquered!!!" *Sunday Argosy*, July 2, 1944.

41. "Recital on Two Pianos," *Daily Argosy*, January 19, 1941, 11.

42. Rita Core, "Oswald Russell in First-rate Concert." *Daily Gleaner*, August 31, 1951, 12.

43. R.A.C. "Legend of Kaieteur: Grand Musical Show in Assembly Rooms." *Daily Argosy*, July 30, 1944.

44. See "Endless Vibrations: 250 Great Songs from the Caribbean." *Caribbean Beat* (September/October 2004): 38–73.

45. "Dawson Music Lovers' Club: Song Recital at Stewartville," *Daily Argosy*, January 4, 1941.

46. Ibid.

47. For further details on James Phoenix, see "James Alexander Phoenix and the British Guiana Police Male Voice Choir." *Black Praxis* (2004): 116–17. Available online at www.guyfolk fest.org/celebrating6.htm.

48. "Annual Distribution of Music Certificates and Prizes." *Daily Argosy*, January 25, 1941.

49. Billy Pilgrim, "Lynette Dolphin: A trail-blazing cultural icon" (manuscript in possession of the author, ca. Febryary 2000); and "Lynette de Weever Dolphin—A Tribute." *Stabroek News*, February 20, 2000. Available online at www.qcguyanaalumny.org/News/dollotrib2.html.

50. Ibid.

51. "Obituary: Mrs. Clarice De Weever Dolphin: Wife of Mr. E. Lugard Dolphin." *Daily Argosy*, June 7, 1936.

52. See Ernie Smith's CD on Jamaican mento music.

53. Celeste Dolphin, "Let the Children Sing." *Kyk-Over-Al* 1:4 (June 1947): 16.

54. Pilgrim, "Lynette Dolphin."

55. Ibid.

56. Ibid.

57. See "BPI Sunday Programme," *Daily Argosy*, date unknown.

58. Lynette Dolphin, "A Short History of the Guyana Music Teachers' Association." *50th Anniversary Souvenir Brochure* (Georgetown, Guyana: Guyana Music Teachers' Association, 1998), 5.

59. Ibid.

60. Ibid.

61. Lloyd Searwar, address at the launch of *A. J. Seymour's Collected Poems*, January 12, 2001, published in the *Stabroek News*, March 4, 2001. Available online at www.triste-le-roi.blogspot.com/ajs_searwar.html. Accessed March 2, 2009. See also N. E. Cameron, *Adventures in the Field of Culture* (Georgetown: Daily Chronicle, 1971).

62. Eleanor Kerry, *First Annual Report of the British Guiana Music Teachers' Association for the Year ended March 31, 1949.*

63. Ibid.

64. Ibid.

65. See Darrell Newton, "Calling the West Indies: The BBC World Service and Caribbean Voices." Available online at www.open.ac.uk/socialsciences/diasporas/conference/pdf/calling_the_west_indies.pdf. Accessed January 7, 2014.

66. The author wrote extended essays on these personalities. They were published in the *Stabroek News* series "Celebrating Our Creative Personalities."

67. Vibert C. Cambridge, "Rudolph Dunbar: A fascinating person, composer, musical conductor, musical journalist, and Caribbean pioneer of the classics"; Alex Pascal (June 16, 1988), "Celebrating Our Creative Personalities," *Sunday Stabroek*, 2004.

68. John Cowley, "Cultural 'fusions': aspects of British West Indian music in the USA and Britain 1918-1951." *Popular Music* vol. 5 (January 1985): 81–96.

69. For further details on the phase of his life when he was "Black balled" by the BBC Radio 4 FM, see documentary broadcast on August 7, 2007, titled "Strange Story of Rudolph Dunbar." Description available online at www.bbc.co.uk/radio4/factual/pip/pp33t/ Accessed January 11, 2013.

70. See Vibert Cambridge, "Rannie Hart—A Virtuoso by Many Names," in the series "Celebrating Our Creative Personalities," *Sunday Stabroek*, ca. 2005. See also Val Wilmer, "Rannie Hart: A Musical Career that took in Brixton, Mayfair–and Rita Hayworth" (obituary). *Guardian* (UK), July 15, 2006. Available online at www.guardian.co.uk/news/2006/jul/15/guardianobituaries.mainsection. Accessed March 2, 2009.

71. Wilmer, "Rannie Hart."

72. See Vibert Cambridge, "James Ingram Fox: A Treasured Composer," in the series "Celebrating Our Creative Personalities," *Sunday Stabroek*, March 13, 2005.

73. Bridget Hart-Doman, "No Sham or Shame: A Conversation with J. Ingram Fox." In *Color It Words* (Unpublished manuscript in author's possession, 1987), 32.

74. "The Franchise Commission." *Daily Argosy*, May 8, 1942, 3.

75. Jagan, *The West on Trial*, 59.

76. Ibid., 61.

77. *PAC Bulletin* no. 1, November 6, 1946, 1.

78. Attributed to Dr. Cheddi Jagan.

79. For an expanded discussion on Burnham's role in the formation of the PPP, see Maurice St. Pierre, *Anatomy of Resistance: Anti-Colonialism in Guyana 1823–1966* (London: Macmillan Education, 1999), especially the chapter "From Exclusion to Inclusion," 87–129. St. Pierre cites Rudy Luck's recall that Burnham played an active role in the creation of the PPP and not the minor role suggested by Janet Jagan, who said that the structure and orientation was already in place prior to Burnham's return to British Guiana in 1948.

80. Denis Williams, "Guiana Today." *Kyk-Over-al*, 2 no. 9 (December 1949): 9–10.

Chapter 6

1. See N. E. Cameron, *Adventures in the Field of Culture* (Georgetown, British Guiana: self-published [printed by the *Daily Chronicle*]), 1971.

2. See Kirk, *Twenty-five Years in British Guiana*, 308.

3. For further details on this theory see Matthew Riley, "Civilizing the Savage: Johan Georg Sulzer and the 'Aesthetic Force' of Music." *Journal of the Royal Musical Association* 127, no. 1 (2002): 1–22.

4. "The Festival: Origin and Progress" from *British Guiana Music Festival*, the Official Program for 1954.

5. For an extended discussion on this topic, see Arthur Phillips, "British Music Competition Festivals." Letters to the editor, *Musical Times* 74, No. 1086 (August 1933): 734–36.

6. Miriam E. David, *The State, the Family, and Education* (London: Routledge and Kagan Paul, 1980).

7. "Preliminary Session of B.G. Music Festival Held in New Amsterdam." *Daily Argosy*, June 28, 1952.

8. "Berbice Artistes Carry Off Three of Four Festival Championship Cups." *Daily Argosy*, July 21, 1952, 1.

9. Ibid.

10. Ibid.

11. Ibid.

12. "Mrs. Ruby McGregor 'Chief Architect of Glorious Festive Record.'" *Berbice Weekly Argosy* in *Daily Argosy*, July 30, 1952, 5.

13. Based on interview with Janet Jagan in Georgetown, Guyana, August 2007.

14. Patricia Benn, from interview with Vibert Cambridge in Guyana, August 2007.

15. Jai Narine Singh, *Guyana: Democracy Betrayed: A Political History 1948–1993* (Kingston, Jamaica: Kingston Publishers, 1996), 41.

16. St. Pierre, *Anatomy of Resistance*, 94–95. Maureen Warner-Lewis suggests the call-and-response pattern is an African retention from a children's game brought to Guyana and other parts of the Caribbean by Kongos. For further details see Maureen Warner-Lewis, *Central Africa in the Caribbean: Transcending Time, Transforming Cultures* (Jamaica: University of the West Indies Press, 2006), 229–32.

17. Warner-Lewis, *Central Africa in the Caribbean*.

18. For further details on Sydney King, see "Eusi Kwayana: The Librettist of Guyana's Political Opera or the Political Musician," in the series "Celebrating Our Creative Personalities," published in *Sunday Stabroek*, July 20, 2003. Available online at www.guyfolkfest.org/celebratings5.htm.

19. Eusi Kwayana, *Guyana: No Guilty Race* (Guyana: Guyana Review, 1999), v–vi.

20. See www.brandenburghistorica.com/page5.html.

21. Tim Blanning, *The Triumph of Music: The Rise of Composers, Musicians, and Their Art* (London: Penguin, 2008).

22. Jagan, *The West on Trial*, 115.

23. "Registration Officer Congratulates B.G. Electorate on Orderly Poll." *Daily Argosy*, May 4, 1953, 1.

24. "British Guiana General Elections: Statistical Summary." *Daily Argosy*, May 3, 1953.

25. "Governor Lifts Ban on Music with Labour Day Parade." *Daily Argosy*, May 1, 1953.

26. "Record Crowd Attends May Day Celebrations." *Daily Argosy*, May 4, 1953, 1.

27. "Sir Alfred is Patron of B.G. Music Festival." *Daily Argosy*, May 1, 1953.

28. Jagan, *The West on Trial*, 117.

29. For details on the responsibilities of each portfolio, see "Executive Council Meets for First Time." *Daily Argosy*, May 30, 1953, 1, 4.

30. See Colin A. Palmer, *Cheddi Jagan and the Politics of Power: British Guiana's Struggle for Independence* (Chapel Hill: University of North Carolina Press, 2010).

31. "Coronation Celebrations: Colony-wide Plans Outline in Broadcast." *Daily Argosy*, May 11, 1953, 1, 2.

32. "Radio Demerara to Start Pre-Coronation Programmes on Monday." *Daily Argosy*, May 1, 1953.

33. "Schools Music Festival Heralds Coronation Week." *Daily Argosy*, June 2, 1953, 4.

34. "Coronation Celebrations: Colony-wide Plans Outline in Broadcast."

35. "Calypso," in "People, Events & Things." *Daily Argosy*, May 31, 1953.

36. "Thousands Converge on City to View Coronation Illuminations." *Daily Argosy*, June 2, 1953, 1.

37. "Carnival Spirit Reigns as Steelbands Roam City." *Daily Argosy*, June 4, 1953, 1.

38. "Festival of Music Ushers in Coronation Week." In *Berbice Weekly Argosy*, *Daily Argosy*, June 3, 1953.

39. "Week Just Past Is One We Shall Long Remember." *Daily Argosy*, June 8, 1953, 1, 2.

40. Ibid.

41. Jai Narine Singh, *Guyana = Democracy Betrayed: A Political History 1948–1993* (Kingston, Jamaica: Kingston Publishers, 1996), 63.

42. "History of PPP." Available online at www.ppp-civic.org/history/historyppp.htm. Accessed November 30, 2008.

43. Martin Carter, "This Is the Dark Time My Love." *Poems of Resistance from Guiana* (London: Lawrence and Wishart, 1954), 35.

44. Jagan, *The West on Trial*, 159.

45. For further details, please visit: www.alanbushtrust.org.uk/music/operas/reapers .asp?room=Music. Accessed January 21, 2012.

46. Vibert C. Cambridge, "John "Bagpipe" Fredericks—There is more to the name," in the series "Celebrating of Creative Personalities" in *Stabroek News*, December 4, 2010. Available online at www.landofsixpeoples.com/gycreperjs.htm. Accessed January 11, 2013.

47. C. Jagan, *The West on Trial*, 161.

48. "Houses for the People of Guiana." *Chronicle Christmas Annual*, 1956.

49. "Industrial Development." *Chronicle Christmas Annual*, 1956.

50. "The Banks Beer Calypso." *Chronicle Christmas Annual*, 1957.

51. "The USIS in B.G.'s Cultural Life." *Chronicle Christmas Annual*, 1957.

52. Ibid.

53. C. Jagan, *The West on Trial*, 161.

54. "British Guiana Goes to the Polls Tomorrow." *Daily Argosy*, August 12, 1957, 1.

55. Clef, "Electioneering with Music" in "Our Music Forum," *Sunday Argosy*, August 11, 1957, 3.

56. Lord Melody, "Apan Jaat." 1958. Lyrics available online at mobilizing-india.cscsarchive .org/gen/lyrics_apanjaat.html Accessed December 11, 2008.

57. "Burnham Says: 'Que Sera, Sera.'" *Daily Argosy*, August 15, 1957, 4.

58. David A. Granger, *Forbes Burnham and the Founding of the People's National Congress 1957-1961*. Draft of a manuscript to be published by Guyana Institute of Strategic and International Studies.

59. Ibid., 3.

60. From PPP 1957 Manifesto.

61. "Interview 7 Brindley H. Benn (Part Two)," Frank Birbalsingh (ed.). *The PPP of Guyana 1950–1992: An Oral History*, 66.

62. Frank Birbalsingh, *The People's Progressive Party of Guyana 1950–1992: An Oral History* (London: Hansib Publications, 2007), 57.

63. A. J. Seymour, et al. *Guianese History and Culture Week October 20-24, 1958: Committee's Report and Proposed Programme of Activities*, 1.

64. Octave. "The Band Moves On." *Guyana Police Force Magazine* (1972): 101–6.

65. For further details see Vibert C. Cambridge, "Vincent De Abreu: A Pioneer." *Writings on Guyanese Music 2003-2004* (Athens, OH: Department of African American Studies, 2004), 52–55.

66. Committee's Report and Proposed Programme of Activities, 1.

67. Cambridge, "Vincent De Abreu," 5.

68. Ibid., 7.

69. Norman Cameron, *Adventures in the Field of Culture* (Georgetown, Guyana: Daily Chronicle, 1971), 77.

70. Trev Sue-A-Quan, "Vivian Lee: Broadcasting Ace." In Trev Sue-A-Quan (ed.), *Cane Ripples: The Chinese in Guyana* (Vancouver: Cane Press, 2003), 193.

71. Ibid.

72. Ibid., 192.

73. Cyril Shaw died in January 2012. For further details on his life and work, see Guyana Cultural Association of New York, *Guyana Folk and Culture* vol. 2:1 (January 15, 2012): 26. Available online at guyaneseonline.files.wordpress.com/2012/01/january-2012-newsletter -_-final.pdf. Accessed January 20, 2012.

74. For further details on Al Seales, see Vibert Cambridge, "Happy Holiday: Al Seales, Billy Moore and music at Christmas." Available online at www.ecaroh.com/bmp/articles/happyholi day.htm. Also see Ray Seales, "Al Seales: The Washboard Orchestra and a Musical Revolution in Guyana." *Black Praxis: Writings on Guyanese Music 2003–2004* (Athens, OH: Department of African American Studies, 2004).
This section draws upon Ray Seale's article.

75. Interview with Ray Seales, Tampa, Florida.

76. Ray Seales, "The making of popular Guyanese music." Available online at www.gems -av.com/themakingofpopguyanesemusic.htm. Accessed November 10, 2010.

77. Bernard Heydorn. "Bing Serrão and the Ramblers—Pure Gold After 50 Years." *Indo Caribbean World* (ca. 2002).

78. Ibid.

79. Ibid.

80. Ibid.

81. For further information on George Simmons, see Vibert C. Cambridge, "George Simmons: Technique is the secret to success," in the series "Celebrating Our Creative Personalities," *Sunday Stabroek*, April 24, 2005. Available online at www.landofsixpeoples.com/gycreperjs.htm. Accessed January 11, 2013.

82. Based on Vibert Cambridge, "Wilfred Robert Adams," in the series "Celebrating Our Creative Personalities," *Sunday Stabroek*, July 25, 2004. Available online at www.landofsixpeo- ples.com/gycreperjs.htm. Accessed March 6, 2009.

83. This section is based on Vibert Cambridge, "Cy Grant: Doing it his way," In the series "Celebrating Our Creative Personalities," *Sunday Stabroek*, April 18, 2004.

84. This section is based on Vibert Cambridge, "Frank Holder: One Hell of an exciting jour- ney," in the series "Celebrating Our Creative Personalities," *Sunday Stabroek*, January 30, 2005. Available online at www.landofsixpeoples.com/gycreperjs.htm. Accessed January 11, 2013.

85. From notes to the recordings for Melodisc on Melo 1230 and Melo 1235, recorded July 8, 1952, and Pa MP 118 and PaMP 117, recorded July 22, 1952.

86. See "Recording for Parlophone and Melodisc in 1952," in Hinds, *The Life and Works of Bill (Bhagee) Rogers*, 42–43.

87. Douglas Harper, *Douglas Harper: A Man and His Music* (Sweden: self-published, ca. 2010).

88. Clef, "Our Music Forum: Notes in Brief," *Daily Argosy*, December 8, 1958.

89. Clef, "New Voice or the Concert Stage, *Daily Argosy*, December 16, 1958.

90. See, for example, "Something New, Something Old" and "Mr. 'Voice' Martin" in "Our Music Forum." *Sunday Argosy*, August 11, 1957, 3.

91. From interview in New Jersey with Charles Knights, November 2005.

92. For a useful exploration of this characteristic of Guyana's political culture, see Hazel Woolford, "A History of Political Alliances in Guyana: 1953–1997." Available online at

www.guyanacaribbeanpolitics.com/commentary/history_guyana1953-1997.html. Accessed December 10, 2008.

Chapter 7

1. Forbes Burnham, "Let Us Create One People, One Nation, One Destiny." *Guyana Graphic Independence Souvenir*, May 26, 1966, 5.

2. Recorder. "Music-Makers." *Guyana Graphic Independence Souvenir*. May 26, 1966, 43.

3. Ibid.

4. Ibid.

5. Ibid.

6. See Vibert Cambridge, "Ray Charles, British Guiana, and My Generation," in the series "Celebrating Our Creative Personalities." *Sunday Stabroek*, June 27, 2004. Available online at www.landofsixpeoples.com/news402/ns4062711.htm. Accessed November 23, 2010.

7. From Secret and Personal Guard note: NOTE FROM SIR RALPH GREY, GOVERNOR OF BRITISH GUIANA, TO R. W. PIPER OF THE COLONIAL OFFICE, LONDON (25 September 1962). Available online at www.guyana.org/govt/declassified_british_documents _1958-1964.html.

8. Cheddi Jagan notes on memorandum from Government Information Services, dated October 16, 1959, available at the Cheddi Jagan Research Center, Georgetown, Guyana.

9. PPP Manifesto for 1961 General Election. Available at the Cheddi Jagan Research Center, Georgetown, Guyana.

10. Taitt, *My Life, My Country*, 36.

11. For further information on Gilli-Danda, see en.wikipedia.org/wiki/Gilli-danda.

12. "Village Girl," from concert program for *The Future Is Bright*. Available at the Cheddi Jagan Research Center, Georgetown, Guyana.

13. *The Future Is Bright*, "If You Leave Me."

14. *The Future Is Bright*, "Believe in Me."

15. *The Future Is Bright*, "Take Yu Cool Time."

16. *The Future Is Bright*, "Girls of Water Street."

17. "Domestics get ready," *Guiana Graphic*, September 16, 1963. Accessed from Guyana Pepperpot in *Sunday Chronicle*, November 21, 2010.

18. "Do Something to Stop Exodus of Guianese from B.G." *Evening Post*, September 11, 1961, 12.

19. *The Future is Bright*, "Right Here."

20. "Music Marvels Meet—And a Song Is Born." *Evening Post*, September 19, 1961, 7.

21. Ibid.

22. For additional perspectives on Oscar, see Godfrey Chin, "A Tribute to Guyana's Newspaper Vendors," in *Nostalgias: Golden Memories of Guyana 1940-1980* (Gotha, FL: Chico Khan Publishing, 2007), 160.

23. *The Future Is Bright*, "Buy a Paper."

24. *The Future Is Bright*, "Lady Guiana."

25. *The Future Is Bright*, "Guy, Ana."

26. Ibid.

27. For more on "Guianisation" see Seecharan, *Sweetening Bitter Sugar*, and Earl John's unpublished 2010 manuscript *Being Personal: With Sugar.*

28. *The Future Is Bright*, "Soldiers in The Town."

29. From concert program for *The Future Is Bright.*

30. Taitt *My Life, My Country*, 35.

31. From e-mail to the author from Hugh Sam, December 10, 2008.

32. Ibid.

33. Taitt, *My Life, My Country*, 36.

34. Ibid., 36.

35. Taitt, *My Life, My Country*, 38.

36. For Sydney King's role in this proposal, see Estherine Adams, "Eusi Kwayana and nationalist politics in British Guiana. Part 3" in the series "History This Week." *Stabroek News*, April 16, 2009. Available online at landofsixpeoples.com/news303/ns3072710.htm. Accessed January 12, 2013.

37. See John Rex, "The Plural Society in Sociological Theory." *British Journal of Sociology* vol. 10, no. 2 (June 1959): 114–24.

38. See Palmer, *Cheddi Jagan and the Politics of Power*, 152.

39. Ved Vatuk, "Protest Songs of East Indians in British Guiana," in Kira Hall (ed.), *Essays in Indian Folk Traditions: Collected Writings of Ved Prakash Vatuk* (Meerut, India: Archana, 2007), 411.

40. Ibid.

41. Ibid., 412.

42. Although Vatuk did not mention the dhatal, I have assumed that this most essential instrument was also used.

43. Vatuk, "Protest Songs of East Indians in British Guiana," 424.

44. Ibid., 425.

45. Ibid.

46. Ibid.

47. Vatuk, *Essays in Indian Folk Traditions.*

48. "All B.G. Says Bring Back The Bacon." *Evening Post*, October 12, 1961, 1.

49. Stephen Rabe, *U.S. Intervention in British Guiana: A Cold War Story* (Chapel Hill: University of North Carolina Press, 2009), 87.

50. Ibid.

51. Jagan, *The West on Trial*, 189.

52. Ibid., 191.

53. Ibid., 208.

54. Ibid., 209.

55. Hamilton Green, *From Pain to Peace: Guyana 1953–1964* (Georgetown: self-published, ca. 1987), 59.

56. For a first-person report on the incident, see Godfrey Chin, "Guyana's Blackest Friday—16 Feb 1962," in *Nostalgias: Golden Memories of Guyana 1940 to 1980* (Gotha, FL: Chico Khan, 2008), 103–9.

57. Jagan, *The West on Trial*, 221.

58. Ibid.

59. Green, *From Pain to Peace: Guyana 1953–1964*, 83.

60. Ibid., 90–91.

61. See www.guyana.org/features/guyanastory/chapter162.html for details on the legislative actions that led to the lapsing of the legislature.

62. For details on the back story between the UK and the USA leading up to Duncan Sandy's decision, see Palmer, *Cheddi Jagan and the Politics of Power*, and Rabe, *U.S. Intervention in British Guiana*.

63. Robert Waters and Gordon Daniels, "Striking for Freedom? International Intervention and the Guianese Sugar Workers' Strike of 1964." *Cold War History* (2010): 1–32.

64. Rabe, *U.S. Intervention*, 126.

65. For further details see Vibert Cambridge, "Nesbit Chhangur," in the series "Celebrating Our Creative Personalities." *Sunday Stabroek*, June 8, 2003. Available online at www.landofsix peoples.com/gycreperjs.htm. Accessed March 7, 2009. Also see Bernard Heydorn, "Our Grand Ole Nesbit Chhangur." *Indian Caribbean World*, March 28. Available online at www.indocarib beanworld.com/archives/march26/artse.html. Accessed March 7, 2009.

66. Green, 95.

67. Ibid., 99.

68. Ibid., 100.

69. Ibid., 99.

70. Rabe, 152.

71. *Hansard* Vol 8A: 1961–62, 534–36, cited in Baytoram Ramharack, *Against the Grain: Balram Singh Rai and the Politics of Guyana* (Trinidad and Tobago: Chakra Publishing House, 2005), 208.

72. Lynette Dolphin, "The Story of the National Anthem of Guyana." *Talking about Education*, a radio program produced by the Broadcast to Schools unit of the Ministry of Education, June 1984. A copy of the program in the possession of the author.

73. Ibid.

74. Arthur and Elma Seymour, *Dictionary of Guyanese Biography* (Georgetown: Arthur and Elma Seymour, 1985), 88.

75. "William Pilgrim Invited to Guyana's Celebrations." *Jamaica Gleaner*, May 29, 1966, 10.

76. "Aback Accepts Federal Govt. Appointment." *Jamaica Gleaner*, March 26, 1959, 11.

77. "Lunch Hour Concert." *Jamaica Gleaner*, June 7, 1967, 22.

78. From e-mail to the author by Carlo Lachmansingh, June 26, 2013,.

79. Facebook contribution by Gordon Burnett on Billy Moore's Sweet Mango Interview. conversation.www.facebook.com/video/video.php?v=1544996778413&comments=.

80. Nona Permaul (e-mail attachment from Wanda Mongal, November 25, 2010).

81. Translated by "Oldie Fan." Song from the 1949 film *Dulari*. Singer: Mohamed Rafi; Lyricist: Shakeel Badayuni; Musician: Naushad. Available online at www.bollywoodlyrics.com/cs/blogs/rafi/archive/2006/08/11/18399.aspx. Accessed December 20, 2008.

82. See "Suhani Raat" on Terry Gajraj's CD *Sweet Love Songs* (New York: Mohabir Records, 1998) and "Sohanni Raat" on Ray Seales and Company CD *Cool Dive* (Tampa, Florida: Ray-GEMS Music, 1997).

83. See Sibille Hart, "Folk singing is too 'Englishified': says 1967 Music Festival Adjudicator." *Guyana Graphic*, Monday, April 10, 1967.

84. David Levering Lewis and Deborah Willis, *A Small Nation of People: W. E. B. Du Bois and African American Portraits of Progress* (New York: Amistad/HarperCollins, 2003), 13.

85. Langston Hughes, "The Negro Artist and the Racial Mountain," in Henry Louis Gates and Nellie McKay (ed.), *African American Literature*, 2nd Ed (New York: W. W. Norton, 2004), 1314.

86. "Society Urged for Preservation of Guyanese Folklore." *Evening Post*, September 28, 1961.

87. From e-mail from Wendell Bunyan to Vibert Cambridge, December 8, 2011.

88. For a description of this scene see Dick Hebdige, *Cut 'n Mix* (London: Routledge, 1987).

89. Claire Goring, "Wayne Nunes." *Guyana Folk and Culture*. vol. 1, no. 9 (December 15, 2011): 9.

90. See Tina K. Ramnarine, *Creating Their Own Space: The Development of an Indian-Caribbean Musical Tradition* (Kingston, Jamaica: University of the West Indies Press, 2001), 33.

91. Ray Seales and Vibert Cambridge, Facebook conversation, November 2010.

92. For further details, please visit: www.alanbushtrust.org.uk/music/operas/reapers.asp?room=Music. Accessed March 7, 2009.

93. For further details on the matter, see Rashleigh Jackson, *Guyana's Diplomacy: Reflections of a Former Foreign Minister* (Guyana: Free Press, 2003), especially 29–39.

94. See Odeen Ishmael, "The Ankoko Incursion." Available online at www.guyanajournal.com/ankoko.html. Accessed December 26, 2008.

95. Ibid.

96. Ibid.

97. Dave Martins, e-mail message to author, March 27, 2009. See also Dave Martins "Not A Blade O' Grass" in the column "Is So It Go." *Stabroek News*, July 29, 2012. Available online at www.stabroeknews.com/2012/features/07/29/not-a-blade-o-grass/. Accessed January 12, 2013.

98. Odeen Ishmael, "Guyana-Suriname Border Issue—from the 1960s to 2004." Available online at www.guyanajournal.com/guyana_suriname_border.html. Accessed December 26, 2008.

99. See Granada TV (UK) documentaries *The Trail of the Vanishing Voters* (December 9, 1968) and *The Making of a Prime Minister* (January 6, 1969), referred to in various publications, including www.guyana.org/features/postindependence/chapter2.html.

100. Odeen Ishmael. See also David Granger, "The Defence of the New River, 1967–1969." *Sunday Stabroek*, February 15, 2009. Available online at www.stabroeknews.com/2009/features/02/15/the-defence-of-the-new-river-1967-1969/. Accessed on March 7, 2009.

101. Gowkarran Sukdeo, "The Rupununi Uprisings Revisited: Need for a Full Account." *Guyana Journal* (October 2005). Available online at www.guyanajournal.com/rupununiuprising.html. Accessed December 26, 2008.

102. Brian Ward, "People Get Ready: Music and the Civil Rights Movement of the 1950s and 1960s." Available online at www.historynow.org/06_2006/print/historian2.html. Accessed December 26, 2008.

103. For further details see Vibert Cambridge, "Eusi Kwayana: The Political Librettist," in the series "Celebrating Our Creative Personalites," *Sunday Stabroek*, July 27, 2003. Available online at landofsixpeoples.com/news303/ns3072710.htm. Accessed January 12, 2013. Also see "Party Battle Song" in *Party Constitution and Meeting Companion* (Georgetown, Guyana: People's National Congress, Secretariat, 1983), 90–91.

Chapter 8

Chapter title from Forbes Burnham, *A Destiny to Mould A Destiny: Selected Discourses by the Prime Minister of Guyana* (Trinidad and Jamaica: Longman Caribbean, 1970), 70.

1. M. Shahabuddeen, *Constitutional Development in Guyana 1621–1978* (Georgetown, Guyana: self-published, 1978), 571.

2. Ibid.

3. Ibid.

4. "'70: The World's First Co-op Republic." *Decade Guyana 1970-1980: A Review of 10 Years of the Republic of Guyana*, 7.

5. Ibid.

6. Ibid.

7. The PPP criticized this date as it was close to Forbes Burnham's birthday.

8. M. Shahabuddeen, *Constitutional Development in Guyana 1621–1978*, 570.

9. See Vibert Cambridge, "Charwin Burnham," in the series "Celebrating Our Creative Personalities." *Sunday Stabroek*, October 30, 2005. Available online at www.landofsixpeoples.com/. Accessed March 11, 2009.

10. Ibid.

11. See Vibert Cambridge, "Bertram De Varell—the father of steel band in British Guiana," in the series "Celebrating Our Creative Personalities," *Sunday Stabroek*, November 27, 2005. Available online at www.landofsixpeoples.com/. Accessed March 11, 2009.

12. Based on conversations with London-based Guyanese steel band pioneer Aubrey Bryan and previous writings by Vibert Cambridge on this matter, specifically the series on steel bands in "Celebrating Our Creative Personalities."

13. See Onpapa Wantaya, "The Sound of Steel in Thailand." Available online at www.ecaroh .com/bmp/lead_act/soundofsteel_thailand.htm. Accessed March 11, 2009.

14. "All Govt. Corporations to Sponsor Steelbands." *Guyana Chronicle* (probably July 31, 1971).

15. Ibid.

16. Ibid.

17. Jerry Daniel, "National Pan Festival: Ignoring Our Own to Copy Others." *Sunday Graphic*, August 1, 1971, 3.

18. Cedric Grant, "Foreword," in Jackson, *Guyana's Diplomacy*, vii.

19. Ibid., viii.

20. See W. R. A. Pilgrim, "Foreword," in Lynette Dolphin, *Zeerenggang Bai* (*Let Us Sing*) (Guyana: Ministry of Education, 2000), 3.

21. Billy Pilgrim, "Lynette de Weever Dolphin." *Stabroek News*, February 20, 2000. Available online at www.qcanalumny.org/News/dollotrib2.html. Accessed November 21, 2008.

22. See Ron Sanders, *Broadcasting in Guyana* (London: Routledge & Kagan Paul, in association with International Institute of Communications, 1978), 24.

23. Ibid., citing *Public Corporations Ordinance 1962 (No. 76 of 1972)*, published in the legal supplement of the *Guyana Official Gazette*, September 30, 1972.

24. From e-mail to Vibert Cambridge from Ron Sanders, December 26, 2008.

25. Ibid.

26. Ibid.

27. Ibid.

28. Peter Lauchmonen Kempadoo, *Our Kind of Folk: Guyana* (Georgetown: National Folk Development Unit of JARAI, September 1972).

29. Based on e-mail to the author, May 17, 2009.

30. Based on liner notes for Kempadoo, *Our Kind of Folk*.

31. For further information on "Dougla" Elsie and "Kaytie" (Kassri Narine), see Rakesh Rampertaub, "'Dougla' Elsie and 'Kaytie' of Grove." in the series "Celebrating Our Creative Personalities," *Sunday Stabroek*, May 29, 2005. Available online at www.landofsixpeoples.com/news502/ns5052955.htm. Accessed on April 7, 2009.

32. For further details on these performers, especially Aunty Nylon and Aunty Margaret, see Vishnu Bisram, letter to the editor, *Stabroek News*, February 12, 2009.

33. Rampertaub, "'Dougla' Elsie and 'Kaytie' of Grove."

34. Ibid.

35. See Harry T. Hergash, *A Collection of Info: Guyanese Words and Phrases and Their Meanings* (Toronto: self-published, 2013), 34.

36. Based on conversation with Taij Singh, April 8, 2009.

37. Ibid.

38. Sibille Hart, "Folk-Singing Is Too 'Englishfied': Says 1967 Music Festival Adjudicator." *Guyana Graphic*, Monday, April 10, 1967.

39. See www.coconutxchange.com/literature/show_item.php?id=49&section_id=107223 4946.

40. Peter Jackson, "The State of Research Work and Publications on African Negro Cultural Presence in Guyana" (Paris: UNESCO, September 28, 1979). Available online at unesdoc. unesco.org/images/0003/000387/038724eb.pdf. Accessed September 5, 2014.

41. Alvin O. Thompson, "Symbolic Legacies of Slavery in Guyana." *New West Indian Guide* Vol. 80, no. 3 & 4 (2006): 191–220. Available online at www.kitlv-journals.nl/index.php/nwig/issue/view/11. Accessed March 21, 2009.

42. For references to the limited range of instruments, see Vibert Cambridge, "On Hearing the Yoruba Singers Again," in *Excuse Me, May I Offer Some Interpretations* (Toronto: WACACRO, 1975), 29.

43. Thompson, "Symbolic Legacies of Slavery in Guyana," 214.

44. See "In an address to the National History & Arts Council on Thursday, November 18, 1971 Hon'ble Elvin McDavid, Minister of Information & Culture gave this charge." *Kaie* no. 8 (December 1971): 2–4.

45. Ibid.

46. Colin Moore, "Importance of Cultural Activity." A Paper presented to the Cultural Committee of the People's Progressive Party, Wednesday, July 15, 1964. Available at the Cheddi Jagan Research Center. Shelf location CJ0012.

47. "The Vision of Carifesta." *Kaie* no. 8 (December 1971): 5.

48. Ibid.

49. Ibid., 5.

50. Ibid., 11.

51. Ibid., 8.

52. Ibid., 7.

53. Invitations were extended to Antigua, Barbados, Bahamas, Belize, Brazil, Colombia, Cuba, Dominica, Dominican Republic, French Guiana, Grenada, Guadeloupe, Haiti, Jamaica, Martinique, Montserrat, Peru, Puerto Rico, Surinam, St. Kitts-Nevis-Anguilla, St. Lucia, St. Vincent, Trinidad and Tobago, and Venezuela.

54. Ibid., 8.

55. *Kaie* no. 8 (December 1971): 8.

56. Colin Moore, "Importance of Cultural Activity."

57. PPP Manifesto for 1957 General Elections in British Guiana.

58. See Rampersaud Tiwari, "A Historical Perspective," in Hergash, *A Collection of Info*, xix. Tiwari served in the Guyana Civil Service from 1953–83 and held several senior executive-level appointments.

59. See also Frank Thomasson, *A History of Theatre in Guyana 1800–2000* (London: Hansib, 2009), 191–92.

60. "Maha Sabha on the Immigration Fund." *Evening Post*, January 17, 1972, 1.

61. Robert E. McDowell, "Interview with Sheik Sadeek—a Guyanese popular writer." *World Literature written in English* 14, no. 2 (1975): 532.

62. Forbes Burnham, "Our World of the Caribbean: Address to the Nation by the Hon. L. F. S. Burnham, S.C., Prime Minister of Guyana on the occasion of the Caribbean Festival of Creative Arts, The National Park, Georgetown, Guyana, August 25, 1972." Georgetown, Guyana.

63. For further details on this topic, see Walker-Lewis, *Central Africa in the Caribbean*.

64. "Organ Recital." *Evening Post*, August 17, 1972, 1. For further details on Ian Hall, see Leo Small, "Guyanese matches the majesty of the masters," *Guyana Graphic*, April 5, 1975, 5.

65. Based on *Carifesta KHONDI*. The tape of this program is available in the Jarai Tapes Collection available at Alden Library, Ohio University, Athens, OH.

66. Ibid.

67. See A. J. Seymour, *Cultural Policy in Guyana* (Paris: UNESCO, 1977), 23, 68.

68. Shahabuddeen, *Constitutional Development in Guyana*, 571.

69. Forbes Burnham, *Declaration of Sophia: Address by the Leader of the People's National Congress at a Special Congress to Mark the 10th Anniversary of the P.N.C. in Government* (Georgetown: People's National Congress, 1974), 12.

70. Halim Majeed, *Forbes Burnham: National Reconciliation and National Unity* (New York: Global Communications, 2005), 21–22.

71. Ibid. See also "PPP won't allow imperialist agents to topple PNC Govt." *Guyana Chronicle*, December 19, 1975; "PPP Pledges to Exploit Healthy Trends in Guyana." *Guyana Chronicle*, December 23, 1975.

72. Forbes Burnham, in *L. F. S. Burnham on National Service: Militant Library Series* vol. 1, no. 1 (undated but definitely 1974): 27.

73. Forbes Burnham, "State Paper on National Service for the Co-operative Republic of Guyana by Prime Minister, Thursday, 20 December, 1973." In *L. F. S. Burnham on National Service* 1, no. 1 (Georgetown: Design and Graphics, ca. 1974), 13.

74. Attributed to L. F. S. Burnham.

75. For further details see Tyrone Ferguson, *To Survive Sensibly or to Court Heroic Death: Management of Guyana's Political Economy 1965-1985* (Georgetown, Guyana: Public Affairs Consulting Enterprise, 1999), 194–95.

76. Ibid., 15.

77. Gora Singh, "Ideological Art: New Approach in Guyana—Cultural Revolution—Bold Step in Development Thrust." *Sunday Chronicle*, December 14, 1975.

78. See Vibert Cambridge, "A New Offering on Racial Conflict Resolution," in the series "Celebrating Our Creative Personalities." *Sunday Stabroek*, May 30, 2004. Accessible online at www.ecaroh.com/bmp/articles/rajkumari_singh.htm. Accessed January 14, 2012.

79. Gora Singh, "Cultural Revolution, bold steps in development thrust." *Sunday Chronicle*, December 14, 1975, 15.

80. Ibid.

81. For details on that career, see Vibert Cambridge, "Rector Malcolm Schultz: Making music from Canje Creek to New York," in the series "Celebrating Our Creative Personalities." *Sunday Stabroek*, May 16, 2004. Available online at www.landofsixpeoples.com/news402/ns4051611.htm. Accessed April 12, 2009.

82. Steve Narine, "Guyana bounces back into cotton race." *Sunday Chronicle*, December 14, 1975, 2.

83. See Vibert Cambridge, "'I Want to Build': An important Guyanese musical achievement." In the series "Celebrating Our Creative Personalities," *Stabroek News*, February 15, 2004. Available online at www.landofsixpeoples.com/news401/ns4021550.htm. Accessed September 5, 2014.

84. See "History of the Band Corps." Available online at gdf-gy.org/index.php?option=com_content&task=view&id=48&Itemid=90. Accessed April 13, 2009. See also Program for Military Tattoo, November 1995, shared by Col. Carl Morgan (retired).

85. For more information on R. H. Bennett see e-mail from Joyce Hendrickson dated September 17, 2010, and received by Vibert Cambridge November 1, 2010. In addition, there was an extended interview (Joyce Hendrickson and Vibert Cambridge) conducted in 2009. Audio recording in possession of the author.

86. "History of the Band Corps."

87. Ibid.

88. Ibid.

89. Based on interview with David Granger, former Commander of the Guyana Defence Force, 2008.

90. See Inspector Cutting, "Male Voice Choir," *Guyana Police Force Magazine* (1970): 61–62; and Octave, "The Band Moves On," *Guyana Police Force Magazine* (1972): 101–6.

91. Shirley Field-Ridley, "Message." *Guyfesta '75* (Georgetown, Guyana: National History and Arts Council, 1975), 1.

92. Ibid., 3.

93. A. J. Seymour, *Studies and Documents on Cultural Policies: Cultural Policy in Guyana* (Paris: UNESCO, 1977), 61.

94. For examples of successful East Indian participants in Guyfesta 75, visit www.guyanaundersiege.com/East%20Indian%20culture/Images%20Music/musiciangall/index1.html. Accessed November 10, 2009.

95. Based on e-mail from Ken Crosbie to the author.

96. Based on interview with Avis Joseph in December 2010.

97. Guyana Music Teachers' Association, *50th Anniversary Souvenir Brochure* (Georgetown, Guyana: Guyana Music Teachers' Association, 1998), 6.

98. George W. Noel, *Sing! Guyana's Children* (Georgetown, Guyana: Department of Culture, January 1979).

99. Ibid., 28.

100. Ibid.

101. Based on e-mail received from Eusi Kwayana, April 12, 2009.

102. Ibid.

103. Norman C. Stolzoff, *Wake the Town and Tell the People: Dancehall Culture in Jamaica* (Durham, NC: Duke University Press, 2000), 65.

104. Based on Vibert Cambridge, "Aubrey Cummings: A Musician of a Generation," in the series "Celebrating Our Creative Personalities." *Sunday Stabroek*, January 18, 2004. Available online at www.landofsixpeoples.com/. Accessed on March 30, 2009.

105. From interview with Aubrey Cummings in Barbados, June 2005.

106. For further details on "Pancho" Carew, see G. I. Chappelle, "Pancho took radio beyond the boundaries of a small studio." *Guyana Chronicle*, October 24, 1999. Available online at www.landofsixpeoples.com/news/nc910246.htm. Accessed April 13, 2009.

107. Based on Cambridge, "Aubrey Cummings: A Musician of a Generation."

108. Here is an extended extract from an e-mail about the contribution Edith Pieters made to Derry Etkins's music education:

Edith had to take the position of "interloper" because the programme there was mainly Theory and Singing; no pedagogy. Realizing that the system of the day was not of much help, she arranged to have Music education included in a three year training series with the Organization for Co-operation in Overseas Development OCOD, a subsidiary of CIDA.

In July/August of 1979, 1980 and 1981, Educators in various disciplines came to Guyana and conducted workshops. During the following academic year, Edith would visit our schools and follow up and monitor us. At the end of this we were given a Certificate of successful completion.

While I don't know if it carried any real weight outside of Guyana, it has contributed in very large part to the teacher I am today.

109. Brook Benton, "How to Make a Hit Record." Mercury, 1962.

110. E-mail from Romesh Singh to Vibert Cambridge, October 7, 2008.

111. Carmen McLean, "Pop and Soul Survey." *Sunday Chronicle*, February 15, 1970, 12.

112. See, for example: "Tomorrow's Children for Caribbean tour." *Daily Gleaner*, February 1, 1971, 6; "Pluto to tour Barbados, T'Dad, Guyana and Antigua." *Daily Gleaner*, January 24, 1976.

113. *Daily Gleaner*, March 12, 1971, 7.

114. "The Magic That's Ken Lazarus." *Daily Gleaner*, June 30, 1972, 8.

115. "Govt. Bans Kung Fu, Sex, Horror Films." *Guyana Chronicle*, December 18, 1976, 1. See also George Baird, "Govt. is praised for films ban decision." *Guyana Chronicle*, December 20, 1975; Carl Blackman (editorial), "Exit Dracula." *Sunday Chronicle*, December 21, 1975, 8.

116. Rashid Osman, "Stirring up a hornets' nest?: The Police and suggestive songs." *Sunday Chronicle*, Family Magazine Section, February 8, 1970, 1.

117. Based on interview with Charles Knights in 2004.

118. For details see A. J. McR. Cameron, *The Berbice Uprising 1763* (Chichester, West Sussex: Dido Press, 2007).

119. Joseph L. H. Nelson, "Malpractices in the Radio Field." *Evening Post*, January 21, 1974, 4.

120. From Facebook group "Anything Guyanese" conversation on Guyanese Hit Parade during February 1970 on January 23, 2012.

121. Joseph L. H. Nelson, "Music as a means to educate the nation." *Evening Post*, April 14, 1974, 4.

122. Roddy Fraser, "Guyanese oldies—They are packing dance floors." *Guyana Graphic*, October 11, 1975, 5.

123. Ibid.

124. Roddy Fraser, "These are my top musicians." *Guyana Chronicle*, December 13, 1975, 18.

125. Roddy Fraser, "Top Musicians of the Year." *Sunday Chronicle*, December 28, 1975, 2.

126. Roddy Fraser, "Top Vocalists for 1975," *Guyana Chronicle*, January 10, 1976, 12.

127. Roddy Fraser, "The Whittaker Genius." *Sunday Chronicle*, March 9, 1975, 13.

128. Roddy Fraser, "Lady Guybau extremely competent." *Sunday Chronicle*, December 21, 1975, 37. For other details on Monica Chopperfield, see Vibert Cambridge, "Monica Chopperfield: From Bay Monica to Lady Guymine—via Lady Monica and Lady Guybau," in the series "Celebrating Our Creative Personalities." *Sunday Stabroek*, August 31, 2003.

129. Roddy Fraser, "Sid—man of tremendous courage." *Guyana Chronicle*, May 6, 1978, 11.

130. Roddy Fraser, "Roddy Fraser Raps with Noel Adams." *Sunday Argosy*, October 21, 1973, 1.

131. Roddy Fraser, "Guyanese sets hot pace in Caribbean." *Sunday Chronicle*, February 1, 1976, 20.

132. Roddy Fraser, "My Top Steel bands for '75." *Guyana Chronicle*, February 14, 1976, 12.

133. Roddy Fraser, "Chronicle Atlantic." *Guyana Chronicle*, August 28, 1976, 13.

134. Roddy Fraser, "Musicians should buy their own instruments." *Sunday Chronicle*, February 16, 1975, 13.

135. Ibid.

136. Roddy Fraser, "Local musicians & the copy-cat craze." *Sunday Chronicle*, June 23, 1974, 11.

137. Roddy Fraser, "What a decade!" *Guyana Chronicle*, February 23, 1980, 29.

138. From interview with Billy Pilgrim.

139. See "Local musicians open G.N.C.B. account." *Sunday Chronicle*, February 12, 1978, 10.

140. Rashid Osman, "Row and rows of empty chairs at this year's Music Festival." *Sunday Graphic*, August 5, 1973, 6.

141. Ibid.

142. Ibid.

143. Rashid Osman, "Guyana Part of Carifesta Fever in J'ca" (ca. July 1976). Also Rashid Osman, "Yoruba Singers—Fine showing at Carifesta—ana silver medal to prove it." *Guyana Chronicle*, August 13, 1976, 15.

144. Harry Milner, "Musical nights." *Daily Gleaner*, August 1, 1976, 4.

145. From advertisement "Carifesta '76: CALLING ALL SINGERS." *Daily Gleaner*, June 11, 1976, 4.

146. "Jimmy Cliff, Jamaican Experience Starts off Carifesta Song Contest Show." *Daily Gleaner*, August 5, 1976.

147. Rashid Osman, "Festac: Guyana part of grand show." *Guyana Chronicle*, February 6, 1967, 1.

148. From interview with Malcolm Hall on Tuesday, April 21, 2009. The tape of the conversation is in the author's collection.

149. Ferguson, *To Survive Sensibly or to Court Heroic Death*, 223.

150. Ibid., 230.

151. Ibid., 236.

152. Ibid., 354.

153. See "Scrapping of EC Railway To Start Next Monday." *Evening Post*, December 29, 1971, 1.

154. "Foreword." *A Review of 10 Years of the Republic of Guyana*, 3.

Chapter 9

1. Anthony Everitt, *The Life of Rome's First Emperor Augustus* (New York: Random House, 2007), 131.

2. See Michael Howard, "Public Finance in Small open societies"; and John Gafar, "Income Distribution, Inequality and Poverty during Economic Reforms in Guyana." *Journal of Developing Areas* 38:1 (2004): 55–77.

3. Hemraj Muniram. "One in every three Guyanese suffers from 'nerves.'" *Guyana Chronicle*, May 31, 1980, 1.

4. Tim Merrill, ed., "The History of the Economy—Post independence," in *Guyana: A Country Study* (Washington: GPO for the Library of Congress, 1992). Available online at countrystudies.us/guyana/55.htm.

5. For further details see Karl Galinsky (ed.), *The Cambridge Companion to the Age of Augustus* (Cambridge: Cambridge University Press, 2005).

6. Other slogans included 1984: The Will to Survive; 1985: The Year of Youthfulness.

7. Based on Jimmy Hamilton's letter to the editor, *Stabroek News*, April 8, 2002. Available online at www.landofsixpeoples.com/news02/gyltns204082.htm. Accessed June 1, 2009.

8. "First Flag-Raising Ceremony at Revolution Square." *Guyana Chronicle*, February 21, 1985, 1.

9. "PM to commission textile mill for Republic." *Guyana Chronicle*, January 10, 1980. 8.

10. "Mashramani is more than an event: Publicity campaign for this year's celebrations launched." *Guyana Chronicle*, January 9, 1983.

11. "Calypso Caravans Clash." *Guyana Chronicle*, January 26, 1980, 10.

12. "National Youth Band Back in Action for Celebrations '80." *Sunday Chronicle*, January 27, 1980. See also Cambridge, "The Rogers Brothers," for further details on Eddie Rogers's musical career.

13. Based on interview with Burchmore Simon in Georgetown, August 2009.

14. "Mash—so let's pack the caravans." *Sunday Chronicle*, ca. February 7, 1982.

15. "Calypso Caravans Clash." *Guyana Chronicle*, January 26, 1980, 10.

16. A mix of calypso and Mari-Mari.

17. "Calypso shows hit the road." *Guyana Chronicle*, January 29, 1980.

18. "The Caravans roll tonight: The ladies aim to capture Mash Crown." *Sunday Chronicle*, February 1, 1980.

19. For more on Lady Guymine, see Vibert Cambridge, "Monica Chopperfield (Lady Guymine)," in *Black Praxis* (Athens, OH: Department of African American Studies, 2004), 43–44.

20. "Houston's road march out." *Sunday Chronicle*, February 1, 1980.

21. "Top Twenty." *Sunday Morning Family Magazine*, February 22, 1981.

22. "Audience boos judges' decision as Lady Guymine wins 1983 Calypso Crown." *Guyana Chronicle*, ca. February 20, 1983.

23. P. H. Day, "The calypso—Entertainment, education, but not protest." *Sunday Chronicle*, February 20, 1983, 17.

24. Lionel Smith, "Calypso contest review." *Sunday Morning Family Magazine*, February 22, 1981, x.

25. Leon Saul, "Local calypsonians need to organize." *Sunday Chronicle*, March 23, 1980, 19.

26. The author served as coordinator of the Mashramani Secretariat in 1983.

27. "Bidco Invaders—back in the top spot." *Guyana Chronicle*, February 26, 1982. See also "Mashramani steel band finals: Judges' comments." *Guyana Chronicle*, February 26, 1982.

28. Rajendra Chandisingh. "The State, the Economy, and Type of Rule in Guyana: An Assessment of Guyana's 'Socialist Revolution.'" *Latin American Perspectives* 10:4 (Autumn 1983): 67.

29. See www.flickr.com/photos/carpe_feline/515775947/ for further details. Accessed January 14, 2013.

30. Quintyn Taylor, "Mass Games here to stay." *Sunday Chronicle*, January 13, 1980. See also Quintyn Taylor, "Mass Games will be household word." *Sunday Chronicle*, January 20, 1980, 5; Cheryl Winter, "Mass Games impressive." *Sunday Chronicle*, January 27, 1980, 17.

31. Quintyn Taylor, "Mass Games a resounding success." *Sunday Chronicle*, February 24, 1980, 20.

32. Leon Saul, "Mass Games score another first." *Guyana Chronicle*, June 2, 1980, 8.

33. "Korean Mass Games team impressed with Guyana's children." *Sunday Chronicle*, March 2, 1980, 13.

34. "It was easy to feel proud." *Guyana Chronicle*, February 25, 1981.

35. Vanessa Cort, "Mass Games '82: A Unique Visual Treat—a warm colorful display by Guyana's children." *Guyana Chronicle*, ca. February 25, 1982.

36. Sase Parasnath, "Best Ever Mass Games." *Guyana Chronicle*, ca. February 20, 1983.

37. Ian McDonald. "On Mass Games and mass views." *Sunday Chronicle*, December 4, 1988, 4. See also "McDonald and *New Nation* agree to differ on Mass Games." *Sunday Chronicle*, December 4, 1988, 8.

38. For details on the Theatre Guild and theatre in Guyana, see Frank Thomasson, *A History of Theater in Guyana* (London: Hansib, 2008).

39. "Musical play for P.M.'s birthday." *Sunday Chronicle*, January 20, 1980.

40. Steve Narine, "First co-op in 1839: 21 bought Victoria for $10,000." *Sunday Chronicle*, February 10, 1980, 13.

41. Rashid Osman. "The Purchase—a resounding success." *Guyana Chronicle*, February 22, 1980.

42. "The President's Birthday Presentation: Pilgrim creates a song and dance fantasy." *Sunday Chronicle*, February 1, 1981.

43. Rashid Osman, "Few Failings, but The Yard raises above them." *Sunday Chronicle*, February 22, 1981, 16.

44. "The President's entertainment: A rich sampling of Guyanese patterns." *Guyana Chronicle*, February 23, 1982.

45. Rashid Osman, "The Birthday Concert: Visually splendid." *Guyana Chronicle*, ca. February 20, 1983.

46. See Cameron. *The Berbice Uprising, 1763*, for a comprehensive exploration of this event.

47. Rashid Osman, "*Rebellion*: Entertainment and a rallying point for freedom." *Sunday Chronicle*, February 26, 1984.

48. Rashid Osman, "*The Inheritance*: As sprawling as its setting." *Sunday Chronicle*, February 24, 1985.

49. See Thomasson, *A History of Theatre in Guyana*, for a comprehensive exploration of this development.

50. "Top Indian Bands clash for Mash." *Guyana Chronicle*, February 18, 1980, 10.

51. "They started in Essequibo 10 years ago: A merry band of musicians." *Guyana Chronicle*, February 20, 1980, 27.

52. "Musical competition finals Friday, Sat." *Guyana Chronicle*, February 17, 1982, 9.

53. "Maha Sabha Culture Corps—newest Indian band on the local scene." *Sunday Chronicle*, August 3, 1986.

54. For further details on Guyana's medals and honors, visit: www.guyanaguide.com/orders.html. Accessed November 18, 2009.

55. "C-C varieties to provide year-round entertainment . . ." *Sunday Chronicle*, January 6, 1980, 13, 24. See also "C-C Varieties: Step to boost arts and culture." *Guyana Chronicle*, January 10, 1980, 8.

56. Hydar Ally, referring to Ken Dann's *Militarization and Development*.

57. See GDF advertisement "Instrumentalists Required." *Guyana Chronicle*, ca. August 16, 1980.

58. From 2008 interview with former commander of the Guyana Defence Force Brigadier (retired) David Granger.

59. Sarojnie Bayney. "I want to build: GNS recording to mark 6th anniversary." *Guyana Chronicle*, September 24, 1980.

60. "Musical Institute." *Guyana Chronicle*, ca. late December 1982.

61. Guyana News Agency, "GNS pan men help establish steel band unit in Tanzania." *Guyana Chronicle*, August 6, 1985.

62. Leon Saul, "Radio Dem, GBC out from next month: GBC to operate to channels from July 1." *Sunday Chronicle*, June 1, 1980, 9.

63. See "Conformatory Notes on Meeting Held in Director General's Office (GNS) on Saturday 11 Oct 80 to Discuss and Implement the Service Sponsored Late Night Programme [Towards the Dawn]" prepared by V. C. Cambridge, Capt., for Director General dated 11 October 1980. Copy of the document in possession of the author.

64. Sarojnie Bayney. "Sammy's back with some big hits." *Sunday Morning Family Magazine*, July 28, 1981, v.

65. Dee Jay, "Feidtkou, Hodge top list in the Caribbean." *Sunday Chronicle*, ca. February 16, 1982.

66. Dee Jay, "Not enough Xmas tunes on the airwaves." *Sunday Chronicle*, December 13, 1981, 13.

67. Dee Jay, "Appeal went unheeded." *Guyana Chronicle*, December 25, 1981, 13.

68. See advertisement in *Guyana Chronicle*, January 10, 1982.

69. See advertisement in *Guyana Chronicle*, ca. February 22, 1983.

70. Leon Saul, "The Saxsational Whittakers: Jazz is back." *Sunday Chronicle*, April 13, 1980, 15.

71. Leon Saul, "The Birdie wows 'em: Calypso King at his effervescent best." *Guyana Chronicle*, March 15, 1980.

72. See advertisement in *Guyana Chronicle*, ca. December 12, 1982.

73. Bert Wilkinson, "Almost a Failure." *Guyana Chronicle*, ca. December 1982.

74. "Something missing in an otherwise good show." *Guyana Chronicle*, ca. early January 1983.

75. Sase Parasnath, "Lata—India's Queen of Song to perform in Guyana." *Sunday Morning Family Magazine*, June 29, 1980.

76. See advertisement "H. Gobind Presents The Show Of Shows." *Guyana Chronicle*, ca. August 20, 1980.

77. Sase Parasnath, "From India with music, song and dance." *Guyana Chronicle*, October 2, 1982.

78. "Baby will dance for you tonight." *Guyana Chronicle*, ca. December 12, 1982.

79. See advertisement in *Guyana Chronicle*, ca. December 12, 1982.

80. See "Chick Corea in Concert: A Novel environment of sound and orchestral color." *Sunday Chronicle*, August 24, 1980, 15. See also advertisement for the September 5 concert by Chick Corea and Friends. *Guyana Chronicle*, ca. late August 1980.

81. Tangerine Clarke, "Corea Brings Fusion." *Guyana Chronicle*, September 5, 1980, 10.

82. Roddy Fraser, "The Flexible Mind of Chick Corea." *Guyana Chronicle*, September 5, 1980.

83. Al Creighton, "Superb performance at Cultural Center." *Guyana Chronicle*, ca. October 8, 1982.

84. See advertisement in *Guyana Chronicle*, ca. July 7, 1985.

85. Vanessa Cort, "Berklee College Rainbow Band workshop session: Local musicians encouraged to practice." *Guyana Chronicle*, July 8, 1985.

86. "Cuban musicians due today for Mash events." *Guyana Chronicle*, ca. February 25, 1981.

87. See Kean Gibson, *Cumfa Religion and Creole Language in a Caribbean Community* (New York: State University of New York Press, 2001).

88. From interview with "Bappy" Roopchand, Guyana, 2009.

89. See "From Sinner to Preacher: Evangelist attracts 20,000 crowd." *Sunday Chronicle*, January 13, 1980; and "Myrtle Hall—Sing songs of faith." *Guyana Chronicle*, September 18, 1980.

90. "Gospel Jewels in concert." *Guyana Chronicle*, February 25, 1981.

91. See *New Age Frontier* vol. 1, no. 13: 17 (published by the United Family). Available online at www.tparents.org/Library/Unification/Publications/.../NAF-1965-07-15.pdf. Accessed November 21, 2009.

92. Based on advertisement provided by Guyana Gajraj in *Guyana Chronicle*, ca. March 1980.

93. See advertisement in *Guyana Chronicle*, ca. October 4, 1981.

94. "New Hymnal for Calypso Caribbean." *Guyana Chronicle*, ca. March 1980.

95. Leon Saul, "Local calypsonians need to organize." *Sunday Chronicle*, March 23, 1980, 19.

96. Roddy Fraser. "Do You Remember him? Mickey D hits targets in the USA." *Guyana Chronicle*, February 16, 1980, 23.

97. See amplifiedsoulnyc.wordpress.com/2010/01/22/randy-muller-and-the-story-of-brass -construction/. Accessed December 17, 2010.

98. Dee Jay, "The Music Scene." *Sunday Morning Family Magazine*, February 22, 1981. See also hem.bredband.net/funkyflyy/salsoul/cameron.html. Accessed December 17, 2010.

99. Beatrice Archer, "Music on her mind." *Guyana Chronicle*, ca. March 24, 1980.

100. "Pamela Maynard back from Toronto with a message for fellow artistes." *Guyana Chronicle*, ca. March 24, 1980.

101. Roddy Fraser, "James—The Travelling Sax Man." *Guyana Chronicle*, April 12, 1980.

102. Ibid.

103. Roddy Fraser. "The return of Souflantis." *Guyana Chronicle*, May 3, 1980, 13.

104. Counterpoint, "Ray Luck Excels." *Sunday Chronicle Family Magazine*, January 10, 1982, FM7.

105. For further details, visit Dr. Ray Luck's website at www.rayluck.com/Biography.htm. Accessed November 21, 2009.

106. Claudette Earle, "Survival instincts and a sense of rhythm." *Sunday Chronicle Family Magazine*, March 1, 1982, FM4.

107. Vibert Cambridge, "Vesta Lowe (1907–1992)." In "Celebrating Our Creative Personalities" series, *Stabroek News*, September 14, 2003.

108. Lionel Luckhoo, "If this be music—stop!" *Sunday Chronicle*, March 16, 1980. See also Lionel Luckhoo, "More Disco?" *Sunday Chronicle*, March 23, 1980, 10.

109. Roddy Fraser, "Where have all our singers gone?" *Guyana Chronicle*, April 7, 1980, 10, 11.

110. See P. A. Brathwaite and Serena Brathwaite, *Musical Traditions: Aspects of Racial Elements with Influence on a Guianese Community. A Short Treatise on the Original Basis of Music, the Rituals and Cultural Trends in the Approach to Guianese Folk-lore.* Volume 1. Georgetown, Guyana: Self-published, 1962, and P. A. Brathwaite and Serena Brathwaite, *Folk songs of Guyana in Words and Music: Queh-Queh, Chanties and Plantation Themes.* Georgetown, Guyana, n.d., ca. 1969.

111. Joycelynne Loncke, "African Survivals in the Music of Guyana." *Sunday Chronicle*, August 2, 1981.

112. See, for example, Olivia Benjamin-Ahyoung, "The Role of Music in Broadcast to Schools," the "final part" in a series on the Broadcast to Schools Unit published by *Sunday Chronicle*, ca. 1980s.

113. "Wheat by Month-end." *Guyana Chronicle*, August 8, 1986, 1.

114. "ERP Support Group meets Jan 10." *Guyana Chronicle*, December 29, 1988, 1.

115. R. M. Austin, "President Hoyte: After one year." *Sunday Chronicle*, August 10, 1986.

116. Dr. Maisha Hazzard, a professor in Ohio University's School of Telecommunications, was in Guyana to conduct training courses in television production for the Ministry of Information when President Burnham died and during the period of mourning. Her first visit to Guyana was in 1984 as a participant in a roundtable to commemorate the 150th anniversary of the abolition of slavery in the West Indies. There she demonstrated her musical prowess with

her lecture/performance, "Through the tears comes a smile," a tribute to role of spirituals in the African American struggle against slavery in the United States.

117. Rashid Osman, "Founder-Leader remembered in song, dance and poetry." *Sunday Chronicle*, August 10, 1986, 10.

118. "Carol Recital at the Residence: Princesville Orchestra, Police Choir together for musical pleasure." *Guyana Chronicle*, December 31, 1986.

119. "Give Us This Land—2 musical versions." *Sunday Chronicle*, January 31, 1982.

120. "Cleveland Hamilton's 'Give Us This Land' set to music." *Sunday Morning*, January 17, 1982, FM1.

121. Dee Jay, "The music scene." *Sunday Chronicle*, August 21, 1988. See also "Top 20." *Sunday Chronicle*, December 18, 1988; and "Top 20." *Sunday Chronicle*, September 3, 1989.

Chapter 10

1. Gail Teixeira, "Cheddi Jagan, Personal Glimpses." *Journal of the Cheddi Jagan Research Center* vol. 1 (2008): 66.

2. Center on Hemispheric Affairs, "Economic Despair and Bleak Prospect for Fair Elections Threaten to Convert Guyana into another Haiti." *News and Analysis*, April 10, 1990.

3. Ibid.

4. Anna Benjamin, *Freedom of Expression and the Birth of Stabroek News* (Georgetown, Guyana: Guyana Publications, 2007), 66–67.

5. Ibid.

6. See "President Hoyte's letter to Sen. Kennedy." *Sunday Chronicle*, May 6, 1990, 9.

7. "Guyana and US sign new PL480 Agreement valued at $M4 facilitating the importation of 24,000 metric tons of wheat." *Guyana Chronicle*, January 10, 1990, 1.

8. "Milk Valued over $1 Million US from French Government." *Guyana Chronicle*, January 23, 1990, 1.

9. In 2010 one ounce of gold was worth more than US$1000.

10. Cheddi Jagan, *Guyana: Two Years with PPP/CIVC Government*, (Georgetown, Guyana: People's Progressive Party, 1994), 19.

11. Ibid., 20–22.

12. See Eusi Kwayana, "Running Out." Commentary at Guyana Caribbean Politics.com. Posted May 21, 2004. Available online at www.guyanacaribbeanpolitics.com/kwayana/kway ana_052104.html. Accessed August 5, 2009.

13. Ibid.

14. These were the Democratic Labour Movement (DLM), National Democratic Party (NDP), National Republican Party (NRP), People's Democratic Movement (PDM), People's National Congress/Reform (PNC/Reform), People's Progressive Party/Civic (PPP/Civic), The United Force (TUF), Union of Guyanese International (UGI), United Republican Party (URP), United Working Party (UWP), and the Working People's Alliance (WPA).

15. Based on e-mail from Gail Teixeira to the author August 12, 2009.

16. See *My Guyana, Eldorado: Songs for All Guyanese* (Georgetown: PPP, 1987), 15; and *Songbook compiled by the Women's Progressive Organization* (Georgetown: Women's Progressive Organization, n.d.), 12.

17. From interview with Gail Teixeira, August 12, 2009.

18. See "Commonwealth Observers declare poll free and fair." *Guyana Chronicle*, October 7, 1992; and "Nothing to suggest integrity of ballot was violated—Carter." *Guyana Chronicle*, October 7, 1992.

19. See "Hoyte accepts results of poll" and "Collins confirms results." *Guyana Chronicle*, October 8, 1992, 1.

20. Deryck M. Bernard, "Folk Traditions and National Development: A Role for African Folk Music from Guyana?" An unpublished paper presented at the conference Soundscapes: Reflections on Caribbean Oral and Aural Traditions, UWI, Cave Hill, July 2005.

21. Ibid., 8.

22. Lynette de W. Dolphin (Complier and Transcriber), *One Hundred Folk Songs of Guyana* (Georgetown: Department of Culture, 1996).

23. See, for example, the songbooks of the Women's Progressive Organization and the Progressive Youth Organization.

24. For a useful perspective on this dynamic, see Alan Fenty, "The Trouble with Mashramani Observations and Expectations." *Stabroek News*, October 16, 2009. Available online at www.stabroeknews.com/2009/archives/10/16/the-trouble-with-mashramani-observations-and-expectations/. Accessed January 15, 2013.

25. Gillian Persaud, "Mighty Rebel is new calypso monarch." *Stabroek News*, February 23, 1993, 12.

26. From "From Step to Step One Makes Progress," an interview President Cheddi Jagan had with Sharief Khan, editor of the *Guyana Chronicle*, on the second anniversary of the PPP/Civic Government of National Unity and published in *Guyana: Two Years with PPP/Civic Government*, 33.

27. *Guyana Chronicle*, January 27, 1990, 10.

28. People's Progressive Party, *PPP/Civic Manifesto: Consolidating Democracy and Unity for Continuous Progress*, 28–31.

29. Based on interview with Gail Teixeira, August 2009.

30. Stacey Bess, "The Canary Is Back." *Guyanese Observer*. Found at http://www.mustrad.org.uk/articles/kaiso08.htm.

31. Based on interview with Gail Teixeira, August 2009.

32. See Laws of Guyana. Chapter 23:01 *Racial Hostility Act*, Sec 2: 1 a, b, and c.

33. Copy of the memorandum in the author's collection.

34. Teixeira, 2009.

35. "Bonny Alves—the under-celebrated Guyanese music pioneer." *Kaieteur News*, September 15, 2007.

36. Ibid. Also from interview with the author in 2008.

37. Ibid.

38. Ibid.

39. Ibid.

40. For a short and personalized summary of the history of this village, see "From Plantation Orange Nassau to Buxton, 168 years later, the struggle continues." Available online at blogs.myspace.com/index.cfm?fuseaction=blog.view&friendId=167572004&blogId=372987087. Among the notable Guyanese with Buxton roots are Eusi Kwayana, Dr. Frank Williams, Randal Butisingh, and Rampersaud Tiwari.

41. Based on interview with Birchmore Simon, August 16, 2009, in Georgetown, Guyana.

42. The band's founding members included Anthony Blair ("Blondie"), Braithwaite (singer, from Plaisance), Burchmore Simon (bass, Buxton/Golden Grove), "Mervin" (keyboard), Headley (singer, Buxton), Mark Walcott, Pepe (trumpet, Mahaica), and "Prick" (drummer, Ann's Grove). The only member who was not from the East Coast was Compton Leacock, who was from the West Coast.

43. Ibid.

44. Ibid.

45. Ibid., 8.

46. www.sweetsoca.com/folk/korokwa_folkguyanastyle.htm.

47. Based on interview with Edith Pieters, August 2000, Georgetown.

48. Based on interview with Russell Lancaster, August 2000, Georgetown.

49. www.yardflex.com/archives/000558.html.

50. See Vibert C. Cambridge, "Winston Ewart Smith (Sir Wins): A promoter of Guyanese music," in the series "Celebrating Our Creative Personalities." *Sunday Stabroek*, October 31, 2004. Available online at www.landofsixpeoples.com/gylinkspeople.htm.

51. For example, Loris Holland won five Daytime Emmy Awards between 2001 and 2005; Alyson Cambridge won the Grand Finals, Metropolitan Opera, National Council Awards, 2003, and has gone on establish an impressive international career.

Chapter 11

1. E. M. T. Moore, "Random Remarks on Social Music." In Marion Rockcliffe and Joseph W. Jackson (ed.), *British Guiana Woman's Centenary Effort 1831–1931* (Georgetown, British Guiana: Daily Argosy, 1931), 81.

2. Lynette Dolphin (Complier), *Ten National Songs of Guyana* (Georgetown, Guyana: National History and Arts Council of the Ministry of Information, 1969).

3. See *Tom Charles and the Syncopaters. Fete For So!!* (Cook 911). Cook Caribbean, 1959.

4. Refer to my essay on Hemerding in the "Celebrating Our Creative Personalities" series in *Sunday Stabroek*.

5. Anil Azeez. Also refer to interview with Alexis Stephens, Georgetown, Guyana, August 2008.

6. A definition of a song generally offered on online sources is "a short metrical musical composition intended or adapted to singing."

7. Herman Snijders and Joycelynne Loncke (ed.), *One Hundred Years of Classical Music in the Guianas: Selected Pieces for Pianoforte* (Guyana: University of Guyana, 2002).

8. Central Rediffusion Services Limited, *Commercial Broadcasting in the British West Indies* (London: Butterworths Scientific Publications, 1956), x.

9. Ibid., 24, 39.

10. Ibid., 23–24.

11. Ibid., 28.

12. Ibid., 53.

13. Ibid., 55.

14. From Facebook conversation with Ray Seales on February 2, 2012.

15. R. Seales, "Al Seales: The Washboard Orchestra and a Musical Revolution Guyana." in, Vibert Cambridge (ed.), *Black Praxis: Writings on Guyanese Music 2003–2004* (Athens, OH: Department of African American Studies, 2004), 141.

16. W. McDavid, "The Progress of Music in B.G." In Rockcliffe and Jackson, *British Guiana Woman's Centenary Effort*, 91.

17. For further discussion on those initiatives, see "Beck" and "I Want to Build" in the "Celebrating Our Creative Personalities" series.

18. Sonjah Stanley Niaah, *Dance Hall: From Slave Ship to Ghetto* (Ottawa: University of Ottawa Press, 2010), 2.

19. From an interview with President Janet Jagan, Georgetown, August 2008.

20. Raymond T. Smith discusses this phenomenon in *The Negro Family in British Guiana: Family Structure and Social Status in Villages* (London: Routledge & Paul, 1956). A similar conclusion was arrived at by Lt. Col (retired) Keith Booker during a conversation in Georgetown in 2009.

Bibliography

Abrahams, R., and Szwed, J. *After Africa: Extracts from British Travel Accounts and Journals of the Seventeenth, Eighteenth, and Nineteenth Centuries concerning the Slaves, their manners, and Customs in the British West Indies*. New Haven: Yale University Press, 1983.

Ackroyd, P. *Albion: The Origins of the English Imagination*. New York: Doubleday, 2002.

Amerindian Languages Project. *An Introduction to the Akawaio and Arekuna Peoples of Guyana*. Guyana: University of Guyana, 1977.

Anderson, B. *Imagined Communities*. London: Verso, 1983.

Arno, W. *History of Victoria Village, East Coast, Demerara*. Georgetown: self-published, ca. 1957.

Arya, U. *Ritual Songs and Folksongs of the Hindus of Surinam*. Leiden: E.J. Brill, 1968.

August, T. *The Selling of the Empire: British and French Imperialist Propaganda, 1890–1940*. Westport, CT: Greenwood Press, 1985.

Bagehot, W. *The English Constitution*. Oxford: Oxford University Press, 1929.

Bacchus, M. *Utilization, Misuse, and Development of Human Resources in the Early West Indian Colonies*. Waterloo, Ontario: Wilfrid Laurier University Press, 1990.

Baptiste, F. *War, Cooperation and Conflict: The European Possessions in the Caribbean, 1939–1945*. Westport, CT: Greenwood Press, 1988.

Benjamin, A. *Freedom of Expression and the Birth of Stabroek News*. Georgetown, Guyana: Guyana Publications Incorporated, 2007.

Berger, B. "How Long is a Generation?" *British Journal of Sociology* 11, no. 1 (March 1960): 10–23.

Bernard, D. "Folk Traditions and National Development: A Role for African Folk Music from Guyana?" Unpublished paper presented at the conference Soundscapes: Reflections on Caribbean Oral and Aural Traditions, UWI, Cave Hill, July 2005.

Best, C. "Technology Constructing Culture: Tracking Soca's First 'Post-.'" *Small Axe* 5, no. 1 (March 2001): 27–43.

Birbalsingh, F. *The PPP of Guyana 1950–1992: An Oral History*. London: Hansib, 2007.

Blackman, C. "Foreword." *A Review of 10 Years of the Republic of Guyana*, Magazine Makers, 1980, 3.

Blanning, T. *The Triumph of Music: The Rise of Composers, Musicians, and Their Art*. Boston: Harvard University Press, 2010.

Blanshard, P. *Democracy and Empire in the Caribbean*. New York: Macmillan, 1947.

Braithwaite, C. "The African-Guyanese Demographic Transition: An Analysis of Growth Trends, 1838–1988." In Winston McGowan, James G. Rose, and David Granger, eds. *Themes in African-Guyanese History*. Georgetown: Free Press, 1998. 201–34.

Brathwaite, P., and Brathwaite, S. *Musical Traditions: Aspects of Racial Elements with Influence on a Guianese Community. Volume 1*. Georgetown, British Guiana: self-published, 1962.

———. *Folk Songs of Guyana in Words and Music*. Georgetown Guyana: self-published, ca. 1966.

———. *Musical Traditions, Vol. 2.* Georgetown, Guyana: self-published, 1979.

British Guiana—British Empire Exhibition, Wembley 1924. 1st ed. London: British Empire Exhibition, 1924.

Browne, R. "The 'Bad Business' of Obeah: Power, Authority, and the Politics of Slave Culture in the British Caribbean." *William and Mary Quarterly* 68, no. 3 (July 2011): 451–80.

Bryan, A. *The Aubrapan: New Pan Invention.* London: Aubrey Bryan, 1986.

Bullivant, J. "Communist Anti-Colonialism: Empire and Nationalism in Alan Bush's *The Sugar Reapers.*" Paper presented to QUB Seminar, University of Nottingham, October 2010.

Bullitt, M. "Toward a Marxist Theory of Aesthetics: The Development of Socialist Realism in the Soviet Union." *Russian Review* 35, no. 1 (January 1976): 53–76.

Burnard, T. *Hearing Slaves Speak.* Guyana: Caribbean Press, 2010.

Burnham, L. *A Destiny to Mould: Selected Discourses by the Prime Minister of Guyana.* Trinidad and Jamaica: Longman Caribbean, 1970.

———. "Let us create One people, One nation, One destiny." *Guyana Graphic, Independence Souvenir,* May 26, 1966. 5.

———. "Our World of the Caribbean." Address to the Nation by the Hon. L. F. S. Burnham, S.C., Prime Minister of Guyana on the occasion of the Caribbean Festival of Creative Arts, National Park, Georgetown, Guyana, August 25, 1972.

———. "Declaration of Sophia." Address by the Leader of the People's National Congress at a Special Congress to Mark the 10th Anniversary of the PNC in Government. Georgetown: People's National Congress, 1974.

Burton, R. *Afro-Creole: Power, Opposition, and Play in the Caribbean.* Ithaca: Cornell University Press, 1997.

Busby, M. "Roy A K Heath: Brilliant, gentle writer whose novels explored the subtle textures of Guyanese life." Obituary, *Guardian* (UK), May 20, 2008. Available online at www.guardian .co.uk/books/2008/may/20/culture.obituaries. Accessed March 21, 2012.

Cambridge, V. *Excuse Me, May I Offer Some Interpretations.* Toronto: WACACRO, 1975.

———. "Nesbit Chhangur." *Sunday Stabroek* (Celebrating Our Creative Personalities), June 8, 2003. Available online at www.landofsixpeoples.com/gycreperjs.htm. Accessed March 7, 2009.

———. "Vincent De Abreu: A Pioneer." *Sunday Stabroek* (Celebrating Our Creative Personalities), April 20, 2003.

———. "Eusi Kwayana: The Librettist of Guyana's Political Opera or the Political Musician." *Sunday Stabroek* (Celebrating Our Creative Personalities), July 20, 2003.

———. "The Mootoo Brothers." *Sunday Stabroek* (Celebrating Our Creative Personalities), August 3, 2003.

———. "Ken "Snakehips" Johnson." *Sunday Stabroek* (Celebrating Our Creative Personalities), May 29, 2003.

———. "Hubert (Bert) and Edward (Eddie)—The Rogers Brothers and Musical Giants," *Sunday Stabroek* (Celebrating Our Creative Personalities), February 29, 2004.

———. "Cy Grant: Doing It His Way." *Sunday Stabroek* (Celebrating Our Creative Personalities), April 18, 2004.

———. "Nigel Hoyow: Musical Success on Both Sides of the Atlantic." *Sunday Stabroek* (Celebrating Our Creative Personalities), May 2, 2004.

———. "Vincent De Abreu: A Pioneer." *Writings on Guyanese Music 2003-2004*. Athens, OH: Department of African American Studies, Ohio University, 2004.

———. "James Alexander Phoenix and the British Guiana Police Male Voice Choir." In *Black Praxis: Writings on Guyanese Music 2003-2004*. Athens, OH: Department of African American Studies, Ohio University, 2004.

———. "Monica Chopperfield (Lady Guymine)." In *Black Praxis: Writings on Guyanese Music 2003-2004*. Athens, OH: Department of African American Studies, Ohio University, 2004, 43-44.

———. "A New Offering on Racial Conflict Resolution." *Sunday Stabroek* (Celebrating Our Creative Personalities), May 30, 2004.

———. "Rudolph Dunbar: 'A fascinating person, composer, musical conductor, musical journalist, and Caribbean pioneer of the classics.'" Alex Pascal (June 16, 1988), *Sunday Stabroek* (Celebrating Our Creative Personalities), 2004.

———. "Wilfred Robert Adams," *Sunday Stabroek* (Celebrating Our Creative Personalities), July 25, 2004.

———. "Rannie Hart—A Virtuoso by Many Names." *Sunday Stabroek* (Celebrating Our Creative Personalities), 2005.

———. "Charwin Burnham." *Sunday Stabroek* (Celebrating Our Creative Personalities), October 30, 2005. Available online at www.landofsixpeoples.com/. Accessed March 11, 2009.

———. "Bertram De Varell—The Father of steel band in British Guiana." *Sunday Stabroek* (Celebrating Our Creative Personalities), November 27, 2005. Available online at www .landofsixpeoples.com/. Accessed March 11, 2009.

———. "Ray Charles, British Guiana, and my generation." *Sunday Stabroek*, (Celebrating Our Creative Personalities), June 27, 2004. Available online at www.landofsixpeoples.com/ news402/ns4062711.htm. Accessed November 23, 2010.

———. "Frank Holder: One Hell of an exciting journey." *Sunday Stabroek* (Celebrating Our Creative Personalities), January 30, 2005.

———. "James Ingram Fox: A Treasured Composer." *Sunday Stabroek* (Celebrating Our Creative Personalities), March 13, 2005.

———. "George Simmons: Techniques is the secret to success." *Sunday Stabroek* (Celebrating Our Creative Personalities), April 24, 2005.

———. "Birdsong and the Guyanese Diaspora in New York: A Preliminary and Orienting Study." Paper presented at the conference Soundscapes: Reflections on Caribbean Oral and Aural Traditions, University of the West Indies, Cave Hill, Barbados, July 25-29, 2005.

———. "Rector Malcolm Schultz: Making Music from Canje Creek to New York." *Sunday Stabroek* (Celebrating Our Creative Personalities), May 16, 2006.

———. "John 'Bagpipe' Fredericks–There is more to the name." *Stabroek News* (Celebrating Our Creative Personalities), November 9, 2003.

———. "'I Want to Build': An important Guyanese musical achievement." *Stabroek News* (Celebrating Our Creative Personalities), February 15, 2004.

———. "Aubrey Cummings: A Musician of a Generation." *Sunday Stabroek* (Celebrating Our Creative Personalities), January 18, 2004. Available online at www.landofsixpeoples.com/. Accessed on March 30, 2009.

——. "Derry Etkins: An Inquisitive Musical Mind." *Sunday Stabroek* (Celebrating Our Creative Personalities), June 12, 2005. Available online at www.landofsixpeoples.com/. Accessed on March 30, 2009.

——. "Winston Ewart Smith (Sir Wins): A promoter of Guyanese music." *Sunday Stabroek* (Celebrating Our Creative Personalities), October 31, 2004. Available online at www.land ofsixpeoples.com/gylinkspeople.htm.

Cameron, A. *The Berbice Uprising, 1763.* Chichester, West Sussex: Dido Press, 2007.

Cameron, N. *The Evolution of the Negro* (Volume 1). Georgetown, Demerara: Argosy, 1929.

—— (ed.). *Guianese Poetry: Covering the 100-year period 1831–1931.* British Guiana: self-published, 1931. Reprint, Nendeln: Kraus-Thomson Organization Ltd., 1970.

——. *Adventures in the Field of Culture.* Georgetown, British Guiana: self-published (printed by the Daily Chronicle), 1971.

Carson, J. *Home Away from Home: The Story of the USO.* New York: Harper & Brothers, 1946.

Carter, M. "This Is the Dark Time My Love." *Poems of Resistance from Guiana.* London: Lawrence and Wishart, 1954.

Center on Hemispheric Affairs. "Economic Despair and Bleak Prospect for Fair Elections Threaten to Convert Guyana into another Haiti." *News and Analysis*, April 10, 1990.

Central Rediffusion Services Limited. *Commercial Broadcasting in the British West Indies.* London: Butterworths Scientific Publications, 1956.

Chandisingh, R. "The State, the Economy, and Type of Rule in Guyana: An Assessment of Guyana's 'Socialist Revolution.'" *Latin American Perspectives* 10, no. 4 (Autumn 1983: 59–67.

Chase, A. *A History of Trade Unionism in Guyana, 1900–1961.* Georgetown, British Guiana: self-published, 1964.

Chin, G. "Best Little Whorehouse," In Trev Sue-A-Quan (ed.). *Cane Ripples: The Chinese in Guyana.* Vancouver: Cane Press, 2003, 180–82.

——. "A Tribute to Guyana's Newspaper Vendors." In *Nostalgias: Golden Memories of Guyana 1940-1980.* Gotha, FL: Chico Khan, 2007, 160.

Christian, G. "The Interwar Years & the Caribbean Soldier in Social Transformation: A Dominican Perspective." Available online at da-academy.org/TheCaribbeanSoldierin SocialTransformation.pdf. Accessed March 19, 2012.

Coe, C. "Educating an African Leadership: Achimota and the Teaching of African Culture in the Gold Coast." *Africa Today* 49:3 (September 2002): 23–46.

Collins, G. "Ringing in the New Millennium—24 times." *Current* (November 15, 1999). Available online at www.current.org/prog/prog921m.html. Accessed March 21, 2012.

Columbus, C. *Letters of Christopher Columbus, with Other Original Documents Relating to his Four Voyages to the New World.* Edited and translated by R. H. Major. London: Hakhyt Society, 1961.

Conn, S., Rose C. Engleman, and Brian Fairchild. *United States Army in World War II—The Western Hemisphere: Guarding the United States and Its Outposts.* Washington: Center of Military History, United States Army, 1964.

Couldry, N. *Listening Beyond the Echoes: Media, Ethics, and Agency in an Uncertain World.* Boulder: Paradigm, 2006.

Cowley, J. "Cultural 'fusions': aspects of British West Indian music in the USA and Britain 1918–1951." *Popular Music* Vol. 5 (January 1985): 81–96.

Cruickshank, G. *Notes on the History of St. Andrew's Kirk, Demerara.* Georgetown, Demerara: Estate of C. K. Jardine, 1911.

——. *Black Talk—Being Notes on Negro Dialect in British Guiana with (Inevitably) A Chapter on the Vernacular of Barbados.* Georgetown, British Guiana: Argosy, 1916.

da Costa, Emilia Viotti. *Crowns of Glory, Tears of Blood: The Demerara Slave Rebellion of 1823.* Oxford: Oxford University Press, 1994.

Daly, V. *A Short History of the Guyanese People.* London: Macmillan, 1993.

David, M. *The State, the Family, and Education.* London and Boston: Routledge and Kagan Paul, 1980.

De Barros, J. "Metropolitan policies and colonial practices at the boys' reformatory in British Guiana." *Journal of Imperial and Commonwealth History* 30, no. 2 (2002): 1–24.

——. *Order and Place in a Colonial Society: Patterns of Struggle and Resistance in Georgetown, British Guiana, 1889–1924.* Montreal: McGill University Press, 2003.

Despres, L. *Cultural Pluralism and Nationalist Politics in British Guiana.* Chicago: Rand McNally, 1967.

de Weever, A. *A Text Book of the Geography of British Guiana, the West Indies, and South America for the Use of Schools* (Georgetown: Daily Argosy, 1907).

de Weever, P. "The History of Music: 1831–1931." *Daily Argosy*, October 1931.

Dolphin, C. "Let the Children Sing." *Kyk-Over-Al* 1:4 (June 1947): 16.

——. "The Vision of Carifesta." *Kaie* 8 (December 1971).

Dolphin, L. (ed.). *Ten National Songs of Guyana.* Georgetown, Guyana: National History and Arts Council, Ministry of Information, 1969.

——. "A Short History of the Guyana Music Teachers' Association." *50th Anniversary Souvenir Brochure.* Georgetown, Guyana: Guyana Music Teachers' Association, 1998, 5.

——. "The Story of the National Anthem of Guyana." *Talking about Education,* radio program produced by the Broadcast to Schools unit of the Ministry of Education, June 1984.

——. *One Hundred Folk Songs of Guyana.* Georgetown: Department of Culture, 1996.

Edwards, W., and Keane Gibson. "An Ethnohistory of Amerindians in Guyana." *Ethnohistory* 26, no. 2 (Spring 1979): 161–75.

Elder, J. *Song Games from Trinidad and Tobago.* Columbus, OH: American Folklore Society, 1965.

Epstein, D. *Sinful Tunes and Spirituals: Black Folk Music to the Civil War.* Chicago: University of Illinois Press, 1977.

Everitt, A. *The Life of Rome's First Emperor Augustus.* New York: Random House, 2007.

Field-Ridley, S. "Message." *Guyfesta '75.* Georgetown, Guyana: National History and Arts Council, 1975.

Ferguson, T. *To Survive Sensibly or to Court Heroic Death: Management of Guyana's Political Economy 1965–1985.* Georgetown: self-published, 1999.

Fraser, C. *Ambivalent Anti-Colonialism: The United States and the Genesis of West Indian Independence, 1940-1964.* Westport, CT: Greenwood Press, 1994.

Galinsky, K. (ed.). *The Cambridge Companion to the Age of Augustus.* Cambridge: Cambridge University Press, 2005.

Garner, S. *Ethnicity, Class, and Gender: Guyana 1838–1985.* Kingston, Jamaica: Ian Randle, 2007.

Gibson, K. *Cumfa Religion and Creole Language in a Caribbean Community.* New York: State University of New York Press, 2001.

GIS. "'70: The World's First Co-op Republic." *Decade Guyana 1970-1980: A Review of 10 Years of the Republic of Guyana.* Georgetown: Government Information Service, 1980.

Gafar, J. "Income Distribution, Inequality and Poverty during Economic Reforms in Guyana." *Journal of Developing Areas* 38, no. 1 (2004).

Goring, C. "Wayne Nunes." *Guyana Folk and Culture* 1, no. 9 (December 15, 2011): 9.

Granger, D. "Civil Violence, Domestic Terrorism and Internal Security in Guyana, 1953-2005." Paper presented to Panel "Threats to Caribbean Security" at Research and Education in Defence and Security Studies, Center for Hemispheric Defence Studies, Santiago, Chile, October 28–30, 2003.

———. *Forbes Burnham and the Founding of the People's National Congress 1957-1961.* Unpublished manuscript.

———. *Guyana's Periodicals: A Brief Survey of the Periodical Press, 1796-2006.* Guyana: Free Press, 2008.

———. "The Defence of the New River, 1967–1969." *Sunday Stabroek*, February 15, 2009. Available online at www.stabroeknews.com/2009/features/02/15/the-defence-of-the-new-river-1967-1969/. Accessed March 7, 2009.

Grant, C. "Foreword." In Rashleigh Jackson, *Guyana's Diplomacy: Reflections of a Former Foreign Minister.* Georgetown, Guyana: Free Press, 2003, vii.

Graziano, J. "The Early Life and Career of the 'Black Patti': The Odyssey of an African American Singer in the Late Nineteenth Century." *Journal of the American Musicological Society* 53, no. 3 (Autumn 2000): 543–96.

Green, H. *From Pain to Peace: Guyana 1953–1964.* Georgetown, Guyana: self-published, ca. 1987.

Green, J. *Black Edwardians: Black People in Britain 1901-1914.* London: Frank Cass, 1998.

Grey, Earl. "Being the substance of a dispatch from Governor Barkly, presented to the Society of the Right Hon. Earl Grey, Her Majesty's late Secretary of State for the Colonies." *Journal of the Statistical Society of London* 15 (September 1852): 234.

Guilbault, J. *Governing Sound: The Cultural Politics of Trinidad's Carnival Musics.* Chicago: University of Chicago Press, 2007.

Guyana Music Teachers' Association. *50th Anniversary Souvenir Brochure.* Georgetown: Guyana, 1998.

Havinden, M., and David Meredith. *Colonialism and Development: Britain and its Tropical Colonies, 1850-1960.* London: Routledge, 1993.

Heath, R. *Shadows Round the Moon.* London: William Collins Sons, 1990.

Hebdige, D. *Cut 'n Mix: Culture, Identity and Caribbean Music.* London: Comedia, 1987.

Heydorn, B. "Bing Serrão and the Ramblers–Pure Gold After 50 Years." *Indo Caribbean World*, ca. 2002.

———. "Our Grand Ole Nesbit Chhangur." *Indian Caribbean World*, March 28, 2002. Available online at www.indocaribbeanworld.com/archives/march26/artse.html. Accessed March 7, 2009.

Herzog, G. "Speech-Melody and Primitive Music." *Musical Quarterly* 20, no. 4 (October 1934): 452–66.

High, S. "The racial politics of criminal jurisdiction in the aftermath of the Anglo-American 'destroyers-for-bases' deal, 1940-1950." *Journal of Imperial and Commonwealth History* 32, no. 3 (2004): 77–105.

Higman, B. "Population and Labor in the British Caribbean in the Early 19th Century." In Stanley L. Engerman and Robert E. Gallman (eds.), *Long-Term Factors in American Economic Growth*. Chicago: University of Chicago Press, 1986, 605–40.

Hillhouse, W. *Indian Notices.* 1825; repr. Georgetown, Guyana: National Commission for Research Materials, 1978.

Hinds, A. "Bhagee," in "Shantos by Bill Rogers." *Forward Guyana: A Magazine to Commemorate the Cooperative Republic of Guyana.* Georgetown: Guyana, February 1970.

Hinds, R. *The Life and Works of Bill (Bhagee) Rogers and the Origins of Shanto Music in Guyana.* Georgetown: Carifesta X Secretariat, 2008.

Howard, M. "Public Finance in Small Open Societies." *Journal of Developing Areas* 38, no. 1 (2004): 55–77.

Howe, G. *Race, War, and Nationalism: A Social History of West Indians in the First World War.* Jamaica: Ian Randle, 2002.

Hughes, L. "The Negro Artist and the Racial Mountain." In Henry Louis Gates and Nellie McKay (general eds.), *African American Literature*, 2nd ed. New York: W. W. Norton, 2004.

Ifill, M. "Creating and Solidifying African Ethnic Identity in Guyana." *Stabroek News*, September 23, 2010. Available online at www.stabroeknews.com/2010/features/09/23/creating-and-solidifying-african-ethnic-identity-in-guiana/. Accessed September 23, 2010.

———. "Federating the British West Indies." *Stabroek News* (History This Week), July 1, 2003. Available online at landofsixpeoples.com/news303/ns3071225.htm. Accessed January 26, 2013.

Ishmael, O. "The Ankoko Incursion." Available online at www.guyanajournal.com/ankoko.html. Accessed December 26, 2008.

———. "Guyana-Suriname Border Issue—From the 1960s to 2004." Available online at www.guyanajournal.com/guyana_suriname_border.html. Accessed December 26, 2008.

Jayawardena, C. *Conflict and Solidarity in a Guianese Plantation.* London: Athlone Press, 1963.

Jackson, R. *Guyana's Diplomacy: Reflections of a Former Foreign Minister.* Guyana: Free Press, 2003.

Jackson, P. "The State of Research Work and Publications on African Negro Cultural Presence in Guyana." Paris: UNESCO, September 28, 1979.

Jagan, C. *The West on Trial: My Fight for Guyana's Freedom.* New York: International Publishers, 1972.

———. *Guyana: Two Years with PPP/CIVC Government.* Georgetown, Guyana: People's Progressive Party, 1994.

John, E. *Being Personal: With Sugar.* Unpublished manuscript, 2010.

———. *Penumbrians.* Unpublished manuscript, 2012.

Johnson, H., and Karl Watson. *The White Minority in the Caribbean.* Kingston, Jamaica: Ian Randle, 1997.

Joseph, C. *The British West Indian Regiment 1914–1918.* Georgetown, Guyana: Free Press, 2008.

Josiah, B. "After Emancipation: Aspects of Village Life in Guyana, 1869-1911." *Journal of Negro History* 82, no. 1 (Winter 1997): 105–21.

——. *Migration, Mining, and the African Diaspora: Guyana in the Nineteenth and Twentieth Centuries*. New York: Palgrave, 2011.

Karenga, M. *Introduction to African American Studies*. Los Angeles: Kawaida, 1982.

Kempadoo, P. *Our Kind of Folk: Guyana*. Georgetown: National Folk Development Unit of JARAI, 1972.

Kerry, E. *First Annual Report of the British Guiana Music Teachers' Association for the Year Ended March 31, 1949*. Georgetown, British Guiana.

Kirk, H. *Twenty-five Years in British Guiana*. Westport, CT: Negro Universities Press, 1970.

Kirk-Greene, A. *On Crown Service: A History of HM Colonial and Overseas Service 1837–1997*. London: I.B. Tauris, 1999.

Kwayana, E. *Guyana: No Guilty Race*. Guyana: Guyana Review, 1999.

——. "Running Out." Commentary at Guyana Caribbean Politics.com. Posted May 21, 2004. Available online at www.guyanacaribbeanpolitics.com/kwayana/kwayana_052104.html. Accessed August 5, 2009.

A Landowner. *British Guiana, Demerara after Fifteen Years of Freedom*. London: T. Bosworth, 1853.

Lewis, D., and Deborah Willis. *A Small Nation of People: W. E. B. Du Bois and African American Portraits of Progress*. New York: Amistad/HarperCollins, 2003.

Liverpool, Hollis "Chalkdust." *Rituals of Power and Rebellion: The Carnival Tradition in Trinidad and Tobago 1763–1962*. Chicago: Research Associates School Times Publications, 2001.

Luckert, S., and Susan Bachrach. *State of Deception: The Power of Nazi Propaganda*. Washington: United States Holocaust Museum, 2011.

Lutchman, H. *Patronage in Colonial Society: A Study of The Former British Guiana*. Georgetown: Critchlow Labour College, 1976.

MacKenzie, J. *Propaganda and Empire: The Manipulation of British Public Opinion, 1880–1960*. Manchester: Manchester University Press, 1984.

MacNeil, W., and William Cran. *The Story of English*. London: Penguin, 2003.

Majeed, H. *Forbes Burnham: National Reconciliation and National Unity*. New York: Global Communications, 2005.

Major, R. (transl. and ed.). *Letters of Christopher Columbus, with Other Original Documents Relating to his Four Voyages to the New World*. London: Hakhyt Society, 1961.

Mangru, B. "Indian Labour in British Guiana." *History Today* 36, no. 4 (1986). Available online at www.historytoday.com/print/3642. Accessed November 26, 2011.

Manuel, P. "Music, Identity, and Images of India in the Indo-Caribbean Diaspora." *Asian Music* 29, no. 1 (Autumn 1997–Winter 1998): 17–35.

——. *East Indian Music in the West Indies: Taan Singing, Chutney, and the Making of Indo-Caribbean Culture*. Philadelphia: Temple University Press, 2000.

Mar, T., and Penelope Edmonds (eds.). *Making Settler Colonial Space: Perspectives on Race, Place, and Identity*. New York: Palgrave Macmillan, 2010.

McDavid, W. "The Progress of Music in British Guiana." In Marion Rockcliffe and Joseph Waterton Jackson (eds.), *British Guiana Woman's Centenary Effort 1831–1931*. Georgetown, British Guiana: Daily Argosy, 1931, 90–91.

McDowell, R. "Interview with Sheik Sadeek—A Guyanese popular writer Georgetown, 11 April 1975." *Journal of Postcolonial Writing* 14, no. 2 (November 1975): 532.

McKenzie, J. *Propaganda and Empire: The Manipulation of British Public Opinion, 1880–1960*, Manchester: Manchester University Press, 1984.

McKinnon, C. "Indigenous Music as a Space of Resistance." In Mar, T., and Penelope Edmonds (eds.), *Making Settler Colonial Space: Perspectives on Race, Place, and Identity.* New York: Palgrave Macmillan, 2010, 255–70.

McTurk, M. *Essays and Fables Written in the Vernacular of the Creoles of British Guiana (1899).* Demerara: Argosy Press, 1899.

Meining, D. W. *The Shaping of America: A Geographical Perspective on 500 Years of History— Atlantic America, 1492-1800.* Vol. 1. New Haven: Yale University Press, 1986.

Menezes, N. *The Portuguese of Guyana: A Study in Culture and Conflict.* Gujarat, India, ca. 1997.

———. "Amerindian Music in Guyana." *Arts Journal* 1, no. 2 (March 2005): 95–99.

Mentore, G. *The Relevance of Myth.* Edgar Mittelholzer Memorial Lectures, Eleventh Series. Guyana: Department of Culture, 1988.

Mentore, L. "Men of Sound Reputation: Achievement in the World of Guyanese Birdsport." In Henrietta Moore and Nick Long (eds.), *The Social Life of Achievement.* Cambridge: Cambridge University Press, 2012.

Meredith, D. "The British Government and Colonial Economic Policy, 1919-1939." *Economic History Review* 28, no. 3 (August 1975): 484–99.

Merrill, T. (ed.). "The History of the Economy—Post Independence." In *Guyana: A Country Study.* Washington: GPO for the Library of Congress, 1992. Available online at countrystudies.us/guyana/55.htm.

Mittelholzer, E. *A Swarthy Boy.* London: Putnam, 1963.

Morgan, D. *The Official History of Colonial Development, Volume 1: The Origins of British Aid Policy, 1924-1945.* London: Her Majesty's Stationery Office and Atlantic Highlands, NJ: Humanities Press, 1980.

———. *The Official History of Colonial Development, Volume 2: Developing British Colonial Resources, 1945-1951.* London: Her Majesty's Stationery Office, 1980.

———. *The Official History of Colonial Development, Volume 3: A Reassessment of British AID Policy, 1951-1965.* London: Her Majesty's Stationery Office, 1980.

———. *The Official History of Colonial Development, Volume 4: Changes in British AID Policy, 1951-1970.* London: Her Majesty's Stationery Office, 1980.

———. *The Official History of Colonial Development, Volume 5: Guidance Towards Self-Government in British Colonies, 1941-1971.* London: Her Majesty's Stationery Office, 1980.

Moore, B. *Cultural Power, Resistance, and Pluralism: Colonial Guyana 1838-1900.* Jamaica: University of the West Indies Press, 1995.

Moore, C. "Importance of Cultural Activity." Paper presented to the Cultural Committee of the People's Progressive Party, Wednesday, July 15, 1964. Available at the Cheddi Jagan Research Center. Shelf location CJ0012.

Moore, E. "Random Remarks on Social Music." In Marion Rockcliffe and Joseph Waterton Jackson (eds.), *British Guiana Woman's Centenary Effort 1831–1931.* Georgetown: Daily Argosy, 1931, 80–84.

Moore, R. "Colonial Images of Blacks and Indians in Nineteenth Century Guyana." In Bridget Brereton and Kevin A. Yelvington (eds.), *The Colonial Caribbean in Transition: Essays on*

Postemancipation Social and Cultural History. Jamaica: Press of the University of the West Indies, 1999, 126–58.

Morris, N. "Cultural Interaction in Latin American and Caribbean Music." *Latin American Research Review* 34, no. 1 (1999): 187–200.

Niaah, S. *Dance Hall: From Slave Ship to Ghetto.* Ottawa: University of Ottawa Press, 2010.

Nehusi, K. "The Causes of the Protest of 1905." In Winston McGowan, James G. Rose, and David Granger (eds.), *Themes in African-Guyanese History.* Georgetown: Free Press, 1998, 251–76.

———. "The Meaning of Queenstown: Tradition, Consciousness and Identity in a Guyanese Village." In *Queenstown Anniversary Publication* (New York: Queenstown, Essequibo New York Association, 1995), 12–16, 23–29, 44–46.

Neptune, N. "White Lies: Race and Sexuality in Occupied Trinidad." *Journal of Colonialism and Colonial History* 2:1 (2001). Available online at journals.ohiolink.edu:6873/journals/journal_of_colonialism_and_colonial_history/v002/2.1neptune.html. Accessed October 24, 2008.

Noel, G. *Sing! Guyana's Children.* Georgetown, Guyana: Department of Culture, 1979.

Octave. "The Band Moves On." *Guyana Police Force Magazine* (1972): 101.

Palmer, C. *Cheddi Jagan and the Politics of Power: British Guiana's Struggle for Independence.* Chapel Hill: University of North Carolina Press, 2010.

People's Progressive Party. *My Guyana, Eldorado: Songs for All Guyanese.* Georgetown: PPP, 1987.

Perris, A. "Music as Propaganda: Art at the Command of Doctrine in the People's Republic of China." *Ethnomusicology* 27, no. 1 (January 1983): 1–28.

Persaud, P. "Preserving Our Literary Heritage: National Songs, Part III." *Guyana Chronicle,* March 2, 2008.

Phillips, A. "British Music Competition Festivals." Letter to the editor, *Musical Times* 74, no. 1086 (August 1933): 734–36.

Pilgrim, W. "Lynette Dolphin: A Trail-Blazing Cultural Icon." Georgetown: Unpublished paper in author's possession, ca. 2000. www.qcguyanaalumny.org/News/dollotrib2.html.

Pugagee Pungus (pseudonym). "Mudland Songs and Bajan Red Legs." *Daily Chronicle,* January 1938.

Rabe, S. *U.S. Intervention in British Guiana: A Cold War Story.* Chapel Hill: University of North Carolina Press, 2009.

Raleigh, Walter. *The discoverie of the large, rich and bewtiful Empire of Guiana.* 1596. Reprint, New York: Da Capo, 1968.

Ramharack, B. *Against the Grain: Balram Singh Rai and the Politics of Guyana.* Trinidad and Tobago: Chakra Publishing House, 2005.

Ramnarine, T. "Brotherhood of the Boat: Musical Dialogues in a Caribbean Context." *British Journal of Ethnomusicology* vol. 7 (1977): 1–22.

———. *Creating Their Own Space: The Development of an Indian-Caribbean Musical Tradition.* Jamaica: University of the West Indies Press, 2001.

Rampertaub, R. "'Dougla' Elsie and 'Kaytie' of Grove." *Sunday Stabroek* (Celebrating Our Creative Personalities), May 29, 2005. Available online at www.landofsixpeoples.com/news502/ns5052955.htm. Accessed April 7, 2009.

Ramphal, S. *Is the West Indies West Indian?* Tenth Sir Archibald Nedd Memorial Lecture. Grenada, January 28, 2011.

Report on British Guiana for the Year 1961. Georgetown: British Guiana Lithographic, 1961.

Rex, J. "The Plural Society in Sociological Theory." *British Journal of Sociology* 10, no. 2 (June 1959): 114–24.

Richards, J. *Imperialism and Music: Britain 1876–1953.* Manchester: University of Manchester Press, 2001.

Richards-Greaves, G. "'Cookup Rice': Guyana's Culinary 'Dougla' as a Performance of Guyanese Identities." Unpublished book chapter, ca. 2011.

Riley, M. "Civilizing the Savage: Johan Georg Sulzer and the 'Aesthetic Force' of Music." *Journal of the Royal Musical Association* 127, no. 1 (2002): 1–22.

Roback, J. "The White-Robed Army: An Afro-Guyanese Religious Movement." *Anthropologica* 16, no. 2 (1974): 233–68.

Rodney, W. "Masses in Action." *New World Quarterly* 2, no. 3 (1966): 30–37. Susan Campbell, transcriber.

———. *A History of the Guyanese Working People, 1881–1905.* London: Heinemann, 1981.

Rodway, J. *Hand-book of British Guiana.* Georgetown: Columbian Exposition Literary Committee of the Royal Agricultural and Commercial Society, 1893.

Rohlehr, Gordon. *Calypso and Society in Pre-Independence Trinidad.* Port-of-Spain: self-published, 1990.

Roopnaraine, R. "Address to QC Reunion." Georgetown: Guyana, October 28, 2009.

Rose, J. "The Coming of Crown Colony Government." In Winston McGowan, James Rose, and David Granger (eds.), *Themes in African-Guyanese History.* Guyana: Free Press, 1998, 296–326.

Roth, W. *Additional Studies of the Arts, Crafts, and Customs of the Guiana Indians: With Special Reference to Those of Southern British Guiana.* Washington: Smithsonian Institution, 1929.

Russell, Roger. "Emory Cook (1913-2002)." Available online at www.roger-russell.com/cook/cook.htm Accessed March 21, 2012.

Safa, H. "Popular Culture, National Identity, and Race in the Caribbean." *New West Indian Guide* 81, no. 3/4 (1987): 115–25.

Sagar, R. "Banshikilli: The Music of the Spanish Arawaks of Moruca, Guyana." Georgetown: unpublished paper in author's possession, ca. 2007.

———. "Chants in the Rainforest: An Essay on the Musical Traditions of the Amerindian People of Guyana." Georgetown,: unpublished paper in author's possession, August 17, 2009.

Sanders, R. *Broadcasting in Guyana.* London: Routledge and Kagan Paul, in association with International Institute of Communications, 1978.

———. "El Dorado may be in sight at last." *Caribbean News Now,* February 18, 2011.

Schomburgk, R. *Travels in British Guiana 1840-1844, Volume 1.* Translated and Edited by Walter E. Roth. Georgetown, British Guiana: Daily Chronicle, 1923.

———. *Travels in British Guiana 1840-1844, Volume 2.* Translated and Edited by Walter E. Roth. Georgetown, British Guiana: Daily Chronicle, 1923.

Schuler, M. *Alas, Alas, Kongo: A Social History of Indentured African Immigration into Jamaica, 1841-1865.* Baltimore: Johns Hopkins Press, 1980.

Schmukler, R. "Public Administration Theory as Musical Theory." *Administrative Theory & Praxis* 24, no. 3 (2002): 415–36.

Seales, R. "The Making of Guyanese Popular Music." Available online at www.gems-av.com/ themakingofpopguyanesemusic.htm. Accessed March 2, 2009.

———. "Al Seales: The Washboard Orchestra and a Musical Revolution in Guyana." In Vibert Cambridge (ed.), *Black Praxis: Writings on Guyanese Music 2003–2004*. Athens: Ohio University Department of African American Studies, 2004.

Seecharan, C. *India and the Shaping of the Indo-Guyanese Imagination 1890s–1920s*. Leeds: University of Warwick and Peepal Tree Brooks, 1993.

———. *Sweetening Bitter Sugar: Jock Campbell, the Booker Reformer in British Guiana, 1934–1966*. Kingston, Jamaica: Ian Randle, 2005.

———. *Muscular Learning: Cricket and Education in the Making of the British West Indies at the End of the 19th Century*. Kingston: Jamaica: Ian Randle, 2006.

Seymour, A. *Guianese History and Culture Week October 20-24, 1958: Committee's Report and Proposed Programme of Activities*. Georgetown: British Guiana, 1958, 1.

———. *Cultural Policy in Guyana*. Paris: UNESCO, 1977.

Seymour, A., and Elma Seymour. *Dictionary of Guyanese Biography*. Georgetown: Arthur and Elma Seymour, 1985.

Shahabuddeen, M. *Constitutional Development in Guyana 1621–1978*. Georgetown: self-published, 1978.

Singh, G. "Ideological Art: New Approach in Guyana—Cultural Revolution—Bold Step in Development Thrust." *Sunday Chronicle*, December 14, 1975.

———. "Cultural Revolution, bold steps in development thrust." *Sunday Chronicle*, December 14, 1975, 15.

Singh, J. *Guyana: Democracy Betrayed: A Political History 1948–1993*. Kingston, Jamaica: Kingston Publishers, 1996.

Smyth, R. "The Development of British Colonial Film Policy, 1927-1939, with Special Reference to East and Central Africa." *Journal of African History* 20, no. 3 (1979): 437–50.

Snijders, H., and Joycelynne Loncke (eds.). *One Hundred Years of Classical Music in the Guianas: Selected Pieces for Pianoforte*. Guyana: University of Guyana, 2002.

Stephens, H. *The Administrative History of the British Dependencies in the Further East*. Ca. 1899. Available online at www.archive.org/details/administrativehioosteprich. Accessed March 21, 2012.

Stoddart, B. "Sport, Cultural Imperialism, and Colonial Response in the British Empire." *Comparative Studies in Society and History* 30, no. 4 (October 1988): 649–73.

Stolzoff, N. *Wake the Town and Tell the People: Dancehall Culture in Jamaica*. Durham, NC: Duke University Press, 2000.

St. Pierre, M. *Anatomy of Resistance: Anti-Colonialism in Guyana 1823–1966*. London: Macmillan Education, 1999.

Swan, M. *British Guiana: The Land of Six Peoples*. London: Her Majesty's Stationery Office, 1957.

Sue-A-Quan, T. (ed.). "Vivian Lee: Broadcasting Ace." In *Cane Ripples: The Chinese in Guyana*. Vancouver: Cane Press, 2003, 193.

Sukdeo, G. "The Rupununi Uprisings Revisited: Need for a Full Account." *Guyana Journal* (October 2005). Available online at www.guyanajournal.com/rupununiuprising.html. Accessed December 26, 2008.

Bibliography

Taitt, H. *My Life, My Country*. Georgetown, Guyana: New Guyana, ca. 2006.

Teixeira, G. "Cheddi Jagan, Personal Glimpses." *Journal of the Cheddi Jagan Research Center* 1 (2008): 66.

Thomasson, F. *A History of Theatre in Guyana 1800–2000*. London: Hansib, 2009.

Thompson, A. *Unprofitable Servants: Crown Slaves in Berbice, Guyana 1803–1831*. Barbados: University of the West Indies Press, 2002.

———. "Symbolic Legacies of Slavery in Guyana." *New West Indian Guide* 80, no. 3/4 (2006): 191–220. Available online at www.kitlv-journals.nl/index.php/nwig/issue/view/11. Accessed March 21, 2009.

Turin, D. "Decolonization and the Collapse of the British Empire." *Student Pulse* 1, no. 10 (2009). Available online at /www.studentpulse.com/a?kl=5. Accessed December 5, 2011.

United Nations Economic and Social Commission for Asia and the Pacific. "What Is Good Governance?" Available online at www.unescap.org/huset/gg/governance.htm. Accessed February 8, 2012.

Van Sertima, F. "Christmas in Georgetown." *Scenes and Sketches of Demerara Life*. Georgetown, 1899.

Vatuk, V. "Protest Songs of East Indians in British Guiana." In Kira Hall (ed.), *Essays in Indian Folk Traditions: Collected Writings of Ved Prakash Vatuk*. Meerut, India: Archana, 2007, 411.

Viotti da Costa, E. *Crowns of Glory, Tears of Blood: The Demerara Slave Rebellion of 1823*. New York: Oxford University Press, 1994.

Waisbord, S. "The Ties that Still Bind: Media and National Cultures in Latin America." *Canadian Journal of Communication* 23, no. 2 (1998): 381–401.

Wantaya, O. "The Sound of Steel in Thailand." Available online at www.ecaroh.com/bmp/lead_act/soundofsteel_thailand.htm. Accessed March 11, 2009.

Ward, B. "People Get Ready: Music and the Civil Rights Movement of the 1950s and 1960s." Available online at www.historynow.org/06_2006/print/historian2.html. Accessed December 26, 2008.

Warner-Lewis, M. *Central Africa in the Caribbean: Transcending Time, Transforming Cultures*. Jamaica: University of the West Indies Press, 2006.

Waters, R., and Gordon Daniels. "Striking for Freedom? International Intervention and the Guianese Sugar Workers' Strike of 1964." *Cold War History* (2010): 1–32.

Webber, A. *Centenary Handbook of British Guiana*. Georgetown, British Guiana: Argosy, 1931.

Westmaas, N. "Revolutionary Centennial: Guyana's 1905 Rebellion." Available online at Solidarity (www.solidarity-us.org/node/1139/print). Accessed September 18, 2007.

Williams, D. "Guiana Today." *Kyk-Over-al* 2, no. 9 (December 1949): 9–10.

———. *Ancient Guyana*. Kingston, Jamaica: Ian Randle, 2005.

Williams, E. "The Historical Background to British Guiana's Problems." *Journal of Negro History* 30, no. 4 (October 1945): 357–81.

Wilmer, V. "Rannie Hart: A Musical Career That Took in Brixton, Mayfair—and Rita Hayworth" (obituary). *Guardian* (UK), July 15, 2006. Available online at www.guardian.co.uk/news/2006/jul/15/guardianobituaries.mainsection. Accessed March 2, 2009.

Wilson, R. *Report of the British Guiana Commission*. London: HMSO, 1927.

Wilson, W. "The Study of Administration." *Political Science Quarterly* 2, no. 2 (June 1887): 197–222.

Woolford, H. "The Origins of the Labor Movement." In Winston McGowan, James G. Rose, and David Granger (eds.), *Themes in African-Guyanese History*. Georgetown, Guyana: Free Press, 1998, 277–95.

———. "A History of Political Alliances in Guyana: 1953–1997." Available online at www.guyana caribbeanpolitics.com/commentary/history_guyana1953-1997.html. Accessed December 10, 2008.

———. "Climate change and the movement of people in Guyana." *Stabroek News*, April 8, 2010. Available online. Accessed August 6, 2011.

Women's Progress Organization. *Songbook Compiled by the Women's Progressive Organization*. Georgetown: Women's Progressive Organization, n.d., 12.

Zeally, E., and J. Ord Hume. "British Guiana Militia Band." In *Famous Bands of the British Empire*. London: J. P. Hull, ca. 1925.

Declassified Documents

From Secret and Personal Guard note NOTE FROM SIR RALPH GREY, GOVERNOR OF BRITISH GUIANA, TO R. W. PIPER OF THE COLONIAL OFFICE, LONDON (25 September 1962). Available online at www.guyana.org/govt/declassified_british_documents_1958-1964 .html.

Index